CONTENTS

Part Three: Literature

PREFACE

Of all the major languages of the world, Bengali has been most neglected by foreign learners. It stands sixth in the world in its number of speakers, has the richest and most developed modern literature in South Asia, was the mother-tongue of many leading reformers and activists of 19th and 20th-century India, and is now the national language of Bangladesh and the state language of West Bengal. There is a sizeable Bengali-speaking diaspora, in India (especially the eastern states of Assam and Tripura), the Middle East, North America and Britain. The East End of London has become as closely associated with its Sylheti-Bengali population as it once was with Huguenot and Jewish migrants. Bengali was the language of Rabindranath Tagore, the greatest and best known modern South Asian writer; and it was the language of India's most celebrated film-maker, Satyajit Ray. Bengali scientists, doctors and academics are prominent all over South Asia, and in Europe and North America. As the language of Bangladesh, Bengali has become internationally identifiable with a people whose increasing numbers and precarious geographical circumstances present a huge challenge not only to the Bangladesh Government but to other governments of good will. By the end of the millennium, there are likely to be more than 250 million Bengali speakers. Yet despite its size, literary wealth, historical importance and growing contemporary profile, there are still remarkably few facilities for foreigners to learn it well. Britain now has only one university lectureship in Bengali, and lectureships in other countries outside South Asia can be counted on the fingers of one hand.

The same can be said of books from which to learn Bengali. Before the Second World War, there were perhaps more grammars and course books for Bengali than for other modern South Asian languages. The Revd. William Sutton Page ran a department of Bengali at the School of Oriental and African Studies, and produced a number of pioneering works; his efforts were extended by Professor T. W. Clark, who briefly held a unique London University Chair in Bengali from 1967 until his death in 1969, and by Dr Tarapada Mukherjee. Western-based scholarship was nourished by the achievements of Suniti Kumar Chatterjee (Dr Mukherjee's teacher) and other scholars in Calcutta and Dhaka in the fields of Bengali philology and lexicography. The materials that Clark and Mukherjee wrote for their students at SOAS were excellent, and served me and other students well. But Dr Mukherjee was aware that they needed updating. He struggled against illness to produce a new course, in collaboration with Professor J. C. Wright, but even while he was writing it the contexts and potential need for Bengali were changing fast. I have therefore adopted a new approach in this book. Apart from the sound and script exercises in **Part One** (which in their methodology go right back to Sutton Page), I have conceived my task afresh, aiming to meet a wide variety of needs and contexts, and to make Bengali as easy and enjoyable to learn as possible.

This is a course in speaking, writing and reading standard Bengali. It assumes that any attempt to go beyond a phrase-book knowledge must teach the script clearly and fully. But a purely 'reading knowledge' of Bengali would not only neglect the wonderful music of its sounds, it would also leave unexplained many discrepancies between spelling and pronunciation. So this course teaches the sounds of Bengali with care, as well as its script and grammar, and the accompanying tape is integral. At the same time, I have tried to enable the learner to progress to higher levels of reading and understanding. In this, as in other aims, I have been influenced by Dr Mukherjee's feeling that the 'leap' between any course in Bengali then available and reading a text, even a newspaper, was too great and dispiriting for most learners (unless they happened to be speakers of another South Asian language).

Those who want primarily to speak Bengali, who are planning to go to Bengal to visit or work, or who are in contact with Bengali communities elsewhere, may feel that they do not wish to make this leap: that a novel sound-system, script, grammar and vocabulary are enough, that the writings of Tagore or Jibanananda Das may have to wait. But I urge them not to be daunted. If they persevere with **Part Three**, not only will they refine their understanding of Bengali grammar, script and pronunciation, but they will encounter a whole new imaginative world, breathtaking in its vigour and variety and delight. And their combined endeavour will help to make the beauties of Bengali known to lovers of language and literature everywhere.

Of the many friends who have assisted me, I should specially like to thank Professor Maniruzzaman, of the Department of Bengali at the University of Chittagong, where I was invited to work on this book as a Visiting Fellow at the end of 1990. **Part Two** is incalculably indebted to his acute linguistic perception, and would never have been written if his personal kindness had not protected me from the political turmoil prevailing at the time. I am also sincerely grateful to Prodosh Bhattacharya, Manoshi Barua, Sukanta and Supriya Chaudhuri, Ghulam Murshid, Priti Kumar Mitra, Sudipta Kaviraj, Yasmin Hossain, Anuradha Roma Choudhury and Professor Sisir Kumar Das. Particular thanks are due to Manoshi Barua, Sonia Kazi, Ajit Banerjee and Nurul Islam for their enthusiastic recording of the cassette that accompanies the book, and to Biman Mullick for his beautiful handwritten script forms. Finally I thank all my pupils at SOAS, who, by cheerfully learning from very imperfect drafts, have helped me to make improvements. I hope that they and other users will not hesitate to let me know of any remaining mistakes or unclarities or omissions.

W.R.
School of Oriental and African Studies, University of London, 1993

Note on the first reprint
Additional thanks are due to Professor Pabitra Sarkar, whose very careful review in the *Statesman* (Calcutta, 28 January 1995) has enabled me to make a number of improvements and corrections, and to Sabia Ali, the most sharp-eyed of my students in the first year of the book's use.

1995

Script diagrams

দ ধ ন

প ফ ব

ভ য ল

ম শ ষ

হ স ৎ

১ ২ ৩ ৪ ৫

৬ ৭ ৮ ৯ ০

In Memoriam

TARAPADA MUKHERJEE
(1928–1990)

PART ONE

SOUNDS AND SCRIPT

1

The languages of South Asia are richly endowed with sounds, particularly consonants; and the Hindus were the first people in the world to realise that the sounds of a language can be grouped scientifically according to where and how they are made in the mouth. Unlike the Greek and Roman alphabets, which follow a haphazard order, Indian scripts are based on a logical table of letters: vowels first, then the 'velar' consonants, the 'palatal' consonants, the 'retroflex' consonants and so on.

The Bengali script, like other South Asian scripts (except Urdu) was originally devised for the writing of Sanskrit. As the modern Indo-Aryan languages developed (growing not exactly from Sanskrit but from the Prakrits, the spoken languages of ancient India), regional varieties of what was essentially the same writing system were used to write them down. Nowadays Sanskrit is usually written and printed in *Devanāgarī*, the script that is also used for Hindi. But it can just as well be written in the Bengali script, and when Bengali children learn their letters, they learn them according to the Sanskrit sequence.

The complete table of letters will be found in the **Review** section at the end of **Part One**. You will need to know it, otherwise you won't be able to use a Bengali dictionary. In the first 12 units, however, you'll be introduced to the sounds and letters according to a different sequence. There are three reasons for this. First, I have found from my experience of teaching Bengali that it is best to begin with sounds that are easy for foreigners to make, and progress gradually to more difficult sounds. Second, it is important to practise the sounds by repeating words and phrases, not by pronouncing them in isolation. There are very few words made of vowels alone, which is what you would start with if you followed the traditional sequence. Third, the pronunciation of Bengali does not fit the spelling perfectly. The mis-match between spelling and pronunciation is nothing like as great as in English, but it is enough to make Bengali pronunciation quite tricky, harder than Hindi. Both languages have essentially 'Sanskritic' spelling systems, but Bengali has diverged from its classical roots more than Hindi. It is essential to explain and learn Bengali sounds and script with care. If I followed the traditional table, I would have to begin by confusing you with the letter that causes more pronunciation problems than any other!

We begin with three vowel sounds. The first vowel is very much the sound you make when the doctor wants to examine your throat:

a   as in English *star*

The second also approximates to an English sound:

i   as in English *see*

The third sound does not really exist in most pronunciations of English, but if you take the 'oo' sound in *moon* and push your lips right forward as if you were whistling, you will get it:

u

Unlike most people's pronunciation of English '*oo*', Bengali u is a *pure* sound: i.e. the lips do not move when uttering it. Most English vowel-sounds are impure: they slide from one sound to another. This is often reflected in English spelling: *break*, *fear*, *boat*, etc. When pronouncing Bengali a, i, u, make sure that the sounds are absolutely pure.

Here are four consonants, none of which should cause any difficulty:

g   as in English *get*
n   as in English *not*
b   as in English *bone*
m   as in English *mat*

The next sound should be rolled or 'trilled' as in Scots or Italian – but don't overdo it. At the end of words, particularly, the tongue flaps only once or twice:

r   as in Italian *Roma*

The last sound is perfectly familiar to English speakers, but make sure you always pronounce it at the front of the mouth:

l   as in English *lend*, **never** as in English *ill*

When pronouncing Bengali consonants on their own, or when referring to them in order to spell a word or name, it is customary to give them a following vowel-sound – the so-called **inherent** vowel ɔ, pronounced as in British English *hot*. (There will be more about the inherent vowel in Unit 2.) The advantage of this is that you don't have to learn **names** for the letters. You simply say:

gɔ   mɔ
nɔ   rɔ
bɔ   lɔ

You now need to learn the Bengali letters for the vowels and consonants above. All South Asian scripts (except Urdu, which is Persian in origin) follow two basic principles:

1   If a syllable consists of a vowel alone, or a vowel followed by a consonant, **full vowels** are used.

2   If a syllable consists of a consonant followed by vowel, **vowel signs** are used.

To see how this works, let's first of all learn the letters for the five consonants above. You need to learn to write them, and also to recognise them in print. You'll see at once that printed forms are not always quite the same as hand-written forms, and of course hand-writing styles vary. If you want to acquire elegant Bengali handwriting, the best thing is to find a native speaker who can teach you. You can also acquire hand-writing books such as Bengali schoolchildren use (see p. 276). For the sequence of strokes, refer to the diagrams on pp. x–xi. You will see that some letters (e.g. the l) begin with a small loop or 'blob':

	Handwriting	**Print**
g	গ	গ
n	ন	ন
b	ব	ব
m	ম	ম
r	র	র
l	ল	ল

If you want to write a on its own, you need the **full vowel**:

a	আ	আ (full vowel)

This letter is also used if the syllable consists of a **vowel + consonant**:

am	আম	আম

A much more common sequence, however, is a **consonant + vowel**, and you'll be relieved to learn that the **vowel sign** is simply ী. Thus:

ga	গা	গা
na	না	না
ma	মা	মা

So far so good. With i and u, however, there are two complications to explain.

(a) Each of these sounds can be represented by one or other of two letters. In Sanskrit, there is a 'short' i and a 'long' i, a 'short' u and a 'long' u. In the standard Roman transliteration of Sanskrit (see p. 47), these are distinguished by the use of a bar or 'macron' over the long vowels, and I propose to adopt the same convention here. The transcription system used in this book derives, with some modifications, from the work of Professor T. W. Clark (see **Preface**, p. viii). It borrows letters from the International Phonetic Alphabet, but it is a transliteration in that it indicates precisely which letters should be used in writing words in Bengali script. The distinction between 'short' and 'long' i and u in Bengali has not survived in Bengali pronunciation, but is still present in Bengali spelling. Thus for two sounds we have four letters and vowel signs to learn.

(b) Bengali is read, like English, from left to right; but the vowel signs do not necessarily follow the consonant on the page. The vowel sign for the short i is written *before* the consonant; the sign for the long i is written *after* the consonant; the signs for the short and long u are written *below* the consonant:

i	ই	ই	(full vowel)
	ি	ি	(vowel sign)
ī	ঈ	ঈ	(full vowel)
	ী	ী	(vowel sign)
u	উ	উ	(full vowel)
	ু	ু	(vowel sign)
ū	ঊ	ঊ	(full vowel)
	ূ	ূ	(vowel sign)

Syllables consisting of, say, **b** + **i, ī, u,** or **ū** would be written as follows:

bi	বি	বি
bī	বী	বী
bu	বু	বু
bū	বূ	বূ

You are now ready to start pronouncing, reading and writing some Bengali words and phrases.

Exercises

1 Practise saying the words and phrases overleaf with the help of the cassette or the previous few pages. In this and in all the first (sound) exercises in Units 1 to 12, you need not worry about analysing the grammar. By the end of the book, you will be able to do so, and you'll know about distinctions between, for example, the different pronouns for *he* and *she*. For the moment, however, concentrate on producing the right sound, and on picking up vocabulary items – particularly nouns and adjectives. You have already seen the first four words:

am	*mango*
ma	*mother*
na	*no, not*
nam	*name*
ga	*body*
gan	*song*
amar	*my*
abar	*again*
bagan	*garden*
ami	*I*
nun	*salt*
ini	*he/she*
uni	*he/she*
rumal	*handkerchief*
nīl	*blue*
lal	*red*
mūl	*root*
ami anini	*I did not bring*
ami anlam	*I brought*

amra niini *we did not take*
amra niina *we do not take*
am anun *Bring (some) mangos.*
nun nii? *May I take (some) salt?*
nin na *Please take (some).*
ini amar ma *She is my mother.*
uni amar mama *He is my (maternal) uncle.*
amar nam raul *My name is Raul.*
amar rumal nin *Take my handkerchief.*
uni umar baba? *Is he Uma's father?*
na, uni rimir baba *No, he's Rimi's father.*

2 Now see if you can write the words and phrases above in Bengali script. If a vowel comes between two consonants, it is always thought of as 'belonging' to the consonant before, **not** the consonant that follows. Thus **amar** is written a-mar, not am-ar:

আমার

If a vowel follows a vowel, it has to be written as a full vowel: so **niina** is written ni-i-na:

নিইনা

The sequence **r** followed by **u** as in **rumal** generally has a special letter-form, perhaps because the ordinary vowel sign for **u** (ꜜ) would interfere with the dot in র:

র+ঊ= রূ

রূ however, does occur in some modern typefaces.

Keys to this and subsequent exercises are on pp. 278–293.

2

In Unit 1, you learnt to give consonants pronounced on their own the **inherent** vowel-sound ɔ. The inherent vowel-sound is frequently given to consonants which have no other vowel attached to them. In Hindi, and the standard north Indian pronunciation of Sanskrit, the inherent vowel is pronounced like the short ə sound in English *the*. It is normally transliterated as *a*. In Bengali, the inherent vowel varies in its pronunciation. It is either pronounced ɔ as in British English *hot*, or as a very pure o such as we don't really have in English, but which speakers of French will know from a word such as *mot*. Sometimes, influenced by the sounds around it, it is half way between these two sounds; but to start with it is best to think of it as having **two** possible pronunciations: ɔ and o.

Romanised spellings of Bengali names often use 'a' for the inherent vowel **and** for the 'long' vowel a that we learnt in Unit 1. Satyajit Ray, for example, the famous film director, would have pronounced his name with an o sound for the first and second 'a', and an a sound for the third. In Bengali spelling, the 'a's in 'Satyajit' are inherent vowels; the 'a' in 'Ray' is a (৷). A Bengali friend of mine writes his name in English 'Sukanta'. The 'a' in the middle is an a; the 'a' at the end is an inherent vowel, pronounced o. Very confusing!

Bengalis are not always consciously aware that their pronunciation of the inherent vowel varies. They think of it as one sound. How is the foreign learner to know whether to pronounce the inherent vowel as ɔ or o? The answer is that he or she will have to develop a 'feel' for which is right, and this only comes gradually. A brief analysis of the processes involved is given on p. 275. Two principles can be remembered at the outset:

(a) In words which have inherent vowels in two consecutive syllables, the sequence will usually be ɔ/o, not o/ɔ. (Exceptions occur with prefixes such as **pro-**, ɔ- or **sɔ-**.) Thus the word for *hot* is pronounced 'gɔrom', not 'gorɔm'.

(b) In words which end with a 'conjunct' consonant + inherent vowel, the inherent vowel is always pronounced o. Thus 'Sukanta' above has to be pronounced 'sukanto', not 'sukantɔ'.

Often the inherent vowel is not pronounced at all. In gɔrom, for example, the inherent vowel is not added to the m at the end of the word. Again, when to pronounce the inherent vowel and when to drop it is something that one can learn only with practice. People with a background in Sanskrit, where the inherent vowel is pronounced unless indicated otherwise by a special sign (see p. 95), sometimes have difficulty with this aspect of Bengali; but most (English-speaking) learners seem to cope with it quite easily and intuitively, perhaps because English has so many words ending with a consonant without a vowel.

So much for the pronunciation of the inherent vowel. There is, however, a further cause for confusion. The o sound in Bengali can be represented **either** by the inherent vowel, or by the 'proper' vowel o, for which there is a separate letter:

o   as in French *mot* or German *so*

Learners of Bengali sometimes have difficulty distinguishing between this sound and u/ū (Unit 1, p. 2). In both the lips are pushed right forward and rounded as when whistling, but in u/ū the tongue is raised higher towards the roof of the mouth. But another sort of confusion arises in the spelling. Because the **inherent** vowel can be pronounced exactly the same as the **proper** vowel o, Bengali spelling is not always consistent in this regard: there are some words, such as the common word bhalo (*good, well*), and many verb forms, which can be spelt either with inherent vowel or with the proper vowel o. In this book, I have tried to settle for the spellings that occur most frequently today. But with verb forms especially, it is difficult to be completely consistent: sometimes one spelling 'looks' better in a particular context than another.

The Romanisation used in this book needs to distinguish between o when it is an inherent vowel, and o when it is a proper vowel. For the former, I have decided to use a circumflex accent: ô. Thus the Bengali word for *good* can either be spelt **bhalo** or **bhalô**. In most Bengali words containing an 'o' sound, the spelling is perfectly fixed: but be prepared to find this inconsistency in some.

Now some consonants: the first is not difficult for most learners, except when the letter is pronounced on its own:

ŋ   as in English *finger*

In referring to this letter, Bengalis generally put an u before it, and you may also find it easier to say `uŋɔ`. When it occurs in words, the hard 'g' element is often softened, so that pronunciation becomes more like 'ng' in English *singer*. This varies from speaker to speaker. In pronouncing the word for the Bengali race or nation, for example, some will say **baŋalī** with a hard 'g' sound in the ŋ; others will soften the 'g' or eliminate it completely.

The next sound does not exist in English. It is a 'd' sound, but unlike the English 'd' it is **dental**, made by pressing the tongue firmly against the top front teeth. Speakers of French or Spanish or the other Romance languages will be used to making their 'd' s dental:

d   as in French *docteur*

The last sound in this chapter can be represented by three different letters in the script. The three 'sibilants' that are distinguished in Sanskrit (ś, ṣ, s) are generally all pronounced as 'sh' in standard Bengali (except sometimes when combined with other letters – see pp. 269–70). In East Bengal (Bangladesh) you will often hear 's' rather than 'sh', even in educated speech. (There is also a tendency to pronounce ch as 's'.) It is safer, however, to stick to 'sh', unless the word is English (*bus, cycle* etc.):

ʃ, ṣ, s   as in English *ship*

All the information given so far in this chapter is easier to understand when you turn to the script. For the **inherent** vowel there is, by definition, no vowel sign: the syllables gɔ, nɔ, bɔ, etc. are simply written with the consonants alone. For a syllable consisting of ɔ on its own, however, a full vowel is used. This is the first letter that Bengali children learn; it is like the letter for a, without the second vertical stroke:

Handwriting	Print

ɔ   অ   অ

The full vowel অ is pronounced ɔ, not ô – but there are exceptions (see p. 275).

The **proper** vowel o has, like the other vowels you have learnt, a 'full' form and a 'vowel sign'. The vowel sign has **two** bits to it: one that goes before the consonant, and one that goes after:

| o | ও | ও (full vowel) |
| | ে া | ে া (vowel sign) |

Thus **bo** is written বো.

The letters for the consonants introduced in this chapter are as follows:

ŋ	ঙ	ঙ
d	দ	দ
ʃ	শ	শ
ş	ষ	ষ
s	স	স

Exercises

1 Listen to the tape, or refer back to previous pages, and practise saying the following words and phrases. Remember to pick up useful vocabulary items, without bothering about grammatical structure at this stage:

o	*he, she*	rôbibar asun	*Come (on)*
ora	*they*		*Sunday.*
or	*his, her*	o dilô	*he/she gave*
dɔʃ	*ten*	ora nilôna	*they did not take*
sɔb	*all*	sombar asbo?	*Shall I/we come*
dada	*elder brother*		*(on) Monday?*
didi	*elder sister*	amra ʃunbo	*we shall listen*
din	*day*	oi bôigulo or?	*Are those books*
aŋul	*finger*		*his/hers?*
masī	*(maternal) aunt*	ora dui bon	*They are two*
ʃunun!	*Listen!*		*sisters.*
biş	*poison*	amra baŋalī nôi	*We are not*
manuş	*man, mankind*		*Bengali.*
o ʃulôna	*he/she did not lie*	aro dôi dao	*Give more dai*
down			*(yoghurt).*
amra asini	*we did not come*		

ami ʃônibar asbona *I shall
not come (on) Saturday.*

oi sɔb amar? *Is all of that
mine?*

or nam bɔlô *Tell (me) his/her
name.*

or didir nam sɔrôla *His/her
elder sister's name is Sarala.*

ami ar bôsbona *I shall not sit/
wait any more.*

uni amar bon nɔn *She is not
my sister.*

2 See if you can write the words and phrases above in Bengali script. For the syllable ʃu there is a variation similar to ru in Unit 1 (p. 6). ru, you remember, is usually written রু. ʃu can be written in the way you would expect:

শ + ু = শু শু

This form occurs in modern typefaces, especially in newspapers. But in handwriting and older typefaces, the form শু is common.

There is also a variation for গু. (See p. 270).

To put in full stops, use a short vertical line. The last sentence above would be written:

উনি আমার বোন নন ।

Question marks and other punctuation marks are the same as English.

3

Speakers of English are used to the same sound being achieved by different spellings. In principle, each letter of the Bengali script represents a separate sound. You have seen, however, that i and ī are pronounced the same, and u and ū; the three sibilants are all pronounced as 'sh'; and the 'o' sound can be achieved either by the proper vowel o or by the inherent vowel.

This unit contains further anomalies of this kind, arising from what is sometimes known as 'phonological decay': phonemic distinctions that existed in Sanskrit have been eroded in speech, while the script remains essentially Sanskritic. 'Decay' is, of course, a rather loaded word; one could say that the evolution of Bengali is a purification and improvement rather than a decline. Certainly its streamlined grammatical system is a relief to those who find complex inflections difficult. One might wish that the writing system had been similarly simplified: but as with English spelling, to reform it would be to sever the language from its history.

The vowel sound introduced in this unit is purer than its nearest English equivalent:

e   as in French *café* rather than in English *play*

The new consonant to learn is quite easy for English speakers to pronounce. It is **aspirated** in a way that is quite normal in English:

kh   as in English *king*

Aspirate it a little more heavily than in English, especially at the beginning of words. When it occurs in the middle or at the end of words, the aspiration is much lighter.

The letter for **e** is:

	Handwriting	**Print**
e	এ	এ (full vowel)
	ে	ে (vowel sign)

The vowel sign is written **before** the consonant; so **be** is written বে. You can see that the vowel sign for **o** (ো , p. 10) is made of **e** + **a**, and this is true for Hindi and other South Asian languages too.

In good Bengali printing, ে is used at the beginning of a word and ে in the middle of a word; but in some modern 'computer' fonts ে is the only form used.

When the sound **e** follows another vowel, especially ɔ, **a**, or **o**, the 'semi-vowel' **y** is used. Words like **bhɔy, khay, pay,** or **dhoy** are therefore pronounced as 'bhɔe', 'khae', 'pae' and 'dhoe'. **y** also serves as a 'glide' between vowels. Between **i** and **e**, **a** and **u**, or **e** and **e** it can sound like an English 'y', and this is the sound you can give it when referring to it on its own. Often, however, it is scarcely pronounced at all. **meye** *(girl)*, for example, is pronounced with a lengthened 'e' sound – the **y** disappears in normal speech. Between **o** and **a** it is pronounced like a light English 'w': in the verbal nouns **khaoya, ʃoya,** and **deoya** for example. This is rather like the 'w' sound in French *oui*. The sound exercise below contains examples of these various pronunciations of **y**. If you have the cassette, listen carefully to it. The letter for **y** is:

y	য়	য

The letter for the consonant **kh** is:

kh	খ	খ

Finally, you need to learn a letter that is sometimes used for the sound ŋ. This is derived from the Sanskrit nasalisation sign, *anusvāra* – frequently used in Sanskrit, but much less so in Bengali (which has a different nasalisation sign with a different function: see Unit 5, p. 19). Bengali ônusvar is used, for example, in the word for the Bengali language itself, **bamŋla** বাংলা

ŋ	ং	ং

There are some words, particularly those where ŋ or ɱ are combined with another letter in a conjunct, where Bengali spelling is not consistent. The word colloquially used for *terrible*, *tremendous*, etc., for example, can be spelt **saŋghatik** (সাঙ্ঘাতিক) or **saɱghatik** (সাংঘাতিক); the word for *colour* can be spelt **rɔŋ** (রঙ) or **rɔɱ** (রং). But for other words, the spelling is fixed (বাঙলা is now an archaic spelling for বাংলা), and it is **never** possible to add a vowel to ং. **baɳalī** (the Bengali race or nation, as opposed to the Bengali language) must always be written বাঙালী.

— Exercises —

1 Listen to the tape, or refer back to previous pages, and practise saying the following words and phrases:

se	*he, she*	amader debenna	*Don't give (it) to us.*
ese	*having come*	o ele khabe?	*Will he/she eat when he/she comes?*
ene	*having brought*		
er	*his/her*	bôikhana niye esô	*Bring the book.*
meye	*girl, daughter*		
biye	*marriage*	ekhane ese bôsun	*Come and sit here.*
khay	*he/she eats*		
rakhe	*he/she puts/keeps*	uni asenni? na	*Hasn't he/she come? No.*
khabe	*he/she will eat*		
khaoya-daoya	*food, meal*	e sɔb likhe nebô?	*Shall I write all this down?*
ʃekhe	*he/she learns*		
khub	*very*	o ekhuni elô	*He/she has just come.*
ɔsukh	*illness*		
nɔkh	*finger/toe nail*	sekhane khub gɔrôm	*It's very hot there.*
maɱsô	*meat*		
sɔŋge	*with*	ami kheye elam	*I came after eating.*
mɔŋgôlbar	*Tuesday*		
ami khabô	*I shall eat*	se mɔŋgôlbar asbena	*He/she will not come (on) Tuesday.*
ami likhbona	*I shall not write*		
amar sɔŋge asun	*Come with me.*		

2 In Unit 1 you learnt the variation ক্রু for **ru**, and Unit 2 included the similar variation শু for শ. This unit contains your first consonantal **conjunct**: **ŋg**. Some Bengali conjuncts are immediately recognisable: they are made up of two letters on top of each other or side by

— 14 —

side. g̲l, for example, is written স্ল (গ + ল). Others are less recognisable, and ŋg is of this type:

ŋg   ঙ্গ   ঙ্গ

In modern typefaces you will sometimes find a more easily recognisable form; but the form above is more common, and always used in handwriting.

Now see if you can write the words and phrases in **Exercise 1** in Bengali script. Watch out for ŋg, which is underlined, like all conjuncts in the transcription used in this book.

4

There are two vowel sounds to learn in this unit. The first is similar to one of the vowel sounds of English:

æ   as in English *bat*

The other sound is a diphthong: i.e. it is made up of two vowels joined together: the vowels **o** and **u** joined to produce:

oŭ

Make sure that you retain the 'purity' of both the **o** and the **u**, but let the stress of the syllable fall on the **o**. You have to push your lips right forward to make this sound.

There is only one new consonant to learn, but it can be difficult for the foreign learner. It's the **un**aspirated version of the consonant you learnt in Unit 3. In order to produce it correctly, say an English word like *break* (notice that we do not normally aspirate the 'k' sound at the end of the word). Now say the Bengali sound, giving it, as usual, the inherent vowel ɔ:

k

The sound **æ** is represented in two ways in Bengali script, but unlike the variations between ô and o or ŋ (ঙ) and m (ং) the spelling is generally fixed nowadays: words spelt in one way will not be spelt in the other.

The first way is to use the letter for **e**, which you learnt in Unit 3.

	Handwriting	**Print**
æ	এ	এ (full vowel)
	ে	ে (vowel sign)

How do you know if এ is pronounced e or æ? The answer is that you don't, from the script alone. But words containing **æ** are generally common words such as **kænô** *(why)* or **kæmôn** *(how)*, or else verbs where there is a regular alternation between **æ** and **e**, according to which tense or person you are using. This will be explained in **Part Two** (see pp. 85–88). Some speakers in East Bengal (Bangladesh) do not distinguish very clearly between **æ** and **e**, but they recognise that in correct speech they should be distinguished, and you should try to do so. As with the ɔ/ô distinction there are some words where the sound is between the two; but such subtleties come with an advanced knowledge of Bengali.

The other way of representing **æ** is explained on p. 26.

The diphthong **oŭ** is written:

oŭ	ঔ	ঔ (full vowel)
	ৌ	ৌ (vowel sign)

The consonant **k** is written:

| k | ক | ক |

Exercises

1 Listen to the tape, or refer back to previous pages, and practise saying the following words and phrases:

ki?	*What?*	dik	*direction*
ke?	*Who?*	lok	*person*
eke	*him, her*	kal	*yesterday/tomorrow*
oke	*him, her*	sɔkal	*morning*
amake	*me*	sɔkôl	*all*
kar?	*Whose?*	kɔlôm	*pen*
kæmôn?	*How?*	ægarô	*eleven*
kænô?	*Why?*	noŭko	*boat*
keu	*anyone*	gælô	*he/she went*
kɔkhôn?	*When?*	ami kôri	*I do*

uni kɔren	he/she does	ækhôn debô?	Shall (I) give
amra kini	we buy		(it) now?
ke kene?	Who buys?	keu amake bɔleni	No one told
or nam ki?	What is his/her		me.
	name?	se noŭko kôre ɔnek dūr gælô	
ekhane golmal kôrona	Don't		He/she went a long way
	make a noise here.		by boat.
e bôikhana kar?	Whose is this	ora sɔbai ʃukrôbar gælô	They
	book?		all went (on) Friday.

2 The last sentence above contained the conjunct k͟r:

ক + র = ক্র ক্র

See Unit 8, p. 30 for more information about conjuncts with r as the second member.

Remember that in this same word ʃu can be written ও (though শ্ is also possible).

Now see if you can write the words and phrases in **Exercise 1** in Bengali script.

5

In Unit 3 you learnt the letter derived from *anusvāra*, the Sanskrit nasalisation sign:

ং   (ṃ)

– which functions in Bengali as an alternative to ঙ (ŋ). To indicate the nasalisation of vowels, Bengali has a different sign called c**ɔndrôbindu**, which means literally *moon-dot*. But first practise saying the nasalised forms of the vowels **e** and **o**. Nasalisation is performed by lowering the soft palate at the back of the mouth so that the air flow is directed through the nose rather than the mouth. There are no nasalised vowels in standard British English. In French there are plenty (*mon père, le pain* etc.) though none of them are quite like the Bengali nasalised vowels:

ẽ

õ

The other sound to learn in this unit is a consonant, easy for English speakers to make:

ch   as in English *chaff*

Make sure this sound is well aspirated (more than in English) when it comes at the beginning of a word. In the middle or at the end of a word, aspiration tends to be much lighter (cf. **kh**, p. 12).

The nasalisation sign, c**ɔndrôbindu**, is written like this:

Handwriting ঁ

Print ঁ

This is placed directly above a full vowel, but if a vowel sign is used it is placed over the **consonant** to which the vowel sign is attached:

ঐঁ ওঁ বৈঁ বৌঁ

In learning to write the letter for **ch**, it is probably helpful to learn the letter for the unaspirated sound **c**, which will be introduced properly in Unit 10. The letter for **c** is contained within the letter for **ch**:

| c | চ | চ |
| ch | ছ | ছ |

 ——————————— **Exercises** ———————————

 1 Listen to the tape, or refer back to previous pages, and practise saying the following words and phrases. Pronouns are more 'polite' when they are nasalised! This will be explained in **Part Two** (see p. 52).

ēke *him, her*
ēra *they*
ēder *their*
ēr *his, her*
ōke *him, her*
ōra *they*
ōder *their*
ōr *his, her*
chele *boy*
chôbi *picture*
chɔy *six*
churi *knife*
ami achi *I am (present)*
amra chilam *we were (present)*
se chilôna *he/she was not (present)*
amra kheyechilam *we ate*
se asche *he/she is coming*

ami bôsechilam *I sat*
ami kôrchi *I am doing*
okhane rekhechi *(I) have put (it) there*
ēke aro mach dao. *Give him/her more fish.*
ēr kache ese bɔsô. *Come and sit near him/her.*
golmal kôrchô kænô? *Why are (you) making a noise?*
ēke bôlbo na ōke bôlbo? *Shall (I) tell this person or that person?*
uni khub rag kôrechen. *He/she is very angry.*
ōr khub ɔsukh kôrechilô. *He was very ill.*

— **20** —

ma ækhôni aschen.   *Mother is just coming.*
bichana rode dao.   *Put the bedding in the sunshine.*
ōke bɔlô amra esechi.   *Tell him/her (that) we have come.*

ēra mach mamsô kichui khanna.   *They don't eat fish (or) meat at all.*

2   There are no conjunct letters to learn in this unit. You may be wondering how you can know whether two consecutive consonants are written as a conjunct or not. The answer to this is that you cannot know just from the sound of a word, but grammar and morphology (the way in which words are put together) will often help you. khanna in the last sentence above is not written with the conjunct ন্ন (ন + ন) because it is made up of the present tense form khan plus the negative suffix na. kôrchô is not written with the conjunct র্ছ (র + ছ) because it consists of the stem kôr- from kɔra and the present continuous ending -chô (see Unit 21, p. 133).

Now see if you can write the words and phrases in **Exercise 1** in Bengali script.

6

You have three more nasalised vowels to learn: this unit introduces you to the nasalised form of the first Bengali sound that you learnt (see p. 2).

ā

This is more or less the sound you would make if you had bad catarrh and the doctor asked to look at your throat.

The two new consonants in this unit introduce you to one of the most important consonantal distinctions to be found in the languages of South Asia. In Unit 2, it was stressed that the consonant d was **dental**: made by pressing the tongue against the upper teeth.

It is essential to pronounce Bengali dental consonants correctly, so as to distinguish them from a corresponding set of **retroflex** or 'cerebral' consonants, made by pressing the tongue against the rear edge of the hard 'alveolar ridge' behind the upper teeth. 'Cerebral', implying the pointing of the tongue up towards the cerebral cortex, is considered to be an archaic term now; 'retroflex', implies the curling of the tip of the tongue backwards. Neither term is very appropriate to Bengali, because the tongue is not curled round or pointed vertically upwards as in some South Asian languages; but the consonants in question are nevertheless quite distinct from the dental consonants. Failure to distinguish dental from retroflex consonants is often parodied in Bengali novels, when Englishmen are shown trying to speak Bengali (or Hindi). This is rather like stereotyped Chinese in English novels confusing 'l' with 'r', or Germans pronouncing 'w' as 'v'.

The two consonants introduced here are both 'unvoiced' and 'unaspirated'. The first is dental, made (like **d**) on the teeth, but without 'voicing' (i.e. you can whisper it if you like):

t   as in French *l'été*

The second consonant is the 'retroflex' equivalent. Put your tongue in much the same position as for an English 't', but point it more. An English 't' is made by flattening the tip of the tongue against the alveolar ridge. The Bengali sound is made with the tip of the tongue:

ţ

Bengalis regard dental **t** as a 'soft' sound, and retroflex **ţ** as a 'hard' sound, and may sometimes correct your pronunciation using these terms.

The nasal **ā**, like the other nasal vowels, is written with c**ɔ**ndr**ô**bind**u**:

Handwriting	Print
আঁ	আঁ

Remember that when the vowel sign is used, the nasal sign goes over the **consonant**:

বাঁ	বাঁ

The letters for the two new consonants are as follows:

t	ত	ত
ţ	ট	ট

Exercises

1   Listen to the tape, or refer back to previous pages, and practise saying the following words and phrases. You may have already noticed a pattern in the forms of the pronouns, which will be explained fully in **Part Two**:

tumi	*you*		tāke	*him, her*
tomar	*your*		ţaka	*money (rupee)*
tomake	*(to) you*		ţukro	*little piece*
tomra	*you (pl.)*		choţô	*small*
tara	*they*		ţebil	*table*
tāra	*they*		æktṭa	*one*

duṭo   *two*

tinṭe   *three*

eṭa   *this*

oṭa   *that*

koṭa   *How much/many?*

eṭuku   *this little bit*

ekṭu   *a little*

tomra ar deri kôrona   *Don't delay any more.*

tumi tôbu bôse achô?   *Are you still sitting/waiting?*

eṭuku kheye nin   *(Please) eat this little bit.*

ṭebilṭa tomar kache ṭene nao   *Pull the table near you.*

tomra kal koṭar somoy ele?   *What time did you come yesterday?*

saṭṭar somoy   *At seven o'clock.*

machṭa beʃ ṭaṭka   *The fish is nice and fresh.*

tomra maṭite ʃuyechô kænô?   *Why did you lie (sleep) on the ground?*

tini ele tāke bôste bôlo   *Tell him to wait when he comes.*

ami kotô ṭaka debô?   *How much shall I pay (you)?*

amṭa sundôr, kintu ṭok   *The mango is beautiful, but sour.*

2   There are two new conjuncts that result from this Unit, n + d and n + t:

ন + দ =   ন্দ্   ন্দ

ন + ত =   ন্ত   ন্ত

As with ʃu (Unit 2, p. 11), there is an alternative way of writing ntu, so that kintu *(but)* can either be written কিন্তু or কিন্তু. In print, the older typefaces usually use the first option, but in modern typefaces (newsprint especially) you will often see the second.

Now see if you can write the words and phrases in **Exercise 1** in Bengali script.

7

There are two new sounds but four new letters to learn in this unit, and some complications to explain with regard to the script. The first sound is like an English 'j', but it can be expressed in Bengali by two different letters. One of these is known as **bôrgīyô** jɔ – the j that belongs to the main **bɔrgô** or *group* of consonants:

j as in English *jam*

The other is known as **ɔntɔhsthô** y̌ɔ – 'semi-vowel' y̌. **ɔntɔhsthô** means 'in between' and is applied to the group of letters that the ancient Indian grammarians regarded as being 'in between' vowels and consonants. Both y̌ and y are derived from the Sanskrit 'y', but in Bengali 'y' at the **beginning** of a word is pronounced like j. To indicate the difference in pronunciation, a dot was added to the latter in the 19th century (য়)

y̌ pronounced like j

In Bangladesh, both j and y̌ can sound more like English 'z', especially in words of Perso-Arabic origin – e.g. **namaj** *(prayers)*, pronounced **namaz**.

The other new sound introduced in this unit is straightforward:

h as in English *hunt* (but sometimes a little 'breathier')

The script for the three letters given above is as overleaf:

	Handwriting	**Print**
j	জ	জ
y̌	য	য
h	হ	হ

When য/য় (originally the same letter, remember) occurs as the second member of a conjunct, it is written ্য and called y̌ɔ-phɔla. This can affect the pronunciation of the conjunct in two ways:

(a) It **lengthens** the sound of the consonant to which it is attached. Thus the common postposition jônyô (জন্য *for*) and its colloquial variant jônye are pronounced 'jônnô' and 'jônne' respectively. Make sure that the double n sound is really double. This applies to all double consonantal sounds in Bengali, which should be akin to Italian *spaghetti* rather than English *penny*.

(b) If ্য is followed by a (ा), the vowel sound often changes to æ. This accounts for the spelling of a word like hyæ *(yes)*, or English words such as byæŋk *(bank)* or myænejar *(manager)*.

্যা is not always pronounced æ: byækhya (ব্যাখ্যা *explanation*), for example, is pronounced with an æ sound in the first syllable and an a in the second. sôndhya (সন্ধ্যা *evening*) has a vowel-sound in the second syllable that is closer to a than æ. As with the ɔ/ô and æ/e distinctions (see pp. 7–8, 16–17), the pronunciation is sometimes in between the two.

Occasionally, in words like bytha *(pain)* or bybôhar *(behaviour)*, ্য occurs without a following ा. It is then pronounced æ, unless followed by i in the next syllable: thus bykti *(person)* is pronounced 'bekti' (see p. 275).

Finally a letter that appears in the script but is often silent in pronunciation. In Sanskrit there is a distinction between 'b' and 'v' which has disappeared in Bengali, so that words and names which in Sanskrit would be spelt with a 'v' in Bengali are spelt (and pronounced) with a b. Thus the Hindu god Viṣṇu is pronounced biṣṇu in Bengali. Sometimes 'v' in Sanskrit occurs in a conjunct, particularly 'jv', 'śv' and 'sv': in which case the Bengali b is written small and attached to the consonant. It is then known as bɔ-phɔla (cf. y̌ɔ-phɔla above). At the beginning of words it is silent in pronunciation, so svamī and jvɔr are pronounced 'shamī' and 'jɔr'. When it occurs between vowels it lengthens the consonant to which it is attached. So biśvô *(universe)* is pronounced 'biʃʃô'. In words of English origin like nɔmbôr, the b is pronounced as a b and will therefore be given as b rather than v in this book.

j, ʃ and s with bɔ-phɔla are written:

জ্ব   জ্ব

শ্ব   শ্ব

স্ব   স্ব

Exercises

1   Listen to the tape, or refer back to previous pages, and practise saying the following words and phrases:

y̆a *which*	ætô jore hāṭbenna *Don't walk so fast.*
y̆e *who*	
jômidar *landlord*	aloṭa ki j̱vele debô? *Shall I turn on the light?*
juto *shoe(s)*	
jɔl *water*	jama gay diye esô *Come with a shirt on.*
jinis *thing*	
s̱vamī *husband*	bɔlô to ækhôn kɔṭa baje? *Tell (me), what time is it?*
ājker kaj *today's work*	
jayga *place*	ōra æk diner jônyô esechen *They have come for a day.*
j̱vɔr *fever*	
hasi *laugh, smile*	
amar jônyô *for me*	tomar ki j̱vɔr hôyeche? *Have you got fever?*
tumi y̆ao *you go*	
amar mône hɔy *I think*	janala diye beʃ rod asche *Nice sunshine is coming through the window.*
ækjɔn lok *a person*	
by̱æmo *disease*	
ʃy̱æm *blue-green*	ōra ei maṯrô elen *They have just come.*
biʃvas *belief*	
by̱bôhar *behaviour*	tāra ei maṯrô gelen *They've just gone.*
biʃvôbidy̱ælɔy *university*	
ote hat diona *Do not touch that.*	

2   Apart from the conjuncts with y̆ɔ-phɔla (ʲ) and bɔ-phɔla (◁) described above, there is one new conjunct in **Exercise 1** – ṯr:

ত + র =   ত্র   ত্র

Be careful not to confuse this with the vowel এ (**e**).

Now see if you can write the words and phrases in **Exercise 1** in Bengali script.

8

There are no new vowels in this unit, but four consonants which are quite difficult for many foreign learners to master. The first is the **aspirated** version of the dental t that you learnt in Unit 6. When English words with an unvoiced 'th' sound *(thin, three)* are transliterated into Bengali, this is the letter that is used (the voiced 'th' as in *then* or *there* is transliterated with a থ). But the sound is actually different from anything in English. To make English 'th' the tongue is placed between the upper and lower front teeth, whereas Bengali th is made by placing the tongue firmly against the upper front teeth as for t, with an additional puff of air following:

th

The next sound is the aspirated labial ph. This is pronounced somewhat variably by native speakers. Some pronounce it as a p with aspiration, but many (especially in Bangladesh) pronounce it more like an English 'f'. In West Bengal it is often pronounced as a 'pf', and this is perhaps the most 'standard' pronunciation to aim for:

ph   as in German *Pfennig*

The third sound in this unit is the 'retroflex' counterpart of d. Place your tongue as for the retroflex t, and add 'voice' to it. Bengalis consider this a 'hard' sound, as opposed to the softer dental consonants. It is like an English 'd', but the tongue should be more pointed and slightly curled back:

ḍ

Finally we come to the sound that is perhaps the most difficult of all for foreign learners of South Asian languages. (In Sanskrit the sound does occur, but only as an 'allophone' of ড় when it occurs between vowels rather than at the beginning of words. As with য/য় the distinguishing dot was added to the Bengali script in the 19th century.) In Unit 1 you learnt the 'rolled' Bengali r. The new sound here is a 'flapped', retroflex ড়. Curl your tongue up and round as if you were about to say ট or ড, but instead of making contact with the alveolar ridge, flap the tongue down smartly so that it audibly slaps against the bottom of the mouth. Or, if you have the tape, ignore this instruction and see if you can simply develop the knack of producing this sound! Some people find it easier to pronounce it between vowels: you can try saying a-ড়-a over and over again. Speakers of American English may find it helpful to compare the sound with the way they pronounce 'tt' in *butter* or *better*:

ড়

The letters for the four sounds above are as follows:

	Handwriting	Print
th	থ	থ
ph	ফ	ফ
ড	ড	ড
ড়	ড়	ড়

Exercises

1 Listen to the tape, or refer back to previous pages, and practise saying the following words and phrases:

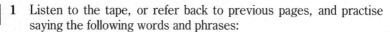

matha *head*	moṭôr gaṛi *motor car*
kɔtha *word, topic*	gôrur gaṛi *bullock-cart*
ami thaki *I stay*	ṭren kɔkhôn chaṛbe? *When*
tumi thamô *you stop*	*will the train leave?*
phul *flower*	ekhane thamô *Stop here.*
phɔl *fruit*	tel phuriye gæche *The oil's*
tini ḍaken *he/she calls*	*run out.*
ækṭa bɔṛô baṛi *a big house*	tumi kothay thakô? *Where do*
ḍal ar tɔrkari *dal and*	*you live?*
vegetables	

ekṭu dāṛan *(Please) wait a little.*

choṭay phire esô *Come back at six.*

ke ḍakche? *Who's calling?*

ogulo deʃi ḍim? *Are those country (free-range) eggs?*

se biṛi khay *He/she smokes biṛis[a].*

aj baṛi theke beriona *Don't go out of the house today.*

oṭa phele diona *Don't throw that away.*

didike ḍakô *Call (your) elder sister.*

thamô, thamô – gaṛi asche! *Stop, stop – there's a car coming!*

rode dāṛabenna *Don't stand in the sun.*

tomar baṛi kothay? *Where is your house?*

phɔlguli sɔb kheye phelechô? *Have you eaten up all the fruit?*

ḍan dik diye gele taṛataṛi hɔbe *If you go to the right it will be quick(er).*

gaṛiṭa thamlei amra nambo *We'll get down when the train stops.*

amar bɔrô baksôṭa kothay? *Where is my big suitcase?*

[a]Small, cheap cheroot, widely smoked throughout the subcontinent.

2 Two new conjuncts occurred in the words and phrases above: ṭr and ks:

ট + র =   ট্র   ট্র

ক + স =   ক্স   ক্স

ট্র is an easily recognisable conjunct, once you know that র when it is written **second** in a conjunct is written ্র attached to the bottom of the first member of the conjunct. Thus:

দ + র =   দ্র   দ্র

ব + র =   ব্র   ব্র

This is known as rɔ-phɔla (cf. y̆ɔ-phɔla and bɔ-phɔla, p. 26). Even in ক্র and ত্র (see pp. 18, 27) rɔ-phɔla is detectable.

Now see if you can write the words and phrases in **Exercise 1** in Bengali script.

9

Five new letters in this unit, but only four new sounds. The first is the nasal version of i (the 'long' ī does not occur in a nasalised form). You should be used to nasalised vowels by now, so this one should present no special difficulty:

ĩ

The next one is the nasalised version of oŭ – a rare sound in Bengali: indeed there are some words whether it is disputed whether the correct pronunciation is oŭ or ōŭ. In transcription the tilda (˜) has to be placed over the first vowel, but be careful to nasalise the whole diphthong:

ōŭ

You might find it interesting at this stage to look at the complete table of letters on p. 45, and tick off the letters you have learnt. You will see that in the fifth group of consonants, the first and the fourth are still remaining. The first is **un**voiced and **un**aspirated. As with other unaspirated consonants, be careful not to aspirate it inadvertently when it occurs at the beginning of a word.

The unaspirated 'p' that occurs at the **end** of English words is similar to the Bengali sound:

p

The letters for these three sounds are as follows:

	Handwriting	**Print**	
ī	ঈ	ঈ	(full vowel)
	ী	ী	(vowel sign)
ōŭ	ঔ	ঔ	(full vowel)
	ৌ	ৌ	(vowel sign)

Remember that when writing the nasal cɔndrôbindu (ঁ) with vowel signs, it should be placed over the consonant, not the vowel sign itself: বিঁ, বৌঁ.

p	প	প

There are two more letters to learn in this unit. The first is really a conjunct made up of k and ṣ. In Sanskrit words and names such as 'kṣatrīya', 'rākṣasa' or 'Lakṣmī', it is pronounced 'ksh'. In Bengali it is pronounced like kh if it occurs at the beginning of a word, and like a double kkh if it occurs between vowels in the middle of a word. Thus the examples above are pronounced in Bengali 'khɔtriyô', 'rakkhôs' and 'lôkkhi' (notice that in the third of these the 'm' is 'assimilated' into the kṣ and is not pronounced at all). In the transcription used in this book, kṣ will be used for this letter, and you will therefore have to remember that the ṣ is not pronounced. The reason for introducing it here rather than merely in passing as a conjunct is that some Bengali dictionaries treat it as a single letter and have a separate section for words beginning with kṣ.

kṣ	ক্ষ	ক্ষ

When referring to this letter on its own, Bengalis call it 'khiyɔ'.

Finally we have the ṇ that belongs to the 'retroflex' group of consonants (see complete table on p. 45). It is pronounced exactly the same as n. It occurs on its own quite frequently, particularly at the end of words, but also in conjuncts with one of the other retroflex consonants. The general rule is that conjuncts involving a nasal use the nasal appropriate to the group: thus 'velar' consonants (k, kh, g, etc.) take ŋ, 'palatal' consonants (c, ch, etc.) take ñ, 'retroflex' consonants take ṇ, 'dental' consonants take n and 'labial' consonants take m.

The three sibilants (see Unit 2, p. 9) are categorised as 'palatal' (শ), 'retroflex' (ষ) and 'dental' (স) , and the same principle applies. The rule is sometimes broken with foreign words: kaunṭar – *counter* – would be written with dental n + retroflex ṭ, and masṭar is written with dental s + retroflex ṭ. The letter for retroflex ṇ is:

ṇ	ণ	ণ

Exercises

1 Listen to the tape, or refer back to previous pages, and practise saying the following words and phrases:

pa *foot, leg*
pɔth *path*
pɔre *after(wards)*
se pɔɾe *he/she reads*
kōŭsulī *legal counsel*
apni bam̩la bôlte paren? *Can you speak Bengali?*
apni kæmôn achen? *How are you?*
ṭaka-pɔysa *money*
apnake ɔpekṣa kôrte hɔbe *You must wait.*
purôno kapôɾ *old clothes*
jamaṭaᵃ chīɾe gæche *The dress has torn.*
eṭa amader pɔṣa beɾal *This is our pet cat.*
ki sundôr pakhi! *What (a) beautiful bird(s)!*
or phuphuᵇ mara gæchen *His (paternal) aunt has died.*
poŭṣ mas *The month of Pausᶜ*
pɔyla tarikh *the first (of the month)*
aj pôrẙôntô *until today*
ækjɔn tôruṇ kôbi *a young poet*
apnara prôṯyeke ɔm̩ʃô nin *(Please) each of you take part.*

tomar mathar upôr *above your head*
ami pa pichle pôɾe gelam *I slipped and fell.*
apni kɔkhôn pōŭchôlen? *When did you arrive?*
tomader pɔɾaʃona kæmôn hôyeche? *How have your studies gone?*
paʃer baɾite kara esechen? *Who has come to the house next door?*
ækhôno alap hɔyni *(We) haven't yet met.*
ēke prôṇam kɔrô *Do praṇāmᵈ to him/her*
jaygaṭar bibɔrôṇ dite parô? *Can (you) give a description of the place?*
seṭa kôruṇ byæpar *That's a sad matter.*
eṭuku pɔth hēṭe ẙete parbo *(I'll) be able to walk this small distance.*
pɔɾaʃona na kôrle, pôrīkṣay paʃ kôrte parbena *If you don't study, you won't pass the exam.*

ᵃjama means any kind of garment for the upper body. jama-kapôɾ is the usual expression for clothes. Nowadays, sarṯ is usually used for a man's shirt, and jama for a girl's blouse or frock.
ᵇA Muslim kinship term. See list on pp. 272–274.
ᶜSee the Review at the end of Part Two (p. 195) for the Bengali months.
ᵈHindu obeisance: 'taking the dust of someone's feet'.

2   There are two new conjuncts in this exercise. One of them is on the same pattern as ট্র in Unit 8 (p. 30):

   প + র =   প্র   প্র

The other conjunct also conforms to a pattern:

   র + য =   র্য

✓ above a consonant is known as **reph**, and is always used when র **precedes** another consonant.

Now see if you can write the words and phrases in **Exercise 1** in Bengali script. Watch out for conjuncts with **y**: remember that ɟ is used if   য/য়   occurs as the second member of a conjunct (see Unit 7, p. 26). Be careful not to miss ŋ   (ণ) , not to be confused with ŋ (ঙ) .

10

The second diphthong in the Bengali alphabet is a combination of **o** and **i**.

oĭ

In Hindi and Sanskrit it would be pronounced 'ai', and the other diphthong, **oŭ**, is pronounced 'au'. Hindu words and names such as 'Vaiṣṇava' and 'Kaurava' become **boĭṣṇôb** and **koŭrôb** in Bengali. Of course other diphthongs are created in Bengali by combinations of vowels: e.g. in words such as **khay** or **keu**, where the stress always falls on the first vowel. Sometimes the diphthongs **oŭ** and **oĭ** are achieved by the inherent vowel + u or i: the words for 'wife' and 'book', for example, are written **bôu** (বউ) and **bôi** (বই) . The combination 'proper' vowel **o** + i can also occur, as in the demonstrative **oi** (ওই) , but **o** + u does not. Remember that the special letters for these diphthongs when they occur are indicated in the transcription used in this book by an accent: **oŭ/oĭ**.

Two new consonants are introduced in this unit. The first is the unaspirated version of **ch** (see Unit 5, p. 19). 'ch' at the end of English words like *touch, bench* or *pitch* is generally free of aspiration: this is the sound you should aim at in Bengali:

c

The second consonant is the aspirated version of **b**. This is a heavy sound, and it takes some considerable heaving of the chest muscles to produce it at first:

bh

The letters for these three sounds are as follows:

	Handwriting	Print
oĭ	ঐ	ঐ (full vowel)
	ৈ	ৈ (vowel sign, written before the consonant, like the vowel sign for এ)
c	চ	চ
bh	ভ	ভ

Exercises

1 Listen to the tape, or refer back to previous pages, and practise saying the following words and phrases:

ca   *tea*

cal   *(uncooked) rice*

cabi   *key*

cokh   *eye*

car   *four*

se cay   *he/she wants*

bhalo   *good*

bhul   *mistake*

ami bhule gechi   *I've forgotten*

bhat   *(cooked) rice*

ki hôcche?   *What's happening?*

cup kɔrô!   *Be quiet!*

bhɔdrôlok   *gentleman*

cɔʃma   *spectacles*

coĭtrô mas   *the month of* Caitra[a]

se amar ceye bɔɽô   *He/she's older than me.*

or bhaike cinina   *(I) do not know his/her brother.*

cɔlô, bæɽate ỹai   *Come, let's go out.*

uni ʈaka dicchen   *He/she is paying.*

bhɔdrôlokke ca dao   *Give the gentleman (some) tea.*

bhat na kheye luci khan   *Don't eat rice, eat lucis.*[b]

kɔy camôc cini debô?   *How many spoon(ful)s of sugar shall (I) give you?*

dui camôc din   *Give (me) two spoon(fuls).*

apnar bhai kæmôn ache?   *How is your brother?*

bhalo ache   *He's well.*

bhɔdrômôhilaʈike cenô?   *Do you know the lady?*

cabiʈa kothay rakhle?   *Where did (you) put the key?*

[a]For the Bengali months, see p. 195.

[b]A kind of puffed chapati: similar to *puri* in North India but smaller and eaten as a snack.

amar bhɔyanôk bhūter bhɔy
kɔre   *I have a terrible fear of*
ghosts.

babar jônyô amar khub bhabna
hɔy   *I'm very worried about*
Father.

baṛiṭa bhalo kintu bhaṛa beʃī
The house is good but the
rent is too high.

cokhe bhalo dekhte paina   *(I)*
don't have good eyesight.

2   The conjunct **c** + **ch** is an obvious combination of the two, and the
conjunct **d** + **r** follows the same pattern as the conjuncts noted in
Units 8 and 9:

চ + ছ =   ছ্ছ   চ্ছ

দ + র =   দ্র   দ্র

Remember how to write **kintu** *(but)* (see Unit 6, p. 24). Now see if
you can write the words and phrases in **Exercise 1** in Bengali script.

11

Five new letters in this unit, but really only three new sounds. First is the voiced aspirated:

jh

This is made by adding aspiration to j. In the same way, aspiration should be added to ţ to create

ţh

This is an easy sound for English speakers, as the English t is normally aspirated when it occurs at the beginning of words: but give the Bengali sound a little more 'punch' than an English t, and remember to press the *tip* of your tongue against the alveolar ridge.

The next sound is rather rare. It is the aspirated version of the voiced retroflex ḍ:

ḍh

It is the sound that occurs in the name of the capital of Bangladesh: ḍhaka. Like ţh, it should be pronounced sharply and forcefully.

The letters for these three sounds are as follows:

	Handwriting	**Print**
jh	ঝ	ঝ
ţh	ঠ	ঠ

ḍh   ড়   ড়

The first of the remaining two letters is theoretically the aspirated version of the retroflex ṛ – but in fact it is not really pronounced with aspiration. It is a very rare letter. The only common word containing it is the Bengali month aṣaṛh (June–July, see p. 195).

ṛh   ঢ়   ঢ়

Like ṛ (ড়) it does not exist as a separate letter in Sanskrit (see Unit 8, p. 29). This is why in the full table of letters ড় and ঢ় are normally given in brackets after ড and ঢ respectively (see p. 45).

Finally a letter which is known as khôṇḍô (*cut-off*) tô. It is used when the dental t occurs **without** the inherent vowel being pronounced, or any other vowel added. It is given as t̲ in the transcription used in this book:

t̲   ৎ   ৎ

It either comes at the end of words – e.g. হঠাৎ (hôṭhat̲, *suddenly*), or before consonants that do not naturally form a conjunct with t – e.g. উৎসব (ut̲sob, *festival*, সৎমা (sot̲ma, *step-mother*). Many such words, however, use ত rather than ৎ. You certainly cannot assume that t without a vowel will always be spelt with ৎ.

Exercises

1   Listen to the tape, or refer back to previous pages, and practise saying the following words and phrases:

jhol *the sauce of a curry*	raṛh bôṇgô (old name for the
jhoṛ *storm*	Western part of Bengal)
jhi *maidservant, charlady*	proūṛhô bôyôs *middle-age*
jhogṛa *quarrel*	kothaṭa ṭhik *What (you) say*
majhi *boatman*	*is right.*
ṭhik *right, correct*	jhi mejhe jhãṭ dicche *The*
ṭhikana *address*	*maid is sweeping the floor.*
thaṭṭa *teasing*	ami bôṇla bujhina *I don't*
maṭh *open land*	*understand Bengali.*
ḍheu *wave, billow*	ḍhil merona *Don't throw*
se bojhe *he/she understands*	*stones.*
tini oṭhen *he/she gets up*	bhat ḍhakô *Cover the rice.*
gaṛhô lal *deep red*	ṭhik ache *all right*

apnar ʈhikanaʈa bôlun *(Please) tell (me) your address.*

aṣaɽh maser majhamajhi *in the middle of Āṣāṛh*

ciʈhiʈa paʈhiye dao *Post the letter.*

mejhete ʃuye or thanḍa legeche *He/she has caught a chill by sleeping on the floor.*

ætô bhore uʈhona *Don't get up so early.*

jhɔgɽa kôrchô kænô? *Why are you quarelling?*

macher jhole ki jhal hôyeche? *Is the fish curry very hot?*[a]

ætô bɔrô gaɽi ki kôre ḍhukbe? *How will such a big vehicle enter?*

hɔʈhat jhɔɽ uʈhlo *Suddenly a storm arose.*

majhi rɔona hôte rajī hôlôna *The boatman was not willing to set out.*

[a]jhal means the quality of hotness or spiciness in a curry.

2 The are two conjuncts in the sound exercise above, ʈʈ and nḍ:

টʈ + টʈ = ট্ট   ট্ট

ণ + ড = ণ্ড   ণ্ড

Now see if you can write out the words and phrases in **Exercise 1** in Bengali script.

12

Three more letters to go! The first is classified as a vowel, but does not seem like a vowel as it is pronounced 'ri' as in the name of the best-loved of all Hindu deities, Krishna. The Sanskritic transliteration for Krishna is 'Kṛṣṇa', and the same symbol for 'ri' has been adopted in the transcription used in this book:

ṛ

It is likely that the letter was originally pronounced rather differently, hence its classification as a vowel. Like other vowels, it has a full form and a vowel sign:

	Handwriting	Print
ṛ	ঋ	ঋ (full vowel)
	ৃ	ৃ (vowel sign)

The vowel sign is attached to the bottom of the consonant, so pṛthibī *(earth)*, for example, is printed পৃথিবী. In some computer typefaces, however, it appears slightly to the right.

The last two sounds are consonants. First, the aspirated version of **g**:

gh

Second, the aspirated version of the dental **d**:

dh

The letters for these sounds are:

| gh | ঘ | ঘ |
| dh | ধ | ধ |

 ——— **Exercises** ———

 1 Listen to the tape, or refer back to previous pages, and practise saying the following words and phrases:

ghi   *ghee (clarified butter)*
gham   *sweat*
ghas   *grass*
ghɔr   *room*
ghoɽa   *horse*
ghôɽi   *watch/clock*
ghoṇṭa   *hour*
dhopa   *washerman*
dhūlo   *dust*
se hat dhoy   *He/she washes his/her hands.*
ekhane bas dhɔra ẏay   *Buses can be caught here*
bam̩ladeʃe chɔṭi ṛtu   *(There are) six seasons in Bangladesh.*
amar ɔnek ṛṇ   *I'm heavily in debt.*
bṛṣṭi hôcche   *It's raining.*
dokanṭa bɔndhô   *The shop's shut.*
amra ʃudhu bôndhu   *We're just friends.*
ami aɽai ghoṇṭa bôse achi   *I've been waiting for two-and-a-half hours.*

adh ser dudh nebô   *I'll take half a seer of milk.*[a]
se sɔmɔstô pṛthibī ghureche   *He's wandered (all over) the world.*
rode ghurbenna – matha dhôrbe   *Don't wander in the sun – you'll get a headache.*[b]
oi baɽi theke dhõya asche!   *There's smoke coming from that house!*
ætôkṣôṇ ghumôcchile?   *Were (you) sleeping all that time?*
budhbar ki skul bɔndhô na khola?   *Is the school closed or open (on) Wednesday(s)?*
bodh hɔy bɔndhô   *Probably closed.*
ei rasta dhôre bajare ẏaoya ẏay?   *Can (I) get to the bazaar by this road?*
ghaṭer pɔthe khub dhūlo   *There's a lot of dust on the path to the ghāṭ.*[c]
ætô sukh amar hṛdɔye![d]   *Such joy in my heart!*

[a]See the **Review** of **Part Two** (p. 196).
[b]See p. 110.
[c]Mooring-place, or steps down to a river or pond for bathing and washing.
[d]For the pronunciation of hṛdɔy, see Note 31 on p. 255.

aj dinṭa ækebare br̥tha
  gælô   *Today the day has been
  absolutely futile.*
se ʃudhu dhuti pɔre   *He only
  wears a dhoti.*

ghoṛaṭa khub dhīre-dhīre
  ṭanche   *The horse is pulling
  very slowly.*

2   There are five conjuncts in the sound exercise above: <u>sk</u>, <u>st</u>, <u>nt</u>, <u>ndh</u>, and <u>st</u>:

স + ক =	স্ক	স্ক
স + ত =	স্ত	স্ত
ণ + ট =	ণ্ট	ণ্ট
ন + ধ =	ন্ধ	ন্ধ
ষ + ট =	ষ্ট	ষ্ট

You also need to note the way in which h + r̥ is written. Older typefaces approximate to the handwritten form – but some modern (computer) typefaces simply put the vowel sign for r̥ under the h in the usual way:

হ + ঋ =	হৃ	হৃ (old)
		হৃ (modern)

Now see if you can write out the words and phrases in **Exercise 1** in Bengali script.

13

———— REVIEW OF ————
PART ONE

You have now, if you have worked through all the exercises in units 1–12, learnt nearly all the basic Bengali letters, and quite a few conjuncts. The complete table of letters, in the traditional order followed by Bengali dictionaries, is shown opposite:

You have also learnt a number of conjuncts. In **Part Two** and **Part Three** your attention will be drawn to other conjuncts as they occur. For reference, a complete table of conjuncts has been supplied in the **Review of Part Three** (pp. 265–70).

The only letters in the table that you have not yet learnt are the nasal for the 'palatal' group of consonants – ñ (এ), and the so-called bisɔrgô (ঃ). এ – called 'niyô' or 'ĩyô' by Bengalis – only occurs in conjuncts such as ñc, ñj, ñjh, or jñ, which will be noted when they occur in **Part Two**. It is pronounced the same as n and ŋ. ঃ is explained on p. 255.

It is essential that the table of letters becomes firmly implanted in your mind, otherwise it will take you ages to find words in the dictionary. The best way to learn the table, and to learn Bengali vocabulary, is to write words on small index cards (with the meaning on the other side of the card), and file them in the correct 'dictionary order'.

Table of letters

<table>
<tr><td colspan="11" align="center">বাংলা বর্ণমালা
Bengali Alphabet</td></tr>
<tr>
<td>অ</td><td>আ</td><td>ই</td><td>ঈ</td><td>উ</td><td>ঊ</td><td>ঋ</td><td>এ</td><td>ঐ</td><td>ও</td><td>ঔ</td>
</tr>
<tr>
<td>ɔ</td><td>a</td><td>i</td><td>ī</td><td>u</td><td>ū</td><td>ṛ</td><td>e</td><td>oĭ</td><td>o</td><td>oŭ</td>
</tr>
<tr>
<td>ং</td><td>ঃ</td><td>ঁ</td><td></td><td></td><td></td><td></td><td></td><td></td><td></td><td></td>
</tr>
<tr>
<td>ṃ</td><td>ḥ</td><td>~</td><td></td><td></td><td></td><td></td><td></td><td></td><td></td><td></td>
</tr>
</table>

ক	খ	গ	ঘ	ঙ
k	kh	g	gh	ŋ
চ	ছ	জ	ঝ	এঞ
c	ch	j	jh	ñ
ট	ঠ	ড(ড়)	ঢ(ঢ়)	ণ
t	th	ḍ (ṛ)	ḍh (ṛh)	ṇ
ত(ৎ)	থ	দ	ধ	ন
t (ṯ)	th	d	dh	n
প	ফ	ব	ভ	ম
p	ph	b	bh	m

য	(য়)	র	ল	শ	ষ	স	হ
y̆	(y)	r	l	ʃ	ṣ	s	h

All the **Conversations** in Units 14 to 25 are given in Bengali script.
When you read them, looking up words in the **Glossary** if necessary,
write down on cards words that you feel would be useful to learn. Even if
you do not have the stamina to write down all the words on cards, the
filing of them will help to ram home the order of the Bengali letters.
Further guidance on the order of words in Bengali dictionaries is given at
the beginning of the **Glossary** (p. 294), and information about which
dictionaries to buy is given on p. 276.

Some of the special names used to refer to particular letters have already been noted. The following list adds a few more:

ই – হ্রস্ব ই	hrɔsvô i	
ঈ – দীর্ঘ ঈ	dīrghô ī	
উ – হ্রস্ব উ	hrɔsvô u	
ঊ – দীর্ঘ ঊ	dīrghô ū	
ং – অনুস্বার*	ônusvar	*or অনুস্বর (ônusvôr)
ঁ – চন্দ্রবিন্দু	cɔndrôbindu	
ঃ – বিসর্গ	bisɔrgô	
জ – বর্গীয় জ	bôrgīyô jɔ	
ণ – মূর্ধন্য ণ	mūrdhônyô ɳɔ	
ন – দন্ত্য ন	dɔntyô nɔ	
য – অন্তঃস্থ য	ɔntɔhsthô y̆ɔ	
য় – অন্তঃস্থ য়	ɔntɔhsthô yɔ*	*pronounced 'ɔntɔhsthô ɔ'
শ – তালব্য শ	talôbyô ʃɔ	
ষ – মূর্ধন্য ষ	mūrdhônyô ʂɔ	
স – দন্ত্য স	dɔntyô sɔ	
্য – য-ফলা	y̆ɔ-phɔla	
্ব – ব-ফলা	bɔ-phɔla	
্র – র-ফলা	rɔ-phɔla	
র্ – রেফ	reph	

When referring to vowel signs, the suffix -kar (কার) is used; and in referring to conjuncts, the locative case ending is applied to the first member of the conjunct (see Unit 17, pp. 83–84). Thus to spell out the word অবিস্মরণীয় (*unforgettable*), one would say:

অ / ব-হ্রস্ব ইকার / স-এ ম / র / মূর্ধন্য ণ-দীর্ঘ ঈকার / অন্তঃস্থ য়

——— **Sanskritic transliteration** ———

If you progress in your study of Bengali, you will come across a standard 'Sanskritic' system of transliteration, used for all South Asian languages. It is not very satisfactory for Bengali, mainly because the inherent vowel is always written *a*, whereas as you know now the Bengali inherent vowel is pronounced ɔ or ô. For reference, the table of letters with Sanskritic transliteration is as follows:

অ	আ	ই	ঈ	উ	ঊ	ঋ	এ	ঐ	ও	ঔ
a	ā	i	ī	u	ū	ṛ	e	ai	o	au

ং	ঃ	ঁ								
ṃ	ḥ									

ক	খ	গ	ঘ	ঙ
k	kh	g	gh	ṅ

চ	ছ	জ	ঝ	ঞ
c	ch	j	jh	ñ

ট	ঠ	ড (ড়)	ঢ (ঢ়)	ণ
ṭ	ṭh	ḍ (ṛ)	ḍh (ṛh)	ṇ

ত (ৎ)	থ	দ	ধ	ন
t (t)	th	d	dh	n

প	ফ	ব	ভ	ম
p	ph	b/v	bh	m

য	(য়)	র	ল	শ	ষ	স	হ
y	(y)	r	l	ś	ṣ	s	h

Some of the names for letters listed opposite would, in Sanskritic transliteration, be:

hrasva, dīrgha, anusvār, candrabindu, bisarga, bargīya, mūrdhanya, dantya, antaḥstha, tālabya, ya-phalā.

PART TWO

CONVERSATION AND GRAMMAR

14

FINDING OUT ABOUT SOMEONE

Conversation

The basic idea behind all the **Conversations** in this book is as follows: you, as a learner, wish to try out your Bengali on native speakers and you do this by meeting as many native speakers as possible, in Bangladesh, West Bengal and among প্রবাসী বাঙালী (expatriate Bengali) communities outside the subcontinent. In the Conversations, you ask them questions about their lives, work, families, ideas, feelings, and so on. Your questions will be simple in structure to begin with, but they will gradually get more complicated as your knowledge of Bengali progresses. Your 'interviewees' will reply in sentences that are natural to them, and they may ask *you* some questions! By the end of Unit 25 you will have reached an equal interraction with the people you are talking to.

The **Grammar** section after each **Conversation** explains nearly all the structures used by *you*: it won't necessarily cover everything said by your 'interviewees'. But when, by the end of **Part Two**, you have completed all the exercises, you can go back and analyse what your interviewees have said in the light of all the grammar you have learnt.

When reading and rehearsing each **Conversation**, try to turn what *you* say into 'active knowledge'. Your understanding of what your interviewees say can be more 'passive': an overall understanding of the meaning will be sufficient. The translation given, and the grammar notes, should enable you to work out the meaning of individual words. Failing that, you can look them up in the **Glossary** at the end of the book.

If you have the tape, you will find all the **Conversations** in the book recorded on it. Listen to it to perfect your pronunciation.

For your first **Conversation**, you try out your Bengali on Mrs Kurshid Rahman, who works in a school office in East London. Noticing a photograph that she keeps on her desk, you ask her about it:

আপনি উনি কে?

মিসেস রাহমান উনি আমার আব্বা ।

আপনি 'আব্বা' মানে বাবা ?

মিসেস রাহমান হ্যা, বাংলাদেশে সাধারণত বাবাকে 'আব্বা' বলে ।

আপনি আর ইনি কে ?

মিসেস রাহমান ইনি আমার আম্মা ।

আপনি 'আম্মা' মানে মা ?

মিসেস রাহমান হ্যা, আমরা সাধারণত 'আম্মা' বলি ।

আপনি ও কে ?

মিসেস রাহমান ও আমার ছোট বোন ।

আপনি ওর নাম কি ?

মিসেস রাহমান ওর নাম রহিমা, কিন্তু ওর ডাক-নাম মিনি ।

আপনি এটা আপনাদের বাড়ি ?

মিসেস রাহমান ঠিক আমাদের বাড়ি নয়, ঢাকায় আমাদের বাসা ।

— 49 —

আপনি	ওটা কার সাইকেল ?
মিসেস রাহমান	আমার ভাই-এর – ও ফটোয় নেই ।
আপনি	ইনি কি আপনার স্বামী ?
মিসেস রাহমান	হ্যা, ফটোটি আমাদের বিয়ের পরে তোলা ।
আপনি	ওটা কি ?
মিসেস রাহমান	ওটা আমাদের প্রতিবেশীর বারান্দা । আমাদের বারান্দা বাসার পিছন দিকে – এ দিক থেকে দেখা যায়না ।

Translation and notes

You	Who's he?
Mrs Rahman	He's my father.
You	Does 'abba' mean father?
Mrs Rahman	Yes, in Bangladesh we usually say 'abba' for father.[a]
You	And who is she?
Mrs Rahman	She's my mother.
You	Does 'amma' mean mother?
Mrs Rahman	Yes, we usually say 'amma'.
You	Who's she?
Mrs Rahman	She's my little sister.
You	What's her name?
Mrs Rahman	Her name is Rahima, but her family name is Mini.[b]
You	Is this your home?
Mrs Rahman	Not exactly our home, but our place in Dhaka.[c]
You	Whose bicycle is that?
Mrs Rahman	My brother's – he's not in the photo.
You	Is he your husband?[d]
Mrs Rahman	Yes, the photo was taken after our marriage.
You	What's that?
Mrs Rahman	That's our neighbour's verandah. Our verandah is at the back of the house – it can't be seen from this side.[e]

[a] baba and ma are the standard words for *mother* and *father*, but abba and amma are used colloquially by Bengali Muslims. Note the conjuncts: ব + ব = ব্ব; ম + ম = ম্ম

[b] Bengalis usually have a formal name by which they are known publicly, and a ḍak-nam (Lit. *call-name*) used within their immediate family.

[c] Mrs Rahman implies here that her family has a home (baṛi) in a village: probably her grandparents still live there. Her parents rent their flat in Dhaka, so it's their basa *(residence)* not their true home.

^dYou may have come across 'Swami' as a title for a Hindu religious teacher. In Bengal it is used by both Hindus and Muslims as the ordinary word for *husband*. For its pronunciation, 'shami', see p. 26.
^eThe 'verandah' in a city flat or house can be an upper-floor balcony.

Grammar

1 Zero verb

In English, sentences like *John is fat*, or *Mary is a policewoman*, or *Is he mad?* are known as **subject-complement constructions**. All the questions in the dialogue above follow this simple structure: in English these require the verb *to be*, whereas in Bengali **no verb is required**.

2 Interrogative ki

The Bengali question word or interrogative ki is pronounced with a slight emphasis or stress when it means *What?* e.g. oṭa ki? *(What's that?)*. But it can also be used to turn a statement into a question, in which case it is unstressed, i.e. pronounced only very lightly: ini ki apnar svamī? *(Is he your husband?)*. The great Bengali writer Rabindranath Tagore tried to establish a convention that 'unstressed ki' should be written with কি and 'stressed ki' should be written with কী but many writers use কি for both, and one has to tell from the context whether it is stressed or not. Unstressed ki can often be omitted, the question being indicated merely by a rising intonation.

3 Personal pronouns

Bengali personal pronouns (*I, you, he*, etc.) and their possessive forms (*my, your, his*, etc.) are not difficult to learn, so although not all of them have been used in the dialogue above, it will be useful to look at a table of them right away. There are three important points to notice:

(a) Bengali (more advanced than English in this respect!) does not distinguish gender even in singular pronouns: there is no distinction between *he* and *she*.

(b) Bengali distinguishes between **polite** and **familiar** pronouns, not only in the second person (*you*) as in French, German and many other

languages, but in the third person too *(he/she/they)*. Polite pronouns are used when addressing or referring to people not well known to you, or people older or more senior than you are. Familiar pronouns are used for friends or children.

(c) In the third person **proximity** is distinguished. ini, for example, means *he* or *she* nearby, and uni means *he* or *she* over there. There is also tini, used for *he* or *she* elsewhere. This is commonly used in written narrative, but in speech the second degree of proximity is often sufficient, even if the person is not actually present. ini, uni, tini are **polite** pronouns: you will see from the table below what the familiar third person pronouns are. You will also see that polite forms are often achieved by 'nasalising' the vowel.

(Note the abbreviations: F = Familiar; P = Polite; H = Here; T = There; E = Elsewhere.)

Subject		Singular	Plural	
1	*I*	ami	amra	*we*
2	*you* [F]	tumi	tomra	*you*
	you [P]	apni	apnara	*you*
3 [H]	*he/she* [F]	e	era	*they*
	he/she [P]	ini	ēra	*they*
3 [T]	*he/she* [F]	o	ora	*they*
	he/she [P]	uni	ōra	*they*
3 [E]	*he/she* [F]	se	tara	*they*
	he/she [P]	tini	tāra	*they*

Possessive		Singular	Plural	
1	*my*	amar	amader	*our*
2	*your* [F]	tomar	tomader	*your*
	your [P]	apnar	apnader	*your*
3 [H]	*his/her* [F]	er	eder	*their*
	his/her [P]	ēr*	ēder*	*their*
[T]	*his/her* [F]	or	oder	*their*
	his/her [P]	ōr*	ōder*	*their*
[E]	*his/her* [F]	tar	tader	*their*
	his/her [P]	tār	tāder	*their*

*The colloquial forms enar, enader, onar, onader are very common in speech.

The interrogative personal pronoun *(Who? Whose?)* follows a similar pattern:

Subject		Singular	Plural
Who?		ke?	kara?

Possessive			
Whose?		kar?	kader?

These forms can be either polite or familiar. They are never nasalized like the non-interrogative personal pronouns. In the subject case, **ke ke** is an alternative for **kara** when separate individuals are implied.

4 Demonstrative pronouns

The demonstrative pronouns *(this, that, these, those)* make use of the same distinctions of proximity as the third person pronouns:

eṭa	*this* (here)
oṭa	*that* (there)
seṭa	*that* (elsewhere)
egulo	*these* (here)
ogulo	*those* (there)
segulo	*those* (elsewhere)

 ———————— **Exercises** ————————

These exercises throughout **Part Two** are based on the grammar covered in each unit. The first exercise is given in script, and is generally very simple in form. The second exercise is given in transcription, and is more complicated. Both sorts of exercise, however, should be answered **either** orally **or** in Bengali script. Do not attempt to write the transcription: the **Key to the exercises** (in Bengali script) is on pp. 278–293.

When script is used, the exercises are numbered with Bengali numerals. You can learn how to write these by referring to the handwriting diagrams on pp. x–xi at the front of the book.

1 *(a)* Imagine that you are being asked questions about a photograph of your own family. Reply affirmatively, following the pattern given in the example:

ইনি কি আপনার বাবা ?
হ্যাঁ, ইনি আমার বাবা ।

> ১ উনি কি আপনার মা ?
> ২ এ আপনার ছোট ভাই ?
> ৩ ওর নাম কি জন ?
> ৪ এটা আপনাদের বাড়ি ?
> ৫ এটা কি আপনার সাইকেল ?
> ৬ ইনি আপনার বোন ?
> ৭ উনি ওঁর স্বামী ?
> ৮ ইনি কি আপনাদের প্রতিবেশী ?
> ৯ ওটা কি ওঁর ?
> ১০ এটা কি আপনার ?

(b) Many words for common articles of modern life have been taken into Bengali from English. See if you can say what the following items are, changing the demonstrative pronoun from এটা to ওটা in each case. Example:

এটা কি ?   **ওটা টেবিল ।**

এটা কি ?   ১ ওটা _____ ।

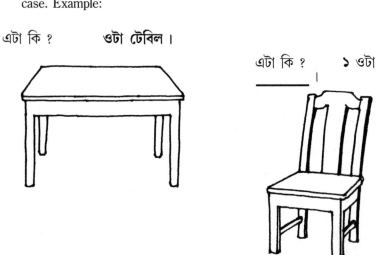

এটা কি ?   ২ ওটা _____ ।

এটা কি ?   ৩ ওটা _____ ।

এটা কি ?   ৪ ওটা _____ ।

এটা কি ?   ৫ ওটা _____ ।

এটা কি ?   ৬ ওটা _____ ।

The last one is a trap, for British learners at least! The English word that is used in Bengali for *trousers* is প্যান্ট ('pant'). Note also that *postage stamps* are ডাকটিকিট ('post-ticket') and *ball-point pen/biro* is ডট-পেন ('dot-pen').

2   Fill in the gaps in the following questions and answers, using the interrogative ki, the personal pronouns, or the demonstrative pronouns. To write the exercise, you will need the following conjuncts, some of which are new to you:

	Handwriting	**Print**
ক + ত =	ক্ত	ক্ত
ঞ + জ =	ঞ্জ	ঞ্জ (see p. 44)
ন + দ =	ন্দ	ন্দ
খ + র =	খ্র	খ্র
ষ + ট =	ষ্ট	ষ্ট
হ + য/য় =	হ্য	হ্য
স + ট =	স্ট	স্ট

(i)   tomar nam ____?
____nam hasan.

(ii)   ami baŋali.
apni ____ iṃrej? *(English)*

(iii)   ____ ki ṭicar? *(teacher)*
na, uni ḍaktar. *(doctor)*

(iv)   oṭa kar?
oṭa ____.

(v)   apni ke?
____ rɔñjit.

(vi)   eṭa ____?
ōr.

(vii)   oṭa ____ koṭ? *(coat)*
na, ____ er koṭ.

(viii)   tara ____ hindu?
na, ____ khriṣṭan. *(Christian)*

(ix)   ____ ki oder baṛi?
hyæ̃, ____ baṛi.

(x)   tomader ṭicar ____?
____ ṭicar misṭar hɔk.

15

TALKING TO A RICKSHAWALLAH

Conversation

You are staying at Santiniketan in West Bengal, where Rabindranath Tagore founded his famous school and university. You've been to Calcutta for a couple of days, and have just returned, travelling on the Visva-Bharati express, arriving at Bolpur station at midday. The rickshawallah who takes you to the university from the station knows you quite well. He knew you were coming back today, and was waiting at the station for you. You ask him some questions as you ride along in the baking midday heat.

আপনি	এই রিকশা কি আপনার ?
রিকশাওয়ালা	হ্যাঁ, এটা আমার ।
আপনি	এখানে কি অনেক রিকশা আছে ?
রিকশাওয়ালা	হ্যাঁ, খুব বেশি । এত রিকশার জন্য যথেষ্ট কাজ নেই ।
আপনি	আপনার কি ছেলেমেয়ে আছে ?
রিকশাওয়ালা	হ্যাঁ, একটি মেয়ে আর দুটি ছেলে ।

আপনি	তাদের বয়স কত ?
রিকশাওয়ালা	মেয়েটির বয়স বার, ছেলেদের বয়স দশ আর সাত ।
আপনি	আপনাদের বাড়ি এখানে কোথায় ?
রিকশাওয়ালা	খুব কাছেই – ওই দিকে, পুকুরের ওপারে ।
আপনি	ওখানে কি গ্রাম আছে ?
রিকশাওয়ালা	ঠিক গ্রাম নেই – ওখানে বাড়িগুলো সব ছড়ানো ।
আপনি	আপনার বাবার কি রিকশা ছিল ?
রিকশাওয়ালা	না, আমার বাবার রিকশা ছিলনা । উনি চাষী ছিলেন ।
আপনি	জমিজমা ?
রিকশাওয়ালা	অল্প-কিছু, তবে এখানে নেই – বিহারে । আমার দাদা এখন ওখানে চাষ করেন ।
আপনি	আপনারা বাঙালী নন ?
রিকশাওয়ালা	না, আমরা বিহারী ।
আপনি	এদিকে কি ক্যামেরার দোকান আছে ?
রিকশাওয়ালা	এদিকে নেই – বোলপুরে অনেক স্টুডিও আছে, তবে দুপুরে খোলা থাকেনা, সন্ধ্যেয় খোলে ।
আপনি	ওটা কি ?
রিকশাওয়ালা	ওটা আপনার ইলেকট্রিক আপিস ।
আপনি	বাড়িটা কি নতুন ?
রিকশাওয়ালা	না, অনেকদিনের পুরনো ।
আপনি	আচ্ছা, বেশ । ভাড়া কত ?
রিকশাওয়ালা	পাঁচ টাকা ।
আপনি	এই যে, নিন । চলি ?
রিকশাওয়ালা	আসুন ।

Translation and notes

You	Is this rickshaw yours?
Rickshawallah	Yes it's mine.
You	Are there lots of rickshaws here?

Rickshawallah	Yes, too many. There isn't enough work for so many rickshaws.
You	Do you have children?
Rickshawallah	Yes, one daughter and two sons.
You	How old are they?
Rickshawallah	The girl is twelve, the boys are ten and seven.
You	Where is your house here?
Rickshawallah	Very near – over there, on the other side of the pond.[a]
You	Is there (a) village there?
Rickshawallah	Not exactly a village – the houses are scattered there.
You	Did your father have a rickshaw?
Rickshawallah	No, my father did not have a rickshaw. He was a farmer.
You	(Did you have) land?
Rickshawallah	A little, but not here – in Bihar. My elder brother farms there now.
You	Aren't you Bengali?
Rickshawallah	No, we're Bihari.[b]
You	Is there a camera shop (near) here?
Rickshawallah	Not this way – in Bolpur there are lots of studios, but they're not open at midday, they'll be open in the evening.[c]
You	What's that (building)?
Rickshawallah	It's the electricity office.[d]
You	Is the building new?
Rickshawallah	No, it's very old.
You	OK, fine. How much is the fare?
Rickshawallah	Five rupees.
You	Here, (please) take (it). May I go?
Rickshawallah	Please.[e]

---

[a]A **pukur** is a common feature of life in Bengal: a pond or 'tank', often with steps down to it, used for communal bathing and washing.

[b]There are many Biharis in the western part of Bengal, and communities of Bengalis in Bihar; they often know each other's languages.

[c]Camera shops, where photos can be developed, are often known as 'studios'.

[d]The rickshawallah uses **apnar** in his reply: it is a common idiomatic usage, informal in tone. It does not of course mean *your* literally.

[e]There are no English equivalents for these phrases. côli literally means *May (I) go?* (see **Verb tables** p. 204). asun means *(Please) come.*

Notice the conjunct গ্র (গ + র) in গ্রাম *(village)*. This makes use of র-ফলা (see Unit 8, p. 30). Other occurrences of র-ফলা will not be specially mentioned from now on.

 —————————— **Grammar** ——————————

1 *Possessive case*

The possessive form of the pronouns is characterised by a final **-r**. This same **-r** ending serves as the possessive case for nouns. If the noun ends in a **vowel**, **-r** alone is added:

    babar kɔlôm   *Father's pen*

If the word ends in a consonant, **-er** is added:

    amader kukurer chana   *our dog's puppy*

Monosyllabic words ending in **-a**, however, usually add **-yer**:

    mayer saɽi   *Mother's sari*
    payer bytha   *pain in the leg*

The **-yer** ending is also used with **bhai** *(brother)* and **bôu** *(wife)*:

    amar bhayer bôndhu   *my brother's friend*
    or bôuyer gɔyna   *his wife's jewellery*

But **bhai-er** and **bôu-er** (spelt with a hyphen) are also found (see the **Conversation** in Unit 14, p. 50).

2 ach- *(to be present)*

You saw in Unit 14 that for one use of the English verb *to be* – subject-complement constructions – **no** verb is required in Bengali. For another use of the English verb *to be*, however, as in sentences like *There is a post-office in my street* or *Is there a telephone here?*, Bengali does use a verb: the appropriate form of the verb **ach-**. (This book generally follows the convention of referring to Bengali verbs in their 'verbal noun' form: **kɔra** *(doing)*, **dækha** (seeing), etc. For **ach-** there is no verbal noun form, so it will be referred to by its 'stem', to which endings are added.) I find it convenient to call this the verb *to be present* though its uses extend beyond presence or location.

ach- has only two tenses, present and past. As with all Bengali verbs, you need to learn the endings for the first person, the familiar second person, the familiar third person, and polite second and third person. The polite form is **always** the same for the second as for the third person. **There are no separate forms for the plural**: in all Bengali verbs, the ending is the same for *we* as for *I*, for *they* as for *he/she*, and so on.

The paradigm given below for the present tense of **ach-** uses the pronouns **ami, tumi, se, apni/tini**. These could be replaced with the plural subject pronouns (see p. 52). The third person pronouns **se** (familiar) or **ini** (polite) could be replaced with the other third person pronouns: **e, o, ini, uni,** or their plural forms:

1		ami achi
2	[F]	tumi achô
3	[F]	se ache
2 & 3	[P]	apni/tini achen

Note that **achô** is often written **acho** (আছো).

The past tense forms are as follows:

1		ami chilam
2	[F]	tumi chile
3	[F]	se chilô
2 & 3	[P]	apni/tini chilen

Note that **chilô** can also be written **chilo** (ছিলো).

ach- is used in sentences involving location:

baba ki baṛi achen?	*Is Father (at) home?*
okhane ɔnek lok chilô.	*There were lots of people there.*

If a locative adverb or phrase is present in the sentence, or the interrogative **kothay** *(Where?)*, **ach-** can be omitted, but only if the present tense is implied:

uni kothay (achen)?	*Where (is) he/she?*
okhane amar kɔlôm (ache).	*My pen('s) there.*

ach- is also used for **possession**. Bengali does not have a verb *to have*: instead an **impersonal** construction is used, of a type that will become familiar to you as you progress with the language. The person *having* or *owning* goes into the possessive case; the verb is always third person [F]. So instead of *Rimi has a bicycle* one says, *Of Rimi a bicycle it is*:

rimir saikel ache.

Remember to make the verb third person [F] even if a polite pronoun is present for the owner or possessor:

apnar ki kukur chilô?   *Did you have a dog?*

Sometimes the 'possessor' is understood from the context and can be left out. ţeliphon ache? could be interpreted as *Is there a telephone (here)?* or *Do (you) have a telephone?*. Bengali grammar expresses here, in a neat and logical way, the overlap between location and possession.

The **negative** of ach- in the present is nei for all persons (nai in Bangladesh). In the past, -na is added to the verb (the usual way of making Bengali verbs negative):

ekhane ţeliphon nei.   *There's no telephone here.*
amader bathrum chilôna.   *We didn't have a bathroom.*

3 Definite article (things)

The definite article *(the)* in Bengali is a suffix added to the noun. For things (as opposed to people or pet animals) by far the most common article is -ţa, which you have already encountered as a component of the singular demonstrative pronouns eţa, oţa, seţa (p. 53):

ţebilţa   *the table*
baŗiţa   *the house*

The singular definite article is quite often omitted when it is clear from the context that a particular item is meant:

cabi kothay?   *Where's (the) key?*

When to use it and when to leave it out is something that can only be learnt through practice, and, like many aspects of the Bengali language, cannot be easily reduced to a rule!

The **plural** definite article for things is -gulo (cf. the plural demonstrative pronouns, p. 53). The noun itself does not change in form:

bôigulo	*the books*
gaɽigulo	*the cars*

This article is obligatory if you want to express a **definite** plural. A sentence like gaɽi odike could mean *The car is over there* or *There is a car over there* or *There are cars over there* but **not** *The cars are over there*. (See Unit 16, p. 72.)

4 Demonstrative adjectives

In English there is no distinction between the demonstrative pronoun (*Give me that*) and the demonstrative adjective (*That letter came yesterday*). In Bengali, demonstrative adjectives are made by putting the two parts of the demonstrative pronoun e/ta, o/ta, se/ta, e/gulo, o/gulo, se/gulo either side of the noun:

e gaɽita ki apnar?	*Is this car yours?*

Usually, in spoken Bengali, an emphatic -i is added:

oi dokanta nôtun.	*That shop's new.*
ei bôigulo or.	*These books are his/hers.*
oi gachgulo khub sundôr.	*Those trees are very beautiful.*

When one is merely drawing attention to an object, not distinguishing *this* one from *that* one, the emphatic ei, oi, sei can be used on their own without -ta:

ei baɽi ki tomar?	*Is this house yours?*

5 Negative of the zero verb

If you want to express the negative of the zero verb (*This is* **not** *my room, He's* **not** *rich*), you must use the appropriate form of the verb nɔ-, which like ach- has no verbal noun form. (Bengali dictionaries only list the literary form nôha.) It exists in the present tense, conjugated as follows:

1		ami nôi
2	[F]	tumi nɔo
3	[F]	se nɔy
2 & 3	[P]	apni/tini nɔn

It is very easy to muddle up these forms, so learn them carefully!

ami baŋalī nôi.	*I am not Bengali.*
oṭa or nɔy.	*That's not his.*
tini ki brahmôn̩ nɔn?	*Isn't he a Brahmin?*

Be careful, too, to distinguish them from nei (see **2** above). In colloquial speech, you will hear people using na *(not)* instead of the correct form of nɔ-: e.g. oṭa bhalo na *(That's not good)*, kɔlômṭa amar na *(The pen's not mine)*. But this practice is probably best avoided by the learner.

 ———————— **Exercises** ————————

1 *(a)* Give negative versions of the following statements, using

নেই
ছিলামনা/ছিলেনা/ছিলনা/ছিলেননা

or নই/নও/নয়/নন and changing the pronoun or demonstrative as indicated. For example:

এদের ছেলেমেয়ে আছে ।
<u>ওদের</u> ছেলেমেয়ে <u>নেই</u> ।

এটা আমার ।
<u>ওটা</u> আমার <u>নয়</u> ।

Do the exercise orally, then write your answers:

আমার বাবার গাড়ি ছিল ।
১ ওর _____ ।

এঁরা বাঙালী ।
২ ওরা _____ ।

এটা আপনার ।

৩ ওটা _____ ।

ওদের টেলিফোন আছে ।

৪ আমাদের _____ ।

এদিকে ক্যামেরার দোকান আছে ।

৫ ওদিকে _____ ।

আমি ওখানে ছিলাম ।

৬ তুমি _____ ।

এ আমার ছেলে ।

৭ ও _____ ।

আমরা বাঙালী ।

৮ আপনারা _____ ।

আমি চাষী ।

৯ তুমি _____ ।

আমি তখন এখানে ছিলাম ।

১০ তিনি _____ ।

(b) Using the pictures as a guide, supply the correct demonstrative adjective forms – *this* (এই ... টা/গুলো) on the left, *that* (ওই ... টা/গুলো) on the right. For example:

এই গাছটা বড় ।   <u>ওই গাছটা</u> ছোট ।

If you can't deduce the meaning, you will find the words in the **Glossary**.

এই নিবটা মোটা ।

১ _____ সরু ।

এই বেড়ালটা মোটা ।

২ _____ রোগা ।

এই সুটকেসটা ভারী ।

৩ _____ হালকা ।

এই চেয়ারগুলো ভালো ।

৪ _____ ভাঙা ।

এই সার্টটা নতুন ।   ৫ _____ পুরনো ।

এই ছবিটা সুন্দর ।   ৬ _____ বিশ্রী[a] ।

[a]In colloquial Bengali the word for *ugly* is often pronounced (and sometimes written) 'bicchiri'.

2 In the following sentences, the words have been jumbled up. Put them into the correct order, so that they make sense. The correct sentences are given in the **Key to the exercises** on p. 280.

   (i)   ache apnader ţelibhiʃɔn ki?
   (ii)   kothay baba tomar?
  (iii)   chile ki okhane tumi?
  (iv)   nɔy amar kɔlômţa.
   (v)   nôtun saikel ache or.
  (vi)   baŋalī nɔn uni.
 (vii)   bhalo khub am amgachţar oi.
(viii)   nam bôiţar ki?
  (ix)   ɔnek chelemeye ache ōder.
   (x)   ţicar amader achen ekhane.
  (xi)   dadar sarţţa ei.
 (xii)   jômijɔma apnar ki chilô babar?

16

____ BUYING FRUIT ____
AND VEGETABLES

 ——————— **Conversation** ———————

You go to a market (বাজার) somewhere in West Bengal, to buy some fruit and vegetables. The shopkeeper sits on the floor of his shop, surrounded by piles of produce, with a cash-box to one side of him and a pair of scales on the other. When you ask him for what you want, he weighs it on his scales and then drops it straight from the pan of the scales into your bag; or he might put delicate items such as tomatoes into a paper-bag first (paper-bags are generally handmade from newspaper). If you have lots of things to buy, he may jot down the prices on a scrap of paper, but most shopkeepers in the subcontinent are very good at mental arithmetic. Many customers serve themselves, picking out whatever they want and handing it to the shopkeeper.

দোকানদার	বলুন ।
আপনি	আলু আছে ?
দোকানদার	অনেক আলু আছে - কত নেবেন ?

আপনি	দেড় কিলো ।
দোকানদার	দিচ্ছি - দেড় কিলো আলু হচ্ছে পাঁচ টাকা ।
আপনি	একটা বেগুন চাই ।
দোকানাদর	এটা ?
আপনি	না, ওগুলোর একটা, ফুলকপির কাছে ।
দোকানদার	আচ্ছা । শুধু একটা চান ?
আপনি	হ্যাঁ - বেশ বড় তো !
দোকানদার	এগুলো তেমন বড় নয় । বর্ষাকালে বেগুন অনেক বড় হবে ।
আপনি	আচ্ছা । বেগুনটা কত ?
দোকানদার	ষাট পয়সা ।
আপনি	আচ্ছা । কয়েকটা টমেটো দেখি ?
দোকানদার	নিশ্চয়ই - কটা নেবেন ?
আপনি	দুটো - ওই বড়গুলো ।
দোকানদার	আচ্ছা, বড় টমেটো, আধ কিলো, তিন টাকা । আর কিছু লাগবে ?
আপনি	একটা বাঁধাকপিও দিন । এইটা, আপনার বাঁ দিকে ।
দোকানদার	দিচ্ছি । আট আনা । ট্যাড়স নেবেননা ? খুব টাটকা ।
আপনি	ঠিক আছে, আড়াই-শ গ্রাম নেব ।
দোকানদার	পাঁচ-শ গ্রাম নিন - খুব সস্তা - চার টাকা কিলো ।
আপনি	বেশ । ভালো ফল কোথায় পাব ?
দোকানদার	রাস্তার ওই পারে । পোস্টাপিসের সামনে, অনেক ফলের গাড়ি আছে । ডিম নেবেন ?
আপনি	না, আজকে ডিম লাগবেনা ।
দোকানদার	খুব ভালো দেশী ডিম আছে । দেখুন ।
আপনি	আচ্ছা, ছটি দিন ।
দোকানদার	দিচ্ছি । এই যে, কাগজের ব্যাগে দিচ্ছি - ভেঙে যাবেনা ।
আপনি	আচ্ছা । আর কিছু লাগবেনা । পুরো দাম কত হল ?
দোকানদার	বার টাকা পঞ্চাশ পয়সা ।
আপনি	আপনি এই কুড়ি টাকার নোটটা ভাঙিয়ে দেবেন ?
দোকানদার	দেব । তের, পনের, কুড়ি - এই নিন ।

Translation and notes

Shopkeeper	Yes?[a]
You	Have you got (any) potatoes?
Shopkeeper	I've lots of potatoes – how many will you take?
You	One-and-a-half kilos.
Shopkeeper	Here you are.[b] One-and-a-half kilos of potatoes makes five rupees.
You	I want an aubergine.
Shopkeeper	This one?
You	No, one of those, near the cauliflowers.
Shopkeeper	OK. Do you only want one?
You	Yes – (they're) nice and big!
Shopkeeper	These are not all that big. In the rainy season they'll be much big(ger).
You	OK. How much will the aubergine be?
Shopkeeper	60 paisa.
You	OK. May I see a few tomatoes?
Shopkeeper	Certainly – how many will you take?
You	Two – those big ones.
Shopkeeper	OK, two big tomatoes, half a kilo, three rupees. Do you need anything else?
You	Give me a cabbage too. This one, to your left.
Shopkeeper	Here you are. Eight annas.[c] Won't you take (some) 'lady's fingers'? (They're) very fresh.
You	Very well, I'll take 250 grammes.
Shopkeeper	Take 500 grammes – (they're) very cheap – four rupees a kilo.
You	Fine. Where will I get good fruit?
Shopkeeper	Across the street – in front of the post-office there are lots of fruit-carts.[d] Will you take (some) eggs?
You	No, I don't need eggs today.
Shopkeeper	I've got very good 'deshi' eggs.[e] Look.
You	OK, give (me) six.
Shopkeeper	Here you are. Here, I'm giving (them to you) in a paper bag – (they) won't break.
You	OK. I won't need anything else. How much did that come to altogether?
Shopkeeper	Twelve rupees, fifty paisa.
You	Will you change this twenty rupee note?
Shopkeeper	Yes.[f] Thirteen, fifteen, twenty – here you are.

^aLit. *Say!, Speak!* – the polite imperative of the verb bɔla (see Unit 19, pp. 110–112). It may seem rather abrupt to the foreign learner, but in West Bengal this would be a normal way in which a shopkeeper would indicate that he is ready for his next customer. In Bangladesh ki lagbe apnar? *(What do you require?)*, ki cai apnar? *(What do you want?)*, or ki neben? *(What will (you) take?)* would be more usual. People don't normally exchange greetings with shopkeepers, unless they know them well.

^bLit. *I am giving*: the present continuous tense of the verb deoya (see p. 133).

^cPaisa (cents) replaced annas in 1957, but people still sometimes use them in colloquial speech. There were sixteen annas to the rupee, so 'eight annas' is equivalent to 50 paisa.

^dSellers of fruit tend to be more itinerant than sellers of vegetables, spreading out their wares on the ground, carrying them around in a basket, or selling them from a trolley or handcart (phɔler gaɽi).

^eDeshi eggs are 'free-range', and are small and flavourful compared to the large white 'poultry' eggs that come from battery hens.

^fLit. *I will give*: it's often more idiomatic in Bengali to reply to a question by repeating the verb, rather than by saying 'yes' or 'no'.

The **Conversation** contains several future tense forms (নেব, পাব etc.) which will be explained fully in Unit 18, and three new conjuncts:

	Handwriting	**Print**
র + ষ =	র্ষ	র্ষ
শ + চ =	শ্চ	শ্চ
এৎ + চ =	ৠ *	ৠ

*In writing conjuncts in which এৎ comes first, it is clearest to retain এৎ in full though handwritten forms do vary.

র্ষ makes use of রেফ (´ – see Unit 9, p. 34). Other occurrences of রেফ will not always be mentioned from now on.

Note that the conjunct স্ত as in সস্তা and রাস্তা is normally pronounced '**st**' rather than '**sht**'. This also happens if স is combined with certain other letters – see pp. 269–70.

Grammar

1 Diminutive form of the article

The definite article, -ṭa, -gulo, which as you learnt in Units 14 and 15 is also used to make up the demonstrative pronoun and demonstrative adjective, has a 'diminutive form', -ṭi, -guli. This is used for people (unless you wish to be rude), and is also used for small or pretty things, pet animals and so on. It can be used for many other things, too, to add a note of politeness, or to indicate some kind of personal relationship with the thing being mentioned. In the conversation above, -ṭi used for eggs suggests that they are small and attractive, and it also adds a friendly, courteous tone to the dialogue.

In Bangladesh, -ṭi is used rather less than in West Bengal, and -ṭa for people is not necessarily pejorative. amar tinṭa chele ache *(I have three sons)* would be perfectly normal usage.

2 Indefinite article

æk *(one)* plus the definite article can form an indefinite article (*a, an*) in Bengali, but is normally only used when you want to make it clear that it is only *one* that you mean. If the diminutive form is used, æk changes to ek:

ækṭa begun cai.	*(I) want an aubergine (just one).*
amader ekṭi meye.	*We have a daughter (only one).*

In many cases where English requires an indefinite article, there is no article at all in Bengali:

tini ḍaktar.	*He's a doctor.*

Note also that there is **no indefinite plural** form in Bengali. alu – on its own without article – can either mean *potato* or *potatoes*, and this is true of all Bengali nouns. Generally the context makes it clear whether one or more than one is meant, but ambiguities do sometimes arise, particularly in written texts where items are not physically in sight. The phrase phulkôpir kache in the **Conversation** above obviously means *near the cauliflowers* if a pile of cauliflowers are visible; but grammatically it would also be correct if there were only one cauliflower.

3 How much? How many?

The word kɔtô was used in the **Conversation** in Unit 15:

tader bɔyôs kɔtô?	*How old are they? (Lit. How much is their age?)*

kɔtô is generally used in questions expecting some kind of measurement in the reply. Don't be confused by the fact that in English we use *How much?* for things that can't be counted as separate objects *(How much sugar would you like?)*, and *How many?* for countable things *(How many potatoes would you like?)*. In Bengali, if the reply expected is a **measurement**, you should use kɔtô:

dam kɔtô?	*How much? (Lit. How much price?)*
dɔʃ ʈaka.	*Ten rupees.*
alu kɔtô kilo?	*How many kilos of potatoes?*
pāc kilo.	*Five kilos.*
kɔtô dūr?	*How far?*
kuɽi mail.	*Twenty miles.*

Instead of kɔtô, kɔy can be used, or the abbreviated and colloquial form kɔ:

kɔy mas?	*How many months?*
kɔ ʈaka?	*How many rupees?*

If the answer expected is not a measurement, but a number of countable objects or people, **the definite article must be added to the interrogative.** kɔy or kɔ, rather than kɔtô, are preferred in this case, kɔy being more formal and literary (or rural) than kɔ. Notice that the same form of the article that is added to kɔy or kɔ in the question should be added to the numeral in the reply:

apnar kɔyʈi chelemeye ache?	*How many children do you have?*
carʈi.	*Four.*
okhane kɔʈa ceyar ache?	*How many chairs are there there?*
satʈa.	*Seven.*
beɽalʈir kɔʈi chana ache?	*How many kittens does the cat have?*
tinʈi	*Three.*

Note that kɔyek *(a few)* takes the article in the same way as the numbers:

kɔyekʈa ʈômeʈo cai	*I want a few tomatoes.*
kɔʈa?	*How many?*
dɔʃʈa.	*Ten.*

4 Numbers

A full table of numbers is given in the **Review of Part Two** (pp. 192–193). Bengali numbers are quite difficult, so for the time being learn the numbers as they occur in the **Conversation** and **Grammar** sections. Note that there are special words for one-and-a-half (deɽ) and two-and-a-half (aɽai), so in the conversation above 250 grammes was aɽai-ʃɔ gram. For the numbers with articles, you need to know the following variant forms:

dui	+ ʈa =	duʈo	2
tin	+ ʈa =	tinʈe	3
car	+ ʈa =	carʈe	4

The remaining numbers take -ʈa as normal. The diminutive is always -ʈi (but remember that æk + ʈi = ekʈi). The variant forms for 2, 3 and 4 are normal in West Bengal; in Bangladesh duʈa, tinʈa, carʈa are heard. Note that dui (2), chɔy (6) and nɔy (9) are generally shortened to du-, chɔ-, nɔ- when the article is added.

5 Postpositions

English has **pre**positions: **on** *the table*, **next to** *me*, **at** *home*, etc. Bengali, like other South Asian languages, has **post**positions, coming after the noun. Most of them require the possessive case (see Unit 15, p. 60) in the noun or pronoun that they follow. In the conversation above, there were several examples:

phulkôpir kache	*near (the) cauliflower(s)*
apnar bā dike	*to your left*
rastar oi pare	*across (the) street*
poʂʈapiser samne	*in front of (the) post-office*

The -e ending that many postpositions have indicates location, as you will see when you learn the locative/instrumental case in Unit 17.

The **Conversation** above includes a number of verb forms, which will be explained in subsequent units. Note for now the future tense marker -b- (nebô, deben, pabô, etc.), and the fact that pronouns are frequently left out in colloquial Bengali:

| (apni) ʃudhu ækʈa can? | *Do (you) only want one?* |

Note too the verb laga, which literally means *to strike* but which has a host of idiomatic uses including the expression of *need* (see Unit 24, p. 172):

| ar kichu lagbe? | *Will (you) need anything more?* |

Exercises

1 *(a)* Several of the Bengali numbers have occurred in the conversations so far, so you can now practise saying the numbers up to 12:

এক, দুই, তিন, চার, পাঁচ, ছয়, সাত, আট, নয়, দশ, এগার*, বার*

*pronounced **ægarô**, **barô** and sometimes spelt এগারো, বারো.

Using the pictures as a guide, answer the following questions, making sure that you use the same form of the article with the number as is used with the interrogative. Remember the special forms for দুই, তিন, চার + টা (p. 74). And remember that **measurements** require no article. Example:

কটা কলম ?
পাঁচটা কলম ।

১ কটি মেয়ে ?

২ কত টাকা ?

৩ কত কিলো চাল ?

৪ ক চামচ চিনি ?

৫ কটা ডিম ?   ৬ কত গ্রাম মাখন ?

(b)   Answer the questions about the picture, below, of a room, using the postpositions কাছে *(near)*, নিচে *(below)*, উপর/উপরে *(above, on top of)*, বাঁ দিকে *(to the left)*, and ডান দিকে *(to the right)*. You don't have to use আছে: it can be left out of questions and statements containing a locative phrase (see Unit 15, p. 61).

Example: বেড়াল কোথায় ?
             মেঝের উপর ।

১ বইগুলো কোথায় ?   ৪ ল্যাম্প[b] কোথায় ?

২ চেয়ার কোথায় ?   ৫ ছবিটা কোথায় ?

৩ মেয়েটি কোথায় ?[a]   ৬ ওয়েস্ট-পেপার বাস্কেট কোথায় ?

[a]*door* is দরজা (dɔrôja).
[b]If you recognise the English word here, you'll identify the conjunct: ম + প = ম্প.

2   Give answers to the following questions, making full use of the
    vocabulary and grammar you have learnt so far. If there are words
    you don't know, you can look them up in the **Glossary** at the end of
    the book. The **Key to the exercises** on p. 280 gives some possible
    answers:

(i)   apnar nam ki?
(ii)   apnar ma-babar nam ki?
(iii)   apnar ki bhai-bon ache?
(iv)   kɔṭi bhai-bon?
(v)   tader bɔyôs kɔtô?
(vi)   apnar ki baŋalī bôndhu
        ache?
(vii)   ôr baṛi ki apnar baṛir
        kache?
(viii) apnar ki gaṛi ache?
(ix)   apni nôtun gaṛi can?
(x)   ki rɔkôm[a] gaṛi?
(xi)   gaṛiṭar ɔnek dam
        hɔbe?[b]
(xii)   apnar baṛir samne ki
        rasta na maṭh?[c]

(xiii) apnar bagan ache ki?[d]
(xiv)   okhane ki rɔkôm gach
        ache?
(xv)   kɔṭa?
(xvi)   apnar baṛir kache ki park
        ache?
(xvii) kɔtô mail dūre?
(xviii) okhane ki khelar maṭh?[e]
(xix)   maṭhṭa bɔrô na choṭô?
(xx)   ʃudhu ækṭa?

[a]*What sort of?*
[b]An idiomatic use of the future of hɔoya, *to be* or *become: Will the car be very expensive?*
[c]*open land.* Note also the use of na to express *or* when posing alternatives in questions.
[d]Note that the interrogative ki can sometimes go at the end of the sentence.
[e]*playing field.*

17

FINDING OUT ABOUT SCHOOLS

 ———————— **Conversation** ————————

You visit a girls' school in a village near Sylhet. It is a বেসরকারী *(private)* school, but all schools in Bangladesh have almost half their costs met by the Government. It is in a well-constructed building and is quite well-equipped: this is partly due to the money brought into the area by 'Londonis' – Sylhetis who have gone to work in Britain and other foreign countries. The classrooms open off a long verandah. Mrs Khan, the headteacher, takes you along the verandah, showing you each classroom in turn and answering your questions. The girls are all in spotless blue and white uniforms: they look round at you with intense curiosity as you look in through the open doors of the classrooms.

আপনি	মিসেস খান, আপনার স্কুলে কটি মেয়ে আছে ?
মিসেস খান	অনেক, মোট তিন-শ হবে । দশটি ক্লাস আছে, ত্রিশটি করে মেয়ে প্রত্যেক ক্লাসে ।
আপনি	সবাই এই উপজেলা থেকেই আসে ?
মিসেস খান	হ্যাঁ, বেশিরভাগই – তবে কয়েকজন আসে সিলেট শহর থেকে, আর কয়েকজন অন্য গ্রাম থেকে ।
আপনি	ওরা কি করে আসে ?

মিসেস খান	বাসে করে। বিশেষ বাসের ব্যবস্থা আছে - নিজেদের নয়, ভাড়া বাস।
আপনি	আপনারা কোন বয়স থেকে নেন ?
মিসেস খান	ছ বছর বয়স থেকে, পনের ষোল পর্যন্ত, তবে সেটা নির্দিষ্ট কিছু নয়।
আপনি	তারপর ওরা কি করে ?
মিসেস খান	মানে, স্কুল শেষ করার পর ? বিভিন্ন কলেজে চলে যায় - কেউ ঢাকায়, কেউ বা চট্টগ্রামে। কোনো কোনো মেয়ে সঙ্গে-সঙ্গে বিয়ে করে, তবে আজকাল মেয়েরা শিক্ষিত হতে চায়।
আপনি	আচ্ছা, ওদের বিয়ে তো লণ্ডনীদের সাথেও হয়, না ?
মিসেস খান	মা-বাবারা প্রায়ই সেটা আশা করেন। তবে এখন ভিসা-টিসা পাওয়া মুশকিল।
আপনি	ওরা কি কি বিষয় এখানে পড়ে ?
মিসেস খান	বাংলা, অঙ্ক, ইংরেজী, ভূগোল, সমাজ, বিজ্ঞান, ধর্ম। ক্লাস ফোর পর্যন্ত ওরা ভূগোল, সমাজ আর বিজ্ঞান সব একটি বইতে একসাথেই পড়ে ; ক্লাস ফাইভ থেকে ক্লাস টেন পর্যন্ত বিষয়গুলো ওরা আলাদা আলাদা বই থেকে শেখে।
আপনি	খেলাধুলা কেমন করে ?
মিসেস খান	ছেলেদের চেয়ে কম। তবে ওরা রোজ ড্রিল করে। ব্রেক-টাইমে হয়তো ওরা নিজেরা-নিজেরা একটু-আধটু খেলে।
আপনি	বল নিয়ে খেলে ?
মিসেস খান	নরম বল দিয়ে হ্যাণ্ড-বল খেলে। আমরা শক্ত বল নিষেধ করি।
আপনি	কজন টিচার আছে ?
মিসেস খান	পনেরজন।
আপনি	জুনিয়ার ক্লাসে কি শুধু একজন করে টিচার থাকেন ?
মিসেস খান	না, আলাদা আলাদা বিষয়ের আলাদা আলাদা টিচার থাকেন।
আপনি	এটা কোন ক্লাস ?

— **79** —

মিসেস খান	এটা ক্লাস টেন – ইংরেজী লেসন চলছে ।
আপনি	ওরা কোন বই থেকে শেখে ?
মিসেস খান	সরকারের নির্দিষ্ট বইও আছে, আবার আমরা অন্য বইও ব্যবহার করি ।
আপনি	কি ধরনের বই ? গল্প-টল্লের বই ?
মিসেস খান	দেখুন না । রমিলা, তোমার ইংরেজী পড়ার বইখানা দাও তো ? এই দেখুন, এতে অনেক কিছুই আছে – গল্প, কবিতা, একটু ইতিহাসের কথা –
আপনি	বাঃ, বেশ তো ! ব্রেক-টাইমে আমি কি মেয়েদের সাথে একটু গল্প করতে পারি ?
মিসেস খান	নিশ্চয়ই । দশটায় আমাদের ব্রেক-টাইম হয় – আর পাঁচ মিনিট আছে – একটু অপেক্ষা করুন ।

Translation and notes

You	Mrs Khan, how many girls are there in your school?
Mrs Khan	A lot, three hundred altogether.[a] There are ten classes, thirty girls in each class.
You	Do they all come from this *upazila*?[b]
Mrs Khan	Yes, most of them – but a few come from Sylhet town, and a few from other villages.
You	How do they get here?
Mrs Khan	By bus. There's a special bus arrangement – not our own, a rented bus.
You	From what age do you take (them)?
Mrs Khan	From six years of age until fifteen or sixteen, but that isn't fixed.
You	What do they do then?
Mrs Khan	You mean, after completing school? They go to various colleges – some to Dhaka, some to Chittagong. Some girls get married straightaway, but nowadays girls want to be educated.
You	Ah, and they also marry 'Londonis', do they?[c]
Mrs Khan	(Their) parents often hope as much. But getting visas and so on is difficult now.[d]
You	What subjects do they study here?
Mrs Khan	Bengali, maths, English, geography, society, science, re-

	ligion. Up to Class 4 they study combined geography, society and science from one book; from Class 5 to Class 10 they learn the subjects from separate books.
You	How about sports?
Mrs Khan	(They do) less than boys. But they do drill every day. At break-time[e] perhaps they play a bit on their own.
You	Do they play ball?
Mrs Khan	They play hand-ball with (a) soft ball. We don't allow hard balls.
You	How many teachers are there?
Mrs Khan	Fifteen.
You	Do the junior classes have only one teacher each?
Mrs Khan	No, there are separate teachers for separate subjects.
You	What class is this?
Mrs Khan	This is Class 10 – an English lesson is going on.
You	Which book do they learn from?
Mrs Khan	There's a book prescribed by the government, but we use other books as well.
You	What kind of books? Story books?
Mrs Khan	Have a look. Romila, will you give (us) your English reading book? Look, there's lots in it – stories, poems, a bit of history.
You	Excellent![f] At break-time, can I chat[g] a little with the girls?
Mrs Khan	Certainly. Our break-time will be at ten – in another five minutes – (please) wait for a bit.

---

[a] Note that the article can be dropped from large numbers: tin-ʃɔ (*300*) rather than tin-ʃɔṭi.

[b] The districts (*zilas*) of Bangladesh are divided into sub-districts (*upazilas*), each with a locally elected council. The Chairman of an *upazila* is a powerful local figure. Note that the emphatic -i in ei is also idiomatically attached to the postposition **theke**.

[c] Lit. *Does marriage with 'Londonis' become (to them)?* – an 'impersonal' construction (see pp. 99–100). Note also the postposition **sathe** *(with)*, common in Bangladesh. In West Bengal sɔŋge is preferred.

[d] *Etc.* is often expressed in Bengali by repeating a word, with the initial consonant changed to ṭ: bhisa-ṭisa *(visas and so on)*; gɔlpô-ṭɔlpô *(stories, etc.)*.

[e] Notice the use of English words, which are natural and idiomatic in many contexts. The Bengali word chuṭi could have been used, but this can also mean the school holidays, or any kind of holiday.

[f] For the spelling and pronunciation of bah!, a warm expression of approval, see p. 44 and p. 255.

[g] gɔlpô means 'story', but gɔlpô kɔra is an idiom meaning *to chat*.

Note the following new conjuncts:

	Handwriting	**Print**
স + থ =	স্থ	স্থ (pronounced 'sth' – see pp. 269–70)
ঙ + ক =	ঙ্ক	ঙ্ক
ল + প =	ল্প	ল্প
জ + এঃ =	জ্ঞ	জ্ঞ

The last of these is pronounced '**g**' at the beginning of a word, and '**gg**' between vowels. It also changes a following **a** to **æ**: so বিজ্ঞান *(science)* is pronouned '**biggæn**' and জ্ঞান *(knowledge)* is pronounced '**gæn**'.

Grammar

1 -jɔn *and* -khana

With people, the ending -jɔn can be used instead of -ṭi with the interrogative and with numbers:

	kɔṭi meye?	
or	kɔjon meye?	*How many girls?*
	triʃṭi.	
or	triʃjɔn.	*Thirty.*

The difference between -jɔn and -ṭi is a subtle matter, and native speakers have varying views on it. The following guidelines are offered rather tentatively:

(a) -jɔn is not normally used for young children; so **pācṭi meye** would suggest that the girls are young (under twelve, say) whereas **pācjon meye** suggests older girls or women.

(b) -jɔn is more 'collective' than -ṭi: **pācjon lok** suggests a group, whereas **pācṭi lok** suggests separate individuals.

(c) -ṭi is not, however, necessarily more respectful than -jɔn. Perhaps because -ṭi can also be used of things (see pp. 71–2), -jɔn is more 'human'. **skule biʃṭi ṭicar ache** suggests 20 separate teachers, but rates them as 'countable objects' rather than as human beings. **biʃjon ṭicar** is, in this context, more respectful.

-jon, unlike -ṭi, can only be used with people, and it can **not** be used as a definite article on its own. You cannot say lokjon if you mean *the person*.

-khana, on the other hand, does function fully as an article. It is an alternative to -ṭa, used with a limited class of objects, usually square or flat objects:

bôikhana amar.	*The book's mine.*
kɔkhana chôbi?	*How many pictures?*
dukhana khata	*two exercise books*

Both -jon and -khana can be combined with æk to form an indefinite article. With people, there is a tendency to use ækjon if the indefinite article is meant, and ekṭi if one wants to stress that it is **one** person; but this is not a hard-and-fast rule.

2 *Participial postpositions*

The postpositions you learnt in Unit 16 all require the possessive case in the noun or pronouns they apply to. There is another class of postposition in Bengali where the possessive case ending is not required. Many of these are actually verbal participles (see pp. 120–123). theke, for example, meaning *from*, is derived from the verb thaka *(to stay)*. kôre, used in the conversation above to mean *by bus*, etc. and after a numeral to mean *each*, is from kɔra *(to do/make)*. Look out for postpositions as they occur in subsequent **Conversations** in the book, and take care to note whether or not they require the possessive case ending. Check them in the **Glossary** if you are unsure.

3 *Locative/instrumental case*

Like the possessive case (see p. 60), the locative case in Bengali can be formed by the application of a simple rule. To words ending in a consonant, add the ending -e. To words ending in a vowel, add the ending -te:

apnar skule	*in your school*
ei klase	*in this class*
tader baṛite	*in their house*
dillite	*in Delhi*

If a word ends in **-a**, however, either **-te** or **-y** (pronounced '**-e**': see p. 13) can be added:

	ḍhakate	
or	ḍhakay	*in Dhaka*
	kôlkatate	
or	kôlkatay	*in Calcutta*

This also applies to words to which the definite article **-ṭa** has been added:

	almariṭate	
or	almariṭay	*in the cupboard*

Note that the adverbs **ekhane** *(here)* and **okhane** *(there)*, and the interrogative **kothay?** *(Where?)* are locative in form.

The locative case also often has an instrumental function. **hate**, for example, can either mean *in (one's) hand* or *by hand*. In the conversation above, **kise?**, the locative form of **ki**, is instrumental in meaning: *By what (means of transport)?* But note too the idiomatic addition of the postposition **kôre** for means of transport:

ora kise kôre ase?	*By what means do they come?*
base kôre.	*By bus.*

4 Plural endings for personal nouns

The endings **-ra** and **-der** that are used to form the subject plural and possessive plural forms of the pronouns (**amra, tomader** etc. – see Unit 14, p. 52) can also be added to personal nouns or names:

meyera	*(the) girls*
cheleder môdhye	*among (the) boys*
coŭdhurīra musôlman.	*The Chaudhuris are Muslims.*

In the subject case, if the noun or name ends in a consonant, **-era** can be added instead of **-ra**:

senera khriṣṭan.	*The Sens are Christian.*
amar bonera calak.	*My sisters are clever.*

The **-ra/-era/-der** endings are not as 'definite' as the plural definite article, but are generally preferred to it. **meyeguli** *(the girls)* is less friendly than **meyera**.

5 Reflexive pronoun

myself, yourself, his own, their own etc. are all neatly expressed by the pronoun nije which comes immediately after a pronoun or noun. It takes the normal endings:

ami nije baŋalī.	*I'm Bengali myself.*
oṭa or nijer saikel.	*That's his own bicycle.*
eṭa amader nijeder baṛi nɔy.	*This is not our own house.*
amra nijera okhane chilam.	*We were there ourselves.*

In Mrs Khan's reply in the Conversation above – nijeder nɔy – the pronoun amader *(our)* is understood from the context.

6 Present tense

As in the **Conversation** in Unit 16, there are quite a few verb forms in the **Conversation** above (infinitive, verbal noun, present continuous tense) which will be dealt with in later units. The time has come, however, to learn how the present tense is formed in Bengali. So far the only verbs you have learnt formally are ach- (pp. 60–62) and nɔ- (pp. 63–64). When nɔ- is conjugated, the **endings** change with each person (ami nôi, tumi nɔo, etc.). But notice that the **stem** vowel also changes between the first person and the rest:

ami nôi	se nɔy
tumi nɔo	apni/tini nɔn

All Bengali verbs mutate between one or other of the following pairs of vowels (see p. 275 for the underlying reason for this):

ɔ/ô	e/i
æ/e	a/e
o/u	

The present tense is harder to learn than the others because, apart from the a/e verbs (and all 'extended' verbs – see Unit 25, pp. 182–184), there is vowel mutation within the tense. But learning the present tense first is the best way of implanting these pairs of vowels securely in your mind.

A problem arises in writing down verbs that mutate between the first two pairs (ɔ/ô and æ/e), because, as you will remember from Units 2 and 4, the Bengali script does not distinguish between the ɔ and ô realisations of the inherent vowel, or the æ and e pronunciations of এ. It is vital, therefore, to know the verb conjugations well, so that you can predict the correct pronunciation from the person and tense of the verb. The other three pairs do not present this problem, as they are clearly distinguished in the script.

As is traditional when learning verbs in a new language, here are **paradigms** for each of the vowel pairs in the present tense. Bengali verbs are almost completely regular. Once you know how to conjugate kɔra *(to do/make)*, you will be able to conjugate pɔra *(to wear/put on)*; once you know how to conjugate dækha *(to see)*, you will be able to conjugate phæla *(to throw)*, and so on. Remember that Bengali verbs are referred to (and listed in dictionaries) in their **verbal noun** form.

ɔ/ô			**kɔra**	
	1		ami kôri	*I do*
	2	[F]	tumi kɔrô	*you do*
	3	[F]	se kɔre	*he/she does*
	2 & 3	[P]	apni/tini kɔren	*you/he/she do(es)*

æ/e			**dækha**	
	1		ami dekhi	*I see*
	2	[F]	tumi dækhô	*you see*
	3	[F]	se dækhe	*he/she sees*
	2 & 3	[P]	apni/tini dækhen	*you/he/she see(s)*

o/u			**ʃona**	
	1		ami ʃuni	*I hear*
	2	[F]	tumi ʃonô	*you hear*
	3	[F]	se ʃone	*he/she hears*
	2 & 3	[P]	apni/tini ʃonen	*you/he/she hear(s)*

e/i			**lekha**	
	1		ami likhi	*I write*
	2	[F]	tumi lekhô	*you write*
	3	[F]	se lekhe	*he/she writes*
	2 & 3	[P]	apni/tini lekhen	*you/he/she write(s)*

All these four types mutate between one vowel in the first person, and another vowel in the other persons. a/e verbs, however, use the e vowel in the past participle and past tenses, but not in the present tense:

a/e			**rakha**	
	1		ami rakhi	*I keep*
	2	[F]	tumi rakhô	*you keep*
	3	[F]	se rakhe	*he/she keeps*
	2 & 3	[P]	apni/tini rakhen	*you/he/she keep(s)*

All the types so far are 'consonant stems'. With the second person [F] forms, you will also encounter spellings with o rather than ô; and o always has to be used with the three remaining three types, which are 'vowel stems'. The pairs of vowels they use have already occurred above, but remember that e after a vowel is written y. Notice also that the polite -en ending contracts to -n.

a/e			**khaoya**	
	1		ami khai	*I eat*
	2	[F]	tumi khao	*you eat*
	3	[F]	se khay	*he/she eats*
	2 & 3	[P]	apni/tini khan	*you/he/she eat(s)*

o/u			**dhoya**	
	1		ami dhui	*I wash*
	2	[F]	tumi dhoo	*you wash*
	3	[F]	se dhoy	*he/she washes*
	2 & 3	[P]	apni/tini dhon	*you/he/she wash(es)*

ɔ/ô			**hɔoya**	
	1		ami hôi	*I become*
	2	[F]	tumi hɔo	*you become*
	3	[F]	se hɔy	*he/she becomes*
	2 & 3	[P]	apni/tini hɔn	*you/he/she become(s)*

Finally there are the slightly anomalous verbs **deoya** *(to give)* and **neoya** *(to take),* which are identical in pattern, but differ from other Bengali verbs in that they mutate between four vowels altogether, three within the present tense:

e/i/a/æ			**deoya**	
	1		ami dii	*I give*
	2	[F]	tumi dao	*you give*
	3	[F]	se dæy	*he/she gives*
	2 & 3	[P]	apni/tini dæn	*you/he/she give(s)*

Like the present tense in English, the Bengali present is used for
habitual present actions (*I play the piano every day, He doesn't drink
alcohol*, etc.). It is also quite often used as a 'historic present' in narrative
(see Unit 27, p. 211, Note 10).

 ───────── **Exercises** ─────────

1 (*a*) Answer the following questions about the Conversation in this
unit, either positively or negatively, using the correct form of the
present tense with or without the suffix না, and changing the
subject-noun to a pronoun (ওরা or ওঁরা). Example:

মেয়েরা কি বাংলা পড়ে ?
হ্যা, ওরা বাংলা পড়ে ।

মেয়েরা কি হিন্দী পড়ে ?
না, ওরা হিন্দী পড়েনা ।

In the third sentence you will need the possessive of সবাই
(*everyone*): সবার .

১ মেয়েরা সবাই কি একইᵃ উপজেলা থেকে আসে ?

২ মেয়েরা কি বাসে করে আসে ?

৩ স্কুল শেষ করার পর কি সব মেয়েদের বিয়ে হয়ে যায় ?

৪ ক্লাস টুতেᵇ কি মেয়েরা আলাদা আলাদা বই থেকে শেখে ?

৫ মেয়েরা কি শক্ত বল দিয়ে খেলে ?

৬ টিচাররা কি খেলাধুলা করেন ?

৭ টিচাররা কি ড্রিল করেন ?

৮ মেয়েরা কি ইংরেজী শেখে ?

৯ মেয়েরা কি শুধু সরকারের নির্দিষ্ট বই ব্যবহার করে ?

১০ টিচাররা কি সবসময় ইংরেজীতে কথা বলেন ?[c]

[a]*the same*
[b]*in Class 2*
[c] কথা বলা – *to speak.*

(b) The map below gives the main *zilas* (জেলা) or districts of Bangladesh, and the four divisions (বিভাগ): Dhaka, Khulna, Rajshahi and Chittagong (ঢাকা, খুলনা, রাজশাহী and চট্টগ্রাম). Answer the questions overleaf by saying where the districts are, giving the Division name with the right locative ending. For Dhaka and Khulna either - য় or - তে is correct, though - য় is perhaps more natural in speech.

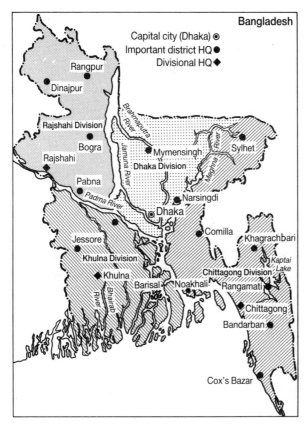

Example: বরিশাল কোন[a] বিভাগে ?
            খুলনায় ।

১ কক্স[b] বাজার কোন বিভাগে ?

২ বগুড়া কোন বিভাগে ?

৩ দিনাজপুর কোন বিভাগে ?

৪ ময়মনসিং কোন বিভাগে ?

৫ সিলেট কোন বিভাগে ?

৬ কুমিল্লা কোন বিভাগে ?

৭ নরসিংদী কোন বিভাগে ?

৮ পাবনা কোন বিভাগে ?

৯ রাঙামাটি কোন বিভাগে ?

১০ যশোর কোন বিভাগে ?

[a]কোন – *which*. See Unit 23, pp. 158–159.
[b]See p. 95.

2   Fill in the gaps in the following sentences, using the words in brackets but in their right form: i.e. with the addition of an article or -jɔn, a locative/instrumental case ending, plural noun ending, or a present tense form. To write the exercise you will need a new conjunct:

হ + ম =   ক্ষ্ম   ক্ষ্ম

brahmôɳ (ব্রাহ্মণ – 'Brahmin') is pronounced '**bramhôn**' or '**brammôn**' in Bengali: the h, if it is pronounced at all, comes **after** the m.

Remember also:

ক + র =   ক্র   ক্র (See Unit 4, p. 18)

(i)   oder _____ gaṛi ache.   (tin)
(ii) ei haspatale ʃudhu _____ ḍaktar.   (pāc)

(iii)	apnar _____ ki ṭeliphon nei?	(baṛi)
(iv)	ei grame _____ jônyô skul nei.	(meye)
(v)	_____ kôbita bhalobase.[a]	(baŋalī)
(vi)	apnar _____ ki ki phuler gach ache?	(bagan)
(vii)	_____ bhalo.	(bôi)
(viii)	apni mɔd _____ ?	(khaoya)[b]
(ix)	tini ki brahmôṇ _____ ?	(nɔ-)
(x)	amar choṭô bhai khub gan _____ .	(kɔra)
(xi)	edeʃe khaoya-daoyar pɔre[c] amra mukh _____ .	(dhoya)
(xii)	tumi krikeṭ _____ ?	(khæla)
(xiii)	oder ʃudhu _____ meye.	(ek)
(xiv)	ami ɔnek ciṭhi _____ .	(lekha)
(xv)	amar baba sɔbsɔmɔy dhuti _____ .	(pɔra)

[a]'Bengalis love poetry.'

[b]**khaoya** means to take anything by mouth: food, liquid, tobacco, etc. **mɔd** means any alcoholic drink.

[c]See p. 108, Note [d].

18

— ARRANGING A VISIT —

 ———— **Conversation** ————

You are in Calcutta, staying with a friend whom you met when he was studying in England. You find it a bit artificial to speak to him in Bengali, because you first got to know each other through the medium of English. But you always speak to his parents in Bengali, and when his married sister dropped in on her parents at the weekend you found it natural to speak Bengali to her. As she is a housewife with a son to look after, your friend suggests that you visit her regularly for conversation practice. You telephone her to fix a time.

আপনি এটা কি ৭২৩৫৬০ ?

অণিমাদি বলুন ।

আপনি আপনি অণিমাদি বলছেন ? নমস্কার, আমি –

অণিমাদি হ্যাঁ, চিনেছি – নমস্কার ।

আপনি আমার কথা বোঝেন ? আমার উচ্চারণ খুব খারাপ ।

অণিমাদি না, কই - স্পষ্টই তো। টেলিফোনে আমার কথা বুঝতে আপনার অসুবিধে হয়না ?

আপনি হ্যাঁ, বেশ শব্দ টেলিফোন-লাইনে, তবে অসুবিধা নেই, একটু জোরে বলুন।

অণিমাদি তা, কি খবর ? কেমন আছেন ?

আপনি ভালো আছি। আপনি ? অমিয়দা কেমন আছেন ? ছেলেটি ভালো আছে তো ?

অণিমাদি আমরা সবাই ভালো আছি। আপনি আমাদের এখানে আসবেন তো একদিন ?

আপনি আসবো, নিশ্চয়ই আসবো। আসলে আমি আপনার সঙ্গে বাংলায় কথা বলতে চাই। আপনার সময় হবে ?

অণিমাদি হ্যাঁ, কেন হবেনা ? আপনি যখন খুশি চলে আসুন। আমি সারাদিন বাড়িতেই থাকি বাচ্চাটির সঙ্গে। মাঝে-মাঝে আমার একা-একাই লাগে।

আপনি 'একা-একা' মানে ?

অণিমাদি বন্ধুবিহীন, বিনা বন্ধু। আপনি আসুন, এই সব কথা শিখতে পারবেন।

আপনি তাহলে আমি কটার সময় আসবো ?

অণিমাদি আজ দুপুরে আসতে চান ? আসুন, আমাদের এখানে লান্চ খাবেন।

আপনি ঠিক আছে। অসুবিধা হবেনা তো ?

অণিমাদি একদম না। বারটার মধ্যে চলে আসবেন। হ্যাঁ ?

আপনি আচ্ছা, বারটার মধ্যে আসতে চেষ্টা করবো। ও - কোন বাসে করে আসবো ?

অণিমাদি আপনি নয়-নম্বর বাস ধরে গোলপার্কে নামবেন। তারপর ওখান থেকে রিকশা নিয়ে সোজা লাল দশতলা বাড়িটার দিকে চলে আসবেন। তারই পাঁচ তলায় আমাদের ফ্ল্যাট। চিনতে কোনো অসুবিধে হবেনা।

আপনি ঠিক আছে, আমি এখন চান-টান করবো, তারপর সাড়ে দশটার মধ্যেই রওনা হব।

অণিমাদি বেশ। দেখা হবে !

আপনি হ্যাঁ, দেখা হবে।

Translation and notes

You	Is that 723560?
Animadi	Yes, go on.[a]
You	Is that Animadi speaking? *Namaskār*, I –[b]
Animadi	Yes, I can tell who you are[c] – *Namaskār*.
You	(Can) you understand me? My pronunciation is very bad.
Animadi	No, it isn't – it's very clear.[d] You don't have any trouble understanding me on the telephone?
You	Yes, there's plenty of noise on the telephone line, but I can manage, (please) speak a little louder.[e]
Animadi	So, what news? How are you?
You	I'm well. And you? How is Amiyada? Is (your) son well?
Animadi	We're all fine. Are you going to come to our place one day?
You	I will come, I'll certainly come. Actually I want to speak Bengali with you.[f] Will you have time?
Animadi	Yes, why not? Come whenever you like. I stay at home all day with (my) little boy. Sometimes I feel rather **æka-æka** *(lonely)*.
You	What does **æka-æka** mean?
Animadi	Friendless, without friends. You come, you'll be able to learn all these words.
You	So what time shall I come?
Animadi	Do you want to come today at midday? Come (and) have lunch here with us.
You	Fine. It won't be inconvenient?
Animadi	Not at all. Come by twelve. All right?
You	OK, I'll try to come by twelve. Oh – what bus shall I come on?
Animadi	Take a No. 9 bus and get off at Gol Park. Then take a rickshaw from there and come straight to a red ten-storey building.[g] Our flat is on the fifth floor. You won't have any difficulty recognising it.
You	Fine, I'll have (my) bath and so on now, (and) then set out by half-past ten.
Animadi	Good. See you!
You	Yes, see you!

[a]People generally use English numbers for telephone numbers, even when speaking Bengali. Notice that one starts a telephone conversation in Calcutta by confirming that one has the right number! bôlun means *(Please) speak*: cf. the shopkeeper in Unit 16, p. 68.

[b]*Namaskār* is the formal (Sanskrit) greeting among Bengali Hindus, corresponding to the (Arabic) *Salaam alaikum* among Muslims. You should reply to *Namaskār* with the same word. To the Muslim greeting, however, you should reply *Alaikum assalaam*. -di (short for didi, *elder sister*) is added to Anima's name partly because she is the elder sister in her family, partly because it is commonly used as an affectionate, respectful addition to a female name. Cf. -da (short for dada, *elder brother*), added to her husband Amiya's name later on in the Conversation.

[c]Lit. *I have recognised (you)*. cena means *to know/recognise a person*, as opposed to jana, which means *to know a fact or thing*.

[d]kôi can mean *where* but has all sorts of idiomatic uses. Notice also the emphatic particle -i; and the 'adversative' particle to, here expressing surprise.

[e]jore – *with force*.

[f]kɔtha bɔla (Lit. *to speak words*) is often used in Bengali rather than bɔla on its own. When referring to a 'word', however (a lexical item), use ʃɔbdô, which you'll see from the translation can also mean *noise* on a telephone line.

[g]When okhane *(there)* is combined with theke *(from)*, the locative case ending is dropped.

The three new conjuncts in the **Conversation** are easily recognisable:

	Handwriting	Print
চ + চ =	চ্চ	চ্চ
স + প =	স্প	স্প
ব + দ =	ব্দ	ব্দ

ফ্ল্যাট *(flat)* is written with the sign known as হসন্ত (্). In Sanskrit this sign indicates that the inherent vowel is not pronounced. In Bengali it can be used (as here) to form conjuncts that are not provided for in the Bengali script, or to 'block' an inherent vowel that the phonology of the language might lead one to expect: e.g. 'Cox Bazaar' in Exercise 1(b), p. 90 – **not** pronounced 'kɔksô bajar'. Note too its use in 'lunch'.

Grammar

1 Appointments

When referring to times in Bengali, a number + -ṭa should be used, either with the postposition sɔmɔy or the locative case ending. sɔmɔy, like many other Bengali postpositions, follows the possessive case:

| pāctar sɔmɔy | *at five o'clock* |
| dɔʃtar sɔmɔy | *at ten o'clock* |

Other postpositions can be used in the same way, such as **age** *(before)*, **pɔre** *(after)*, or **môdhye** *(within, by)*.

For the interrogative, use **kɔta** in the possessive case:

| kɔtar sɔmɔy? | *At what time?* |

The locative case can be used with the number + **ta**, and with the interrogative, instead of **sɔmɔy**:

| kɔtay? | *At what time?* |
| sattay. | *At seven.* |

Divisions of the hours will be dealt with in detail in Unit 19 (pp. 108–109). Note here, however, the use of **saṛe** ('half-past'):

| saṛe dɔʃtar môdhye | *by half-past ten* |

2 Future tense

The future tense is easier to form than the present, because there is no vowel mutation within the tense. The first person ending **-bo** can be spelt either with proper vowel **o**, or with the inherent vowel **ô**. The first spelling is generally followed in this book for the consonant stems: **kôrbo** (করবো) , not **kôrbô** (করব); **bôsbo** (বসবো) not **bôsbô** (বসব) etc. For the vowel stems it is more usual to use the inherent vowel: **khabô** (খাব) not **khabo** (খাবো) ; **hɔbô** (হব) not **hɔbo** (হবো) etc.

		kɔra	
1		ami kôrbo	*I shall do*
2	[F]	tumi kôrbe	*you will do*
3	[F]	se kôrbe	*he/she will do*
2 & 3	[P]	apni/tini kôrben	*you/he/she will do*

	dækha	
1	ami dekhbo, etc.	*I shall see*
	ʃona	
1	ami ʃunbo, etc.	*I shall hear*

1	**lekha** ami likhbo, etc.	*I shall write*
1	**rakha** ami rakhbo etc.	*I shall keep*
1	**khaoya** ami khabô etc.	*I shall eat*
1	**dhoya** ami dhobô etc.	*I shall wash*
1	**hɔoya** ami hɔbô etc.	*I shall become*
1	**deoya** ami debô	*I shall give*

In West Bengal, 'dôbo' is heard for the first person of **deoya**, but it is never written. In written Bengali, you will sometimes encounter the literary form দিব/দিবো , even in texts that are not in literary Bengali as such (see Unit 33, pp. 250–257).

For the future of ach- the verb thaka (to stay) should be used, though sometimes hɔoya is possible: cf. apnar sɔmɔy hɔbe? *(Will you have time?)* in the **Conversation** above.

The future tense in Bengali often has a greater sense of volition than the future in English: thus whereas in English we use expressions like 'would like', in Bengali the future tense will do:

apni ca khaben? *Would you like (some) tea?*

There is also no construction in Bengali comparable to 'going to'. Again, the future tense in Bengali covers it:

brsti hɔbe. *It's going to rain.*
(Lit. *There will be rain.*)

amra cartey rɔona hɔbô *We're going to leave at four.*
(rɔona hɔoya is an expression meaning *to set out*)

3 Infinitive

The infinitive ending in Bengali is -te. Notice that with the exception of the rakha verb type, infinitives (like the future tense) are formed on the second of the pair of mutating vowels (see Unit 17, pp. 85–88):

kɔra	kôrte	*to do*
dækha	dekhte	*to see*
ʃona	ʃunte	*to hear*
lekha	likhte	*to write*
rakha	rakhte	*to keep*
khaoya	khete	*to eat*
dhoya	dhute	*to wash*
hɔoya	hôte	*to become*

The infinitive of deoya uses the second of its four vowels:

deoya	dite	*to give*

The infinitive has several uses not comparable with English, which will be shown in later units. In this unit it is used, as in English, with verbs meaning *want* or *am able*, and to express purpose:

apni bamla bôlte paren?	*Can you speak Bengali?*
ami bamla ʃikhte cai.	*I want to learn Bengali.*
tɔrkari kinte bajare ẏabô.	*(I)'ll go to the bazaar to buy vegetables.*

The infinitives above are from bɔla, ʃekha and kena respectively. Remember that if you want to look up verbs in the **Glossary** at the end of this book (or in a dictionary), you will need to work out from your knowledge of Bengali verb conjugation which vowel will be used in the 'verbal noun' form.

4 Object case

In Unit 14 (pp. 51–53), you learnt the Bengali personal pronouns in the subject and possessive cases. One more case needs to be added: the object case, which serves both for direct objects (*me*, *him*, *us*, etc.) and indirect objects (*to me*, *to him*, *to us*, etc.). In the following table, note that the **plural** object pronouns are the same as the possessive:

		Singular	**Plural**	
1	*me*	amake	amader	*us*
2	*you* [F]	tomake	tomader	*you*
	you [P]	apnake	apnader	*you*
3 [H]	*him/her* [F]	eke	eder	*them*
	him/her [P]	ēke*	ēder*	*them*
[T]	*him/her* [F]	oke	oder	*them*
	him/her [P]	ōke*	ōder*	*them*
[E]	*him/her* [F]	take	tader	*them*
	him/her [P]	tāke	tāder	*them*

*The colloquial forms enake, enader, onake, onader are very common in speech. Cf. Unit 14, p. 52.

Like the plural subject and possessive endings (-ra and -der: see Unit 17, p. 84), the object case endings -ke and -der can be added to personal nouns or names – either directly, or to the definite article:

se meyeṭike roj bɔke.	*He/she scolds the girl every day.*
rimike ḍakbo?	*Shall I call Rimi?*
cheleder anbo?	*Shall I bring (the) boys?*

Occasionally -ke can be added to the plural definite article: chelegulike would be grammatically possible in the sentence above, but as was pointed out on p. 84 -ra and -der are preferred to the definite article with personal nouns.

In Bangladesh, forms such as oderke, amaderke, chelederke are commonly used for the plural object case in pronouns and personal nouns. This is not 'standard' usage, but it is sometimes convenient to be able to distinguish between the possessive and the object in this way.

5 Impersonal constructions

These are a very important area of Bengali grammar, and many varieties of them will be noted in subsequent units. You have already learnt how to express *have* in Bengali by using ach- in an impersonal construction (Unit 15, p. 62). In the **Conversation** in this chapter, there were two more impersonal constructions. subidha *(convenience)* and ɔsubidha *(inconvenience)* are very important words in Bengali (especially in Calcutta, which is not the most convenient city in the world!). They are used in an impersonal construction with hɔoya *(to be/become)*:

apnar ɔsubidha hɔbe?	*Will it be inconvenient to you?* (Lit. *Of you inconvenience it will be?*)
kolkatar gɔrôme amar khub ɔsubidha hɔy.	*Calcutta's heat bothers me a lot.* (Lit. *In the heat of Calcutta of me much inconvenience it is.*)

The colloquial variants **subidhe/ɔsubidhe** are particularly common in Calcutta, and have been used in the conversation above because of its Calcutta setting.

Impersonal constructions are often used in Bengali to express 'things that happen to you' rather than things which you do actively or deliberately. Animadi also uses an impersonal idiom using **laga** (*to strike*: cf. Unit 16, p. 74). As often happens in colloquial speech, the possessive pronoun is omitted:

majhe-majhe (amar) æka-æka-i lage.	*Sometimes (I) feel rather lonely.* (Lit. *Sometimes of me lonely it strikes.*)

Often 'active' constructions have corresponding impersonal forms. Compare **ami khub rag kôri** *(I am very angry deliberately)* with **amar khub rag hɔy** *(I am helplessly angry)*. Normally for a man marrying a woman the active verb **biye kɔra** is used; for a woman marrying a man, a 'passive' impersonal construction is used:

amar meyeṭir samner sɔptahe biye hɔbe.	*My daughter is getting married next week.*

Modern women, however, are beginning to marry 'actively' and can say of themselves **ami biye kôrbona** *(I shall not get married)* if they like! The active form was used of the girls at the school in Unit 17 (p. 79).

 ———————— **Exercises** ————————

1   *(a)   Too, also* is commonly expressed in Bengali by the use of the particle ও . Complete the following questions with the right future form of the verb and the particle ও added to the noun or pronoun. The interrogative কি is not always necessary, but it is a good idea to get into the habit of using it. Example:

আজ বিকেলে আমি বাজারে যাব ।
তুমিও কি বাজারে যাবে ?

আমি বাসে করে যাব ।
১ আপনি _____ ?

তিনি বাংলায় কথা বলবেন ।
২ তুমি _____ ?

আমার ছেলেমেয়ে আসবে ।
৩ তোমার ছেলেমেয়ে _____ ?

আমরা পাঁচটায় খাব ।
৪ তোমরা _____ ?

আমার বাবা চিঠি লিখবেন ।
৫ তোমার বাবা _____ ?

আমার একা-একা লাগবে ।
৬ তোমার _____ ?

ও এখন চান-টান করবে ।
৭ তুমি _____ ?

উনি যেতে চেষ্টা করবেন ।
৮ আপনার স্বামী _____ ?

আমার খুব অসুবিধা হবে ।
৯ তোমার _____ ?

আমি কিছু বুঝবোনা ।
১০ আপনি _____ ?

(b)　Overleaf there is a page from Anima's engagement diary. See if you can answer the questions about it:
১ বুধবারে কে আসবেন ?
২ কটার সময় ?

এপ্রিল ১৯৯২

১৩ সোমবার

১৪ মঙ্গলবার

আনিমার সঙ্গে আ-বাবার বাড়ীতে লান্চ খাব।

১৫ বুধবার

১২·০০ - অবলা আসবে।

১৬ বৃহস্পতিবার

অমিয় অমিথ্য প্লেনে করে দিল্লি যাবে।

১৭ শুক্রবার

১৮ শনিবার

৪·০০ বৃষ্টিনাথ গাড়িতে যেতে হবে।

১৯ রবিবার

অমিথ্য ফিরবে।

৩ অণিমা রমিলার বাড়িতে যাবেন কোন দিনে ?[a]

৪ কটার সময় ?

৫ মঙ্গলবার অণিমা কোথায় লান্চ খাবেন ?

৬ আর কে যাবেন লান্চ খেতে ?

৭ অমিয় কোন দিনে দিল্লি যাবেন ?[b]

৮ বিকেলে না সকালে ?

৯ উনি প্লেনে করে যাবেন, না ট্রেনে করে যাবেন ?

১০ উনি কোন দিনে ফিরবেন ?[c]

[a]*On which day?* Cf. Unit 17, Exercise 1(b), p. 90. Alternatively you can say কি বারে ?

[b]*to Delhi*: the locative case-ending is often left out for 'motion towards' a place.

[c] ফেরা *(to return)*.

2   Imagine that you are planning your week. In your mind, list the things
    you will have to do and give them each a time when you might do
    them. The days of the week are:

rôbibar	*Sunday*
sombar	*Monday*
mɔŋgôlbar	*Tuesday*
budhbar	*Wednesday*
brhɔspôtibar	*Thursday*
ʃukrôbar	*Friday*
ʃônibar	*Saturday*

For *on Sunday*, etc., use the locative case (rôbibare, sombare, etc.).
For the times, you need expressions like:

bhore	*at dawn*
sɔkale	*in the morning*
dupure	*at noon*
bikele	*in the afternoon*
sôndhyey	*in the evening*
(sôndhyay in Bangladesh)	
ratre	*at night*
ɔnek ratre	*very late at night*

With all these, you can also use the word bæla, which means a period
of the day:

bhor bælay
sɔkal bælay
etc.
(ratri bæla, not ratre bæla)

You can also use the hours of the day, using sɔmɔy or the locative
case. If you use the day of the week as well, one locative case ending
(on the time rather than the day) will be sufficient. A possible
sentence might therefore be:

sombar dɔʃṭar sɔmɔy ami   *(On) Monday at ten o'clock I*
   byæŋke ỹabô.   *shall go to the bank.*

Using the following verbal 'clues' (or any others that you can think
of), construct similar sentences:

(i)	baṛi pôriṣkar kɔra	*to clean the house*
(ii)	dokan kɔra	*to do the shopping*
(iii)	ṭelibhiʃɔn dækha	*to watch television*

(iv)	snan kɔra	*to have a bath*[a]
(v)	brekphaṣṭ khaoya	*to eat breakfast*[b]
(vi)	ciṭhi lekha	*to write a letter*
(vii)	khɔbôrer kagôj pɔṛa	*to read a newspaper*
(viii)	parke ÿaoya	*to go to the park*
(ix)	sinema dekhte ÿaoya	*to go to the cinema*
(x)	jama-kapôṛ kaca	*to wash clothes*
(xi)	pɔṛaʃona kɔra	*to study*
(xii)	apis theke phera	*to return from the office*
(xiii)	ḍaktarke dækhate ÿaoya	*to see the doctor*[c]
(xiv)	biʃram kɔra	*to have a rest*
(xv)	ʃute ÿaoya	*to go to bed*
(xvi)	kɔyekjɔn bôndhuder phon kɔra	*to phone a few friends*
(xvii)	oṭha	*to get up*
(xviii)	saradin khabar toïri kɔra	*to spend all day preparing food*[e]
(xix)	sɔkôle æksɔŋge khaoya	*to eat all together*
(xx)	gan ʃona	*to listen to songs*

The conjunct **sn** (pronounced as in English *sneeze*) is a predictable স + ন = স্ন . You should be able to work out the conjuncts **rk** and **ʃr** for yourself!

[a]The more 'correct' form of **can kɔra**, which was used in the Conversation in this unit, and in Exercise 1(*a*) above. In Bangladesh, **gosol kɔra** is used.

[b]**nasta khaoya** in Bangladesh.

[c]Lit. *to show (oneself) to the doctor*. **dækhano** is an 'extended' verb: see Unit 25, pp. 182–184.

[d]Lit. *to go to lie down* (**ʃoya**).

[e]A Bengali might say **rannar ayojɔn kɔra** – i.e. to cut up the vegetables, grind the spices, etc., which is what takes the time in Bengali cooking. **ranna kɔra** (with the obvious conjunct ন + ন = ন্ন) is to cook regularly: e.g. **ei baṛite baba ranna kɔren** (*Father does the cooking in this house*).

19
— HEALTH AND DIET —

———— **Conversation** ————

You are staying in the house of a professor at Rajshahi University, Bangladesh. It is Friday (equivalent to Sunday in Muslim countries), and your hosts were going to take you to have lunch with relatives. You have a cold, and have been suffering rather from the heat (the two often go together in tropical climates), so you ask if you can rest for the day. Your hosts' fifteen-year-old daughter stays behind to organise your lunch, etc. As you eat you talk to her. Notice that she addresses you with **apni**, whereas you address her with **tumi**.

মেয়েটি আমার মনে হয় আপনার খুব সর্দি হয়েছে ।

আপনি হ্যাঁ, বোধ হয় গত রাত্রের গরমের জন্যে, আমার ঠাণ্ডা লেগেছে ।

মেয়েটি আপনার কি ঘাম হয়, রাত্রি বেলায় ?

আপনি হ্যাঁ, খুব ঘামি ।

মেয়েটি	তাহলে আর ফ্যান ব্যবহার করবেননা - আরো ঠাণ্ডা লাগবে। একটু ডালের সুপ নিন ? সর্দি-কাশির জন্য খুব ভালো।
আপনি	বেশ। তুমি সুপ খাবেনা ?
মেয়েটি	না, আমি পরে ভাত খেয়ে নেব। আপনার কিন্তু আর একটু বেশি খাওয়া উচিত। আর একটু ভাত আর এক-টুকরো মাছ নিন ?
আপনি	কেন ? আমার তো অত খিধে পায়নি, এগুলো বেশি হবে।
মেয়েটি	আপনি হয়তো গরমের জন্য একটু দুর্বল হয়ে গেছেন। গরম কালে অনেক ভাত খেতে হয়।
আপনি	চেষ্টা করবো। তুমিও খাও না।
মেয়েটি	না, আপনার খাওয়া-দাওয়ার পর আমি বসে খাব।
আপনি	না না, তা কেন ? তুমি এক্ষুণি বসে খাও ! পরে খাবে কেন ?
মেয়েটি	আচ্ছা, ঠিক আছে। আর একটু তরকারি দেব ?
আপনি	দিতে পারো, তবে আর একটু মাছের ঝোলও দাও।
মেয়েটি	এই যে। খাওয়া-দাওয়ার পর আপনার বিশ্রাম করা উচিত। ফল খাবেন ?
আপনি	না, থাক। পেট ভরে গেছে।
মেয়েটি	বিশ্রামের পর ফল খাবেন ? আমি ফল আর চা নিয়ে আসবো ? কটার সময় আসবো ?
আপনি	এখন কটা বাজে ?
মেয়েটি	দেড়টা।
আপনি	আচ্ছা, আমি ঘণ্টা দুয়েক বিশ্রাম নেব। খবরের কাগজ আছে ?
মেয়েটি	এই যে – বাংলা না ইংরেজী ?
আপনি	ইংরেজী। আমি ক্লান্ত, বাংলার উপর এখন অত মনযোগ দিতে পারবোনা।
মেয়েটি	মাথা ধরেছে ? ওষুধ খাবেন ?
আপনি	না না, চিন্তা কোরোনা।
মেয়েটি	জ্বর আসেনি তো ?
আপনি	আরে না। তুমি এখন কি করবে ?
মেয়েটি	আমি ? এই দুই-একটা ঘরের কাজ করবো, তারপর আমিও একটু বিশ্রাম করবো। যা গরম !

Translation and notes

Daughter I think you have a bad cold.

You Yes, perhaps because of the heat last night,[a] I caught a chill.

Daughter Do you sweat at night?

You Yes, I sweat a great deal.

Daughter Then don't use a fan any more – you'll get a worse chill. (Will you) take a little *dal* soup? (It's) very good for colds and coughs.

You Fine. Won't you have (some) soup?

Daughter No, I'll have my meal later. But you should eat a bit more. (Will you) have some more rice and a piece of fish?

You Why? I'm not all that hungry,[b] this will be more than enough.

Daughter You're perhaps a little weak from the heat. (You) must eat a lot in the hot season.

You I'll try. But you (must) eat too.[c]

Daughter No, after (you've had) your meal,[d] I'll sit down and eat.

You No, no, why? Sit down and eat right now! Why eat afterwards?

Daughter OK, all right. Shall I give you a little more vegetable (curry)?

You You can give me (some), but give (me) a little sauce from the fish curry as well.[e]

Daughter Here you are. After eating you ought to rest. Will you have (some) fruit?

You No, please. I'm full up.[f]

Daughter Will you have some fruit after your rest? Shall I bring you some fruit and tea? What time shall I come?

You What time is it now?

Daughter Half-past one.

You OK, I'll rest (for) one or two hours. Do you have a newspaper?

Daughter Here – Bengali or English?

You English. I'm tired, I won't be able to concentrate so much now on Bengali.

Daughter Do you have a headache? Do you want some medicine?

You No, no, don't worry.

Daughter You haven't got a fever?[g]

You Not at all. What will you do now?

Daughter   Me? I shall do one or two things in the house, and then I shall also rest a bit. What heat!

[a]ratri bæla (*night time* – see Unit 18, p. 103), but when bæla is dropped, ratri is abbreviated to rat. The locative case is ratre, and the possessive case (as here) is ratrer. rater is also possible in colloquial speech.

[b]Notice the use of the 'adversative' particle to here and elsewhere in the conversation.

[c]Notice the use of the particle -o here and elsewhere to express *too, as well*, etc.

[d]khaoya-daoya (*meal*) is a reduplicative or 'echo' form, typical of colloquial Bengali. Here it takes the possessive case-ending, because it is followed by the postposition pɔr. pɔr and pɔre (*after*) are alternative forms, like upôr/upôre (*on*).

[e]jhôl is the sauce of a curry. macher jhôl (*fish curry*) can be regarded as the national dish of Bengal.

[f]thak (*let it stay*) – See pp. 204–205 of the **Verb tables** at the end of **Part Two**. peț bhôre gæche, Lit. *stomach has filled* – a common idiom. The verb is in the perfect tense, which is introduced in Unit 20.

[g]Remember that jvɔr is pronounced 'jɔr' (see Unit 7, p. 26).

Apart from conjuncts with রেফ (দ and ব), there is one very easily recognisable new conjunct:

ক + ল =   ক্ল   ক্ল

 ——————— **Grammar** ———————

1   Telling the time

In Unit 18 (pp. 95–96) you learnt how to refer to appointments at fixed times. To express the time **now**, the article -ța should also be used with the number (remember the special forms of -ța that are used with 2, 3 and 4: see Unit 16, pp. 73–74). In asking the time, the interrogative kɔta is used, with the third person of the present tense of the verb baja (*to strike*):

kɔta baje?	*What time is it?*
tințe baje.	*It's three o'clock.*

The words for *quarter past*, *half past* and *quarter to* respectively are sɔoya, saɽe, pôune:

sɔoya carțe baje.	*It's a quarter past four.*
saɽe pãcța baje.	*It's half past five.*
pôune chɔța baje.	*It's a quarter to six.*

For *1.30* and *2.30,* however, the special words for *one-and-a-half* and *two-and-a-half* must be used:

derta baje.	*It's half past one.*
araita baje.	*It's half past two.*
(Or araite baje, especially in West Bengal.)	

For times in minutes, the past participle (see Unit 2, pp. 120–123) of baja is used for times 'after' the hour:

dɔʃta beje kuri.	*(It's) twenty past ten (Lit. ten having struck twenty).*

and the infinitive is used for times 'before' the hour:

dɔʃta bajte kuri.	*(It's) twenty to ten (Lit. twenty to strike ten).*

For railway timetables and the like the equivalent of English *6.35, 8.40,* etc. can be used, using beje or sometimes omitting beje:

tinte beje pɔytalliʃ	*3.45*
nɔta-sɔterô	*9.17*

2 Obligation

The most common way of expressing obligation *(must, have to)* in Bengali is by an impersonal construction: object case + infinitive + third person of the verb hɔoya *(to be/become)*. hɔoya can be in any tense, depending on the time of the obligation:

tomake aro kaj kôrte hɔbe.	*You must do more work.*
apnake byæŋke ўete hɔbe.	*You must go to the bank.*
bɔrṣa kale lokder noŭko kôre ўete hɔy.	*In the rainy season people have to go by boat.*

Sometimes the possessive case is used instead of the object case, especially if the obligation arises from circumstances, rather than from anyone actively imposing an obligation:

amar roj osudh khete hɔy.	*I have to take medicine every day.*

You will also often hear, especially in West Bengal, a contracted form of the (singular) object case in this construction: amay, apnay, tomay:

apnay pɔre aste hɔbe.	*You will have to come later.*

Moral obligation, equivalent to English *ought* or *should*, is expressed by the construction: possessive of person obliged + verbal noun + ucit. In the present tense no main verb is required, because ucit acts as a 'complement' to the verbal noun (see Unit 14, p. 51):

apnar aro ṭaka deoya ucit.   *You should give more money.*

To make such a sentence negative, use nɔ- as in other subject-complement constructions:

æto beʃī khaoya ucit nɔy.   *(You) oughtn't to eat so much.*

For the future use hɔbe(na), and for the past use chilô(na). (This is done with all subject-complement constructions set in the future or past, not just with ucit constructions.) Notice too that the possessive can go **after** the verbal noun:

eṭa kɔra amar ucit hɔbena.   *It won't be right for me to do this.*
amar seṭa kɔra ucit chilô.   *I ought to have done that.*

3 More impersonal constructions

The conversation above includes some other idiomatic impersonal constructions:

apnar sôrdi-kaʃi hôyeche.   *You have a cold.*
                            (Lit. Of you cold it has become.)
amar ṭhaṇḍa legeche.   *I have caught a chill.*
(apnar) matha dhôreche?   *Have (you) got a headache?*

The tense used here is the perfect, which will be dealt with properly in Unit 20.

4 Imperative

Imperative verb forms are needed for commands and prohibitions. As you would expect from your knowledge of the Bengali verb so far, there are polite and familiar imperatives. There is also a distinction between present and future imperative: present for immediate actions, future for things you want done in the future.

		kɔra	
Present	[F]	kɔrô	*Do!*
	[P]	kôrun	
Future	[F]	kôro	
	[P]	kôrben	

		dækha	
Present	[F]	dækhô	*See!*
	[P]	dekhun	
Future	[F]	dekho	
	[P]	dekhben	

		ʃona	
Present	[F]	ʃonô	*Hear!*
	[P]	ʃunun	
Future	[F]	ʃuno	
	[P]	ʃunben	

		lekha	
Present	[F]	lekhô	*Write!*
	[P]	likhun	
Future	[F]	likho	
	[P]	likhben	

		rakha	
Present	[F]	rakhô	*Keep!*
	[P]	rakhun	
Future	[F]	rekho	
	[P]	rakhben	

		khaoya	
Present	[F]	khao	*Eat!*
	[P]	khan	
Future	[F]	kheo	
	[P]	khaben	

		dhoya	
Present	[F]	dhoo	*Wash!*
	[P]	dhon	
Future	[F]	dhuo	
	[P]	dhoben	

		hɔoya	
Present	[F]	hɔo	*Be!*
	[P]	hɔn	
Future	[F]	hôo	
	[P]	hɔben	

		deoya	
Present	[F]	dao	*Give!*
	[P]	din	
Future	[F]	dio	
	[P]	deben	

As with other verb forms ending with ô/o, you may, with the consonant stem verbs, come across o for the last syllable of the present (F) imperative, or ô for the future (F). Note that the (F) imperative of asa *(to come)* is esô (or eso) in the present **and** future.

It is an important rule in Bengali that for **negative** commands or prohibitions the future **must** be used, whatever the time referred to. If the negative suffix -na is added to the present imperative, the meaning is politely emphatic, **not** negative. With ɔ/ô and æ/e verbs, written (F) imperatives can be ambiguous, because Bengali spelling does not indicate the mutation of the vowel sound. In speech, however, the emphatic form is indicated by a special intonation, as well as by the vowel:

bɔsô na!	*Please sit!*
bôsona.	*Don't sit.*
dækhô na!	*Please look!*
dekhona.	*Don't look.*

With polite imperatives, there is no danger of ambiguity:

gan kôrun na!	*Please sing!*
gan kôrbenna.	*Don't sing.*

In Bangladesh it is normal to use the polite present tense forms – **kɔren, bɔsen,** etc. – as imperatives instead of **kôrun, bôsun,** etc. But the latter forms are recognised throughout Bengal as 'standard'.

5 *Negative of past tenses*

You have no doubt gathered by now that Bengali verbs are normally made negative by adding -na:

ami dhūmpan kôrina.   *I don't smoke.*

To the perfect and past perfect tenses, however (see Unit 20, pp. 123–124 and Unit 22, pp. 146-147), -na should not be added. Instead -ni is added to the **present** tense:

apnar jvɔr aseni?   *You haven't got a fever?*
                                  ('**esechena**' never occurs)
matha dhɔreni?   *You haven't got a headache?*

Note that in written Bengali -ni must **always** be attached to the verb. In this book -na has also been attached to help the learner achieve the right intonation. In the texts in **Part Three**, however, you will see that it is commonly written as a separate word.

Exercises

1   *(a)*   First, a simple but important exercise in telling the time. Answer the question কটা বাজে ? by reading the clock faces below. Use সওয়া, সাড়ে and পৌনে for a quarter past, half past and a quarter to, and for times in minutes use either বেজে or বাজতে . Then repeat the exercise using বেজে throughout (the 'railway-timetable method' – p. 109). You will need, in addition to the numbers up to 12, the following numbers (the complete table of Bengali numbers is given in the **Review of Part Two**, pp. 192–193):

15   পনের
20   বিশ(or কুড়ি)
30   ত্রিশ [a]
45   পঁয়তাল্লিশ

[a]often pronounced 'tiriʃ'.

(Notice the obvious conjunct ল + ল = ল্ল.)

Remember the variants for the numbers plus article (see Unit 16, p. 74), and the special words for *one-and-a-half* and *two-and-a-half* that have to be used for 1.30 and 2.30 (unless you are using the railway-timetable method). Examples:

কটা বাজে ?   সাড়ে দশটা বাজে / দশটা বেজে ত্রিশ ।

কটা বাজে ?   চারটে বাজতে কুড়ি / তিনটে বেজে চল্লিশ ।

১ কটা বাজে ?

৪ কটা বাজে ?

২ কটা বাজে ?

৫ কটা বাজে ?

৩ কটা বাজে ?

৬ কটা বাজে ?

(b)   Health is as frequent a topic of conversation in Bengal as the weather is in Britain. Even the most minor ailments are earnestly discussed, and detailed advice is freely given. Fall into this mode by giving your own list of prescriptions to someone suffering from a cold, cough and low fever. Use the উচিত construction, and the verbs and phrases indicated. Example:

বিশ্রাম করা ।   আপনার বিশ্রাম করা উচিত ।

শুতে যাওয়া   ১ _____ ।
সোয়েটার পরা[a]   ২ _____ ।
গরম চা খাওয়া   ৩ _____ ।
ঠাণ্ডা জল না খাওয়া   ৪ _____ ।
সুপ খাওয়া   ৫ _____ ।
ওষুধ খাওয়া   ৬ _____ ।
কাজ না করা   ৭ _____ ।
সিগারেট না খাওয়া   ৮ _____ ।
মাফলার[b] পরা   ৯ _____ ।
ডাক্তারকে দেখানো[c]   ১০ _____ ।

[a]*to wear a sweater.* পরা means *to wear* or *put on.*
[b]*muffler, scarf.*
[c]*'extended' verb. See Unit 18, p. 104 and Unit 25, pp. 182–184.*

2   You've been spared traditional translation exercises so far, but you now have enough Bengali grammar to translate the following simple sentences. Do the exercise orally, as fast as you can, repeatedly, to consolidate the grammar that has been covered so far; then write it.

   (i) Who are you? [F]
   (ii) He's [P] my friend.
   (iii) What's that there?
   (iv) We have two sons.
   (v) My sister's house is not big.
   (vi) The trees are beautiful.
   (vii) How old is your [F] father?
   (viii) The post-office is near the station.

   (ix) How many children are there in your [F, plural] class?
    (x) Isn't he [F] Bengali?
   (xi) He [P] doesn't eat rice.
  (xii) Put [F] the books on the table.
 (xiii) What time will your [F] mother come?
 (xiv) Will you [P, plural] eat at nine?
  (xv) Can you [F] sing?
 (xvi) He [F] doesn't want to work.
(xvii) It won't be inconvenient to you [P]?
(xviii) You [F] must go there on Thursday.
 (xix) Please [P] sit next to my elder brother.
  (xx) You [F] didn't catch a chill?

20
– MEETING AN ARTIST –

Conversation

You visit a Bengali painter who lives in New Delhi, near the Triveni Arts Centre. Bengali Market, a pleasant conglomeration of sweet shops and coffee-houses is also nearby, and the artist has just finished a painting based on sketches he has made of his favourite coffee-house. You ask him about the painting, his work and life generally, and about Bengalis living in Delhi.

আপনি	এই ছবিটা হয়ে গেছে ?
শিল্পী	হ্যাঁ, মোটামুটি হয়ে গেছে ।
আপনি	আপনি নিজে এই কফি-হাউসে যান ?
শিল্পী	হ্যাঁ, প্রায় রোজই যাই । সেখানে আরো শিল্পীদের সঙ্গে দেখা হয়, আড্ডা হয় ।
আপনি	সবাই বাঙালী ?
শিল্পী	সবাই নয়, তবে বেশিরভাগই বাঙালী ।

আপনি সমস্ত ছবিটা এখানে এঁকেছেন, না শুরুটা কফি-হাউসে বসে করেছেন ?

শিল্পী প্রথমে আমি কফি-হাউসে বসে এর খসড়াটা করি। এই যে, আমার স্কেচ-বুক দেখুন। পরে স্কেচ-বুকটা আমার স্টুডিওতে নিয়ে এসে বড় ক্যানভাসে ধীরে-ধীরে তুলে দিই।

আপনি অনেক কিছু এনেছেন এই ছবিতে - লোকজন, খাওয়া-দাওয়া, কাপ, প্লেট, টেবিল, দেওয়ালে ছবি - আর বাইরে একটা ফুলের দোকান। সব কিছু মিলে বেশ সুন্দর লাগছে।

শিল্পী হ্যাঁ, ফুলের দোকানের লাল গোলাপগুলি দেখুন - এখানে কেমন লাগে ? ফুল-ওয়ালা একটা বড় গাছের নিচে শান্ত-ভাবে বসে আছে, তবে কফি-হাউসের ভিতরে অনেক ভিড়। এই দুটো ভাব - ফুল-ওয়ালার শান্ত ভাব, আর কফি-হাউসের আড্ডা ও ব্যস্ততাকে - আমি এখানে ধরে রাখতে চেষ্টা করেছি।

আপনি আপনি ফ্রান্সে গিয়েছেন ? বেঙ্গলী মার্কেটের কফি-হাউসের সমাজ প্যারিসের প্রায় ক্যাফে সমাজের মত।

শিল্পী আমি প্যারিসে গিয়েছি একবার। খুব ভালো লেগেছে, তবে আমার খুব অল্প টাকা ছিল বলে ক্যাফেতে বেশি যেতে পারিনি।

আপনি হয়তো আবার যাবেন একদিন ?

শিল্পী নিশ্চয়ই, তবে এখনও পর্যন্ত সুযোগ পাইনি।

আপনি বিদেশে আপনি ছবি বিক্রি করেছেন ?

শিল্পী দু-একজন বিদেশী আমার কয়েকটা ছবি কিনেছেন, তবে বিদেশে আমার কোনো এক্সিবিশন হয়নি।

আপনি 'এক্সিবিশন'-এর জন্য কোনো বাংলা শব্দ নেই ?

শিল্পী আছে বই কি - 'প্রদর্শনী' ! কিন্তু শব্দটা একটু কঠিন। ইংরেজী থেকে অনেক শব্দ আমাদের বাংলায় ঢুকেছে।

আপনি দিল্লিতে বাঙালী ছেলেমেয়েরা সবাই বাংলা জানে ?

শিল্পী বাংলা বুঝতে পারে, কথাও বলতে পারে, তবে অনেকে লিখতে পড়তে পারেনা। একটা বড় বাংলা স্কুল আছে, তবে অনেকে ইংরেজী মাধ্যমের স্কুলে যায়।

আপনি আপনার ছেলেমেয়ে ?

শিল্পী ওরাও ইংরেজী স্কুলে যায়, মানে ইংরেজী মাধ্যমে পড়ে।

আপনি ও - বুঝেছি । আচ্ছা, আজ উঠি । আমি বোধ হয় আপনার
সময় নষ্ট করেছি !

শিল্পী একটুও না । আপনার সঙ্গে আলাপ করে আমার খুব ভালো
লেগেছে ।

Translation and notes

You Is this picture finished?

Artist Yes, more or less finished.

You Do you go to this coffee-house yourself?

Artist Yes, I go almost every day. One can meet and talk with other artists there.[a]

You (Are they) all Bengali?

Artist Not all, but most of them are Bengali.

You Did you paint all the picture here, or[b] did you begin (it) sitting in the coffee-house?

Artist First I sat in the coffee-house and did the sketches for it. Here, look at my sketch-book. Then I brought the sketch-book (back) to my studio and slowly worked it up on a large canvas.[c]

You You've brought lots (of things) into this picture – people, food, cups, plates, tables, pictures on the wall – and a flower-stall outside. I love the way you've combined everything.

Artist Yes, look at the red roses of the flower-stall – how do you like (them) here? The flower-seller is sitting peacefully under a big tree, but inside the coffee-house there's a great crowd. I've tried to capture here these two feelings: the peaceful expression of the flower-seller, and the coffee-house's gossip and busy activity.

You Have you been to France? Bengali Market's coffee-house society is rather like Paris café society.

Artist I've been to Paris once. I liked it a lot, but because I had very little money I couldn't go to cafés much.

You Perhaps you'll go back one day?

Artist Certainly, but up till now I haven't had a chance.

You Have you sold pictures abroad?

Artist One or two foreigners have bought a few of my pictures, but I haven't had an exhibition abroad.

You	Isn't there any Bengali word for 'exhibition'?
Artist	Of course there is – 'প্রদর্শনী' ! But the word is a bit difficult. Lots of words have come into our Bengali from English.
You	Do the Bengali children in Delhi all know Bengali?
Artist	They can understand Bengali, (and) can speak it too, but many[d] can't read or write it. There is a big Bengali school, but many go to English medium schools.
You	Your children?
Artist	They also go to an English school, i.e. they study through English medium.
You	Oh – I see. Well, I must go now.[e] I've probably wasted your time!
Artist	Not at all. It's been a pleasure to meet you.

[a]ad̪d̪a is a favourite Bengali pastime: it means sociable chatting and gossiping. Note the conjunct.

[b]Remember that na is used to mean *or* when you are posing alternatives in questions.

[c]Notice the idiomatic use of a compound verb – **tule deoya** (Lit. *to lift up*). See the **Grammar** section below.

[d]The -e ending on ɔnek, giving it the meaning *many people*, is not a locative, but an archaic plural ending that has survived in a few words. **loke bole** *(people say)* is another common idiom.

[e]uṭhi literally means *May I get up?*: this is not the first person of the present tense but a first person imperative. See **Verb tables**, p. 204.

 ——————— **Grammar** ———————

1 Past participle

The past participle is very important in Bengali grammar. Many functions that in English are handled by conjunctions and subordinate clauses are expressed in Bengali by participles. They are also used to form compound verbs. The forms of the participles for the paradigms given in earlier chapters are as follows:

| **kɔra** | kôre | *having done* |
| **dækha** | dekhe | *having seen* |

ʃona	ʃune	*having heard*
lekha	likhe	*having written*
rakha	rekhe	*having kept*
khaoya	kheye	*having eaten*
dhoya	dhuye	*having washed*
hɔoya	hôye	*having become*
deoya	diye	*having given*

Participles were used in the **Conversation** above in various ways:

(a) They connect two sentences where in English it would be natural to use *and*:

ami kôphi-hause bôse khɔsôɽa kôri.	*I sit in the coffee-house and make sketches (Lit. Having sat in the coffee-house I make sketches).*
apni dɔrôjaṭa bon̪dhô kôre asun.	*(Please) shut the door and come (in).*

Or participles can be used where English uses a subordinate clause introduced by conjunctions such as *when* or *after*:

ciṭhiṭi ʃeʂ kôre ami b̠yæn̠ke y̆abô.	*When I've finished the letter I shall go to the bank.*

You can see that this makes for considerable concision in Bengali:

bhat kheye esô.	*Come when you have had your meal.*

(b) Participles are used to form a very frequent type of compound verb in Bengali. In English you make compound or 'phrasal' verbs by combining a verb with a preposition: *get up, carry on, take after*, etc. A similar (colloquial) role is played by Bengali verbs that combine the participle of one verb with the finite form of another:

niye asa	*to bring (Lit. having taken come)*
niye y̆aoya	*to take something somewhere (Lit. having taken go)*
phire asa	*to come back (Lit. having returned come)*
phire y̆aoya	*to go back (Lit. having returned go)*
côle y̆aoya	*to go away, move off (Lit. having moved go)*
kheye phæla	*to eat up (Lit. having eaten throw)*
ghure asa	*to go for a stroll, to come by a round-about route (Lit. having wandered come)*

Be alert to compound verbs of this type as they occur in the **Conversations** and texts in the chapters that follow – especially as they are rarely listed in Bengali dictionaries. (They are, however, given in the **Glossary** at the end of this book.)

(c) The participles of certain verbs are combined with **ach-** to express **states**: thus ami bôse achi means *I am sitting*. The present continuous tense (see Unit 21, p. 133) would mean *I am in the act or process of sitting down*. The past of ach- would be used if you wanted to say *I was sitting*: ami bôse chilam. Because ach- has no future form (see Unit 18, p. 97), thaka is used with the participle if you want to express states in the future:

ami tomar jônyô gol parke bôse thakbo.	*I will sit (wait) for you in Gol Park.*

(d) The past participle kôre *(having done)* is used to turn adjectives into adverbs in Bengali. Some adverbs are special words: e.g. taratari *(quickly)*, dhīre-dhīre *(slowly)*, or ʃiggir *(soon)*, but almost any adjective can be turned into an adverb by adding kôre:

bhalo kôre	*well*
kharap kôre	*badly*
sundôr kôre	*beautifully*, etc.

There are, however, other idiomatic ways of making adverbs, using words like bhab or rɔkôm, meaning *way* or *manner*:

ʃantô bhabe	*calmly (in a calm way)*
bicchiri rɔkôme	*nastily (in a nasty, ugly way)*

(e) As has already been noticed in Unit 17 (see p. 83), some past participles are used as postpositions. Remember that this type of postposition does **not** require the possessive case in the preceding noun or pronoun:

skul theke pãcʈay phire asbo.	*(I'll) return from school at five.*
dɔʃ nɔmbôr bas bajar hôye y̆ayna.	*Bus No. 10 does not go via the bazaar.*
ṭyæksi kôre asun.	*Come by taxi.*

Participial and non-participial postpositions can be combined:

bɔner bhitor diye y̆eona.	*Don't go through the forest.*
ami majhe-majhe babar kach theke ciṭhi pai.	*I sometimes get letters from Father.*

kach theke is used instead of **theke** when people rather than places are involved. Notice that the non-participial postpositions drop their locative **-e** ending when they are combined with participles.

2 Perfect tense

Past participles are used to form two of the Bengali past tenses: the perfect and the past perfect. The first of these occurs several times in the **Conversation** above. It is roughly equivalent to the English perfect tense, which is used to express past facts or actions where the exact time is not significant:

apni ki amerikay giyechen?	*Have you been to America?*
hy æ, ami giyechi.	*Yes, I have been (there).*

The use of the various past tenses in Bengali is, however, rather mysterious. Several of the perfect tense forms in the **Conversation** above would be translated most naturally by a simple past form in English (*Did you paint the picture here?*, rather than *Have you painted the picture here?*). Notice also how the artist slipped into the present: **prôthôme ami kɔphi-hause bôse er khɔʃôɽaṭa kôri**, where, in English, you would use the past.

The perfect of **kɔra** is conjugated as follows:

1		ami kôrechi
2	[F]	tumi kôrechô
3	[F]	se kôreche
2 & 3	[P]	apni/tini kôrechen

For all the other verb-types, take the past participles given above, and add the same endings. (There is the usual variation in the spelling of the ô/o ending.) Note that **y̆aoya** *(to go)* uses a different root for its past participle (**giye**) and for the perfect tense formed on it. And it has an alternative contracted form common in colloquial speech:

1		ami giyechi	or	gechi
2	[F]	tumi giyechô	or	gæchô
3	[F]	se giyeche	or	gæche
2 & 3	[P]	apni/tini giyechen	or	gæchen

There is also a common colloquial variant of the perfect tense (for any verb) using the past participle plus **gechi, gæchô**, etc. Thus instead of **plețța pôŗeche** *(The plate has fallen)*, you can say **plețța pôŗe gæche**. At the beginning of the **Conversation** above, a common idiom meaning *is finished* was used:

ei chôbița hôye gæche?   *Is this picture finished?*

(**pɔŗa** and **hɔoya** can be combined with **y̆aoya** in other tenses too, but don't assume that this is possible with all verbs.)

Remember that to form the **negative** of the perfect tense, **-ni** is added to the present (see Unit 19, p. 113):

ami chôbița ʃeʂ kôrini.   *I have not finished the picture.*
amar eksibiʃɔn hɔyni.   *I haven't had an exhibition.*

The second sentence above is an impersonal construction (Lit. *Of me exhibition has not become*). The **Conversation** also includes an important impersonal use of **laga** to express like and dislike: this will be dealt with in the next unit.

 ———————— **Exercises** ————————

1   *(a)*   It has been mentioned several times in the units so far that the Bengali script does not indicate whether করে is the (familiar) third person present tense of করা, in which case it would be pronounced **kɔre**, or the past participle, in which case it would be pronounced **kôre**. A similar problem arises with দেখে (= **dækhe/dekhe**). Read the following sentences, predicting the right pronunciation of the word in bold in accordance with its grammatical function. The answers are given in transcription on p. 282. Example:

সে ভালো গান করে।
se bhalo gan kɔre

১ আমি **দেখে** এসেছি।
২ সে রোজ ফুটবল **খেলে**।
৩ আমরা নৌকো **করে** যাব।
৪ মেয়েটি সুন্দর **করে** চিঠি লেখে।
৫ উনি অনেকক্ষণ **ধরে** বসে আছেন।
৬ আমি সুট **পরে** যাব।

৭ দশটার **পরে** আসুন ।
৮ সে সারাদিন টেলিভিশন **দেখে** ।
৯ ছেলেটি খুব পড়াশোনা **করে** ।
১০ ওরা এই বাড়ি থেকে **চলে গেছে** ।

[a]*for a long time.* ধরে , used as a postposition, is from the verb ধরা (*to hold*).

(b) Now practise the perfect tense by filling in appropriate verb forms. The statements above each picture describe the action that has just been performed. Describe the action, using the verb indicated. Example:

ছেলেটি মাটিতে _____ ।
ছেলেটি মাটিতে বসেছে ।
(বসা)

১ উনি মেয়েটিকে উপহার _____ ।
(দেওয়া)

২ ভদ্রলোকটি চিঠি পোষ্ট _____ ।
(করা)

৩ ছেলেটি এক গেলাস জল _____ ।
(খাওয়া)

4 গাছটা মরে _____ ।
(যাওয়া)[a]

৫ লোকটি ধুতি _____ ।
(পরা)

৬ ট্রেন স্টেশন _____ ।
(ছেড়ে দেওয়া)

[a] মরে যাওয়া is appropriate for a plant dying, but for a person dying মারা যাওয়া should be used – a compound unusual in that it uses the verbal noun instead of the participle.

2   One of the most important things to master in speaking Bengali is the frequent use of participles to connect ideas. Try turning each of the following pairs of short sentences into one sentence, by turning the verb in the first sentence into a participle. If a negative is involved, put na before the participle, as a separate word. Notice that the subject of the two clauses is usually the same but not always, e.g. (vii) and (xi). Remember that the past participle of y̆aoya is giye.

(i)   ami bhat khabô.
        ami apise y̆abô.
(ii)   apni koṭ pôrenni.
        apni kænô esechen?
(iii)   tumi pôrīkṣay pas kôrechô.[a]
        tumi kɔleje y̆ete parbe.
(iv)   ami bajar kôri.
        ami baɽi phire asbo.
(v)   tini bamla ʃikhechen.
        tini edeʃe esechen.
(vi)   soja y̆an.[b]
        bā dike y̆an.
(vii)   brṣṭi hôye gæche.
        akaʃ beʃ pôriṣkar hôyeche.[c]
(viii) lokṭike ʃudhu tin ṭaka din.
        côle asun.
(ix)   tumi hat dhooni.
        tumi khete aste parôna.
(x)   se gaɽi kineche.[d]
        se bɔɽôloke hôye gæche.
(xi)   tumi côle gæchô.
        amader ɔsubidha hôyeche.
(xii)   se pagôl hôyeche.[f]
        se strī baccader khun kôreche.[g]
(xiii) ami biʃram niyechi.
        ami ɔnek bhalo achi.
(xiv)   cheleṭi khub beʃi miṣṭi kheyeche.[h]
        cheleṭir bômi hôyeche.[i]

(xv)   ami prôdhanmôntrīr[j] sɔŋge kɔtha bôlbo.
       ami sɔb bybôstha kôrbo.[k]

[a]*You have passed the exam.* Note the use of the locative case ending on pôrīk̲ṣa – *exam.*
[b]*Go straight.*
[c]*The sky has become nice (and) clear.*
[d]**kena,** *to buy.*
[e]*rich man* (Lit. *big man*).
[f]*He has gone mad.*
[g]*He has murdered his wife (and) children.*
[h]*The boy has eaten too many sweets.*
[i]*The boy has been sick* – impersonal construction.
[j]*prime minister.*
[k]*I shall arrange everything.*

(xii) and (xv) contain 'triple' conjuncts:

	Handwriting	Print
স + ত + র =	স্ত্র	স্ত্র
ন + ত + র =	ন্ত্র	ন্ত্র

The স in the first, like the স in ব্যবস্থা in (xv), is pronounced 's' not 'sh' (see Unit 2, p. 9, and pp. 269–270).

Sometimes Bengali sentences contain a whole string of participles. See if you can link the following eleven sentences into one long sentence by using participles. Look up in the **Glossary** any words whose meaning you cannot guess.

se khub bhore ɔṭhe. se ca khay. se dāt maje. se snan kɔre.
se paṭ-bhaŋa dhuti pɔre.
se juto paliʃ kɔre. se beʃi bhat[a] khayna.
se chata næy. se taṛataṛi hēṭe y̌ay.
se apise ase. se nɔṭar môdhye kaj kôrte ʃuru kɔre.

[a]Office workers in Calcutta often have **bhat** (a rice meal) at home before they leave for work.

The solution is in the **Key to the exercises** on pages 282–283.

21

TALKING TO A CHILD

Conversation

A friend in Calcutta takes you to his uncle's house for tea. Various other friends and relatives turn up at the same time, and the conversation gets too fast and jocular for you to follow very well. You decide to practise your Bengali at a gentler pace with your friend's uncle's five-year-old grandson. You pick up a picture book that he has been reading, and also a খাতা *(exercise-book)* in which he has been practising his hand-writing. Speaking to children is a good way of building up your linguistic competence, but remember that they are unable to make the kind of allowances that adults can: you must work hard to pronounce what you say as correctly as possible, otherwise you won't be understood!

আপনি   এটা কি তোমার বই ?

নাতি   আমার নয়, দিদিমার, তবে আমি পড়ছি । শোন – 'সেনদের বাড়ির কাছে এখন মেলা হচ্ছে । লোক আসছে, লোক যাচ্ছে ।'

আপনি   তুমি খুব ভালো পড়তে পার তো !

নাতি   আমি সব-ই পড়তে পারি । এখন হাতের লেখা শিখছি । এই যে আমার খাতা দেখ । এখানে দিদিমার হাতের লেখা, আর

নিচে-নিচে আমার ।

আপনি হাতের লেখা শিখতে তোমার ভালো লাগছে ?

নাতি একই রকম । বই পড়াও ভালো লাগে – দিদিমার সঙ্গে অনেকগুলো বই পড়েছি ।

আপনি তোমার হাতের লেখা ইংল্যাণ্ডের ছেলেমেয়েদের চেয়ে অনেক ভালো । খুবই সুন্দর ।

নাতি ওরা লিখতে পড়তে পারেনা ?

আপনি তোমার বয়সের ছেলেমেয়েরা এত ভালো করে লিখতে পড়তে পারেনা । আচ্ছা, এই ছবিতে কি হচ্ছে ?

নাতি এটা তো মেলা ! ওটা নাগরদোলা । বাচ্চারা খুব তাড়াতাড়ি ঘুরছে ।

আপনি তুমি মাঝে মাঝে মেলাতে যাও ? নাগরদোলায় ঘুরেছ ?

নাতি একবার । বাবার সঙ্গে গেছি । অনেক লোক ছিল ।

আপনি এখানে কি লেখা আছে ? 'ম্যাজিকের তাঁবু ।' এরা সব তাঁবুতে ঢুকছে কেন ?

নাতি কি জানি, তা আমি বুঝতে পারছিনা ।

আপনি এই নিচের ছবিখানা তুমি নিজে রং করেছ ? ওই রং-পেনসিলগুলো দিয়ে ?

নাতি করেছি । আমি অনেক ছবি-টবি আঁকি । আমার খাতা দেখ ।

অপনি এটা তোমার নিজের আঁকা ছবি ? এই মেয়েটি কি করছে ? মেয়েটি কে ?

নাতি মেয়েটি নাচছে । ও আমার কেউ নয় ।

আপনি ওর চুল হলদে রঙের কেন ?

নাতি বিদেশী মেয়ে তো, তাই । চুলের রং হলদে । চোখের রং নীল । ওর বন্ধু এদেশের ।

আপনি তা আমি বুঝতে পারছি । সুন্দর লম্বা কালো চুল । তুমি কোন স্কুলে যাও ?

নাতি 'হার্মোনি স্কুল'-এ যাই । আমার টিচার খুব স্ট্রিক্ট । বাচ্চাদের খুব বকে ।

আপনি ইংরেজী শিখেছ ?

নাতি না, শুধু বাংলা । তবে কিছু কিছু ইংরেজী জানি – ডগ, ক্যাট, মাদার, ফাদার –

আপনি   ইংরেজী সংখ্যা জান ?

নাতি   ওয়ান, টু, থ্রি, ফোর, ফাইভ – আর জানিনা ।

আপনি   বাংলা সংখ্যা খুব শক্ত । আমি বিশ পর্যন্ত জানি, তারপর
আমার মাথা ঘোরে ।

নাতি   এস, আমি তোমাকে পরীক্ষা করি । এই যে, আমার খাতায়
দিদিমা সব নম্বরগুলো লিখেছে । বল তো এটা কি ?

আপনি   ছত্রিশ । তবে ওটা আমি জানিনা । আরো শিখে নিতে হবে ।
আচ্ছা, এখন দাদা আমাকে ডাকছে । তোমার সঙ্গে গল্প করে
আমার খুব ভালো লেগেছে । আসি – আবার দেখা হবে ।

নাতি   আমি তোমাদের ওখানে আসবো একদিন ।

আপনি   বেশ তো । খুব ভালো লাগবে, একদিন এস ।

Translation and notes

You	Is this your book?
Grandson	Not mine, Grandmother's, but I'm reading (it). Listen: 'There's a fair going on now near the Sens' house. People are coming and going.'
You	You can read very well!
Grandson	I can read everything.[a] I'm learning handwriting now. Look at my exercise book. Here is Grandmother's writing, and mine below.
You	Are you enjoying learning to write?
Grandson	It's all right.[b] I like reading books too – I've read lots of[c] books with grandmother.
You	Your handwriting is much better than English children('s). Very beautiful.
Grandson	Can't they read and write?
You	Children of your age can't write or read so well. Well, what's happening in this picture?
Grandson	It's a fair![d] That's a big wheel. The children are spinning (round) very fast.
You	Do you sometimes go to the fair? Have you been on a big wheel?
Grandson	Once. I've been with Father. There were lots of people.

You	What's written here?[e] 'Magic tent.' Why are all these (people) going into the tent?
Grandson	I don't know, I don't know about that.
You	Did you colour this picture below yourself? With those coloured pencils?
Grandson	I did. I draw lots of pictures and things. Look at my exercise-book.
You	Is this your own picture? What is this girl doing? Who is she?
Grandson	She's dancing. She isn't anyone I know.[f]
You	Why is her hair yellow-coloured?[g]
Grandson	A foreign girl, that's why. Her hair's yellow. Her eyes are blue. Her friend's from this country.
You	I can see that. Beautiful long black hair. Which school do you go to?
Grandson	I go to 'Harmony School'. My teacher is very strict. She scolds the children a lot.
You	Have you learnt English?
Grandson	No, just Bengali. But I know some English – dog, cat, mother, father –
You	Do you know English numbers?
Grandson	One, two, three, four, five – I don't know any more.
You	Bengali numbers are very hard. I know (them) up to twenty, after that my head spins.
Grandson	Come, let me test you. Here, Grandmother has written all the numbers in my book. Tell me, what's this?
You	Thirty-six. But I don't know that (one). I must learn (some) more. OK, (your) *Dada* is calling me now. I've much enjoyed chatting to you. I'll be off now[h] – (I'll) see you again.
Grandson	I'll come to your place one day.
You	That would be fine. I'd like that very much, come one day.

[a]As elsewhere in the **Conversations** so far, the particle -i attached to sɔb conveys emphasis. In English, you would simply stress the word 'everything'.

[b]æk(-i) rɔkôm (Lit. *one kind*) is used idiomatically to express lukewarm approval.

[c]ɔnek *(much, many)* sometimes takes -gulo when applied to countable objects.

[d]It's obvious that it's a fair! Hence the use of the particle to.

[e]An idiomatic use of ach- with lekha: Lit. *What writing is here?*

[f]Lit. *She's not anyone of mine.*

[g]Notice that the word for *colour*, rɔm (রং) is spelt with ঙ when it takes the adjectival

possessive ending -er (রঙের), meaning *coloured*. This is because you cannot add vowels to ২ (see Unit 3, p. 14).

hLit. *May (I) come?* – a polite way of taking leave, to which the normal (adult) reply would be **esô** or **asun**. Like **ami tomake pôrīkṣa kôri** (*Let me test you*) this is a first person imperative (see **Verb tables**, p. 204). (ami) **asi?** can also be used when you want to enter a room: *May I come in?*

◪ ——— Grammar ———

1 Present continuous tense

The present continuous tense corresponds closely to its English equivalent. It is used for actions or events that are taking place at the present time *(It's raining)* or for pre-arranged future actions or events *(I'm flying to Calcutta tomorrow)*. The forms for the present continous of **kɔra** are:

1		ami kôrchi
2	[F]	tumi kôrchô (or kôrcho)
3	[F]	se kôrche
2 & 3	[P]	apni/tini kôrchen

There is no vowel mutation within the tense, so you can, from the following first person forms, work out the forms for the other persons:

dækha	ami dekhchi
ʃona	ami ʃunchi
lekha	ami likhchi
rakha	ami rakhchi
khaoya	ami khacchi
dhoya	ami dhucchi
hɔoya	ami hôcchi
deoya	ami dicchi

Notice the double sound with the vowel-stem verbs – written with the conjunct: চ + ছ = চ্ছ.

2 Comparisons

The participle **ceye** from **caoya** *(to want, ask for)* is used to make comparisons in Bengali. The person or thing with which the comparison is being made goes into the possessive case:

se amar ceye buddhiman.	*He/she (is) more intelligent than I (am).*
ami tomar ceye ɔnek kɔm jani.	*I know much less than you.*

There are no special comparative forms for the adjectives like English *bigger, smaller, less,* etc. If you want to make an adjective comparative without making an explicit comparison with anything, you can do so with the word **aro** (আরো – *more,* sometimes spelt আরও) or with **ɔnek** *(much)*:

seṭa aro bɔrô.	*That's (even) bigger.*
seṭa ɔnek bhalo!	*That's much better!*

Superlatives are expressed with the compound **sɔbceye** *(than all)*:

oṭa amar sɔbceye priyô bôi.	*That's my favourite (dearest) book.*
ami klaser sɔbceye boka chele chilam.	*I was the stupidest boy in the class.*

In the **Conversation** above, strictly speaking **tomar hater lekha imlyænḍer chelemeyeder ceye ɔnek bhalo** means *Your handwriting is much better than England's children.* It would be more grammatical to say **tomar hater lekha imlyænḍer chelemeyeder hater lekhar ceye ɔnek bhalo** *(Your handwriting is much better than the handwriting of England's children)* – but the meaning is perfectly clear in context.

theke/sɔbtheke can be used instead of **ceye/sɔbceye**, in exactly the same way, with the same meaning.

3 Like/dislike

The **Conversation** contains several occurrences of the very common impersonal construction with **bhalo** and **laga** to express like and dislike. To say *I like mangoes,* you say, Lit. *Of me mangoes it strikes well*:

amar am bhalo lage.

In the present continuous tense, the meaning is close to English *enjoy*:

apnar ki bôiṭa bhalo lagche?	*Are you enjoying the book?*

Sometimes the word order is switched round:

oi philmṭa amar bhalo lagbena.	*I won't enjoy that film.*

To express *like* + a verb, either the infinitive (see Unit 18, p. 98) or the verbal noun can be used:

bamla ʃikhte apnar ki bhalo lagche?	*Are you enjoying learning Bengali?*
tomar ei mɔd khaoya amar ækdɔm bhalo lagena.	*I don't like your drinking alcohol at all.*

In the second example above, the infinitive would not be possible, because different persons are involved (**your** *drinking*: **my** *reaction to it*). If the persons are the same, the verbal noun sounds slightly more 'general' than the infinitive, but as in English there is really very little difference:

oi ṭrene kôre y̆ete amar khub bhalo lage	*I like to go on that train.*
ṭrene kôre y̆aoya amar khub bhalo lage.	*I like going by train.*

If like/dislike is directed at a person, the person goes into the **object** case:

se lokṭike amar ekṭuo bhalo lagena.	*I don't like that person at all.*

Various intensifying words can be added, as in the last sentence, which you will pick up gradually. kharap *(bad)* can be used instead of bhalo . . . na to express strong dislike:

oi ṭicarke amar khub kharap lage.	*I can't stand that teacher.*

Or sundôr *(beautiful)* can be used to express strong liking:

oi ʃaṛiṭay tomake sundôr lagche!	*You're lovely in that sari!*

There are other ways of expressing like and dislike in Bengali: with the verb bhalobasa *(to love)*, for example, often applied to favourite foods; or the verb pɔchôndô kɔra *(to like, prefer)*; but bhalo laga is an indispensable element in the language.

Exercises

1 *(a)*   Practise making comparisons by describing the pairs of pictures on pp. 136–137, and by using the demonstrative adjectives এই/ওই and the appropriate form of the definite article. Some of the words have been filled in for you. Example:

এই গাড়িটা ওই গাড়িটার চেয়ে বড় ।

১ _____ বেঁটে ।

---

^aLit. *of less age.*
^bLit. *This man that man than in age small.*

২ _____ লম্বা ।

৩ _____ মোটা ।

4 _____ কম বয়সের[a] ।

৫ এই লোকটি ওই লোকটির _____ বয়সে

_____ ।[b]

৬ _____ রোগা ।

(b) Now 'disagree' with the following expressions of like and dislike by repeating the statements in the negative or affirmative. Remember the use of নি for the negative of the past tenses (see p. 113). If খুব is used in the affirmative, use বেশী in the negative. The emphatic খুবই can become একটুও (*at all*) in the negative. Example:

আমার আম খুব ভালো লাগে ।
আমার আম বেশী ভালো লাগেনা ।

১ এই খাবার আমার ভালো লাগছে ।

২ ফিল্মটা আমার ভালো লেগেছে ।

৩ ওই মেয়েটিকে আমার একটুও ভালো লাগেনা ।

৪ ওখানে যেতে আমার খুবই ভালো লাগবে ।

৫ গানগুলি আমার বেশী ভালো লাগেনি ।

৬ বাগান করা আমার খুব ভালো লাগে ।

৭ এখন আম খেতে আমার খুব ভালো লাগবে ।

৮ বাংলা শেখা আমার বেশী ভালো লাগছেনা ।

৯ ওর কবিতা আমার ভালো লাগেনি ।

১০ বৃষ্টিতে হেঁটে যাওয়া আমার খুবই ভালো লাগে ।

2 You have now been introduced to four Bengali tenses – the present, the future, the perfect and the present continuous – as well as the infinitive, the past participle, the present and past of **ach-** (with its special present tense negative **nei**), and **nɔ-** (the negative of the zero verb). Remember also that **thaka** *(to stay)* functions as a future tense for **ach-**. See now if you can supply the missing verbs in the following sentences, judging from the context what would be the most appropriate tense or form, and whether to give it a negative suffix or not. The verbs you should use are given in brackets in their verbal noun form (apart from **ach-** and **nɔ-**, which have no verbal noun).

(i) akaʃe megh kôrche. jhɔr _____.[a]
(asa)

(ii) ami bajare yacchi. tumi barite _____, na amar sɔŋge asbe?
(thaka)

(iii) ætô bɔrô gari ei rastay _____ parbena.[b]
(ḍhoka)

(iv) ami khub klantô. ækhôn ar pɔraʃona _____.[c]
(kɔra)

(v) dækhô ki hôyeche! kukurta beralṭike mere _____.
(phæla)

(vi) ami roj dɔʃ kap ca _____.
(khaoya)

(vii) apni sɔmɔstô rôbīndrôrɔcônabôlī[d] _____?
(pɔra)

(viii) amra tin ghɔnṭa dhôre _____ achi.
(bɔsa)

(ix) na, ei jamaṭa ami kinbona. er rɔŋṭa amar bhalo _____.
(laga)

(x) amader pɔraʃona bhalo _____. amra ɔnek ʃikechi.
(cɔla)

(xi) uni bamla bôlte parenna. uni baŋalī _____.
(nɔ-)

(xii) ækhôn amader barite bathrum hôyeche.[e] age amader bathrum _____.
(ach-)

(xiii) se sara din nôdīr dhare bôse ache, tôbu kono mach
_____.[f]
(paoya)

(xiv) apnar æto sundôr upôhar ami prôtyaʃa _____.
(kɔra)[g]

(xv) basṭa koṭar sɔmɔy _____? ami ɔpekṣa kôrte parina.[h]
(chaṛa)

[a]*In the sky clouds are making (forming). A storm is coming.*

[b]*Such a big car will not be able to enter (ḍhoka) this street.*

[c]*ar means more here.*

[d]*all of Rabindranath's collected works.*

[e]*has become, i.e. has been built.*

[f]*He has been sitting by the river all day, but he has not got any fish.* tôbu is stronger than kintu or tɔbe, and means *nevertheless, notwithstanding,* etc. For kono *(some, any)* see Unit 23, p. 158. Note that there is no Bengali perfect continuous tense (*has been sitting*). The present continuous, or participle + ach- construction (p. 122) is used.

[g]prôtyaʃa kɔra, *to expect.*

[h]*What time will the bus leave? I cannot wait.*

22

__ CONVERSATION ON __
A TRAIN

Conversation

You are staying in Chittagong, and are returning there by train after a few days in Dhaka. You start talking to a student who is travelling back to Chittagong university to start the new term. You tell him about what you did and saw in Dhaka, and ask him about his studies and ambitions.

ছাত্র	আপনি চিটাগাঙ যাচ্ছেন ?
আপনি	হ্যাঁ, আপনিও ?
ছাত্র	জি, আমি ছাত্র, চট্টগ্রাম বিশ্ববিদ্যালয়ে যাচ্ছি । আপনি ওখানে কখনও গেছেন ?
আপনি	একবার গিয়েছিলাম । আমার একজন জার্মান বন্ধু আছে চট্টগ্রাম শহরে । একদিন সে আমাকে নিয়ে গিয়েছিল, ওখানকার বিজ্ঞান অনুষদে ।
ছাত্র	কোনো অধ্যাপকের সঙ্গে দেখা করতে গিয়েছিলেন ?
আপনি	হ্যাঁ, প্রফেসার হোসেনের সঙ্গে ।
ছাত্র	ও - তিনি তো আমারও অধ্যাপক ! অঙ্ক বিভাগে পড়ান ।
আপনি	আপনি অঙ্কে অনার্স পড়ছেন ?
ছাত্র	শুরুতে আমি তাই পড়তে চেয়েছিলাম, তবে অঙ্ক নিয়ে পাশ

— 141 —

করে স্কুল-মাস্টারী ছাড়া তো আর কোনো চাকরি পাওয়া যায়না । তাই আমি এখন পরিসংখ্যানে চলে এসেছি - তবে অবশ্য এখনও অঙ্ক পরীক্ষা দিতে হবে, সাবসিডিয়ারি হিসেবে ।

আপনি   আপনি ঢাকার লোক ?

ছাত্র   জি ।

আপনি   তাহলে ঢাকা বিশ্ববিদ্যালয়ে ঢুকতে চাননি কেন ?

ছাত্র   ঢাকা বিশ্ববিদ্যালয়ে খুব বেশী রাজনীতি হয় - গোলমাল লেগেই থাকে । আমি রাজনীতি করিনা, সেজন্য ওখানে যেতে আমার ইচ্ছে হয়নি । চিটাগাঙ ঢাকার চেয়ে একটু চুপ-চাপ । ঢাকা ইউনিভার্সিটি আপনি দেখেছেন ?

আপনি   দূর থেকে আপনাদের কার্জন হল তো দেখেছি । ক্যাম্পাসের ভেতরে যাইনি । ঢাকায় আমার বন্ধুর বাসা থেকে ছাত্রদের মিছিল দেখা যায় মাঝে-মাঝে, আর খুব শব্দ শোনা যায় ।

ছাত্র   গত মঙ্গলবারে একটা ছিল । আপনি দেখেছিলেন ?

আপনি   না, দেখিনি । সেদিন আমরা বেড়াতে গিয়েছিলাম, ঢাকার বাইরে । তবে পরের দিন কাগজে মিছিলের খবর বেরিয়েছিল - আমি পড়েছি ।

ছাত্র   ঢাকার আর কোন কোন জায়গায় গিয়েছিলেন ? জাদুঘরে ? পুরনো ঢাকা ? শহীদ মিনারে ? স্মৃতি-সৌধের দিকে ?

আপনি   পুরনো ঢাকায় গিয়েছিলাম । জাদুঘরে এখনও যাইনি । শহীদ মিনারে গিয়েছিলাম, একুশে ফেব্রুয়ারিতে । হ্যাঁ, এবারে স্মৃতি-সৌধটা দেখতে গিয়েছিলাম ।

ছাত্র   কিসে করে গেলেন ?

আপনি   আমার বন্ধুর গাড়ি করে । জায়গাটা ভারী সুন্দর - ওখানে গিয়ে আমার মনের উপরে খুব ছাপ পড়েছিল । ওর চারদিকে বাগান, জলধারা খুব চমৎকার ।

ছাত্র   স্বাধীনতা যুদ্ধের সময় এদেশে আমরা অনেক বীর ও অনেক শ্রেষ্ঠ সন্তানকে হারিয়েছিলাম । এটা তাঁদেরই স্মৃতিতে গড়া ।

আপনি   আমি জানি । এই মুক্তি যুদ্ধ সম্বন্ধে আমার একটা ভালো বই আছে ।

ছাত্র   আমার জন্ম হয়েছিল বাহাত্তর সালে, স্বাধীনতার পরেই । কিন্তু আমার আত্মীয়-স্বজনের মুখে আমি যুদ্ধের অনেক কথা শুনেছি ।

আপনি	ডিগ্রি পাশ করে আপনি কি করতে চান ?
ছাত্র	সম্ভব হলে, আমি আমেরিকা চলে যাব, আরো পড়াশোনা করতে । জনসংখ্যা বিক্ষোরণ নিয়ে কিছু কাজ করায় আমার ইচ্ছা আছে । এদেশে এখন এটা একটা মস্ত সমস্যা ।
আপনি	আমেরিকা গিয়ে পি এইচ ডি পাশ করে ভালো চাকরির সুযোগ পেলে, আপনি কি বাংলাদেশে ফিরে আসবেন ?
ছাত্র	আশা করি । এই দেশটা তো গরীব । তাই আমি দেশের সেবা করতে চাই । তবে আপনি ঠিকই বলেছেন, অনেকে পড়াশোনার জন্য বিদেশে গিয়ে আর দেশে ফিরে আসেনা । আর একটা সমস্যা হচ্ছে বেকার-সমস্যা - এদেশে চাকরির খুব অভাব ।
আপনি	শিক্ষিত-লোকের মধ্যেও কি তাই ?
ছাত্র	জি, তাদের মধ্যেও । দু বছর আগে আমার বড় ভাই অর্থনীতিতে ভালো ডিগ্রি নিয়ে পাশ করেছিল । এখনও চাকরি পায়নি ।
আপনি	আজকাল পাশ্চাত্য দেশগুলিতেও বেকার-সমস্যা বাড়ছে, তবে ভালো ডিগ্রি থাকলে সাধারণত তেমন অসুবিধা হয়না ।
ছাত্র	দেখুন, চট্টগ্রামে এসে গেছি । ক্যাম্পাসে আসবেন একদিন - আমাদের হলে আসবেন, অন্য ছাত্রদের সাথেও আলাপ হবে ।
আপনি	আমি খুব খুশি হব । আশা করি আপনার পড়াশোনা ভালো ভাবে চলবে, আর আমেরিকা থেকে ফিরে এসে এদেশে ভালো কাজ করবেন ।
ছাত্র	চেষ্টা করবো । দেখা হবে ! খোদা হাফিজ ।
আপনি	খোদা হাফিজ ।

Translation and notes

Student	Are you going (to) Chittagong?[a]
You	Yes, and you?
Student	Yes, I'm a student, I'm going to Chittagong university. Have you ever been there?
You	I've been once. I have a German friend in Chittagong city. One day he took me to the Science Faculty there.[b]
Student	You went to meet some professor?
You	Yes, Professor Hossain.

Student Oh, he's my professor! He teaches in the Mathematics department.

You Are you studying for Mathematics Honours?

Student At the beginning I wanted to study that, but with a maths degree, there isn't any employment available apart from school-teaching.[c] So I've moved now into Statistics – but I will still have to take an exam in maths as a subsidiary (subject).

You Are you a Dhaka person?

Student Yes.

You Then why didn't you want to enter Dhaka University?

Student There's too much politics at Dhaka University – constant trouble. I don't engage in politics, so I had no wish to go there.[d] Chittagong is a bit quieter than Dhaka. Have you seen Dhaka University?

You I've seen your Curzon Hall from the distance. I didn't go into the campus. From my friend's house in Dhaka students' demonstrations can sometimes be seen, and a lot of noise can be heard.

Student There was one last Tuesday. Did you see (it)?

You No, I didn't. That day we had gone on a jaunt, outside Dhaka.[e] But the meeting was reported in the newspaper the next day – I read (about it).

Student What other places in Dhaka have you been to? The Museum? Old Dhaka? Shahid Minar? To the Smriti Soudha?

You I've been to Old Dhaka. I haven't yet been to the museum. I went to the Shahid Minar, on 21st February. Yes, this time I went to see the Smriti Soudha.

Student How did you get (there)?

You In my friend's car. It's a very beautiful place – going there made a great impression on me. The gardens and fountains all around it are very fine.

Student During the Independence war we lost many heroes and many (of our) finest young people. It was built in memory of them.

You I know. I have a good book about the Liberation War.

Student I was born in '72, after Liberation.[f] But I've heard a lot about the war from my relatives.

You What do you want to do after (your) degree?

Student If possible, I shall go to America, to do further study. I want to do some work on the population explosion. This is now a major problem in this country.

You   If you go to America, get your Ph.D and (then) a chance of
              a good job, will you return to Bangladesh?
Student   I hope (so). This country is poor, you know. I want to do it
              service. But you are right, many (people) go abroad for
              study and do not return to (their) country. Another prob-
              lem is the problem of unemployment – in this country
              (there's) a great lack of jobs.
You   Even among educated people?
Student   Yes, among them too. Two years ago my elder brother
              got a good Economics degree.[g] He still hasn't got a job.
You   In Western countries too the problem of unemployment is
              growing, but if you have a good degree you don't usually
              have much trouble.
Student   Look, we've arrived at Chittagong. Come to the campus
              one day – come to our hall (of residence), (you'll) meet the
              other students.
You   I'd be very happy (to). I hope your studies go well, and
              that after returning from America you will do good work in
              this country.
Student   I shall try. See you! Khoda Hafiz.[h]
You   Khoda Hafiz.

---

[a] People with a knowledge of English shift freely from English words to Bengali words (e.g.
biʃvôbidyælôy/iunibharsiṭi) or from Bengali names to anglicised forms of those names
(coṭṭôgram/ciṭagaṇ).

[b] okhankar is a possessive (adjectival) form of okhane (see **3** in the **Grammar** section
below). Remember that bijñæn *(science)* is pronounced 'biggæn' (see Unit 17, p. 82).

[c] chaṛa *(to leave)* is frequently used to mean *apart from.*

[d] Notice this common impersonal construction with icche/iccha *(wish)*. It is either combined
with the infinitive (as here) or with the verbal noun in the possessive case.

[e] bæṛate ẏaoya is a rather unusual compound using an infinitive rather than a participle,
meaning to *go out and about, to go on a trip,* etc. bæṛate is the infinitive of bæṛano, an
'extended' verb (see Unit 25, pp. 182–184).

[f] The full date would be uniʃ-ʃɔ-bahattôr sale *(1972)*. sal not bɔchôr is used in dates. See the
Review of Part Two (p. 195).

[g] bɔṛô bhai is used by Muslims for 'elder brother' rather than dada. See the list of **Kinship
terms** on pp. 272–274.

[h] A common Arabic valediction used by Bengali Muslims: Lit. *May God protect you.*

In আত্মীয়-স্বজন note that ত্ম (ত + ম) is pronounced 'tt', and
remember that the ব-ফলা in স্বজন is silent (see Unit 7, p. 26). Of the
other new conjuncts, three are easily recognisable:

	Handwriting	**Print**
ম + ভ =	ম্ভ	ম্ভ
র + থ =	র্থ	র্থ
স + ফ =	স্ফ	স্ফ

There are two, however, that are not so predictable:

ত + ত =	ত্ত	ত্ত
দ + ধ =	দ্ধ	দ্ধ

 ———————————— **Grammar** ————————————

1 Past perfect tense

In English, the past perfect (also known as the pluperfect) tense is used for actions and events that happen earlier than some past action or event: *He told me that the parcel* **had arrived**.

In Bengali, the past perfect is commonly used for any past action or event at a particular time, except things that have happened in the very recent past (for which the simple past is used – see Unit 23, p. 156). Like the perfect tense it is formed on the past participle, and the endings added are identical to the past of **ach-** (see Unit 15, p. 61). So the past perfect of kɔra would be:

1		ami kôrechilam
2	[F]	tumi kôrechile
3	[F]	se kôrechilô (or kôrechilo)
2 & 3	[P]	apni/tini kôrechilen

The other verb types form the tense similarly. (Remember that the past participle of y̆aoya is **giye**.) The first person forms are:

dækha	ami dekhechilam
ʃona	ami ʃunechilam
lekha	ami likhechilam
rakha	ami rekhechilam
khaoya	ami kheyechilam
dhoya	ami dhuyechilam
hɔoya	ami hôyechilam
deoya	ami diyechilam

As with the perfect tense, there is no negative form: instead, -ni has to be added to the present tense (this is the normal rule although you will hear some people saying giyechilamna, etc.):

gɔtô bɔchôre ami baɱladeʃe giyechilam.	*Last year I went to Bangladesh.*
amar <u>strī</u> y̆anni.	*My wife didn't go.*

2 Verbal noun + y̆aoya

In English 'active' sentences can be converted into 'passive' sentences:

John drove the car.
The car was driven by John.

Passive constructions are possible in Bengali (see Unit 23, p. 158), but are not usually very idiomatic. Instead, events that affect people passively are expressed by impersonal constructions, many of which you know by now. There is, however, a very common construction using the verbal noun with y̆aoya, which is equivalent in meaning to the English *can be* construction. y̆aoya can be in any tense, but is always in the third person:

ekhan theke <u>s</u>teʃɔn dækha y̆ay.	*The station can be seen from here.*
oi dokane ɖim paoya y̆abena.	*(You) won't be able to get eggs in that shop.*

y̆aoya can be used with itself in this way:

oi dike y̆aoya y̆ay.	*(You) can go that way.*

If the verbal noun has a personal object, the object ending -ke should be used:

oke kothao khūje paoya y̆ayni.	*He couldn't be found anywhere.*

3 Adjectival postpositions

You are familiar now with the main types of postposition found in Bengali:

(a) postpositions that follow the possessive case:

amar kache	*near me*
po<u>s</u>tapiser samne	*in front of the post office*

(b)   postpositions which do not follow the possessive case, some of
which are verbal participles:

janala diye	*through (the) window*
saikel kôre	*by bicycle*
rajniti sɔmbɔndhe*	*concerning politics*
pā̃cṭa nagad	*by 5 o'clock*

*In this word (সম্বন্ধে) the b is derived from Sanskrit *b* rather than *v*, but even so the
conjunct tends to be pronounced 'mm' rather than 'mb'.

(c)   combined participial/non-participial postpositions (see Unit 20,
p. 122):

| bɔner bhitôr diye | *through the forest* |
| amar kach theke | *from me* |

It is very natural in Bengali to create adjectival phrases by giving type *(a)*
postpositions a possessive case ending. Sometimes the noun or pronoun
to which the postposition applies is dropped:

(amader) paʃer baṛite ora khub golmal kɔre.	*They make a lot of noise in the house next door (to us).*
nehru parker samner hoṭelṭa bhalo.	*The hotel opposite Nehru Park is good.*
pɔrer din tini mara gæchen, ʃunechi.	*He/she died the next day, (so I) have heard.*

4   Words ending in conjuncts

You should be well aware by now that the inherent vowel is frequently not
pronounced at the end of Bengali words: **gach, bon, phul**, etc. If a word
ends in a conjunct, however, the inherent vowel **is** pronounced: sɔmɔstô,
y̆uddhô. If the possessive case ending is added to such words, the
inherent vowel is dropped:

| y̆uddher pɔre | *after the war* |
| ɔŋker khata | *maths exercise-book* |

If the locative case ending is added, you can either drop the inherent
vowel and add **-e**, or keep it and add **-te** or **-y** (see Unit 17, pp. 83–84).
The first method is probably more common:

| | oi bakse | |
| or | oi baksôte/baksôy | *in that box (suitcase)* |

somudre
or   somudrôte/somudrôy   *in (the) sea*

──────────── **Exercises** ────────────

1 *(a)* Practise the past perfect tense by saying after each of the statements below that you (or whoever is mentioned) did the action in question yesterday, last Tuesday, last year, etc. Example:

আমি আজ বিকেলে ব্যাঙ্কে যাব ।
আমি গতকালও ব্যাঙ্কে গিয়েছিলাম ।

আমি আজ ওকে চিঠি লিখবো ।
১ _____ গত সপ্তাহেও[a] _____ ।

ইনি চিটাগাঙ যাচ্ছেন ।
২ _____ গত রবিবারেও _____ ।

আগামীকাল[b] ওর সঙ্গে আমার দেখা হবে ।
৩ কয়েকদিন আগেও _____ ।

ঠিক তিনটের সময় উনি লণ্ডন থেকে ফোন করবেন ।
৪ গত পরশুদিনও[c] _____ ।

এই বছরে বাবার জন্মদিনে[d] বৃষ্টি হল ।
৫ গত বছরেও _____ ।

আমার ছেলেমেয়েরা আজকে[e] জাদুঘরে যাবে ।
৬ _____ গত বুধবারেও _____ ।

আমি পেট ভরে খেয়েছি ।
৭ কালকেও _____ ।

আমার মা রবীন্দ্রনাথকে দেখেছেন ।
৮ উনি ১৯৪০[f] সালে ওঁকে _____ ।

দাদা আমেরিকায় চলে যাচ্ছে ।

৯ আমার দাদাও গত বছরে _____ ।

বইটি আমি এইমাত্র পড়েছি ।

১০ সরলা _____ গত মাসে _____ ।

[a] Note the conjunct প + ত = প্ত .

[b] কাল can mean yesterday or tomorrow according to the tense, but it is possible to say unambiguously আগামীকাল *(tomorrow)* or গতকাল *(yesterday)*.

[c] পরশুদিন means *the day after tomorrow* or *the day before yesterday* depending on the time.

[d] জন্মদিন means *birthday*. Note the conjunct ন + ম = ন্ম , pronounced as written, 'nm'. হল is simple past tense (see Unit 23, p. 156).

[e] There is no difference between আজ and আজকে (or কাল and কালকে).

[f] 'উনিশ-শ চল্লিশ' .

(b) You are staying at a friend's house in a suburb of Calcutta. Below is what you can see from the window of your bedroom. Describe the view, using the verbal noun + যাওয়া construction (p. 147). You can also hear things, so you might wish to use the verb *to hear* শোনা, as well as the verb *to see* (দেখা). Example:

আমার জানালা থেকে রাস্তা দেখা যায় ।

2 See if you can convert the following pairs of sentences into single sentences by using an adjectival postposition. For example:

phulguli amar samne.
phulguli sundôr.

amar samnèr phulguli sundôr.

The flowers (are) in front of me.
The flowers are beautiful.

The flowers in front of me are
  beautiful.

(i)   boner bhitôre poth.
       pothta khub ondhôkar.[a]
(ii)   pukurer opare môndir.[b]
       môndirta purôno noy.
(iii) barir caridike jongôl.
       jongôle onek pakhi thake.
(iv)   īder pore[c] chuti hobe.
       chutite bari ÿabô.
(v)   amader upôre ækta ghor
       ache.   se ghore tini
       thaken.

(vi)   brstir pore rod hobe.
       rode amader
       caragulo sotej hobe.[d]
(vii) byæger bhitôre taka.
       takagulo bideʃī.
(viii) amar desker nice baksô
       ache.   baksôta niye
       asbo?
(ix)   taker upôre upôharti
       ache.   upôharti amake
       dao.
(x)   dupurer age lekcar[e]
       chilô.   lekcarta khub
       kharap chilô.

[a] *dark.*
[b] *temple.*
[c] *after Eid.*
[d] *In the sunshine my plants will shoot up.* sotej *means vigorous, full of energy.*
[e] *lecture.*

Sometimes in Bengali you can have a whole string of these possessive postpositional phrases. See if you can join the following sentences into one long sentence, using this method. Of course such a
grotesque sentence would never normally be spoken or written in
Bengali! Look up any words you don't know in the **Glossary**.

skultar pichône pukur.
pukurer dhare bon.
boner môdhye purôno bari.
purôno barir paʃe botgach.
botgacher tolay[a] pathôr.
pathôrer nice gortô.
gorter bhitore baksô.
baksôte prôcur sonar mohor chilô.

[a] tolay, *at the bottom of,* becomes tolar in its possessive form.

23
— TELLING STORIES —

 Conversation

You are in England, in Birmingham, visiting a community centre where, among other things, a 'community school' for Bengali children meets on Saturday mornings. On the morning of your visit, Putul, a Bengali lady who has a talent for entertaining young children with stories, has been talking to the children. Over coffee, you talk to her about her work and ask to look at some of the pictures and stories she has been showing and telling the children. (The second story mentioned in the conversation can be found in Unit 27, p. 208.)

আপনি	আমি আপনাকে পুতুল বলে ডাকতে পারি ?
পুতুল	নিশ্চয়ই । সবাই আমাকে তাই বলেই ডাকে ।
আপনি	আপনি কি নিয়মিত এই সেন্টারে আসেন ?
পুতুল	না, আমি নানা জায়গাতে ঘুরি । তবে আগেও আমি এখানে দু-তিনবার এসেছি ।
আপনি	বাচ্চাদের সঙ্গে আপনি আজকে কি করলেন ?
পুতুল	আমি প্রথমে তাদের পাঁচটা ছবি আঁকতে বললাম – বাড়ি, বল্, কুকুর, নাচের ভঙ্গিতে তিনটি বাচ্চা, আর একটি বেড়াল – এই

সবের । এই যে দেখুন, তাদের আঁকা কয়েকটি ছবি । খুবই সুন্দর, তাই না ?

আপনি চমৎকার ! ছবিগুলো আঁকার পর, আপনি তখন কি বললেন ?

পুতুল তখন একটা মজার খেলা দিলাম ওদেরকে । আমি বললাম, 'আমি একটা গল্প বলবো আর তোমরা গল্পের যেখানে যেখানে আমি কোনো শব্দ বাদ দেব, সেখানে এই ছবিগুলো দেখাবে ।' এইভাবে আমি ফাঁকে ফাঁকে শব্দ বাদ দিয়ে গল্পটা শেষ করলাম, আর ওরা সেই সব বাদ দেওয়া শব্দের জায়গায় ছবিগুলো তুলে ধরে শব্দটা বুঝিয়ে দিল । গল্পটা ছিল এই রকম -

একদিন বাবুরাম আর পুপুয়া খেলতে গেল তাদের বন্ধু পটলদের ... । তারা অনেকক্ষণ ... খেললো । ওদের সঙ্গে ছুটোছুটি করলো পটলদের পাশের বাড়ির ... । তিনটি ... নাচানাচি করলো । ওদের চেঁচামেচি শুনে এসে হাজির হল একটা ... । পুপুয়া তাকে ডেকে বললো, 'পুসি বেড়াল, তুমি গান করতে পার ?' 'দূর বোকা, আমি শুধু মিউমিউ করতে পারি !' হেসে বললো ... ।

আপনি বেশ মজার তো । সঠিক শব্দগুলি তাহলে হচ্ছে - প্রথমে বাড়ি, তার পরেরটা বল, তারপর এখানে বেড়াল ?

পুতুল না, কুকুর । বেড়াল ছুটোছুটি করেনা ।

আপনি আচ্ছা, হ্যাঁ, কুকুর । তার পরে তিনটি বাচ্চা, তার পরে বেড়াল, শেষটাও বেড়াল । ঠিক হয়েছে ?

পুতুল একদম ঠিক-ঠিক হয়েছে ।

আপনি তার পরে আপনি কি করলেন ?

পুতুল তারপর, একটা গান শুনিয়ে দিলাম, আর এই সব দেশী খেলনাগুলো তাদের দেখালাম । এই ঘোড়ার-গাড়িটা তাদের বিশেষ করে ভালো লাগলো ।

আপনি এটা কলকাতায় বানানো, না ?

পুতুল না, বোধ হয় ঢাকায় । কি সুন্দর করে রং করা, দেখেছেন ?

আপনি হ্যাঁ । খেলনাগুলো দেখিয়ে আপনি শেষ করলেন, তাই না ?

পুতুল না, আমি আর একটা গল্প বললাম । গল্পটি উপেন্দ্রকিশোর রায়চৌধুরীর নাম করা 'টুনটুনির বই' থেকে নেওয়া । এই যে,

বইটি দেখুন ।

আপনি   বইটি কবে লেখা হয়েছিল ?

পুতুল   উনিশ-শ দশ-এ । লেখক সত্যজিৎ রায়ের ঠাকুরদা ।

আপনি   সেই নাম করা সিনেমা পরিচালক সত্যজিৎ রায় ?

পুতুল   হ্যাঁ । গল্পটি বেশ মজার । এই ধরনের গল্পগুলোতে একটা চালাক পশু আর একটা বোকা পশু থাকে । টুনটুনি পাখি আর শেয়াল, এরা হচ্ছে চালাক ; আর বেড়াল, বাঘ, কুমির এরা হচ্ছে খুব বোকা । এই বিশেষ গল্পটিতেও বেড়ালটি খুব বোকা, তবে আর একটা খুব জনপ্রিয় গল্পে বেশ বুদ্ধিমতী একটা বেড়াল আছে - মজন্তালি সরকার নামে ।

আপনি   আমি কি বইটি কিনতে পারি ?

পুতুল   এই দেশে বইটি পেতে আপনার বোধ হয় অসুবিধা হবে । তবে এই কপিটি আপনি ধার নিতে পারেন ।

আপনি   আমি খুব কৃতজ্ঞ । আপনার ঠিকানা কি ? বইটি পড়ে শেষ করে, আমি পরে আপনাকে পোস্টে ফেরৎ পাঠিয়ে দেব ।

পুতুল   কোনো তাড়া নেই । বইটি আমার এখুনি লাগছেনা । বইটি আপনার ভালো লাগবে । ভাষাটা খুব সহজ ।

আপনি   আচ্ছা, আমার ভাগ্য বেশ ভালো যে আপনার সঙ্গে দেখা হল । বাচ্চাদের ভাগ্য তো ভালো বটেই ।

পুতুল   কাজটা আমি ভালোবাসি । সারা সপ্তাহ আমি অফিসে খাটি । এখানে পালিয়ে এসে আমি বাঁচি । আবার দেখা হবে একদিন !

আপনি   নিশ্চয়ই হবে ।

Translation and notes

You   Can I call you Putul?[a]

Putul   Certainly. Everyone calls me that.

You   Do you come to this Centre regularly?

Putul   No, I go round various places. But I've been here two or three times before.

You   What did you do with the children today?

Putul   First I told them to draw five pictures: a house, a ball, a dog, three children dancing, and a cat – all that. Look, here are some of their pictures. Very beautiful, aren't they?

You   Superb! What did you do after painting the pictures?[b]

Putul   I then gave them a funny game. I said, 'I shall tell you a story and you will show these pictures for any words that I shall leave out.' I finished the story leaving out words like this, and they held up[c] the pictures in all the places where words were left out, to indicate the (right) word. The story (was) like this:

'One day Baburam and Pupuya went to play at their friend Patol's _____. They played _____ for a long time. The _____ from the house next to Patol's house[d] ran around with them. The three _____ danced around. Hearing the noise they were making a _____ turned up. Pupuya called it and said, "Pussy cat, can you sing?" "Don't be silly, I can only go mew-mew," laughed _____.'

You   Very funny. The right words are:[e] first house, the next one (is) ball, then cat here?

Putul   No, dog. Cats don't rush around.

You   OK, yes, dog. Then three children, then cat, and the last one is also cat. Is that right?

Putul   Absolutely right.

You   Then what did you do?

Putul   I then sang them a song, and I showed them all these toys from Bengal. They particularly liked this horse and cart.

You   It (was) made in Calcutta, I suppose?

Putul   No, probably in Dhaka. Have you seen how beautifully painted (it is)?

You   Yes. When you'd shown them the toys, you finished, did you?[f]

Putul   No, I told them another story. The story is taken from Upendrakishore Raychaudhuri's famous book *Ṭuṇṭunir Bai*. Here, have a look at the book.

You   When was the book written?

Putul   In 1910. The author was Satyajit Ray's grandfather.

You   The famous film-director Satyajit Ray?

Putul   Yes. The story is very amusing. In stories of this kind there is a clever animal and a stupid animal. The tailor-bird and the jackal, they're clever; and the cat, the tiger and crocodile, they're very stupid. In this particular story too the cat is very stupid, but in another very popular story there is a very intelligent cat – called Majantali Sarkar.

You   Can I buy the book?

Putul	In this country you will perhaps find it difficult to get the book. But you can borrow this copy.
You	I'm very grateful (to you).ᵍ What's your address? When I've finished reading the book, I'll post it back to you.
Putul	There's no hurry. I don't need the book right now. You'll enjoy the book. The language is very easy.
You	Well, I was very lucky to meet you. And the children are really lucky.
Putul	I love the work. I slave away in an office all week. It's a relief to escape and come here.ʰ See you again one day!
You	Certainly.

ªPutul might be her ḍak-nam, or pet-name. See Unit 14, p. 50.

ᵇNotice the use of the postposition pɔr after the verbal noun in the possessive case – chôbi-gulo ākar pɔr.

ᶜNotice the compound verb tule dhɔra *(to lift up)*, here used participally.

ᵈpoṭôlder: the possessive plural ending added on to Poṭol implies *Poṭol's family*. See Unit 17, p. 84.

ᵉSometimes hɔoya in the present continuous or simple past tense (see **Grammar** section below) is used instead of the zero verb – especially if you are explaining something to someone else. Notice that Putul uses hôcche in this way later when she is talking about the Ṭunṭuni stories.

ᶠ tai na? or tai naki? is commonly used as a 'question tag' equivalent to English *isn't it?, aren't you?, did you?, isn't she?*, etc.

ᵍkɪtôjñô – pron. 'kɪtôggô' (see Unit 17, p. 82).

ʰLit. *Having escaped here I live.* paliye is the past participle of the extended verb palano (see 4 in the **Grammar** section below), and bāci is the first person of the present tense of bāca *(to live, survive)*.

 —————————— **Grammar** ——————————

1 Simple past tense

The simple past tense in Bengali is generally used for actions or events occurring in the very recent past – say within the same day. For things that happened as recently as yesterday, the past perfect is preferred. The simple past is also used as the main narrative tense in story telling (though writers often slip into the present – see Unit 27, p. 211). In the **Conversation** above, Putul uses it to describe the things she has done earlier in the morning, and also in the story that she tells. For kɔra the forms are as follows:

1		ami kôrlam
2	[F]	tumi kôrle
3	[F]	se kôrlo
2 & 3	[P]	apni/tini kôrlen

For the third person [F] the spelling kôrlô (করল) is often found and is particularly common with the vowel stems – hôlô, khelô, etc. The other verb-types take the same endings, so you can easily derive them from the following first person forms:

dækha	ami dekhlam
ʃona	ami ʃunlam
lekha	ami likhlam
rakha	ami rakhlam
khaoya	ami khelam
dhoya	ami dhulam
hɔoya	ami hôlam
deoya	ami dilam

As with the perfect and past perfect tenses, y̆aoya *(to go)* uses a different root for the simple past tense. Notice the vowel mutation too:

ami gelam
tumi gele
se gælô
apni/tini gelen

asa *(to come)* has a slightly irregular form: ami elam, tumi ele, etc., though in Bangladesh you will often hear ami aslam, tumi asle, etc.

2 Verbal noun as adjective

You already know Bengali verbal nouns as the forms by which verbs are named and listed in dictionaries. They have several grammatical functions, one of which is to behave like adjectives:

æk̨ta bhaŋa ceyar	*a broken chair*
amar āka chôbi	*a picture painted by me (*Lit. *my painted picture)*
ækjɔn nam kɔra kôbi	*a famous (named) poet*

Like other adjectives, these adjectival verbal nouns can be placed as 'complements' to the subject of the sentence, with zero verb:

| machgulo ekhane dhɔra. | *The fish (are) caught here.* |

or with the negative of the zero verb:

| ei payjamaṭa chēṛa nɔy. | *These pyjamas are not torn.* |

If you want to put structures of this kind into a tense other than the present, hɔoya can be used. This creates something very similar to an English passive construction:

| ciṭhiṭa lekha hôlô. | *The letter was written.* |

Any tense of hɔoya is possible. Remember the negative is -ni for the past tenses:

baṛiṭa ækhôno rɔŋ kɔra hɔyni.	*The house has not yet been painted.*
ca satṭay deoya hɔbe.	*Tea will be served at seven.*
ei ʃɔbdôṭa bad deoya hôyeche.	*This word has been left out.*

If you want to add *by me, by you,* etc. you can say amar <u>d</u>vara, tomar <u>d</u>vara (দ্বারা), etc. With nouns and names, this postposition is sometimes used without the possessive case.

3 Which, any

It is very easy to confuse kon *(Which?)* with kono *(any)* – especially as the latter word can be spelt in three different ways:

kon	কোন
kono	কোনো
kon-o	কোনও
konô	কোন

Sometimes writers add the হসন্ত (্ – see Unit 18, p. 95) to kon meaning *Which?*, to indicate that the inherent vowel at the end is not pronounced:

| kon | কোন্ |

– but you cannot rely on this. The context will generally make clear which word is meant:

kon nam <u>b</u>ybôhar kôrbo?	*Which name shall I use?*
apnar konô chelemeye ache?	*Have you any children?*
o konô kɔtha ʃonena.	*He/she doesn't listen to anything.*

kon only means *Which?* in an interrogative sense (the relative pronoun *which* – y̆e – will be dealt with in Unit 28). The definite article can be added:

ami konʈa nebô?	*Which one shall I take?*
konʈi tomar?	*Which one (is) yours?*

kono (kon-o, konô) in negative or interrogative sentences is equivalent to English *any*:

ei basay kono ʈeliphon nei.	*There isn't any telephone in this house.*
okhane kono gaʈi ache?	*Is there any car there?*

When quantities are involved in questions, however, **kichu** *(some)* is preferred:

tomar hate kichu sɔmɔy ache?	*Do you have any time on your hands?*

kichu is used in affirmative statements where in English *some* is used:

hyæ̃, ækhôn amar kichu sɔmɔy ache.	*Yes, I have some time now.*

Used on its own in a negative sentence, it means *anything*:

oi almarite kichu nei.	*There isn't anything in that cupboard.*

If **kono** is repeated, it can mean *some*: there was an example of this usage in the **Conversation** in Unit 17, (pp. 78–80):

kono kono meye sɔŋge-sɔŋge biye kɔre.	*Some girls get married at once.*

4 *Compound verbs with* deoya/neoya

The **Conversation** above contains several extended verbs such as **dækhano** *(to show)*, **bojhano** *(to explain)*, and **palano** *(to flee)*. Extended verbs will be dealt with properly in Unit 25. Notice also the compound form **bujhiye deoya**. Most extended verbs have a causative meaning (**dækhano**, *to cause to see*; **bojhano**, *to cause to understand*) and it is natural to combine them with **deoya** to create a sense of *doing something for someone else*:

ami ækṭa rekɔrḍ ʃuniye debô? *Shall I play you (cause you to hear) a record?*

This usage of **deoya**, however, is not limited to extended verbs:

ami oke bôle debô. *I'll tell him/her (for you).*

If you are doing something for yourself, use **neoya** instead of **deoya**. Compare:

ami likhe nebô. *I'll write it down (for myself).*
ami likhe debô. *I'll write it down (for you).*

ami kaṭ̣a kôriye nebô. *I'll have the work done (for myself).*

ami kaṭ̣a kôriye debô. *I'll have the work done (for you).*

 —————————— **Exercises** ——————————

1 *(a)* Fill in the gaps in the following sentences with কোন *(Which?)*, কোনো *(any)* or কিছু *(some)*. Example:

ওদের _____ ছেলেমেয়ে নেই ।
ওদের কোনো ছেলেমেয়ে নেই ।

১ _____ বাস নেব ?
২ তোমার কাছে[a] _____ টাকা আছে ?
৩ হ্যাঁ, আমার কাছে _____ টাকা আছে ।
৪ আপনি _____ দেশ থেকে এসেছেন ?
৫ ওখানে _____ নেই ।
৬ _____ লোক রাস্তায় মারা যায় ।
৭ আপনি _____ টা কিনবেন ?
৮ বাচ্চাটি _____ খেয়েছে ?
৯ না, ও _____ খায়নি ।
১০ বাংলাদেশে আমাদের _____ গাড়ি ছিলনা ।

[a]Notice this idiomatic use of কাছে : *Have you any money on you?*

(b) Now see if you can read the following simple story from a child's primer (Part 3 of the popular *Ānanda Pāṭh* series, published in Calcutta), looking up words in the **Glossary** if necessary. Then answer the comprehension questions beneath it. You'll notice that the spelling used here favours the inherent vowel rather than o (ে া) in verb forms.

এক গ্রামে তিন বন্ধু ছিল । তিনজনের মধ্যে সবচেয়ে বোকা[a] ছিল দামু ।
ওদের মধ্যে সবচেয়ে বুদ্ধিমান ছিল গ্রামের নাপিত রামু । শামুর মাথায়
ছিল একটা মস্ত টাক ।

একদিন ওরা ঠিক করল[b] গ্রাম ছেড়ে অন্য দেশে যাবে । হাঁটতে
হাঁটতে[c] ওরা একটা জঙ্গলে পৌঁছল[d] । তখন সন্ধ্যা । আকাশ অন্ধকার ।

[a]*the stupidest.* For the use of সবচেয়ে see Unit 21, p. 134.
[b]*they decided.*
[c]*while walking along.*
[d]For the extended verb পৌঁছানো *(to arrive),* see Unit 25, p. 183.

ঝিঝি পোকা ডাকছে[e] । তিনজনের খুব ক্লান্ত লাগছে আর ঘুম
পেয়েছে । সবচেয়ে ক্লান্ত হয়েছিল বোকা দামু ।

রামু বলল, ঐ যে বট আর তেঁতুল দুটো গাছ দেখছ ওর মধ্যে
বটগাছটা বেশী বড় । চল, আমরা বট গাছের নিচে ঘুমাই । তবে সবাই
একসঙ্গে ঘুমোব না[f] । এখন আমি জাগব । তারপর বোকা দামু জাগবে ।
সবচেয়ে শেষে জাগবে টেকো শামু ।

রামুর খুব ঘুম পাচ্ছিল[g] । ও খুর বের করে বোকা দামুর মাথাটা
কামিয়ে দিল[h] । তারপর বোকা দামুকে ঘুম থেকে তুলে দিয়ে রামু ঘুমিয়ে
পড়ল । বোকা দামু হঠাৎ মাথায় হাত দিয়ে দেখে তার মাথায় একটুও
চুল নেই । দামু তো খুব বোকা । তাই ও ভাবল, আমি বোধ হয় বোকা

দামু নই । আমি নিশ্চয়ই টেকো শামু । রামু আর শামুর ভেতর মাঝরাতে দামুর জাগবার কথা[e]। আমি কেন জাগব ? এই ভেবে দামু ঘুমিয়ে পড়ল ।

যেই দামু শুয়েছে অমনি[j] জঙ্গলে একটা বাঘ গর্জন শুরু করল । রামু তাড়াতাড়ি উঠে আগুন জ্বালাল । রামু আর শামু দামুকে খুব বকল । তারপর রামু বলল, আমাদের তিনজনের মধ্যে তুমি সবচেয়ে বোকা । আমাদের গ্রামের সব লোকদের মধ্যে তুমি সবচেয়ে বোকা । দামু বলল, আমি ভেবেছিলাম[k] আমার সবচেয়ে বেশী বুদ্ধি । দামুর কথা শুনে রামু আর শামু খুব হাসতে লাগল[l]।

[e] Here, as often in Bengali story-telling, it is quite natural to slip into the present tense sometimes. Cf. Unit 27, p. 211.

[f] Another extended verb, meaning to sleep. See Unit 25, p. 183. Notice too that the negative **না** has been separated from the verb. Many writers do this (see p. 113).

[g] Past continuous tense of **পাওয়া**. See Unit 25, pp. 181–182.

[h] Extended verb **কামানো** *(to shave)* combined with **দেওয়া** . See pp. 159–160 above.

[i] See Unit 31, Note 5, p. 239.

[j] **যেই . . . অমনি**, *as soon as . . . then immediately*.

[k] Past perfect tense of **ভাবা** *(to think)*.

[l] *began to laugh*. Note this very common use of **লাগা**.

   (b) **১** তিন বন্ধুর নাম কি ?

       ২ তিন বন্ধুর মধ্যে সবচেয়ে বুদ্ধিমান কে ?

       ৩ তিন বন্ধুর মধ্যে সবচেয়ে বোকা ছিল কে ?

       ৪ টাক ছিল কার মাথায় ?

       ৫ বটগাছ আর তেঁতুল গাছের মধ্যে কোনটা বড় ?

       ৬ জঙ্গলে পৌঁছে কে সবচেয়ে বেশী ক্লান্ত হয়েছিল ?

       ৭ সবচেয়ে আগে কে জেগেছিল ?

       ৮ দামু জেগে উঠে মাথায় হাত দিয়ে কি দেখল ?

       ৯ রামু বাঘের গর্জন শুনে কি করল ?

      ১০ শেষে দামুর কথা শুনে রামু আর শামু কি করল ?

2   As the simple past tense is the main 'story-telling' tense in Bengali, it is what you would naturally use if you wrote a diary. Using the following verbs and phrases as hints, see if you can construct your diary for an ordinary sort of 'day off work'. Try to make full use of past participles to connect phrases (see Unit 20, p. 121):

(i) aj
(ii) deri kôre oṭha
(iii) b̲r̲e̲k̲p̲h̲a̲s̲ṭ̲ khete khete[a] khɔbôrer kagôj pɔṛa
(iv) tarpɔr
(v) dui-ækṭa ciṭhi lekha
(vi) dokane/bajare y̆aoya
(vii) ras̲ṭay durg̲h̲ɔṭôna[b] dekha
(viii) æ̲k̲jɔn buṛo bhɔdrôlok
(ix) aghat paoya
(x) puliʃ
(xi) æmbulyæns[c]
(xii) par̲k̲er bhitôr diye phire asa
(xiii) mône pɔṛa
(xiv) kal bhaipor jɔnmôdin[d]
(xv) lanc-er pɔre a̲b̲ar beriye y̆aoya[e]
(xvi) bôi-er dokane y̆aoya
(xvii) nam kɔra krikeṭar sɔmbɔndhe ækṭa bôi kena
(xviii) baṛi phire ese dækha
(xix) bathrumer sɔmɔstô mejhete jɔl[f]
(xx) mis̲t̲r̲ī̲ke[g] ṭeliphon kôre ḍaka
(xxi) bɔl̲a̲
(xxii) 'kalke abar asbo'
(xxiii) sɔb jɔl bɔndhô kɔrar jônyô ɔsubidha hɔoya
(xxiv) rag hɔoya[h]
(xxv) _____ ṭeliphon kɔra[i]
(xxvi) b̲y̲s̲tôj
(xxvii) samner ʃônibar dækha kɔrar byb̲ô̲s̲t̲h̲a kɔra
(xxviii) ṭelibhiʃɔne bic̲c̲hiri chôbi dækha

---

[a]*while eating*. Note that a repeated infinitive can have this kind of meaning. Cf. p. 218, Note 12.

[b]*accident*.

[c]For the spelling of *ambulance* see p. 226, Note 2.

[d]Use future of hɔoya.

[e]A compound verb meaning *to go out* that uses the past participle of the extended verb berôno.

[f]Use past of ach-, and use pani for *water* instead of jɔl if you have a Muslim context in mind (see p. 275).

[g]mistrī is a general term for *artisan*: here it means *plumber*.

[h]Use impersonal construction (see Unit 18, pp. 99–100).

[i]Insert the name of a suitable friend.

[j] ব্যস্ত *(busy)*, used with ach-.

24
— MEETING A WRITER —

 ———————— **Conversation** ————————

You attend a lecture at the Bangla Academy in Dhaka, and during the reception afterwards you meet a young woman writer. She shows you a volume of poems she has published. She would like you to help her translate some of her poems into English. You discuss this, her plans for the future, the role of poetry in Bangladesh, and other related matters.

আপনি   এটা অপনার নিজের লেখা বই ?

লেখক   হ্যাঁ, আমার নিজের কবিতার বই ।

আপনি   বইটা কবে বেরিয়েছে ?

লেখক   প্রায় এক বছর হল ।

আপনি   অনেক কপি বিক্রি হয়েছে, আশা করি ?

লেখক   সেটা আমি বলতে পারবোনা, তবে বইটা বেরলে আমি একটা পুরস্কার পেয়েছিলাম – তাতে বই বিক্রিতে সাহায্য হয়েছিল ।

আপনি   মানে আপনি বেশ প্রশংসা পেয়েছিলেন ?

লেখক   যথেষ্ট প্রশংসা পেয়েছিলাম, তবে সমালোচকদের প্রশংসা পাওয়া আর পাঠকদের ভালো লাগা এক কথা নয় ।

আপনি   বইটিতে কি ধরনের কবিতা আছে ?

লেখক নানা ধরনের । প্রেমের কবিতা, প্রকৃতি-বিষয়ক কবিতা, আর দেশপ্রেম মূলক, মানে কিছু রাজনৈতিক কবিতাও আছে এতে ।

আপনি এগুলি কি প্রথম এই বইটিতেই ছাপা হল, না অন্য কোথাও আগে বেরিয়েছিল ?

লেখক কয়েকটি প্রথমে মাসিক পত্রিকায় আর কয়েকটি অন্য কাগজে প্রকাশিত হয় ; অন্য কবিতাগুলোর বেশিরভাগই নতুন । বইটি আপনি পড়তে পারবেন ? সম্ভব হলে, আমি আমার কবিতাগুলি ইংরেজী অনুবাদে বার করতে চাই । আমাদের মুশকিল হচ্ছে যে বিদেশে প্রায় কেউ বাংলা জানেনা, তাই আমাদের সাহিত্য তাদের কাছে অজানা থেকে যায় ।

আপনি একেবারে অজানা নয় ! রবীন্দ্রনাথের নাম অনেকে জানেন ।

লেখক রবীন্দ্রনাথ ছাড়া অন্য লেখকের নাম কি তারা বলতে পারবে ? আসলে ভালো অনুবাদের খুব অভাব । ভালো অনুবাদ থাকলে রুশ-ভাষার ইংরেজী অনুবাদের মত, বাংলা সাহিত্য আরো পরিচিত হত ।

আপনি তবে বাংলাদেশে শুনেছি কবিতা খুব জনপ্রিয় - কিন্তু কবিতার অনুবাদ তো খুব শক্ত ।

লেখক ঠিকই বলেছেন । যাঁরা করতে পারেন তারা সংখ্যায় খুব কম । কবিতা অনুবাদ করতে চাইলে, নিজে কবি হতে হয় । আপনি তো কবিতা লেখেন ?

আপনি আমি ? লিখতাম একসময় । তবে আজকাল আর কবিতা লিখিনা । আমার দেশে কবিতার পাঠক খুব কম । এদেশের মত ওখানে কবিতার অনুষ্ঠান করা অসম্ভব ।

লেখক আপনি আমার কবিতা অনুবাদ করবেন ?

আপনি সম্পূর্ণ নিজে করতে পারবোনা । আপনি আমাকে সাহায্য করলে, হয়তো পারবো । প্রথমে একটা খসড়া থাকলে, অনুবাদটা আরো ভালো করে করা যেত - সেই রকম করে পারা যাবে ?

লেখক ঠিক আছে । তাহলে আমি খসড়াটা করি, পরে আবার আপনার সাথে দেখা করবো ?

আপনি আমি এখন ঢাকায় নেই - বরিশালে । আপনি খসড়াগুলো আমাকে পাঠিয়ে দিলে, আমি দেখে রাখবো । পরে, ঢাকায়

এলে, আপনার সঙ্গে যোগাযোগ করে অনুবাদটা নিয়ে আমরা তখন আলোচনা করতে পারি ।

লেখক বেশ । আমি খুব কৃতজ্ঞ থাকবো ।

আপনি বাংলা কবিতা ছাড়া, আপনি আর কি লেখেন ? ছোটগল্প ? প্রবন্ধ ?

লেখক প্রবন্ধ লিখি মাঝে-মাঝে, পত্রিকার জন্য । আমি ইংরেজী কবিতাও লিখতাম, তবে বেশ আগে ।

আপনি ইংরেজী কবিতা লিখতেন ! তাহলে আপনি নিজেই তো অনুবাদ করতে পারেন !

লেখক মোটেই না । একজন কবি নিজের কবিতা অনুবাদ করতে পারেনা ।

আপনি রবীন্দ্রনাথ তো নিজেই করতেন ।

লেখক রবীন্দ্রনাথের নিজের অনুবাদ কি ভালো ?

আপনি ওঁর ভাষা একটু সেকেলে বটে, তবে –

লেখক মূল বাংলার সঙ্গে তুলনা করলে, আপনি দেখবেন যে অনেক ফাঁক আছে । অনেক সময় উনি পুরো কবিতা অনুবাদ করেননি । আর তাছাড়া উনি শুধু এক ধরনের কবিতাই অনুবাদ করতেন – প্রধানত গান ।

আপনি হতে পারে । আমার ওঁর আরো কবিতা পড়া উচিত । আমি শুধু দুয়েকটা পড়েছি ।

লেখক আরো পড়লে, আপনার ভালো লাগবে । নজরুলের কবিতাও পড়া উচিত, আর জসীমুদ্দিন –

আপনি বাস, বাস, আর না ! বাংলা ভাষা এত সহজ নয় ! আমি কেবল আস্তে-আস্তেই পড়তে পারি ।

লেখক রোজ কিছু কিছু বাংলা পড়লে ঠিক হয়ে যাবে ।

আপনি আপনার মনে হয় তাই ?

লেখক নিশ্চয়ই । এর মধ্যে আপনি অনেক শিখেছেন । আর কয়েক মাস পরে, আপনার কোনো অসুবিধাই হবেনা । আমার বইটি নেবেন ?

আপনি ধন্যবাদ । আমি প্রতিদিন শোয়ার আগে আপনার এই বাংলা কবিতাগুলি দুয়েকটা করে পড়তে চেষ্টা করবো ।

লেখক আশা করি আপনার ভালো লাগবে । শুভরাত্রি !

Translation and notes

You	Is this your own book?[a]
Writer	Yes, my own book of poems.
You	When did the book come out?
Writer	About a year ago.
You	Lots of copies have sold, I hope?[b]
Writer	I can't say that, but when the book came out I got a prize – and that was a help in selling the book.[c]
You	You mean you received plenty of praise?
Writer	I got enough praise, but the praise of critics and the approval of readers are not the same thing.
You	What kind of poems are in the book?
Writer	Lots of kinds. Love poems, poems about Nature, and (poems) based on love of (one's) country – that is to say, some political poems too are in it.
You	Have these been printed for the first time in this book, or have they come out before anywhere else?
Writer	A few were published first in monthly magazines and a few in other papers; most of the rest of the poems are new. Will you be able to read the book? If possible, I would like to bring out my poems in English translation.[d] Our problem is that hardly any (people) abroad know Bengali, so our literature remains unknown to them.
You	Not totally unknown! Lots of people know Rabindranath's name.
Writer	Apart from Rabindranath can they name other writers? Actually (there is) a great lack of good translations. If there were more good translations like English translations of Russian, Bengali literature would be better known.
You	I've heard though (that) in Bangladesh poetry is very popular – but it's surely very hard to translate poetry.
Writer	That's right. Those who can do (it) are very few in number. If (you) want to translate poetry, you have to be a poet yourself. Do you write poetry then?
You	Me? I wrote (it) at one time. But I don't write poetry any more these days. In my country (there are) very few readers of poetry. (It's) impossible to hold poetry functions there as in this country.[e]
Writer	Would you like to translate my poems?
You	I can't all on my own. If you help me, perhaps I'll be able to. If (I) had a draft first, the translation could be done

	better – could it be done in that way?
Writer	Very well. Let me then do a draft,[f] (and) later meet you again, shall I?
You	I'm not staying in Dhaka now – (I'm) in Barisal. If you send me the drafts, I'll look (at them) and keep (them). Later, when I come to Dhaka, I shall get in touch with you, bring the translation, and we can discuss (it) then.
Writer	Fine. I shall be very grateful.
You	Apart from Bengali poems, what else do you write? Short stories? Essays?
Writer	I sometimes write essays, for journals. I used to write English poems too, but (that was) long ago.
You	You used to write English poems! In that case you can do your own translations!
Writer	Not at all. A poet cannot translate his own poems.
You	But Rabindranath used to do (so) himself.
Writer	Are Rabindranath's own translations good?
You	His language is indeed a little out-of-date, but –
Writer	If you compare (them) with the original Bengali, you will see that there are lots of gaps. Often he hasn't translated the whole poem. And moreover he translated only one kind of poem – mainly song(s).
You	Maybe. I should read more of his poems. I've only read one or two.
Writer	If you read more, you'll like them. (And) you ought to read Nazrul's poems, and Jasimuddin –
You	Stop, stop, that's enough! Bengali is not an easy language! I can only read slowly.
Writer	If you read some Bengali every day it'll come all right.
You	You think so?
Writer	Certainly. You've already learnt a lot. In a few months, you won't have any trouble at all. Will you take my book?
You	Thank you. I'll try to read one or two of the poems each night before I go to bed.
Writer	I hope you will like them. Good night![g]

[a]Lit. *your own written book*: the verbal noun lekha is used as an adjective. (See Unit 23, pp. 157–158).

[b]bikri kɔra means *to sell*; bikri hɔoya means *to be sold*.

[c]Lit. *In that in selling the book help was*. ta is a pronoun meaning *it* or *that* and is commonly used to refer to a previous statement. Here it has the locative case ending -te. The phrase is really an impersonal construction, as amar could be inserted.

^d**bar kɔra**: *to bring out.* **bar** is short for **bahir** or **bair** *(outside)* which, with the locative ending, can also be used as a postposition – **baɽir baire**, *outside the house.*

^e*Functions* (**ônusthan**) at which poems are recited, speeches given and songs are sung are very popular in Bangladesh and attract large audiences.

^fA first person imperative, *Let me do . . .* See **Verb tables** p. 204.

^gBoth **dhônyôbad** *(Thank you)* and **ʃubhôratri** *(Good night)* are Anglicisms, not really natural in Bengali: but in conversations with a foreigner they can be appropriate, and through Western influence they are becoming more common among the younger generation. If you feel the need to say *Thank you,* don't be afraid to use the English words.

Note the conjunct ষ + ঠ = ষ্ঠ in অনুষ্ঠান (it also occurred on p. 142), and the triple conjunct in রবীন্দ্রনাথ : ন + দ + র = ন্দ্র

Grammar

1 Conditional participle

In Unit 20 you learnt about the Bengali past participle. There is another very important participle, the **conditional** participle, which is used where English would use a subordinate clause headed by 'if' or 'when'. To form it, simply take the infinitive (see Unit 18, p. 98) and change the **-te** ending to **-le**:

kɔra	kôrle	*if (one) does*
dækha	dekhle	*if (one) sees*
ʃona	ʃunle	*if (one) hears*
lekha	likhle	*if (one) writes*
rakha	rakhle	*if (one) keeps*
khaoya	khele	*if (one) eats*
dhoya	dhule	*if (one) washes*
hɔoya	hôle	*if (one) becomes*
deoya	dile	*if (one) gives*

There are two exceptions to these forms: the conditional participle for **asa** *(to come)* is **ele** (although in Bangladesh **asle** is common), and the conditional participle for **y̆aoya** *(to go)* is **gele**.

Watch out for compound verbs in the conditional form: **paṭhiye dile**, for example, consists of the participle of the 'extended' verb **paṭhano** (see Unit 25, pp. 182–184) and the conditional participle of **deoya**.

To construct complex conditional sentences in Bengali, the conjunction ўôdi *(if)* is used, and this will be explained in Unit 25. Simple conditional sentences make use of the conditional participle. For present or future conditions, the present or future tense is used in the 'main' clause. The subject of the two clauses need not be the same:

se ele ami ўabô.   *I shall go if he/she comes.*
bôn̲ya hôle ghɔr-baɽi ɖube ўay.   *If a flood occurs, the house(s) are*
                                    inundated.

If it *is* the same, it can be left out of the conditional clause, or even both clauses if the context is clear:

pôrīk̲ṣay pas kôrle (ami) nôtun   *If (I) pass the exam (I) shall get*
   saikel pabô.   *(be given) a new bicycle.*

Impersonal constructions can be made conditional by putting the verb in its conditional form:

baccaṭir ɔsukh kôrle kothay   *If the child is ill where will (you)*
   ɖaktar pabe?   *get a doctor?*

In all the above sentences, 'when' would be just as good a translation of the participle as 'if'.

In English there are two further types of condition:

If he came I would go.
If he had come I would have gone.

The first of these can often be treated in Bengali as a future condition ('If he comes I will go'); but if the meaning is truly 'hypothetical', then one can use the habitual past tense (see next section) which also has a 'subjunctive' rôle. The habitual past tense would **have to be** used for the second sentence above, which is a hypothetical statement referring to the past. **Hypothetical conditions in Bengali can therefore refer either to the past or to the future, depending on the context.**

If a conditional participle is used rather than a clause headed by ўôdi, the 'hypothetical' nature of the condition is indicated by the tense in the main clause. The habitual past tense is easily formed by taking the simple past tense (ami kôrlam, tumi kôrle, etc.) and changing the l to t – with the exception of ўaoya, which goes ami ўetam, tumi ўete, etc., not 'ami getam'. The second of the two sentences above (and possibly the first) would therefore be translated as:

se ele ami ўetam.

If the condition is negative, **na** comes **before** the participle (cf. the negative with the past participle – Unit 20, p. 127):

pôrīkṣay pas na kôrle, tumi saikel pabena.	*If (you) don't pass the exam, you will not get a bicycle.*
o rag na kôrle ami oke kichu ṭaka ditam.	*If he/she hadn't got angry I would have given him/her some money.*

2 Habitual past tense

The other function of the habitual past tense is (as its name suggests) to express past actions or events that happened habitually or regularly. It is thus equivalent to English *I used to live*. . ., *She used to sing*. . ., etc. In English, however, the simple past tense is often used for past habits:

When I lived in Paris I ate in restaurants every day.

In Bengali, you **must** use the habitual past tense in such sentences. Often it is used where *used to* would not be appropriate in English:

chelebælay ami iṃrejī kɔtha bôlte partamna.	*I couldn't speak English as a child.*
ami jantamna!	*I didn't know (that)!*

ami janini would be possible, but only if it referred to a specific item of information (i.e. *I was never told that, I didn't hear about that*), rather than to a past state of knowledge.

As indicated in the previous section, the forms of the habitual past can be easily constructed from the simple past, by changing **l** to **t**:

kɔra	ami kôrtam
	tumi kôrte
	se kôrto
	apni/tini kôrten

dækha	ami dekhtam, etc.
ʃona	ami ʃuntam
lekha	ami likhtam
rakha	ami rakhtam
khaoya	ami khetam
dhoya	ami dhutam

| **hɔoya** | ami hôtam |
| **deoya** | ami ditam |

As with the simple past, spellings with inherent vowel in the third person (F) are common, especially with vowel stems – hôtô, khetô, etc.

3 Need

Need in Bengali can be expressed by an idiomatic use of **laga**:

| na, amar rikʃa lagbena. | *No, I won't need a rickshaw.* |
| bilete ẙete ɔnek ʈaka lage. | *To go to England you need a lot of money.* |

But the word **dɔrkar** *(need, necessity)* is also commonly used, in an impersonal construction: possessive + noun/verbal noun in possessive case + **dɔrkar**. Past, future and negative are achieved in the same way as with **ucit** (see Unit 19, p. 110):

amader aro ʈakar dɔrkar.	*We need more money.*
tyæksi beʃ sɔkal-sɔkal asar dɔrkar hɔbe.	*The taxi will need to come very early.*
bamʃladeʃe amader moʈa poʃak pɔrbar* dɔrkar chilôna.	*In Bangladesh we didn't need to wear thick clothes.*

In colloquial speech the possessive ending is often dropped:

| tomar ækbar bhisa-apise ẙaoya dɔrkar. | *You'll have to make a visit to the visa-office.* |

*Note this variant of the verbal noun in the possessive case: **pɔrbar** instead of **pɔrar**.

 ——————— **Exercises** ———————

1 *(a)* On page 173 there is a map of central Calcutta, with the metro railway and its stations clearly marked. Fill in the gaps in the following sentences by reading information off the map. They are all about what you will see or find if you get off at particular metro stops, so they all contain the conditional participle নামলে .

1 Museum
2 Maidan
3 Planetarium
4 Jagu Babu's Bazaar
5 Ashutosh College
6 Kali Temple
7 Rabindra Sarobar
8 Golf Club

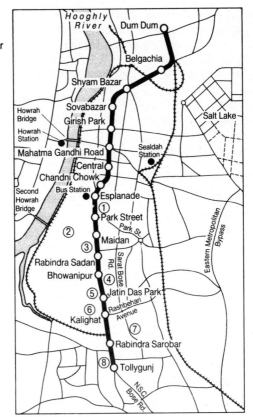

Example:

_____ নামলে, বড় বাস স্টেশনটা কাছে পাবেন ।

এসপ্লেনেডে নামলে, বড় বাস স্টেশনটা কাছে পাবেন ।

১ _____ নামলে, কালীমন্দির দর্শন করে আসতে পারেন ।

২ _____ নামলে, জগু বাবুর বাজারে যেতে পারবেন ।

৩ _____ নামলে, তারামণ্ডল দেখে আসবেন ।

৪ _____ নামলে, জাদুঘরে যেতে পারেন ।

৫ _____ নামলে, গল্‌ফ ক্লাবে যেতে পারেন ।

৬ _____ নামলে, রবীন্দ্রসরোবরের কাছে বেরিয়ে আসতে পারেন ।

৭ _____ নামলে, আশুতোষ কলেজ দেখতে যেতে পারেন ।

৮ _____ নামলে, ময়দান সামনে পাবেন ।

(b) Now pretend that you have made the shopping list below. Say or write in full what you need to buy. You can use a variety of need or obligation constructions: hints in English as to which one to use are given alongside each item. It is not necessary to keep repeating the first person pronoun (আমি/আমার). Example:

চিনি   *(to strike)*

(আমার) চিনি লাগবে ।

কলম	*(need)*
পোস্টাপিসে	*(must go)*
দশটা এক টাকার টিকিট [a]	*(must bring)*[b]
দিদির জন্য উপহার	*(must buy)*
শামসুর রাহমানের নতুন কবিতার বই	*(must buy)*
ভালো চা	*(must bring)*
খাম	*(need)*
~~আঠা~~	*(I won't need glue.)*
আম ?	*(If I find*[c] *some good mangoes, I'll buy them.)*
~~ছাতা~~	*(I **must** buy an umbrella!)*[d]

[a] i.e. *postage-stamp* (ডাকটিকিট).
[b] আনা *(to bring)* is often used instead of কেনা *(to buy)* in connection with shopping.
[c] Use পাওয়া.
[d] To emphasise the obligation construction, add the emphatic ই to the infinitive.

2   Bengali participles, and especially the conditional participle, make for extreme concision, as does the use of **ucit** or **dɔrkar**. See if you can translate the following three or four word sentences into English. You will often have to supply pronouns, and most of the sentences will be ambiguous in terms of the sex or number of people referred to (*he/she, I/we,* etc.). You will be surprised at how many English words you will need compared to the Bengali:

(i)   o ele khabe?
(ii)   oṭa dile y̌abô.
(iii)   br̥ṣṭi hôle esôna.
(iv)   ɔsukh hôye mara gæchen.
(v)   okhane gele pabe.

(vi)   beʃī dam diye kinbenna.

(vii)   pɔre kôrle bhalo hɔbe.

(viii)   oṭa bɔla ucit.

(ix)   age khele bhalo hôtô.

(x)   deri hôyechilô, tai ÿaini.

(xi)   ṭyæksi thakle nitam.

(xii)   am miṣṭi hôle khabô.

(xiii)   rag kɔra ucit nɔy.

(xiv)   iji-ceyare[a] bôse khabô.

(xv)   oṭa kine khuʃi hôini.

(xvi)   cād uṭhle chade ÿeo.

(xvii)   dɔrkar hôle asbo.

(xviii) okhane ÿaoyar ki dɔrkar?

(xix)   ṭaka lagbena.

(xx)   okhane giye paini.

[a]*in an easy chair.*

25
– LEARNING BENGALI –

Conversation

Sooner or later, people in Bangladesh and West Bengal will ask you where and how and why you learnt Bengali. If you learn to speak it well, you may even find yourself being interviewed by a journalist! Obviously each learner will have a different story, and the **Conversation** below may not fit your case at all. But if you have worked through all the units so far, you should be ready now to answer questions as well as ask them.

সাংবাদিক	বাংলা জানেন ?
আপনি	হ্যাঁ, কিছু বাংলা শিখেছি।
সাংবাদিক	কোথায় শিখেছেন ?
আপনি	আমি প্রথমে নিজে নিজে শিখেছি, 'Teach Yourself Bengali' ব্যবহার করে। তারপরে এদেশে এসে আমি নানা লোকের সঙ্গে মেলামেশা করে আরো কিছুটা উন্নতি করেছি – তবে এখনো আরো অনেক শিখতে হবে।
সাংবাদিক	আপনার উচ্চারণ খুবই ভালো।
আপনি	না, না মোটেও না। দুয়েকটা ব্যঞ্জন-ধ্বনি আছে যেগুলি উচ্চারণ করা আমার পক্ষে খুব শক্ত – বিশেষ করে র, ফ, ক ইত্যাদি – এছাড়া দ আর ড, এবং ত আর ট-এর মধ্যে পার্থক্যটা আমি এখনো ভালো করে শুনতে পাইনা।
সাংবাদিক	আমরাও ইংরেজী 'th' বলতে পারিনা। আর আমরা ব্যাকরণেরও ভুল করি।

আপনি	নাঃ, আপনারা খুব ভালো ইংরেজি জানেন। আপনাদের সুবিধা হচ্ছে, স্কুলে ইংরেজী শেখেন। আমি একটু দেরি করে বাংলা শিখতে শুরু করেছি।
সাংবাদিক	আপনি এখন সহজে না ঠেকে বাংলা পড়তে পারেন? গতকাল আমি দেখলাম, আপনি বাংলা খবরের কাগজ পড়ছিলেন।
আপনি	খবরের কাগজ আমি সহজে বুঝতে পারিনা। অনেক জটিল রাজনৈতিক আর অর্থনৈতিক শব্দ থাকে, যেগুলো ধরতে কষ্ট হয়। তবে যখন আমার বিষয়টা জানা থাকে, তখন আর তেমন অসুবিধে হয়না।
সাংবাদিক	আপনি বাংলা সাহিত্য পড়েছেন?
আপনি	খুব কম। আমি বাচ্চাদের বই মাঝে-সাঝে পড়ি। এখন আমি রবীন্দ্রনাথের চিঠিপত্র পড়তে চেষ্টা করছি।
সাংবাদিক	আপনাকে কেউ শেখাচ্ছে?
আপনি	যে বন্ধুর বাড়িতে আমি উঠেছি, তার মা-বাবা আমাকে খুব সাহায্য করেন। আমি রোজ বাংলায় ডায়েরি লিখি। ব্রেকফাস্টের সময় আমি ডায়েরি ওঁদের পড়ে শোনাই। ওঁরা আমার ভাষার ভুল সংশোধন করে দেন।
সাংবাদিক	বেশ। একদিন হয়তো ডায়রিটা প্রকাশ করলে, আপনার অভিজ্ঞতা আর চিন্তাধারার সাথে আমরা পরিচিত হব।
আপনি	অসম্ভব! আমার বাংলা খুব কাঁচা। আর আমার হাতের লেখা খুবই খারাপ।
সাংবাদিক	আমার হাতের লেখার চেয়ে অনেক পরিষ্কার। আমার হাতের লেখা তো পড়াই যায়না। কালকে আমি বাংলায় চিঠি লিখছিলাম - আমার সাত বছরের মেয়েটি কাছে এসে সেটা পড়তে চেষ্টা করছিল। কিছুই পড়তে পারেনি!
আপনি	আজকে আমাকে একটা চিঠি লিখতে হবে। যদি আমি একটা লেখা তৈরি করে আনি, আপনি দেখে দিতে পারবেন?
সাংবাদিক	নিশ্চয়ই। আমি খুব খুশি হব। আপনি কখন আসবেন?
আপনি	সাড়ে পাঁচটার দিকে। আর রবীন্দ্রনাথের চিঠিপত্রে দুই-একটা অংশ আছে যা আমি ভালো বুঝতে পারিনি।

অভিধানে শব্দগুলো খুঁজে পেয়েছি, তবু অর্থটা এখনও আমার কাছে স্পষ্ট হয়নি ।

সাংবাদিক যদি আমি বুঝতে পারি, তাহলে আমি বুঝিয়ে দেব । তবে আমাদের কাছেও রবীন্দ্রনাথের ভাষা মাঝে-মাঝে খুব শক্ত লাগে । আচ্ছা, আপনি বাংলা সিনেমা দেখেছেন ?

আপনি সত্যজিৎ রায়ের ছবি আমি দেখেছি । খুব ভালো লেগেছে । যে ফিল্মটা আমার মনের ওপর বিশেষ ছাপ ফেলেছিল সেটা হল 'অপুর সংসার' । ষোল বছর বয়সে সেই ফিল্মটা দেখেই বোধ হয় আমি বাংলা শিখতে উৎসাহ বোধ করেছিলাম ।

সাংবাদিক তাই নাকি ! তবে ফিল্মটা বুঝতে পেরেছিলেন ?

আপনি ইংরেজী সাব-টাইটেল ছিল । এখন ফিল্মটা আবার দেখতে পারলে হয়তো বাংলাটাও অনেকখানি বুঝতে পারবো ।

সাংবাদিক নিশ্চয়ই পারবেন । আচ্ছা, বাংলা শিখে ভাষার সুবিধা-অসুবিধা সম্বন্ধে এখন আপনার মত কি ? কোন দিক থেকে সহজ আর কোন দিক থেকে কঠিন ?

আপনি শেখার শুরুতে ভাষাটা উচ্চারণ করতে আর লিখতে খুবই কঠিন লাগে । ব্যাকরণ তেমন কঠিন নয় - ক্রিয়াপদ বিশেষ করে নিয়মিত আর সহজ, ইংরেজী আর জার্মানের অনিয়মিত ক্রিয়াপদগুলোর মত নয় । তবে বাংলা বাক্যের পদক্রমের নিয়ম খুব শক্ত - ইংরেজীর একেবারে উলটো । সবচেয়ে কঠিন ব্যাপার হচ্ছে আপনাদের বিশাল শব্দকোষ । যদি আমরা একটা অন্য ইউরোপীয় ভাষা শিখি, সেখানে অনেক শব্দই পরিচিত পাই - শুধু সামান্য তফাৎ থাকে, তার উচ্চারণ আর শব্দরূপে ।

সাংবাদিক সেই । আমাদের পক্ষে যেমন হিন্দী । আপনার ছেলেমেয়ে আছে ? তারা বাংলা জানে ?

আপনি আছে, তবে ওরা বাংলা জানেনা । একদিন আমার পরিবারের সবাইকে নিয়ে আমি আসবো । হয়তো তখন ওরা একটু বাংলা শিখবে ।

সাংবাদিক নিয়ে আসুন । আমি ওদের শিখিয়ে দেব ।

আপনি বেশ, তাই হবে । আমার নিজের দ্বারা তো কখনো হবেনা

- বরং আপনার কাছে হয়তো শিখবে ।

Translation and notes

Journalist	Do you know Bengali?
You	Yes, I have learnt some Bengali.
Journalist	Where did you learn (it)?
You	First I learnt by myself, using *Teach Yourself Bengali*. Then by coming to this country and mixing with various (sorts of) people, I've improved a bit more[a] – but I've still got a lot more to learn.
Journalist	Your pronunciation is very good.
You	No, no not at all. There are one or two consonants which are very difficult for me to pronounce – especially rɔ, phɔ, kɔ, etc. – also I still can't hear the difference well between dɔ and ɖɔ, tɔ and ʈɔ.
Journalist	*We* can't say the English 'th'. And we make grammatical mistakes, too.
You	No, you know English very well.[b] You have the advantage (that) you learn English at school. I have started to learn Bengali a little late.
Journalist	Can you read Bengali easily or with difficulty[c] now? Yesterday I saw (that) you were reading a Bengali newspaper.
You	I can't read a newspaper easily. There are lots of complicated economic and political words, which I find hard to grasp. But when I have knowledge of the subject, I don't have so much difficulty.[d]
Journalist	Have you read Bengali literature?
You	Very little. I sometimes read children's books. Now I am trying to read Rabindranath's letters.
Journalist	Is anyone teaching you?
You	The parents of the friend whose house I'm staying in[e] help me a lot. I write a diary in Bengali every day. At breakfast I read out the diary to them. They correct my language-mistakes (for me).
Journalist	Good. One day perhaps if you publish the diary, we'll be able to become acquainted with your experiences and ideas.
You	Impossible! My Bengali is very childish.[f] And my handwriting is very bad.
Journalist	(It's) much clearer than my handwriting. My handwriting is quite illegible. Yesterday I was writing a

letter in Bengali: my seven-year-old daughter came up and was trying to read it. She couldn't read anything!

You I've got to write a letter today. If I make a rough version, will you be able to look at it for me?[g]

Journalist Certainly. I'll be delighted. When will you come?

You At about half-past five.[h] And in Rabindranath's letters there are one or two bits that I couldn't understand well. I've found the words in the dictionary, but the meaning is still not clear to me.[i]

Journalist If I can understand (them), then I'll explain (them to you). But for us too Rabindranath's language is sometimes very hard. Well now, have you seen (any) Bengali films?

You I have seen Satyajit Ray's films. I liked them very much. The film that made a special impression on me was *The World of Apu*. After seeing that film at the age of 16 maybe I felt an eagerness to learn Bengali.

Journalist Really! But could you understand the film?

You There were English sub-titles. Now if I could see the film again, perhaps I could understand quite a lot of the Bengali, too.

Journalist Of course you could. OK, now that you have learnt Bengali, what do you think about the pros and cons of the language? In what way (is it) easy, and in what way (is it) difficult?

You When (you) start to learn it is very difficult to pronounce and write the language. The grammar is not so hard – the verbs are especially regular and easy, not like English or German irregular verbs. But the rules for word-order in Bengali sentences are very hard – the complete opposite of English. The hardest matter of all is your vast vocabulary. If we learn another European language, we find we are familiar with many words there – there are only trivial differences, in their pronunciation and form.[j]

Journalist That's right.[k] Like Hindi for us. Do you have children? Do they know Bengali?

You I do have (children), but they don't know Bengali. One day I'll come with my whole family. Perhaps then they will learn a little Bengali.

Journalist Do bring (them). I'll teach them for you.

You   Good, that's a deal. (They)'ll never be (taught) by me
             myself – perhaps in preference (they)'ll learn from you.

[a]Notice that kıchu *(some)* can take the article -ṭa – especially when 'uncountable' quantities
are involved. kɔyek *(a few)*, ɔnek *(a lot)* and khanik *(a little)* can also take -ṭa in the same
way. khanikṭa is also commonly used with adjectives to mean 'fairly, moderately' (e.g.
khanikṭa bhalo – *fairly good*).

[b]nah – an emphatic form of na, written with বিসর্গ (see p. 255). It could also be written নাহ্
(i.e. with হ+হসন্ত – see p. 95).

[c]theke – an idiomatic use of the contracted past participle of the verb ṭhekano *(to obstruct)*.
See p. 182.

[d]Notice the very common pair of conjunctions y̆ɔkhôn . . . tɔkhôn *(when . . . then)*. The
tense is **always** the same in both clauses, unlike conditional sentences. *When he comes I
will tell him* would be y̆ɔkhôn se asbe, tɔkhôn ami oke bôle debô.

[e]Notice this idiomatic use of oṭha *(to rise)*.

[f] kāca *(unripe)*: used for mangoes, etc. as well as in this sort of way.

[g]Notice here (and elsewhere in the **Conversation**) the use of deoya to express something
done for someone else (see Unit 23, pp. 159–160).

[h]Lit. *in the direction of half-past five*. Use dike if you are expressing an approximate
appointment, pray if you are giving the approximate time. kɔṭa baje? pray pāc. *(What time is
it? About five.)*

[i] amar kache spɔṣṭô hɔyni. Lit. *To me clear it has not become* (impersonal construction).

[j] For the spelling of rūp *(form, way, manner)* see Note 29, p. 255.

[k]Note this very common idiomatic use of the demonstrative pronoun, to express agree-
ment with what someone has just said.

Grammar

1 Past continuous tense

This is the last Bengali tense that you have to learn. It is equivalent to
English *I was waiting, He was writing*, etc., but it is not as frequent in
Bengali as in English, perhaps because of the tendency to slip into the
present when describing past events. A Bengali speaker, especially
when he or she wants to be vivid and immediate, will often prefer the
present continuous to the past continuous.

It is easy to form. Simply take the present continuous (see Unit 21,
p. 133), and instead of the -chi/chô/che/chen endings add -chilam/chile/
chilô/chilen – which is the same as the past tense of ach-. Thus the past
continuous of kɔra would be:

1		ami kôrchilam
2	[F]	tumi kôrchile
3	[F]	se kôrchilô (or kôrchilo)
2 & 3	[P]	apni/tini kôrchilen

The other verb types can be formed in the same way. The vowel stems would go ami khac̲c̲h̲ilam, ami dhuc̲c̲h̲ilam, ami hôc̲c̲h̲ilam, ami dic̲c̲h̲ilam (and ami ẙac̲c̲h̲ilam for ẙaoya).

2 Extended verbs

Several 'extended' verbs have occurred in the **Conversations** in this and previous units, but so far all the verbal paradigms given have been formed on **monosyllabic** stems. Many Bengali verbs can, however, be extended, usually with the vowel -a, thereby acquiring a causative meaning. The verbal noun then ends in -ano (or -anô). Thus:

ʃekha	*to learn*	ʃekhano	*to cause to learn*
pɔʈa	*to read*	pɔʈano	*to cause to read*

(Both these verbs mean *to teach*, ʃekhano being used for a craft or skill, pɔʈano for more academic things.)

kɔra	*to do*	kɔrano	*to cause to do, have something done*
bojha	*to understand*	bojhano	*to cause to understand, explain*

If the unextended verb is intransitive (i.e. it cannot take an object), the extended form will be transitive. Thus:

bheja	*to get wet*, as in kapôʈgulo bhijeche *(The clothes have got wet.)*
bhejhano	*to wet, moisten, soak*, as in ca-pata bhijiyechi *(I have soaked the tea leaves.)*
bhɔra	*to fill up with*, as in amar peʈ bhôreche *(My stomach is full.)*
bhɔrano	*to fill*, as in ami gɔrtôʈa bhôriyechi *(I have filled the hole.)*

Extended participles are often contracted to their unextended form in colloquial Bengali, especially when combined with other verbs in compounds:

aloṭa j̲vele debô?	*Shall I turn on the light?*
oder pōŭche diye esô	*See them (home).*

j̲vele should really be j̲valiye, and pōŭche, from pōŭchano *(to arrive)* should really be pōŭchiye.

Some extended verbs only occur in an extended form and carry no causative meaning. pōŭchano is one; dāṛano *(to stand, wait)* is another. Some extended verbs can be extended with the vowel -ô- (or -o-) instead of -a-. Thus we have se ghumôcche *(he/she is sleeping)* instead of ghumacche; se doŭṛôcche *(he/she is running)* instead of doŭṛacche. Dictionaries, however, list all extended verbs with the -ano ending, not -ôno, in the verbal noun.

As the stem of extended verbs is extended with -a-, they all conjugate like khaoya except for the infinitive, participles and tenses formed on the past participle. Thus for kɔrano and all extended verbs the forms are:

Verbal Noun			kɔrano	*causing to do*
Infinitive			kɔrate	*to cause to do*
Present	1		ami kɔrai	*I cause to do,*
	2	[F]	tumi kɔrao	*etc.*
	3	[F]	se kɔray	
	2 & 3	[P]	apni/tini kɔran	
Present	1		ami kɔracchi	*I am causing to do,*
continuous	2	[F]	tumi kɔracchô	*etc.*
	3	[F]	se kɔracche	
	2 & 3	[P]	apni/tini kɔracchen	
Future	1		ami kɔrabo	*I shall cause to do,*
	2	[F]	tumi kɔrabe	*etc.*
	3	[F]	se kɔrabe	
	2 & 3	[P]	apni/tini kɔraben	
Simple past	1		ami kɔralam	*I caused to do,*
	2	[F]	tumi kɔrale	*etc.*
	3	[F]	se kɔralô	
	2 & 3	[P]	apni/tini kɔralen	
Habitual past	1		ami kɔratam	*I used to cause to do,*
	2	[F]	tumi kɔrate	*etc.*
	3	[F]	se kɔratô	
	2 & 3	[P]	apni/tini kɔraten	

Conditional participle			kɔrale	*if one causes to do*
Past participle			kôriye	*having caused to do*
Perfect	1		ami kôriyechi	*I have caused to do,*
	2	[F]	tumi kôriyechô	*etc.*
	3	[F]	se kôriyeche	
	2 & 3	[P]	apni/tini kôriyechen	
Past perfect	1		kôriyechilam	*I caused to do,*
	2	[F]	tumi kôriyechile	*etc.*
	3	[F]	se kôriyechilô	
	2 & 3	[P]	apni/tini kôriyechilen	
Past continuous	1		ami kɔracchilam	*I was causing to do,*
	2	[F]	tumi kɔracchile	*etc.*
	3	[F]	se kɔracchilô	
	2 & 3	[P]	apni/tini kɔracchilen	

Vowel stem verbs add -oya rather than -a-: thus khaoya becomes khaoyano *(to cause to eat, to feed)*. The past participles for all extended verbs end in -iye, but notice the vowel changes in the stems:

kɔrano	–	kôriye
dækhano	–	dekhiye
ʃonano	–	ʃuniye
ʃekhano	–	ʃikhiye
dãɽano	–	dãɽiye
khaoyano	–	khaiye
dhoyano	–	dhuyiye
lɔoyano*	–	lôiye

*Extended form of the verb lɔoya, which is a rather formal and archaic alternative for neoya. See note 20 on p. 255.

For extended verb imperatives, see p. 207.

3 y̆ôdi

In the last chapter you learnt about the conditional participle in -le. This participle is very convenient for short conditional clauses; but for longer, more complex ones it is often clearer to use the conjunction y̆ôdi *(if)*. The tense of the verb in the y̆ôdi clause will be present for present or future conditions, and habitual past for 'hypothetical' conditions. The 'main' clause is generally headed by tɔbe or tahôle, which mean *then* or *in consequence* (these words can also be used in sentences using the conditional participle, but they are not so necessary):

y̆ôdi bas ase tahôle ami hēṭe y̆aina.	*If the bus comes I don't walk.*
y̆ôdi se ase tɔbe ami y̆abô.	*If he/she comes I shall go.*
y̆ôdi o ṭeliphon kôrto tahôle ami khuʃi hôtam.	*If he/she had telephoned I would have been pleased.* or *If he/she were to telephone I would be pleased.*

Note that in Bengali the conditional clause normally comes before the main clause, but occasionally the order can be reversed as in English. *I won't come if it rains* could be ami asbona y̆ôdi brʃṭi hɔy, but y̆ôdi brʃṭi hɔy tahôle ami asbona would be more usual.

For negative conditions using y̆ôdi, na should go **before** the verb, in the same way that it goes before the past participle and conditional participle (see Unit 20, p. 127 and Unit 24, p. 171):

y̆ôdi se na asto tɔbe ami thaktam.	*If he/she had not come I would have stayed.* or *If he/she were to come I would stay.*

y̆ôdi with the particle -o tacked on to it means *although* – in which case tɔbe becomes tôbu *(nevertheless)*.

y̆ôdio khub brʃṭi chilô, tôbu ami okhane giyechilam.	*Although it was raining hard, I nevertheless went there.*

-o can be added to the conditional participle, with the same effect:

ōr ṭaka na thakleo, uni khuʃi.	*Although he/she has no money, he/she is happy.*

If you now complete the exercises in this unit, you will have covered the main elements of Bengali grammar. There remains one important area exemplified in several places in the **Conversation** above: relative clauses, using y̆e, y̆a, y̆eṭa, etc. (*who, which*, etc.). These will be dealt with in **Part Three**.

——————— **Exercises** ———————

1 *(a)*   The following conditional sentences are constructed with যদি
. . . তাহলে/তবে. Convert each one into a sentence using the
conditional participle (see Unit 24, pp. 169–170). You can leave out
the তাহলে/তবে. Example:

আপনি যদি চান, তাহলে আমি যাব ।
আপনি চাইলে[a] **আমি যাব ।**

[a]Note this slightly irregular conditional participle for the verb চাওয়া *(to want)*. See
Verb tables p. 202.

১   যদি বৃষ্টি হয়, তবে আমাদের ভিতরে খেতে হবে ।

২   যদি ও চিঠি লিখতো, তাহলে আমি রাগ করতাম না ।

৩   তুমি যদি পড়াশোনা কর, তবে পরীক্ষায় পাশ করবে ।

8   ছেলেটা যদি বেশী আম খায়, তাহলে ওর অসুখ করবে ।

৫   যদি তুমি ভদ্রভাবে না বল, তাহলে তোমার অসুবিধা হবে ।

৬   আমার যদি টাকা থাকতো, তবে আমি আমেরিকায় চলে যেতাম ।

৭   যদি সে ওইভাবে ব্যবহার করে, তাহলে তার স্ত্রীর তাকে ছেড়ে
দেওয়া উচিত ।

৮   আপনি যদি আমাকে সাহায্য না করতেন, তবে আমি কাজটা করতে
পারতামনা ।

৯   তুমি যদি টাকা দাও, তাহলে আমি করবো ।

১০ যদি আপনি এই বইটা শেষ করেন, তাহলে আপনি অনেক বাংলা
জেনে যাবেন ।

You will have noticed that যদি can come before or after the subject of
its clause.

(b) The pictures below and overleaf show various kinds of childish reluctance. Complete the sentences that explain the reluctance by supplying the right verb in the ordinary form and in its extended ('causative') form. Remember that it is often appropriate to combine the extended verb with দেওয়া. Example:

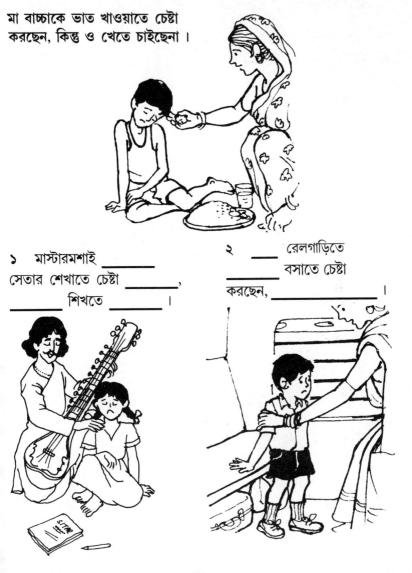

মা বাচ্চাকে ভাত খাওয়াতে চেষ্টা করছেন, কিন্তু ও খেতে চাইছেনা ।

১ মাস্টারমশাই _____ সেতার শেখাতে চেষ্টা _____, _____ শিখতে _____ ।

২ _____ রেলগাড়িতে _____ বসাতে চেষ্টা করছেন, _____ ।

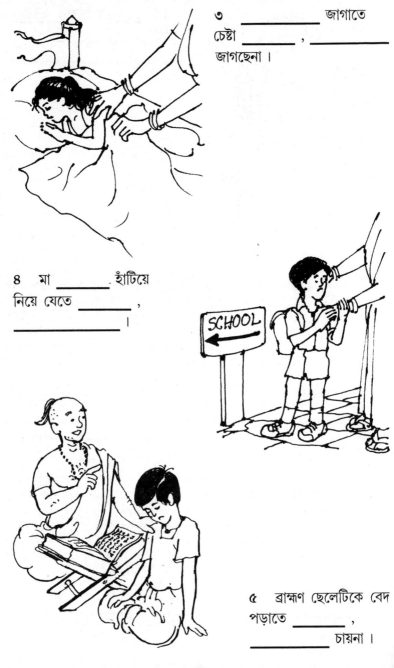

৩ _____ জাগাতে চেষ্টা _____ , _____ জাগছেনা ।

4 মা _____ হাঁটিয়ে নিয়ে যেতে _____ , _____ ।

৫ ব্রাহ্মণ ছেলেটিকে বেদ পড়াতে _____ , _____ চায়না ।

৬ ___ মেয়েকে ___
পরাতে ___ ,
___ ও ___ ।

2 You are equipped now to write your first continuous piece of Bengali prose. See if you can turn the following words and phrases into a sequence of grammatical sentences, by giving the verbs their correct forms, and the nouns and pronouns their correct cases. The words that have to be adjusted are given between brackets. To help you, a translation of the passage is supplied below.

ami (ʃīter deʃ) lok, tɔbe (baŋladeʃ) gɔrôm (ami) kharap lagena. (rasta) ami iuropīyô poʃak (pɔra) kintu baṛite ami baŋalī poʃak (pɔra) (bhalobasa). ami roj khub (bhor) (oṭha). ca (khaoya khaoya) ami (pakhi) ḍak (ʃona) ar sūryodɔy (dækha). tɔkhôn (ami) mône gôbhir bhab (jaga). tar pɔre ami bôi (pɔṛa) ba ciṭhi (lekha).

gɔtôkal (ami) bôndhu nɔren (asa) (brekphasṭ) age. (se) aʃi (bɔchôr) (ma) jônyô (se) khub bhabna (hɔoya). uni (bat) (bytha) khub (bhoga) ar (hãṭa) (para) na. tachaṛa nɔren ækṭa nôtun (maṭi) ghɔr (kɔrano). kajṭa nije tɔdarôk (kɔra) jônyô se ẏothesṭô sɔmɔy (paoya) na. kɔyek din age ækṭa kal-boïʃakhīr jhoṛ (oṭha) – nôtun (ghɔrṭa) ɔrdhek ʃeṣ kɔra chad (batas) (jhapṭa) uṛe (ẏaoya). ækhôn (se) abar ʃuru (kɔra) hɔbe – khalikhali ɔnekguli ṭaka nɔsṭô (hɔoya).

mône (hɔoya) (ami) ækhôn (se) kichu ṭaka dhar deoya ucit. tate (se) ekṭu sahaẏẏôᵃ (hɔoya). nɔren (ami) jônyô age ɔnek (kɔra).

ᵃ য + য = য্য

I am a cold-country person, but I don't find the heat of Bengal[b] too bad. I wear European dress in the street, but in the house I love to wear Bengali clothes. I get up very early every day. I drink tea and listen to the birdsong and watch the sunrise. Deep feelings awake in my mind then. Next I read a book or write a letter.

Yesterday my friend Naren came before breakfast. He is very worried about his 80-year-old mother. She suffers terribly from rheumatic pain, and cannot walk. In addition, Naren is having a new mud-house built. He doesn't get enough time to look after the work. A few days ago a Kāl-baiśākhī storm[c] blew up: the half finished roof of the new house was blown off by the force of the wind. He will now have to start again – lots of money has been wasted for nothing.

I think I should lend him some money. That way he will be helped a bit. Naren has done a lot for me in the past.

[b]Although 'Bangladesh' has become the name of a nation state, traditionally it means the whole Bengali-speaking area.

[c]These are freak storms that blow up in the month of *Baiśākh* (p. 195).

26

—— **REVIEW OF** ——
PART TWO

—— **Numbers, dates, etc.** ——

The Arabic numerals that are now used the world over actually originated in India. The exercises in Units 13–25 have already shown you that the Bengali figures for 1, 2, 3, 4, 5, 6, 7, 8, 9 and 0 are:

১   ২   ৩   ৪   ৫   ৬   ৭   ৮   ৯   ০

For the handwritten forms, refer to the diagrams on pp. x–xi at the front of the book.

The words for the numbers from 1 to 100 are as follows:

		10+	20+	30+	40+	50+
1	এক æk	এগার* ægarô	একুশ ekuʃ	একত্রিশ æktriʃ	একচল্লিশ ækcôlliʃ	একান্ন ækannô
2	দুই dui	বার* barô	বাইশ baiʃ	বত্রিশ bôtriʃ†	বিয়াল্লিশ biyalliʃ	বাহান্ন bahannô
3	তিন tin	তের* tærô	তেইশ teiʃ	তেত্রিশ tetriʃ	তেতাল্লিশ tetalliʃ	তিপ্পান্ন tippannô
4	চার car	চৌদ্দ* coŭddô	চব্বিশ côbbiʃ	চৌত্রিশ coŭtriʃ	চুয়াল্লিশ cuyalliʃ	চুয়ান্ন cuyannô
5	পাঁচ pāc	পনের* pônerô	পঁচিশ pỗciʃ	পঁয়ত্রিশ pỗytriʃ	পঁয়তাল্লিশ pỗytalliʃ	পঞ্চান্ন pɔ̃cannô
6	ছয় chɔy	ষোল* ʃolô	ছাব্বিশ chabbiʃ	ছত্রিশ chɔtriʃ	ছেচল্লিশ checôlliʃ	ছাপ্পান্ন chappann
7	সাত sat	সতের* sɔterô	সাতাশ sataʃ	সাঁইত্রিশ sāitriʃ	সাতচল্লিশ satcôlliʃ	সাতান্ন satannô
8	আট at	আঠার* aṭharô	আঠাশ aṭhaʃ	আটত্রিশ āṭtriʃ	আটচল্লিশ aṭcôlliʃ	আটান্ন aṭannô
9	নয় nɔy	উনিশ ūniʃ	উনত্রিশ ūnôtriʃ	উনচল্লিশ ūnôcôlliʃ	উনপঞ্চাশ ūnôpɔ̃caʃ	উনষাট ūnôʃaṭ
10	দশ dɔʃ	বিশ/কুড়ি biʃ/kuɽi	ত্রিশ triʃ	চল্লিশ côlliʃ	পঞ্চাশ pɔ̃caʃ	ষাট ʃaṭ

*Also written with o: এগারো, বারো , etc.
†32–37 are pronounced with a doubling of the t in triʃ.

		60+	70+	80+	90+
1	এক æk	একষট্টি ækṣôṭṭi	একাত্তর ækattôr	একাশি ækaʃi	একানব্বই ækanôbbôi
2	দুই dui	বাষট্টি baṣôṭṭi	বাহাত্তর bahattôr	বিরাশি biraʃi	বিরানব্বই biranôbbôi
3	তিন tin	তেষট্টি teṣôṭṭi	তিয়াত্তর tiyattôr	তিরাশি tiraʃi	তিরানব্বই tiranôbbôi
4	চার car	চৌষট্টি coŭṣôṭṭi	চুয়াত্তর cuyattôr	চুরাশি curaʃi	চুরানব্বই curanôbbôi
5	পাঁচ pāc	পঁয়ষট্টি pɔ̃yṣôṭṭi	পঁচাত্তর pɔ̃cattôr	পঁচাশি pɔ̃caʃi	পঁচানব্বই pɔ̃canôbbôi
6	ছয় chɔy	ছেষট্টি cheṣôṭṭi	ছিয়াত্তর chiyattôr	ছিয়াশি chiyaʃi	ছিয়ানব্বই chiyanôbbôi
7	সাত sat	সাতষট্টি satṣôṭṭi	সাতাত্তর satattôr	সাতাশি sataʃi	সাতানব্বই satanôbbôi
8	আট aṭ	আটষট্টি aṭṣôṭṭi	আটাত্তর aṭattôr	অষ্টাশি ɔṣṭaʃi	আটানব্বই aṭanôbbôi
9	নয় nɔy	ঊনসত্তর ūnôsɔttôr	ঊনআশি ūnôaʃi	ঊননব্বই ūnônôbbôi	নিরানব্বই niranôbbôi
10	দশ dɔʃ	সত্তর sɔttôr	আশি aʃi	নব্বই nôbbôi	এক-শ æk-ʃɔ

100, 200 etc. are এক-শ, দুই-শ, etc. Remember that the words for *one-and-a-half* and *two-and-a-half* are দেড় and আড়াই , so 150 and 250 are দেড়-শ and আড়াই-শ .

1000, 2000, etc. are এক হাজার, দুই হাজার, etc.

In the whole of South Asia, **lakhs** and **crores** are used rather than millions and billions:

1 lakh (এক লাখ or লক্ষ) = 100,000
1 crore (এক কোটি or ক্রোড়) = 10,000,000

When writing such numbers in figures, commas are put after two noughts instead of three: 7 lakhs would be 7,00,000 and 20 crores would be 20,00,00,000.

For the numbers + definite article, and rules for their use, see Unit 16, pp. 72–74. The article is often dropped from very large numbers: e.g. ভূকম্পতে তিন হাজার লোক মারা গেছে *(Three thousand people have died in the earthquake)*.

Percentages are expressed by শতকরা : e.g. 10 per cent would be শতকরা দশ .

For fractions, use পোয়া for a quarter, আধ for a half (as in, for example, আধ ঘণ্টা – *half-an-hour*; but *a half* on its own would be অর্ধেক), তিন পোয়া for *three quarters*, দেড় for *one-and-a-half*, আড়াই for *two-and-a-half*. To express *five-and-a-quarter, six-and-a-half, seven-and-three-quarters*, etc., use the words সওয়া, সাড়ে and পৌনে that are used in telling the time (see Unit 19, pp. 108–109).

There is a Sanskritic series of ordinal numbers, but only the first three are used commonly in speech:

প্রথম	*first*	ষষ্ঠ	*sixth*
দ্বিতীয়	*second*	সপ্তম	*seventh*
তৃতীয়	*third*	অষ্টম	*eighth*
চতুর্থ	*fourth*	নবম	*ninth*
পঞ্চম	*fifth*	দশম	*tenth*

Above *third* the possessive case of the ordinary numbers can be used – চারের, পাঁচের , etc.

Dates, etc.

There are special words for the first four days of the month: পয়লা *(first)*,

দোসরা *(second)*, তেসরা *(third)*, চৌঠা *(fourth)*, generally used with তারিখ (date): পয়লা তারিখ, দোসরা তারিখ, etc.

From the 5th to 18th use the ordinary numbers with ই – পাঁচই, ছয়ই, সাতই, etc. From the 19th to the 31st use the ordinary numbers with এ – ঊনিশে, বিশে, etc.

Alternatively you can simply say এক তারিখ, দুই তারিখ, তিন তারিখ, etc.

The Bengali months are as follows:

বৈশাখ	*April–May*
জ্যৈষ্ঠ (The J is not pronounced.)	*May–June*
আষাঢ়	*June–July*
শ্রাবণ	*July–August*
ভাদ্র	*August–September*
আশ্বিন	*September–October*
কার্তিক	*October–November*
অগ্রহায়ণ	*November–December*
পৌষ	*December–January*
মাঘ	*January–February*
ফাল্গুন	*February–March*
চৈত্র	*March–April*

To refer to a year, সাল should be used: so *in 1993* would be ঊনিশ-শ তিরানব্বই সালে.

There is a Bengali era, that should be used if you are using Bengali months, beginning in 593; so 1993 is 1399 or 1400 depending on whether you are referring to a time before or after April.

The days of the week are:

রবিবার	*Sunday*
সোমবার	*Monday*
মঙ্গলবার	*Tuesday*
বুধবার	*Wednesday*
বৃহস্পতিবার	*Thursday*
শুক্রবার	*Friday*
শনিবার	*Saturday*

For their pronunciation and usage, and for the times of day (ভোর বেলা, সকাল বেলা etc.), see Unit 18, p. 103.

As regards weights and measures, older books on Bengali give all the traditional terms of weight; but nowadays metric terms are used, and the only traditional measure you are likely to encounter is the 'seer' (সের), by which milk is sold, rather as the British stick obstinately to pints. Tailors continue to use British imperial inches (ইঞ্চি), but cloth is sold by the metre. Height is measured by feet (ফুট); but for body-weight kilos are used. In referring to money, annas (আনা – 16 annas to the rupee) are still sometimes used: see Unit 16, p. 71.

Verb tables

In the following verb tables, transliterated forms are given only when the script does not indicate the correct pronunciation of the vowel. For the use of the 'very familiar' **tui** forms, see Unit 27, Note 8 (p. 211).

Consonant stems

১/ô

Verbal noun	করা	kɔra
Infinitive	করতে	kôrte
Present	আমি করি	kôri
	তুই করিস	kôris
	তুমি কর/করো	kɔrô/kɔro
	সে করে	kɔre
	আপনি/তিনি করেন	kɔren
Present continuous	আমি করছি	kôrchi
	তুই করছিস	etc.
	তুমি করছ/করছো	
	সে করছে	
	আপনি/তিনি করছেন	
Future	আমি করব/করবো	kôrbô/kôrbo
	তুই করবি	etc.
	তুমি করবে	
	সে করবে	
	আপনি/তিনি করবেন	
Simple past	আমি করলাম *	kôrlam
	তুই করলি	etc.

	তুমি করলে	
	সে করল/করলো	
	আপনি/তিনি করলেন	
Habitual past	আমি করতাম*	kôrtam
	তুই করতিস	etc.
	তুমি করতে	
	সে করত/করতো	
	আপনি/তিনি করতেন	

*In West Bengal, the variant endings –লুম and –তুম are frequently heard for the first person of the simple past and habitual past tenses of all verbs.

Conditional participle	করলে	kôrle
Past participle	করে	kôre
Perfect	আমি করেছি	kôrechi
	তুই করেছিস	etc.
	তুমি করেছ/করেছো	
	সে করেছে	
	আপনি/তিনি করেছেন	
Past perfect	আমি করেছিলাম	kôrechilam
	তুই করেছিলি	etc.
	তুমি করেছিলে	
	সে করেছিল/করেছিলো	
	আপনি/তিনি করেছিলেন	
Past continuous	আমি করছিলাম	kôrchilam
	তুই করছিলি	etc.
	তুমি করছিলে	
	সে করছিল/করছিলো	
	আপনি/তিনি করছিলেন	

æ/e

Verbal noun	দেখা	dækha
Infinitive	দেখতে	dekhte
Present	আমি দেখি	dekhi
	তুই দেখিস	dekhis
	তুমি দেখ/দেখো	dækhô/dækho
	সে দেখে	dækhe
	আপনি/তিনি দেখেন	dækhen

Present continuous	আমি দেখছি etc.	dekhchi
Future	আমি দেখব/দেখবো etc.	dekhbô/ dekhbo
Simple past	আমি দেখলাম etc.	dekhlam
Habitual past	আমি দেখতাম etc.	dekhtam
Conditional participle	দেখলে	dekhle
Past participle	দেখে	dekhe
Perfect	আমি দেখেছি etc.	dekhechi
Past perfect	আমি দেখেছিলাম etc.	dekhechilam
Past continuous	আমি দেখছিলাম etc.	dekhchilam

o/u

Verbal noun	শোনা
Infinitive	শুনতে
Present	আমি শুনি তুই শুনিস তুমি শোন/শোনো সে শোনে আপনি/তিনি শোনেন
Present continuous	আমি শুনছি etc.
Future	আমি শুনব/শুনবো etc.
Simple past	আমি শুনলাম etc.
Habitual past	আমি শুনতাম etc.
Conditional participle	শুনলে
Past participle	শুনে

Perfect	আমি শুনেছি
	etc.
Past perfect	আমি শুনেছিলাম
	etc.
Past continuous	আমি শুনছিলাম
	etc.

e/i

Verbal noun	লেখা
Infinitive	লিখতে
Present	আমি লিখি
	তুই লিখিস
	তুমি লেখ/লেখো
	সে লেখে
	আপনি/তিনি লেখেন
Present continuous	আমি লিখছি
	etc.
Future	আমি লিখব/লিখবো
	etc.
Simple past	আমি লিখলাম
	etc.
Habitual past	আমি লিখতাম
	etc.
Conditional participle	লিখলে
Past participle	লিখে
Perfect	আমি লিখেছি
	etc.
Past perfect	আমি লিখেছিলাম
	etc.
Past continuous	আমি লিখছিলাম
	etc.

a/e

Verbal noun	রাখা
Infinitive	রাখতে
Present	আমি রাখি

	তুই রাখিস
	তুমি রাখ/রাখো
	সে রাখে
	আপনি/তিনি রাখেন
Present continuous	আমি রাখছি
	etc.
Future	আমি রাখব/রাখবো
	etc.
Simple Past	আমি রাখলাম
	etc.
Habitual past	আমি রাখতাম
	etc.
Conditional participle	রাখলে
Past participle	রেখে
Perfect	আমি রেখেছি
	etc.
Past perfect	আমি রেখেছিলাম
	etc.
Past continuous	আমি রাখছিলাম
	etc.

আসা has the following variant forms (the regular forms are also heard, especially in Bangladesh):

Simple past	আমি এলাম
	তুই এলি
	তুমি এলে
	সে এল/এলো
	আপনি/তিনি এলেন
Conditional participle	এলে

Vowel stems

a/e

Verbal noun	খাওয়া
Infinitive	খেতে
Present	আমি খাই
	তুই খাস

	তুমি খাও
	সে খায়
	আপনি/তিনি খান
Present continuous	আমি খাচ্ছি
	etc.
Future	আমি খাব/খাবো
	etc.
Simple past	আমি খেলাম
	etc.
Habitual past	আমি খেতাম
	etc.
Conditional participle	খেলে
Past participle	খেয়ে
Perfect	আমি খেয়েছি
	etc.
Past perfect	আমি খেয়েছিলাম
	etc.
Past continuous	আমি খাচ্ছিলাম
	etc.

যাওয়া goes like খাওয়া but has a different root for the following:

Simple past	আমি গেলাম	gelam
	তুই গেলি	geli
	তুমি গেলে	gele
	সে গেল/গেলো	gælô/gælo
	আপনি/তিনি গেলেন	gelen or gælen
Conditional participle	গেলে	gele
Past participle	গিয়ে	
Perfect	আমি গিয়েছি	
	or গেছি	gechi
	তুই গিয়েছিস	
	or গেছিস	gechis
	তুমি গিয়েছ/গিয়েছো	
	or গেছ/গেছো	gæchô/gæcho
	সে গিয়েছে	
	or গেছে	gæche
	আপনি/তিনি গিয়েছেন	
	or গেছেন	gæchen

Past perfect	আমি গিয়েছিলাম	
	or গেছিলাম	gechilam
	etc.	

চাওয়া and গাওয়া differ from the normal pattern as follows:

Infinitive	চাইতে	
Present continuous	আমি চাইছি	or চাচ্ছি
	etc.	
Future	আমি চাইব/চাইবো	
Simple past	আমি চাইলাম	
Habitual past	আমি চাইতাম	
Conditional participle	চাইলে	
Past continuous	আমি চাইছিলাম	or চাচ্ছিলাম

o/u

Verbal noun	ধোয়া
Infinitive	ধুতে
Present	আমি ধুই
	তুই ধুস
	তুমি ধোও
	সে ধোয়
	আপনি/তিনি ধোন
Present continuous	আমি ধুচ্ছি
	etc.
Future	আমি ধোব/ধোবো
	etc.
Simple past	আমি ধুলাম etc.
Habitual past	আমি ধুতাম
	etc.
Conditional participle	ধুলে
Past participle	ধুয়ে
Perfect	আমি ধুয়েছি
	etc.
Past perfect	আমি ধুয়েছিলাম
	etc.

Past continuous	আমি ধুচ্ছিলাম etc.	

ɔ/ô

Verbal noun	হওয়া	hɔoya
Infinitive	হতে	hôte
Present	আমি হই তুই হস তুমি হও সে হয় আপনি/তিনি হন	hôi hôs hɔo hɔy hɔn
Present continuous	আমি হচ্ছি etc.	hôcchi
Future	আমি হব/হবো etc.	hɔbô/hɔbo
Simple past	আমি হলাম etc.	hôlam
Habitual past	আমি হতাম etc.	hôtam
Conditional participle	হলে	hôle
Past participle	হয়ে	hôye
Perfect	আমি হয়েছি etc.	hôyechi
Past perfect	আমি হয়েছিলাম etc.	hôyechilam
Past continuous	আমি হচ্ছিলাম etc.	hôcchilam

e/i/a/æ

Verbal noun	দেওয়া	
Infinitive	দিতে	
Present	আমি দিই তুই দিস তুমি দাও সে দেয় আপনি/তিনি দেন	 dæy dæn

Present continuous	আমি দিচ্ছি
	etc.
Future	আমি দেব/দেবো
	তুই দিবি*
	তুমি দেবে
	etc.
Simple past	আমি দিলাম
	etc.
Habitual past	আমি দিতাম
	etc.
Conditional participle	দিলে
Past participle	দিয়ে
Perfect	আমি দিয়েছি
	etc.
Past perfect	আমি দিয়েছিলাম
	etc.
Past continuous	আমি দিচ্ছিলাম
	etc.

*Note the vowel change here. The first person form is sometimes pronounced (but never written) 'dôbo'; likewise 'nôbo' for the first person future of **neoya**.

Imperatives

In addition to the imperative forms given in Unit 19, pp. 110–112, the first person imperative (*Let me . . ./May I . . .*, see Note 14, p. 211) is given, the 'very familiar' **tui** forms (see Note 8, p. 211), and the third person imperative (*Let him/her . . .*, see Note 17, p. 212). For the polite present imperative (consonant stems), the forms করেন, দেখেন, শোনেন, লেখেন and রাখেন are commonly used in Bangladesh.

Consonant stems	Present imperative		Future imperative	
১/ô				
(আমি)	করি	kôri		
(তুই)	কর	kɔr	করিস	kôris
(তুমি)	কর/করো	kɔrô/kɔro	কর/করো	kôrô/kôro
(আপনি)	করুন	kôrun	করবেন	kôrben
(সে)	করুক	kôruk		

æ/e

(আমি)	দেখি	dekhi		
(তুই)	দেখ	dækh	দেখিস	dekhis
(তুমি)	দেখ/দেখো	dækhô/dækho	দেখ/দেখো	dekhô/dekho
(আপনি)	দেখুন	dekhun	দেখবেন	dekhben
(সে)	দেখুক	dekhuk		

o/u

(আমি)	শুনি		
(তুই)	শোন	শুনিস	
(তুমি)	শোন/শোনো	শুন/শুনো	
(আপনি)	শুনুন	শুনবেন	
(সে)	শুনুক		

e/i

(আমি)	লিখি		
(তুই)	লেখ	লেখিস	
(তুমি)	লেখ/লেখো	লিখ/লিখো	
(আপনি)	লিখুন	লিখবেন	
(সে)	লিখুক		

a/e

(আমি)	রাখি		
(তুই)	রাখ	রাখিস	
(তুমি)	রাখ/রাখো	রেখ/রেখো	
(আপনি)	রাখুন	রাখবেন	
(সে)	রাখুক *		

*With the verb থাকা, which goes like রাখা, the contracted form থাক, is also commonly heard. See Note 17, p. 212.

আসা, (*to come*) has a special very familiar present imperative আয় (see Unit 29, Note 9, p. 224), and its familiar imperative is এস/এসো in the present and future.

Vowel stems

a/e

(আমি)	খাই		
(তুই)	খা	খাস	
(তুমি)	খাও	খেও	
(আপনি)	খান	খাবেন	
(সে)	খাক		

o/u

(আমি)	ধুই		
(তুই)	ধো	ধুস	
(তুমি)	ধোও	ধুও	
(আপনি)	ধোন	ধুবেন	
(সে)	ধুক		

ɔ/ô

(আমি)	হই	hôi		
(তুই)	হ	hɔ	হস	hôs
(তুমি)	হও	hɔo	হও	hôo
(আপনি)	হন	hɔn	হবেন	hɔben
(সে)	হোক	hok		

e/i/a/æ

(আমি)	দিই		
(তুই)	দে	দিস	
(তুমি)	দাও	দিও	
(আপনি)	দিন	দেবেন	
(সে)	দিক		

Extended verbs

Since the stem of most extended verbs ends in **-a**, only one paradigm is needed. A few verbs extend (in colloquial speech) with **-ô** or **-o** rather than **-a**, but the endings are the same, and the past participle and tenses formed on the past participle are as normal (see Unit 25, pp. 182–184). The 'first' vowel is used in the stem for all forms and tenses other than the past participle, perfect and past perfect: i.e. kɔranô/kɔrano but kôriye, dækhanô/dækhano but dekhiye, ʃonanô/ʃonano but ʃuniye etc. a/e verbs, however, use the **a** vowel throughout: dāɽanô/dāɽano – dāɽiye, khaoyanô/khaoyano – khaiye (খাইয়ে), etc.

Verbal noun	করান/ করানো	kɔranô/kɔrano
Infinitive	করাতে	kɔrate
Present	আমি করাই	kɔrai
	তুই করাস	etc.
	তুমি করাও	
	সে করায়	
	আপনি/তিনি করান	
Present continuous	আমি করাচ্ছি	kɔracchi
	তুই করাচ্ছিস	etc.
	তুমি করাচ্ছ/করাচ্ছো	
	সে করাচ্ছে	
	আপনি/তিনি করাচ্ছেন	
Future	আমি করাব/করাবো	kɔrabô/kɔrabo
	তুই করাবি	etc.
	তুমি করাবে	

	সে করাবে	
	আপনি/তিনি করাবেন	
Simple past	আমি করালাম	kɔralam
	তুই করালি	etc.
	তুমি করালে	
	সে করাল/করালো	
	আপনি/তিনি করালেন	
Habitual past	আমি করাতাম	kɔratam
	তুই করাতিস	etc.
	তুমি করাতে	
	সে করাত/করাতো	
	আপনি/তিনি করাতেন	
Conditional participle	করালে	kɔrale
Past participle	করিয়ে	kôriye
Perfect	আমি করিয়েছি	kôriyechi
	তুই করিয়েছিস	
	তুমি করিয়েছ/করিয়েছো	
	সে করিয়েছে	
	আপনি/তিনি করিয়েছেন	
Past perfect	আমি করিয়েছিলাম	kôriyechilam
	তুই করিয়েছিলি	
	তুমি করিয়েছিলে	
	সে করিয়েছিল/করিয়েছিলো	
	আপনি/তিনি করিয়েছিলেন	
Past continuous	আমি করাচ্ছিলাম	kɔracchilam
	তুই করাচ্ছিলি	
	তুমি করাচ্ছিলে	
	সে করাচ্ছিল/করাচ্ছিলো	
	আপনি/তিনি করাচ্ছিলেন	
Present imperative	(আমি) করাই	kɔrai
	(তুই) করা	kɔra
	(তুমি) করাও	kɔrao
	(আপনি) করান	kɔran
	(সে) করাক	kɔrak
Future imperative	(তুই) করাস	kɔras
	(তুমি) করিয়ো	kôriyo*
	(আপনি) করাবেন	kɔraben

*Note that here too the 'second' vowel is used. Thus **dækhanô/dækhano** goes **dekhiyo**, **ʃonanô/ʃonano** goes **ʃuniyo**, etc.

PART THREE

LITERATURE

27

__ THE TAILOR-BIRD __ AND THE CAT

In this and the remaining units, you will be introduced to some of the finer points of Bengali grammar and idiom through a series of short texts by authors from West Bengal and Bangladesh. The texts have been reproduced in their published form: i.e. spellings of verb forms, etc. have not been altered. So be prepared particularly for spellings with ô/o different from those used in **Parts One** and **Two** of the book.

The first text is from the book that Putul mentioned in Unit 23: Upendrakishore Raychaudhuri's টুনটুনির বই *(The Tailor-bird's Book)*. This charming collection of fable-like animal stories by the grandfather of Satyajit Ray, published in Calcutta in 1910 and reprinted many times since, makes an excellent first reader in Bengali, and my own translation of the book (*The Stupid Tiger and Other Tales*, Andre Deutsch, 1981, 1988) is, I hope, accurate enough to be a useful aid. The first story in the book is short enough to be given complete.

টুনটুনি আর বিড়ালের কথা[1]

গৃহস্থের ঘরের পিছনে বেগুন গাছ আছে । সেই বেগুন গাছের পাতা ঠোঁট দিয়ে সেলাই করে[2] টুনটুনি পাখিটি তার বাসা বেঁধেছে ।

বাসার ভিতরে তিনটি ছোট-ছোট[3] ছানা হয়েছে ।[4] খুব ছোট ছানা, তারা উড়তে পারে না, চোখও মেলতে[5] পারে না । খালি হাঁ করে, আর চি চি করে ।[6]

গৃহস্থের বিড়ালটা ভারী দুষ্টু । সে খালি ভাবে 'টুনটুনির ছানা খাব ।' একদিন সে বেগুন গাছের তলায় এসে বললে,[7] 'কি করছিস[8] লা টুনটুনি ?'

টুনটুনি তার মাথা হেঁট হয়ে বেগুন গাছের ডালে ঠেকিয়ে[9] বললে, 'প্রণাম হই, মহারাণী !' তাতে বিড়ালনী ভারী খুশি হয়ে চলে গেল ।

এমনি সে রোজ আসে, রোজ টুনটুনি তাকে প্রণাম করে আর মহারাণী বলে, আর সে খুশি হয়ে চলে যায় ।[10]

এখন টুনটুনির ছানাগুলি বড় হয়েছে, তাদের সুন্দর পাখা হয়েছে ।[11] তারা আর চোখ বুজে[12] থাকে না । তা দেখে টুনটুনি তাদের বললে, 'বাচ্চা, তোরা উড়তে পারবি ?'[13]

ছানারা বললে, 'হাঁ মা পারব ।'

টুনটুনি বললে, 'তবে দেখ তো দেখি,[14] ঐ তাল গাছটার ডালে গিয়ে বসতে পারিস কিনা ।'[15]

ছানারা তখনি[16] উড়ে গিয়ে তাল গাছের ডালে বসল । তা দেখে টুনটুনি হেসে বললে, 'এখন দুষ্টু বিড়াল আসুক দেখি ।'[17]

খানিক বাদেই[18] বিড়াল এসে বললে, 'কি করছিস লা টুনটুনি ?'

তখন টুনটুনি পা উঠিয়ে তাকে লাথি দেখিয়ে[19] বললে 'দূর হ,[20] লক্ষ্মীছাড়ী[21] বিড়ালনী !' বলেই[22] সে ফুড়ুক করে উড়ে পালাল ।

দুষ্টু বিড়াল দাঁত খিচিয়ে গাছে লাফিয়ে উঠে টুনটুনিকে ধরতে পারল না, ছানাও খেতে পেল[23] না । খালি বেগুন কাঁটার খোঁচা খেয়ে নাকাল হয়ে ঘরে ফিরল ।

The Story of the Tailor-bird and the Cat

In the yard of a house there was a brinjal-plant. A tailor-bird had sewn up the leaves of the plant with her beak, to make a nest.

Inside the nest there were three tiny chicks. They were so tiny that they couldn't fly or open their eyes. They could only open their mouths and cheep.

The householder had a very wicked cat. She kept thinking, 'I'd like to eat that tailor-bird's chicks.' One day she came to the base of the brinjal-plant and said, 'Hello, little bird, what are you doing?'

The tailor-bird bowed her head till it touched the branch beneath the nest, and said, 'Humble greetings, Your Majesty.'

This made the cat very pleased and she went away. She came like this every day, and every day the tailor-bird bowed down before her and called her Your Majesty; and the cat went away happily.

The tailor-bird's chicks grew big, and they grew beautiful wings. Their eyes were open now, so the tailor-bird said to them, 'Children, do you think you can fly?'

'Yes, mother we do,' said the chicks.

'Well,' said the tailor-bird, 'let's see first whether you can go and perch on a branch of that palm tree.'

The chicks flew off at once and perched on a branch of the palm tree. Then the tailor-bird laughed and said, 'Now let's see what happens when the wicked cat comes.'

In a little while the cat came and said, 'Hello, little bird, what are you doing?'

This time the tailor-bird kicked her leg at her and said, 'Go away, you good-for-nothing cat!' Then she darted into the air and flew away.

Baring her teeth, the cat jumped up into the plant; but she couldn't catch the wicked tailor-bird, or eat the chicks. She just scratched herself badly on the thorns of the brinjal, and went home feeling very silly.

Notes

[1] কথা can mean *story*, *word*, *speech*, etc., but can also act as a postposition meaning *about*. So the title can be translated as *The Story of the Tailor-bird and the Cat* or *About the Tailor-bird and the Cat*.

[2] সেলাই করে is a participial phrase, *having sewn*. Remember that kɔre (third person present tense) and kôre (past participle) are both spelt করে in Bengali script.

[3] A diminutive form of ছোট : *very small, tiny*.

[4] *have become* – i.e. *have been born*.

[5] মেলা meaning *to open* is mostly used with eyes. The normal verb for *open* is খোলা .

[6] করে in this sentence (occurring twice) is a present tense form, not a participle.

[7]The normal third person simple past form would be বললো or বলল *(he/she said)*. But in the colloquial language of West Bengal the ending -লে (i.e. the same ending as for the second person familiar) is used, with any common verb.

[8]As well as the pronouns তুমি and আপনি and their corresponding verb forms that you learnt in **Part Two**, Bengali has a 'very familiar' pronoun তুই . This has a variety of uses, none of which are likely to be needed by the foreign learner. It can be used when speaking affectionately to children or animals, and children in lower class families often use it to address their mothers. It is also used by schoolchildren or college students when addressing friends of the same age. Intimate appeals or prayers to God can use তুই , but it is not normally used by lovers or between husband and wife. It can be used in anger, or in deliberate rudeness, when a speaker wants to 'do down' someone from a lower social class than himself, but it would not be used to a complete stranger. The cat uses it patronisingly to the tailor-bird! The verb forms for তুই end in -i or -is depending on the tense, and are best learnt as they occur (they are given in the **Verb tables** in the **Review of Part Two**, pp. 196–207). The particle লা here gives the cat's question a rustic air: *What are you doing, pray?* This particle (or its East Bengal form লো) also has a 'feminine' association: women use it when addressing each other.

[9]Past participle of the extended verb ঠেকানো (thækano) (see Unit 25, pp. 182–184).

[10]Notice this shift into the present tense, as often happens in Bengali story-telling.

[11]This phrase is probably best construed as an impersonal construction: *Of them beautiful wings it had become.* Remember that impersonal constructions are often used for things that happen to you, rather than things which you do deliberately.

[12] বোজা meaning *to close* is used for the eyes or mouth, and has some other idiomatic uses: e.g. পুকুর বুজে গেছে *(The pond has silted up).* The usual verb for *close* is বন্ধ করা .

[13]The future tense তুই form of পারা *(to be able).*

[14]An idiomatic phrase meaning *Then let's try and see.* The imperative of দেখা is often used to mean *Try, have a go,* etc. Here we have the তুই imperative, pronounced dækh, though the ordinary familiar imperative can be spelt the same way (see Unit 19, p. 111). দেখি is not the

first person of the present tense, but a first person imperative: *May I
. . .*, *Let me . . .* Cf. Unit 15, p. 59 and Unit 20, p. 120, Unit 21, p. 133,
Unit 24, p. 169, and see the **Verb tables** on p. 204.

[15] কিনা , *whether or not*, is normally placed at the end of the clause.
[16] তখন means *then*, and the emphatic form তখনি means *right then*
or *at once*. It can also be spelt তখনই . An even more emphatic form
তক্ষুণি is also found, especially in children's literature. এখনি *(right now)*
has similar variations.

[17]Another idiomatic phrase, this time using the 'third person imperative'
form আসুক *(Let her come)*. These forms – করুক, লিখুক, হোক , etc.
have a variety of idiomatic uses. থাকুক , for example, from থাকা, *to
stay*, means *Let it be*, *Never mind*, etc. though the abbreviated form
থাক is more common in this meaning.

[18]*in a short while*. খানিক means *some, a little*, and বাদ means *a gap,
interval*, etc. The emphatic ই suggests a **very** short while.

[19]More extended verb past participles, from ওঠানো *(to cause to rise,*
i.e. *to lift)*, and দেখানো *(to cause to see*, i.e. *to show)*. The tailor-bird
shows a kick, makes as if to kick the cat.

[20] তুই imperative of হওয়া (Lit. *Be distant)*.

[21]Note the conjunct ক্ষ + ম = ক্ষ্ম in লক্ষ্মীছাড়ী *(good-for-nothing)*, in
which the ম is silent ('lôkkhichaṛi'). Cf. লক্ষ্মী মেয়ে, a common expression for a nice, well-behaved girl.

[22]Past participle with the emphatic particle ই : *Immediately after saying
(that) . . . .*

[23] পাওয়া *(to get, receive)* can be used instead of পারা *(to be able)* with
certain verbs. With verbs of sensation like শোনা or দেখা the
meaning can be different according to which one is used:
ওর কথা শুনতে পাইনা means *I can't hear what he says*, but
ওর কথা শুনতে পারিনা can mean *I can't bear what he says*. Sometimes
পারা can be used with verbs of sensation without this special meaning (on the telephone, for example, one can shout
আপনার কথা শুনতে পারছিনা ! , *I can't hear what you're saying)*, but be
careful!

 ——————— **Exercise** ———————

Fill in the table below, by defining the verb forms as indicated. All the
verbs have been taken from the story above, and you should define them
according to their use there.

	Tense or participle or infinitive	Person 1,2,3 P or F	Verbal noun	Meaning as in text
বেঁধেছে	*perfect*	3 F	বাঁধা	*has built*
হাঁ করে				
ভাবে				
খাব				
হেঁট হয়ে				
চলে গেল*				
চলে যায়*				
উড়তে				
পারব				
বসতে				
এসে				
পালাল				
লাফিয়ে				
ধরতে				
ফিরল				

*Compound verb (see Unit 20, pp. 121–122).

28

—— SAKUNTALA ——

The text in this unit is from a prose version by Abanindranath Tagore (1871–1951) of the classic story, *Śakuntalā*. The oldest version of the story is in the *Mahābhārata*, the great epic of India; but it was Kalidasa (in about 400 AD) who gave it classic status by making it the subject of the most celebrated of all Sanskrit plays. Abanindranath Tagore, the son of a cousin of Rabindranath Tagore, wrote his version for children, but the beautiful lucidity of his prose appeals to all ages. Abanindranath was primarily a painter, and his version of *Śakuntalā* was first published in 1895 with his own illustrations.

Sakuntala is the daughter of a heavenly nymph, Menaka, who leaves her in a forest soon after her birth. She is found and brought up by the sage Kanva and his disciples, in the idyllic peace and beauty of a forest hermitage. One day King Dushmanta (Dushyanta in Kalidasa) is out hunting in the forest. He sees Sakuntala watering plants with her companions Anasuya and Priyamvada, and immediately falls in love with her. They meet, and he plights his troth to her by giving her a ring. He leaves, saying he will come back to fetch her. The passage below begins with Sakuntala pining for the absent king.

রাজা রাজ্যে গেলে একদিন শকুন্তলা কুটির-দুয়ারে গালে হাত দিয়ে বসে বসে[1] রাজার কথা ভাবছে[2] – ভাবছে আর কাঁদছে, এমন সময়[3] মহর্ষি দুর্বাসা দুয়ারে অতিথি এলেন, শকুন্তলা জানতেও[4] পারলে না, ফিরেও

দেখলে[5] না । একে[6] দুর্বাসা মহা অভিমানী,[7] একটুতেই মহা রাগ হয়, কথায়-কথায় যাকে-তাকে[8] ভস্ম করে ফেলেন,[9] তার উপর শকুন্তলার এই অনাদর - তাঁকে প্রণাম করলে না,[10] বসতে আসন দিলে না, পা ধোবার জল দিলে না !

দুর্বাসার সর্বাঙ্গে[11] যেন আগুন ছুটল, রাগে কাঁপতে কাঁপতে[12] বললেন - 'কী ! অতিথির অপমান ? পাপীয়সী, এই অভিসম্পাত করছি - যার জন্যে[13] আমার অপমান করলি সে যেন[14] তোকে[15] কিছুতে না চিনতে পারে ।'

হায়, শকুন্তলার কি তখন জ্ঞান ছিল যে দেখবে কে এল, কে গেল ![16] দুর্বাসার একটি কথাও তার কানে গেল না ।

মহামানী মহর্ষি দুর্বাসা ঘোর অভিসম্পাত করে চলে গেলেন - সে কিছুই জানতে পারলে না, কুটির-দুয়ারে আনমনে যেমন[17] ছিল তেমনি রইল ।

অনসূয়া প্রিয়ংবদা দুই সখী উপবনে ফুল তুলছিল, ছুটে এসে দুর্বাসার পায়ে লুটিয়ে পড়ল । কত[18] সাধ্য-সাধনা করে, কত কাকুতি-মিনতি করে, কত হাতে পায়ে ধরে দুর্বাসাকে শান্ত করলে !

শেষে এই শাপান্ত[19] হল - 'রাজা যাবার সময় শকুন্তলাকে যে-আংটি[20] দিয়ে গেছেন সেই আংটি যদি রাজাকে দেখাতে পারে তবেই রাজা শকুন্তলাকে চিনবেন ; যতদিন[21] সেই আংটি রাজার হাতে না পড়বে ততদিন রাজা সব ভুলে থাকবেন ।'[22]

দুর্বাসার অভিশাপে তাই পৃথিবীর রাজা সব ভুলে রইলেন ! বনপথে সোনার রথ আর ফিরে এল না !

Soon after the king's return to his kingdom, and while Sakuntala sat one day at the door of her cottage thinking about him with her cheek resting against her hand – thinking and crying – the great sage Durbasa had come expecting hospitality; and Sakuntala had not noticed him, had not even turned her head. Durbasa was a proud and touchy man, who lost his temper at tiny things, burnt everyone to ashes at the slightest provocation: and here was Sakuntala treating him so rudely – she had not greeted him, had not asked him to sit down, had not given him water for his feet!

Blazing all over his body, trembling with fury, Durbasa said, 'So! Insult to a guest? You sinful girl, I curse you, so that from now on whoever it is who is causing you to neglect me will never be able to recognize you.'

Alas, had Sakuntala any thought for who was coming or going? Not one of Durbasa's words entered her ears.

The high and mighty sage Durbasa delivered this terrible curse and then went on his way – but Sakuntala was completely unaware of him, she remained just as she was at the door of the hut, with her thoughts far away.

Her two companions Anasuya and Priyamvada were picking flowers in a grove nearby. They came running and threw themselves at Durbasa's feet. They appealed to him, they begged him, they held his hands and feet and implored him to relent.

At last the curse was modified: 'If Sakuntala can show the king the ring that he gave her when he left her, then the king will recognize her; for as long as the ring is not in the king's hands, the king will not remember anything about her.'

It was because of Durbasa's curse that the king of the world had forgotten everything.

The golden chariot never came back along the forest-paths.

The sage Kanva has been away during this episode, travelling in search of a husband for Sakuntala. When he returns and hears about her bethrothal to Dushmanta, he is delighted, and decides to send her to the king. Tearfully, she takes her leave of the hermitage, and her companions Anasuya and Priyamvada, who carefully tie the king's ring into the corner of her sari. But Durbasa's curse has a further, unexpected twist to it: Sakuntala loses the ring while bathing, so that when she confronts the king he still doesn't remember or recognize her. You will have to turn to Kalidasa's play to find out how the situation is finally resolved. Meanwhile, here is Abanindranath's exquisite description of Sakuntala's loss of the ring:

ঋষির অভিশাপ কখনো মিথ্যে হয় না । রাজপুরে যাবার পথে শকুন্তলা একদিন শচীতীর্থের জলে গা ধুতে গেল । সাঁতার-জলে গা ভাসিয়ে, নদীর জলে ঢেউ নাচিয়ে[23] শকুন্তলা গা ধুলে । রঙ্গভরে অঙ্গের শাড়ি জলের উপর বিছিয়ে দিলে ; জলের মতো চিকণ আঁচল জলের সঙ্গে মিশে গেল, ঢেউয়ের সঙ্গে গড়িয়ে গেল । সেই সময় দুর্বাসার শাপে রাজার সেই আংটি শকুন্তলার চিকন আঁচলের এক কোণ থেকে অগাধ জলে পড়ে গেল, শকুন্তলা জানতেও[24] পারলে না । তারপর ভিজে কাপড়ে তীরে উঠে, কালো চুল এলো করে, হাসিমুখে শকুন্তলা বনের ভিতর দিয়ে রাজার কথা ভাবতে ভাবতে শূন্য আঁচল নিয়ে রাজপুরে চলে গেল, আংটির কথা মনেই[25] পড়ল না ।

A sage's curse is never idle. On her way to the royal city, Sakuntala stopped one day to bathe in a watering-place sacred to Sachi. Floating in the buoyant water, splashing and sending out ripples, Sakuntala washed herself clean. She merrily let her sari spread out over the water; the shimmering sari blended with the water like water, moulded itself to the waves. Because of Durbasa's curse, the king's ring slipped from the corner of Sakuntala's sari of shining silk, and fell into the bottomless water; and she knew not a thing.

Then with soaking sari and her black hair bedraggled, Sakuntala got out on to the bank, smiling. She went on through the forest with her thoughts on the king. She approached the royal city with the end of her sari empty, but not once did she remember the ring.

Notes

[1]The repeated past participle বসে বসে suggests a continuous state or action, like a present participle in English: *Sitting with her hand against her cheek, Sakuntala was thinking . . .*

[2]Note the present continuous tense *(is thinking)* in vivid narrative, where English would use the past continuous *(was thinking)*.

[3] এমন সময় *(at such a time)*. This phrase is commonly used in Bengali to link simultaneous actions, where English would use the conjunction *while*.

[4]The repeated particle ও in জানতেও পারলে না ফিরেও দেখলে না conveys **neither** *was she able to know,* **nor** *did she look round.*

[5] ফেরা means *to return*; the compound ফিরে দেখা means *to look round.*

[6] একে, pronounced æke, means *in the first place*, and goes with তার উপর, *on top of that*, later in the sentence.

[7] অভিমান is a notoriously untranslatable Bengali emotion. Here it just expresses pride, haughtiness, touchiness; but it is commonly used for *a feeling of being hurt by someone you love.* Abstract nouns in Bengali often have adjectival forms ending in ী .

[8]Bengali idioms often involve verbal duplication – কথায়-কথায় যাকে-তাকে – and are hard to translate literally into English. *He turned to ashes everyone and anyone at any or every word . . .* This is not just metaphorical – Brahmins in Indian mythology have the power literally to blast people to ashes with their curse.

[9]Verbal compounds with ফেলা *(to throw)* often express sudden or aggressive actions, or thoroughly completed actions. Cf. খেয়ে ফেলা, which means *to eat up*. Note the conjunct in ভস্ম : স + ম = স্ম , in which the ম is silent, lengthening and perhaps nasalising the স ('bhɔʃʃo'). In স্মৃতি *(memory)* the conjunct is pronounced 's' ('srti').

[10]The third person simple past ending in **-e** rather than **-ô/o**, which was noticed in the Tailor-bird story in Unit 27, also occurs frequently here.

[11]সর্ব (sɔrbô – *all*) and অঙ্গ (ɔŋgô – *limb*) combine to form sɔrbaŋgô – *whole body*. ô + ɔ = a according to Sanskrit *sandhi* rules. These rules, governing the way sounds change when words are joined to form compounds, are not systematic in Bengali, but survive in many compounds derived from Sanskrit.

[12]Remember that repetition of the infinitive – কাঁপতে কাঁপতে – turns it into a present participle: *trembling with anger he said . . .* (cf. Unit 23, p. 163).

[13] যার জন্যে . . . সে   This is the first of several relative/correlative constructions in this passage. Bengali relative clauses are difficult to translate literally into English because English does not make use of **correlatives**. Most Bengali relative clause constructions use a correlative as well as a relative pronoun – but not all: sometimes the correlative is left out. Here the relative pronoun occurs in the possessive case with the postposition জন্য and the correlative is the subject case pronoun সে : Lit. *He because of whom you insulted me may he not be able to recognise you at all.*

[14] যেন picks up the previous clause: *I am cursing you to this effect, namely. . .* যেন can be a conjunction meaning *so that. . .*, referring to possibilities or probabilities in the future. It can also mean *as if*, and is used to express a sense of *seeming*: cf. যেন আগুন ছুটল earlier in the sentence.

[15]Note the object case of the very familiar pronoun তুই . The possessive is তোর .

[16]Lit. *Alas, did Sakuntala have knowledge then that she will see who came, who went?* Remember that জ্ঞান is pronounced 'gæn' (see Unit 17, p. 82.)

[17]The principle of the relative/correlative governs many kinds of clause and phrase construction in Bengali. You already know the pair যখন . . . তখন *(when . . . then)* from **Part Two** (p. 181). Here we have: *In the way (* যেমন *) that she was, absent-minded at the cottage-door, so (* তেমনি *) she remained.*

[18]কত can mean *so much, such a lot* as well as *how much/many.*

[19]Another *sandhi*, between শাপ *(curse)* and অন্ত *(end)*. But the compound means *modification of the curse* here, rather than complete release from it.

[20]Another relative/correlative construction: যে-আংটি . . . সেই আংটি, *That ring which . . . that ring . . . .* The emphatic particle ই is often attached to the correlative.

[21]Another construction comparable to যেমন . . . তেমনি above: *for as*

many days (যতদিন) . . . *for so many days* (ততদিন). Note the negative না is placed **before** the verb, as in conditional constructions (see Unit 25, p. 185).

[22]Verbs are combined with থাকা *(to stay)* to convey sustained action: *will keep forgetting everything.* রওয়া *(to remain)* can also be used with the same meaning: so in the next sentence we have সব ভুলে রইলেন, *went on forgetting everything.*

[23]Notice the extended past participles to express a causative or transitive meaning: *causing her body to float . . . causing the waves to dance.*

[24]Lit. *Sakuntala wasn't even able to know.* The emphatic particle ও expresses *even.*

[25]The emphatic particle ই, attached to মনে intensifies the phrase: *The matter of the ring did not fall into (her) mind at all.*

Exercise

In the following sentences, either the relative pronoun or the correlative has been left out. Fill in the gaps, by chosing the right word from the list below. Note that two main types of relative clause occur in these sentences: (*a*) **named** clauses, in which a specific person or thing or place is mentioned to which the relative clause applies (b) **un-named**, in which the relative pronoun means *the thing which, the place where,* etc.

In type (*a*), the relative pronoun is always যে , whereas the correlative can be any of the third person pronouns or demonstrative pronouns. In type (*b*) যে is used for people and যা for things, but the polite form যিনি , the possessive form যার and the object form যাকে also occur for people, and demonstrative forms যেটা , যেটি , যেগুলো and যেগুলি occur for things.

A complete and systematic exposition of Bengali relative clauses would be a complicated affair: it is simpler to pick up the various possibilities gradually. Bear in mind that relative clauses in spoken Bengali can sound rather precious or pompous: short sentences linked with demonstrative pronouns are generally preferred.

১ যে লোকটি পাশের বাড়িতে থাকতো _____ হঠাৎ মারা গেল ।
The man who lived next door has suddenly died.

২ _____ চেয়ারের কথা আপনাকে বলেছিলাম সেটা এই ।

This is the chair which I told you about.

৩ তোমাদের মধ্যে _____ বাঙালী, তারা আমার সাথে এস ।

Those of you who are Bengali come with me.

৪ যে চাবি দিয়ে এই আলমারি খোলা যায় _____ কোথায় ?

Where is the key which opens this cupboard?

৫ যে জায়গা থেকে পাহাড় দেখা যায় _____ থাকতে চাই ।

I want to live in a place from which mountains can be seen.

৬ রবীন্দ্রনাথের যে গল্পগুলি তুমি পড়েছ, _____ মধ্যে কোনটি তোমার সবচেয়ে প্রিয় ?

Of the stories by Rabindranath that you have read, which of these is your favourite?

৭ যে জামা-কাপড় ধোয় _____ ধোপা বলে ।

One calls a man who washes clothes a dhopa.

৮ _____ দোষ নেই সে মানুষ নয় ।

Anyone who has no faults is not human.

৯ যা অসম্ভব _____ কেউ করতে পারেনা ।

No one can do what is impossible.

১০ _____ জল নেই সেখানে কি করে থাকবো ?

How can I live where there is no water?

১১ তুমি আমাকে যা-ই দেবে _____ আমি সারাজীবন কাছে রাখবো ।

What you give me I shall keep by (me) all my life.

১২ _____ পরিষ্কার নয় তা ব্যবহার না করাই ভালো ।

It is better not to use what is unclean.

যে, সেখানে, সেগুলির, যার, তা, যারা, সেটা, তা-ই, যা, তাকে, সে, যেখানে

29

—— SATYAJIT RAY ——

From writing for children we move to adult memories of childhood. The following extract is from Satyajit Ray's charming book of reminiscences, *When I was small* (যখন ছোট ছিলাম), published in Calcutta in 1982. Ray's family was one of the most talented in Calcutta. His grandfather Upendrakishore Raychaudhuri was a printer as well as writer for children, founding his own printing company in 1895. Upendrakishore's son Sukumar, Satyajit's father, has achieved lasting fame and popularity as a writer of nonsense verse, which he illustrated himself in inimitable style.

Satyajit was only two when his father died in 1923, so his reminiscences revolve round his mother, uncles, aunts and cousins, the house at 100 Garpar Road, Calcutta, where the family printing press was housed, and the magazine for children, *Sandesh*, that was published there. The keen observation that has served him so well as a film-maker was with him from an early age, and his reminiscences are full of fascinating vignettes of life in Calcutta in the 1920s and 1930s. Here, after describing a European stage magician called Sephalo, he recalls a Bengali master magician.

এর কিছু দিন পরে এক বিয়ে বাড়িতে[1] একজন বাঙালীর ম্যাজিক দেখেছিলাম যার কাছে[2] শেফালো সাহেবের স্টেজের কারসাজি কিছুই

না । স্টেজ ম্যাজিকে নানান যন্ত্রপাতির ব্যবহার হয়, আলোর খেলা আর প্যাটারের জোরে লোকের চোখ মন ধাঁধিয়ে যায় । ফলে জাদুকরের কাজটা অনেক সহজ হয়ে যায় ।[3] এই ভদ্রলোক ম্যাজিক দেখালেন প্যাণ্ডেলের[4] তলায় ফরাসের উপর বসে, তাঁর চারিদিক ঘিরে চার পাঁচ হাতের মধ্যে বসেছেন নিমন্ত্রিতরা ।[5] এই অবস্থাতে একটার পর একটা এমন খেলা দেখিয়ে গেলেন ভদ্রলোক[6] যা ভাবলে[7] আজও তাজ্জব বনে যেতে হয় ।[8] এই জাদুকরকে অনেক পরে আমার একটা ছোট গল্পে ব্যবহার করেছিলাম । ফরাসের উপর দেশলাইয়ের কাঠি ছড়িয়ে দিয়েছেন ভদ্রলোক, নিজের সামনে রেখেছেন একটা খালি দেশলাইয়ের বাক্স । তারপর 'তোরা আয়[9] একে একে' বলে ডাক দিতেই[10] কাঠিগুলো গড়িয়ে গড়িয়ে[11] এসে বাক্সয় ঢুকেছে । আমাদেরই চেনা এক ভদ্রলোকের কাছ থেকে চেয়ে নিলেন[12] একটা রুপোর টাকা, আর আরেকজনের কাছ থেকে একটা আংটি । প্রথমটাকে রাখলেন হাত চারেক[13] দূরে, আর দ্বিতীয়টাকে নিজের সামনে । তারপর আংটিটাকে উদ্দেশ্য করে বললেন, 'যা[14] টাকাটাকে নিয়ে আয় ।' বাধ্য আংটি গড়িয়ে গেল টাকার কাছে, তারপর দুটো একসঙ্গে গড়িয়ে এল ভদ্রলোকের কাছে । আরেকটা ম্যাজিকে এক ভদ্রলোকের হাতে এক প্যাকেট তাস ধরিয়ে দিয়ে[15] আরেকজনের হাত থেকে লাঠি নিয়ে ডগাটা বাড়িয়ে দিলেন তাসের দিকে । তারপর বললেন, 'আয়রে ইস্কাপনের টেক্কা !' প্যাকেট থেকে সড়াৎ করে ইস্কাপনের টেক্কাটা বেরিয়ে এসে লাঠির ডগায় আটকে থরথর করে[16] কাঁপতে লাগল ।

ম্যাজিক দেখার কয়েকদিন পরে হঠাৎ জাদুকরের সঙ্গে দেখা হলো বকুলবাগান আর শ্যামানন্দ রোডের মোড়ে । বয়স পঞ্চাশ-পঞ্চান্ন, পরনে ধুতি আর শার্ট, দেখলে কে বলবে ভদ্রলোকের এত ক্ষমতা । আমার ম্যাজিকের ভীষণ শখ, মনে মনে আমি তাঁর শিষ্য হয়ে গেছি । ভদ্রলোককে বললাম আমি তাঁর কাছে ম্যাজিক শিখতে চাই । 'নিশ্চয়ই শিখবে' বলে ভদ্রলোক তাঁর পকেট থেকে এক প্যাকেট তাস বার করে রাস্তায় দাঁড়িয়ে দাঁড়িয়েই আমাকে একটা খুব মামুলি ম্যাজিক শিখিয়ে দিলেন । তারপর আর ভদ্রলোকের সঙ্গে দেখা হয়নি । হঠাৎ সামনে পড়ে ঘাবড়ে[17] গিয়ে ওঁর ঠিকানাটাও নেওয়া হয়নি ।[18] পরে ম্যাজিকের বই কিনে হাত সাফাইয়ের অনেক ম্যাজিক আয়নার সামনে দাঁড়িয়ে নিজেই অভ্যেস করে শিখেছিলাম । কলেজ অবধি ম্যাজিকের নেশাটা ছিল ।

Some time later, at a wedding-ceremony, I saw the conjuring of a Bengali, compared to whom the stage trickery of Sephalo was nothing. In stage magic various devices are used – the play of light and the power of patter – to confuse people's eyes and minds. The magician's work consequently becomes much easier. This gentleman showed his magic sitting on a cloth on a pandal, with the invited guests sitting all around within four or five arms' length of him. In this position he performed trick after trick, such that even today I feel amazed if I think of them. Much later I used this gentleman in one of my short stories. He scattered matchsticks on the cloth, and put an empty matchbox in front of him. Then as soon as he called out, 'Come, one by one', the sticks came rolling towards him and entered the box. He asked for a silver rupee from a gentleman we knew, and a ring from someone else. He placed the first item about four arms' length away, and the second in front of him. Then he said to the ring: 'Go and fetch the coin.' The obedient ring rolled off towards the coin, and then the two of them came rolling back together towards him. In another trick he gave a gentleman a pack of cards to hold, took a stick from someone else, and pointed the tip of it at the pack. Then he said, 'Come, Ace of Spades!' The Ace shot out of the pack and was caught on the end of the stick, fluttering.

A few days after seeing this display, I suddenly met the magician at the crossing of Bokul Bagan and Shyamananda Road. He was fifty or fifty-five years of age, dressed in a shirt and dhoti: to see him, who would say he had such powers? I had a passion for magic, and I pictured myself as his disciple. I told him I wanted to learn magic from him. 'Certainly you can learn,' he said, took a pack of cards from his pocket, and standing in the street taught me a very feeble trick. I never met him again after that. Suddenly bumping into him like that, I hadn't taken his address. Later I bought books on magic and standing in front of a mirror taught myself lots of sleights of hand. I had a craze for magic until I went to college.

Notes

[1]Although large houses are sometimes hired for wedding ceremonies, বিয়ে বাড়ি really just means the ceremony itself.

[2]There is a relative pronoun here – যার কাছে , near (compared to) whom – and no correlative. When is it necessary to have a correlative and when is it not? This is not an easy question to answer, but the logical distinction between 'restrictive' and 'non-restrictive' relative clauses seems to have some bearing on the matter. English punctuation recognises the distinction by requiring commas for the second sort of relative

of clause, but not the first. Compare:

People who live in glass houses shouldn't throw stones.
and
Sukumar Ray, who wrote good books for children, lived in that house.

The first sentence, a restrictive relative clause in which people who live in glass houses are distinguished from those who don't, would require a relative/correlative construction. The second, which merely adds more information about Sukumar Ray, can be expressed in Bengali by using a relative pronoun only:

ওই বাড়িতে থাকতেন সুকুমার রায়, যিনি ছোটদের জন্য ভালো ভালো বই লিখতেন ।

However, this theory does not stand up completely, because if you turn the sentence round (to a rather anglicised and artificial word order in Bengali, but grammatically acceptable), a correlative **is** required:

সুকুমার রায়, যিনি ছোটদের জন্য ভালো ভালো বই লিখতেন, তিনি ওই বাড়িতে থাকতেন ।

3 ধাঁধিয়ে যায় *(become confused)*; অনেক সহজ হয়ে যায় *(becomes much easier)*. Note how verbs can be combined with যাওয়া to express a sense of *becoming*.

4A 'pandal' is an area set apart for sitting (on the ground), often incorporating a raised platform for musicians, magicians, etc.

5 নিমন্ত্রিত from নিমন্ত্রণ *(invitation)* means *invited*, and is here given the plural personal ending to mean *the ones who were invited*.

6 ভদ্রলোক is the subject of the verb দেখিয়ে গেলেন (another colloquial compound). The subject can sometimes come after the verb in Bengali, for a particular stylistic effect.

7 যা , another relative without correlative: *which when (I) think (about it) even today . . .* It refers to খেলা in the main clause.

8Lit. *I have to be reduced to faintness*: an obligation construction (see Unit 19, pp. 109–110) using the verb বনা, *to be reduced to*. বনা is not a common verb, but occurs in some common idiomatic expressions: e.g. আমি বোকা বনে গেলাম *(I was reduced to idiocy)*.

9The plural of the very familiar pronoun তুই , and a special, very familiar imperative of আসা *to come* (see **Verb tables**, p. 205).

10 ডাক দিতেই *(as soon as he called)*. The infinitive with an emphatic ই added can have this participial meaning.

11The past participle of the extended verb গড়ানো. The meaning is not causative here (the repetition of the participle suggests continuous movement), but গড়ানো can be used causatively: e.g. আমি বলটা গড়িয়ে দিলাম *(I rolled the ball)*.

[12] চাওয়া can mean to *ask for* as well as to *want*. Combined with নেওয়া the meaning is *ask for and get*. Notice that the object follows the verb here (একটা রুপোর টাকা): Bengali word order is really very flexible! For the spelling of রুপো *(silver)* see Note 29, p. 255.

[13] চারেক *(about four)*. Any number combined with এক in this way becomes approximate. With দুই the pronunciation is 'æk'; with other numbers it is 'ek'.

[14] Not the relative pronoun, but the very familiar imperative of যাওয়া.

[15] Lit. *having caused to hold/having given to hold.* Extended verb participle combined with দেওয়া, as so often happens. Later in the sentence we have বাড়িয়ে দিলেন. বাড়া means *to grow*, and বাড়ানো means *to cause to grow, extend, increase*, etc., and is therefore used for pointing a stick.

[16] Where English has vivid verbs (e.g. *to flutter*) Bengali has vivid adverbs, often reduplicative in form (see Unit 30, pp. 233–234).

[17] The participle ঘাবড়িয়ে from ঘাবড়ানো *(to be taken aback, lose one's balance)*, here contracted colloquially to ঘাবড়ে and combined with যাওয়া: Lit. *Suddenly in front having fallen having been taken aback . . .*

[18] Lit. *even taking his address had not been done.* This is a passive construction. The agent concerned *(by me)* can be understood from the context.

The passage contains three 'same-letter' conjuncts that have not occurred before:

দ + দ = দ্দ

জ + জ + জ্জ

ক + ক = ক্ক

Exercise

See if you can translate the next two paragraphs from Satyajit Ray's reminiscences, looking up words in the **Glossary** at the end of the book. They are about the circus and annual 'carnival' in pre-war Calcutta. Beware of English words and names: one can spend much time looking for a word in a dictionary, only to realise that it is a name, or an English word.

সার্কাস তো এখনও প্রতি বছরই আসে, যদিও তখনকার[1] দিনে হার্মস্টোন সার্কাসে সাহেবরা খেলা দেখাত, আর আজকাল বেশিরভাগই মাদ্রাজি সার্কাস । যেটা আজকাল দেখা যায় না সেটা হল কার্নিভ্যাল । আমাদের ছেলেবেলায় সেন্ট্রাল অ্যাভিনিউ-এর[2] দুধারে ছিল বড় বড় মাঠ । কলকাতায় প্রথম 'হাই-রাইজ' দশ তলা টাওয়ার হাউস তখনও তৈরী হয়নি, ইলেকট্রিক সাপ্লাই-এর ভিক্টোরিয়া হাউস তৈরী হয়নি । এই সব মাঠের একটাতে সার্কাসের কাছেই বসত কার্নিভ্যাল ।

কার্নিভ্যালের মজাটা যে কী সেটা[3] আজকালকার ছেলেমেয়েদের বোঝানো মুশকিল । মেলায় নাগরদোলা সকলেই দেখেছে, কিন্তু কার্নিভ্যালের নাগরদোলা বা জায়ান্ট হুইল হত পাঁচ তলা বাড়ির সমান উঁচু । বহু দূর থেকে দেখা যেত ঘুরন্ত হুইলের আলো । এই নাগর-দোলা ছাড়া থাকত মেরি-গো-রাউণ্ড, এরোপ্লেনের ঘুর্ণি, খেলার মটর গাড়িতে ঠোকাঠুকি, ঢেউখেলানো অ্যালপাইন রেলওয়ে, আর আরো কত কী । এসবেরই চারিদিকে ছড়িয়ে ছিটিয়ে থাকত নানা রকম জুয়ার স্টল । এত লোভনীয় সব জিনিস সাজানো থাকত এই সব স্টলে যে[4] খেলার লোভ সামলানো কঠিন হত । শেষ পর্যন্ত প্রকাশ্যে জুয়া খেলাটা সরকার বেআইনী করে দেওয়ার ফলে কলকাতা শহর থেকে কার্নিভ্যাল উঠে গেল ।[5] আসল রোজগারটা হত বোধহয় এই জুয়া থেকেই ।

[1] Note this possessive form of তখন *in those days).* At the beginning of the second paragraph you have আজকালকার *(of today).* Cf. the possessive forms of ওখানে and এখানে : এখানকার and ওখানকার.

[2] English words beginning with an **æ** sound are sometimes spelt with an initial এ্যা , sometimes with an initial অ্যা (as here).

[3] যে is not a relative: without it the phrase would not be so balanced, but would still be grammatical. সেটা refers to কী : *What . . . that . . .*

[4] Not a relative pronoun, but the conjunction *that* following এত *(such)* at the beginning of the sentence.

[5] A colloquial meaning of the compound verb উঠে যাওয়া *to close down, pack up, be abolished.* ওর চুল উঠে গেছে means *He's gone bald.*

30

_____ TAGORE IN _____
ENGLAND

Now for something by the greatest Bengali writer, Rabindranath Tagore, from a little-known early work of great charm, his যুরোপ-প্রবাসীর পত্র *(Letters from Europe)*. Tagore first came to England when he was 18 years old, in 1878, accompanied by his elder brother Satyendranath (who was the first Indian to qualify for the Indian Civil Service). They stayed over a year, in lodgings in London, Brighton, Tunbridge Wells and Torquay, and experienced Victorian social life at various middle-class and upper-middle class levels.

The letters that Rabindranath wrote home describing his stay were first printed in the journal *Bhāratī*, and were published as a book in 1881. Later Tagore became embarrassed by some of the things he said in the letters, and the book was cut down when it appeared in his collected works. The complete text has only been reprinted once, in 1961, the centenary of Tagore's birth.

The following passage describes a couple of Dickensian eccentricity in whose house Tagore lodged for a short while.

আমি দিন-কতক[1] আমার শিক্ষকের পরিবারের মধ্যে বাস করেছিলুম ।[2] সে বড়ো অদ্ভুত পরিবার । **Mr. B** মধ্যবিত্ত লোক । তিনি লাটিন ও

গ্রীক খুব ভালো রকম জানেন । তাঁর ছেলেপিলে কেউ নেই - তিনি, তাঁর স্ত্রী, আমি আর একটা দাসী, এই চার জন মাত্র একটি বাড়িতে থাকতুম । Mr.B আধবুড়ো লোক, অত্যন্ত অন্ধকার মূর্তি,[3] দিনরাত খুঁৎখুত খিটখিট করেন, নীচের তলায় রান্নাঘরের পাশে একটি ছোট্ট-জানালা-ওয়ালা[4] দরজা-বন্ধ অন্ধকার ঘরে থাকেন, একে তো সূর্যকিরণ সে ঘরে সহজেই প্রবেশ করতে পারে না[5] তাতে[6] জানালার উপর একটা পর্দা ফেলা,[7] চার দিকে পুরোনো ছেঁড়া ধুলো-মাখা নানা প্রকার আকারের ভীষণ-দর্শন গ্রীক লাটিন বইয়ে[8] দেয়াল ঢাকা - ঘরে প্রবেশ করলে এক রকম বদ্ধ হাওয়ায় হাঁপিয়ে উঠতে হয় ।[9] এই ঘরটা হচ্ছে তাঁর study, এইখানে তিনি বিরক্ত মুখে পড়েন ও পড়ান । তাঁর মুখ সর্বদাই বিরক্ত, আঁট বুট জুতো পরতে বিলম্ব হচ্ছে,[10] বুট জুতোর উপর মহা চটে উঠলেন ; যেতে যেতে দেয়ালের পেরেকে তাঁর পকেট আটকে গেল, রেগে ভুরু কুঁকড়ে[11] ঠোঁট নাড়তে লাগলেন । তিনি যেমন খুঁৎখুতে মানুষ তার পক্ষে তেমনি খুঁৎখুতের কারণ প্রতি পদে জোটে ; আসতে যেতে তিনি চৌকাঠে হুঁচট খান, অনেক টানাটানিতে তাঁর দেরাজ খোলে না, যদি বা খোলে তবু যে জিনিস খুঁজছিলেন তা পান না, এক-এক দিন সকালে তাঁর study তে এসে দেখি তিনি অকারণে বসে বসে ভুকুটি করে উ-আ করছেন[12] - ঘরে একটি লোক নেই । কিন্তু Mr. B আসলে ভালোমানুষ, তিনি খুঁৎখুতে বটে কিন্তু রাগী নন, তিনি খিটখিট করেন কিন্তু ধমকান না । নিদেন তিনি মানুষের ওপর কখনো রাগ প্রকাশ করেন না — Tiny বলে তাঁর একটা কুকুর আছে তার ওপরেই তাঁর যত আক্রোশ,[13] সে একটু নড়লে-চড়লে তাকে ধমকাতে থাকেন[14] আর দিন রাত তাকে লাথিয়ে লাথিয়ে একাকার করেন । তাঁকে আমি প্রায় হাসতে দেখিনি । তাঁর কাপড়-চোপড় ছেঁড়া অপরিষ্কার । মানুষটা এই রকম । তিনি এক কালে পাদ্রি[15] ছিলেন ; আমি নিশ্চয় বলতে পারি, প্রতি রবিবারে তাঁর বক্তৃতায় তিনি শ্রোতাদের নরকের বিভীষিকা দেখাতেন । Mr. B র এত কাজের ভিড়, এত লোককে তাঁর পড়াতে হয় যে, এক-এক দিন তিনি ডিনার খেতে অবকাশ পেতেন না । এক-এক দিন তিনি বিছানা থেকে উঠে অবধি[16] রাত্রি এগারোটা পর্যন্ত কাজে ব্যস্ত থাকতেন । এমন অবস্থায় খিটখিটে হয়ে ওঠা কিছু আশ্চর্য নয় ।

Mrs. B খুব ভালো মানুষ, অর্থাৎ রাগী উদ্ধত লোক নন । এক

কালে বোধ হয় ভালো দেখতে ছিলেন । যত বয়স তার চেয়ে তাঁকে বড়ো দেখায়,[17] চোখে চশমা পরেন — সাজগোজের বড়ো আড়ম্বর নেই । নিজে রাঁধেন, বাড়ির কাজকর্ম করেন (ছেলেপিলে নেই, সুতরাং কাজকর্ম বড়ো বেশি নয়) আমাকে খুব যত্ন করতেন । খুব অল্প দিনেতেই বোঝা যায় যে, Mr. & Mrs.Bএর মধ্যে বড়ো ভালোবাসা নেই । কিন্তু তাই বলে যে দুজনের মধ্যে খুব ঝগড়াঝাঁটি হয় তা নয়,[18] নিঃশব্দে সংসার চলে যাচ্ছে । Mrs. B কখনো Mr. Bর studyতে যান না, সমস্ত দিনের মধ্যে খাবার সময় ছাড়া দুজনের মধ্যে আর দেখাশুনা হয় না,[19] খাবার সময়ে দুজনে চুপচাপ বসে থাকেন, খেতে খেতে আমার সঙ্গে গল্প করেন, কিন্তু দুজনে পরস্পর গল্প করেন না । Mr. Bর আলুর দরকার হয়েছে, তিনি গোঁ গোঁ করতে করতে Mrs. Bকে বললেন: Some potatoes! (Please কথাটা বললেন না কিন্তু শোনা গেল না ।) Mrs. B বলে উঠলেন: I wish you were a little more polite. Mr. B বললেন : I did say please. Mrs. B বললেন : I didn't hear it. Mr. B বললেন It was no fault of mine that you didn't! কথাটা সমস্তটা ভালো করে শোনা গেল না, এইখেনেই[20] দুই পক্ষে চুপ করে রইলেন । মাঝের থেকে[21] আমি অত্যন্ত অপ্রস্তুতে পড়ে যেতেম । একদিন আমি ডিনারে যেতে একটু দেরি করেছিলাম, গিয়ে দেখি Mrs. B Mr. Bকে ধমকাচ্ছেন, অপরাধের মধ্যে Mr. B মাংসের সঙ্গে একটু বেশি আলু নিয়েছিলেন । আমাকে দেখে Mrs. B ক্ষান্ত হলেন, Mr. B সাহস পেয়ে প্রতিহিংসা তোলবার জন্যে দ্বিগুণ করে আলু নিতে লাগলেন । Mrs. B তাঁর দিকে একটু নিরুপায় মর্মভেদী কটাক্ষপাত করলেন ।

I stayed for a few days with my tutor's family. It is a very strange household. Mr B is a middle-class man. He knows Latin and Greek very well. He has no children. He and his wife, me and a servant-girl – it was just the four of us in the house. Mr B is middle-aged and has a scowling expression: he fusses and complains about things all day long, and spends his time in a dark room on the ground floor next to the kitchen, with one small window and the door tight shut. The sun's rays can't easily enter the room, but even so he keeps a curtain drawn over the window; the walls are covered with various formidable-looking Greek and Latin books – old, torn and dusty. When you go into the room you feel suffocated from the lack of air. This room is his study, where he does his reading and teaching, with a bad-tempered expression on his face. He always looks bad-tempered: if it takes him a long time to put on tight boots or shoes he gets furious with them. If he catches his pocket on a nail in the wall, he screws up his eyebrows and his lips tremble. He is such an irascible individual that there seems to be something to infuriate him at every step: he trips on the threshold when he goes in and out; he cannot get a drawer open without a struggle; if he gets it open he cannot find what he is looking for. One morning when I went into his study I found him sitting and frowning and groaning for no apparent reason – there was no other person in the room. But actually Mr B is not a bad person: he is irritable but is not violent; he carps and cavils but he doesn't threaten – or at least he doesn't behave aggressively towards people. He has a dog called Tiny, though, on whom he works out all his fury; if he so much as moves he threatens him continually, and kicks him to a pulp day and night. I have never seen him smile. His clothes are ragged and dirty. He is this sort of man. At one time he was a priest; I am sure that in his sermons on Sunday he regaled his congregation with the terrors of Hell. Mr B is so overworked, he has to teach so many people, that some days he has no time to eat his dinner. Sometimes he is busy from the moment he gets up till eleven at night. In such a situation it is not very surprising that he is irritable.

Mrs B is a very good person – she never shows any anger. She must have been quite attractive once. But she looks older than her years and wears spectacles – and does not take much trouble over her dress. She does the cooking herself, and the housework (there are no children, so there is not very much to do) – and she took good care of me. Within a few days it was apparent that there was very little love lost between Mr and Mrs B. But this did not mean that they quarrelled a lot: the household functioned quite silently. Mrs B never goes into Mr B's study, and throughout the day they see nothing of each other any more except at mealtimes, when they sit quietly, talking to me but not to each other. If Mr B needs more potatoes, he says gruffly to Mrs B, 'Some potatoes!' (he never says please, or at least it is inaudible). Mrs B then says, 'I wish you were a little more polite.' 'I did say please,' says Mr B. 'I didn't hear it,' says Mrs B. 'It was no fault of mine that you didn't!' says Mr B. I did not hear everything they said – at this point both sides lapsed into silence. I felt very ill-at-ease between the two of them. One day I arrived a little late for dinner, and found Mrs B rebuking Mr B: among his other faults, he had taken too many potatoes with his meat. Mrs B fell silent when she saw me, and Mr B seized his chance to have his revenge by taking a double helping of potatoes. Mrs B looked at him with a heart-rendingly helpless expression.

Notes

যুরোপ প্রবাসীর পত্র was the first Bengali book to be written entirely in the *calit bhāṣā*, as opposed to the literary *sādhu bhāṣā* that will be illustrated by the passage in Unit 33. *Calit bhāṣā* is often translated as 'colloquial language'. Its verb endings and pronouns do indeed conform to the West Bengal speech on which Modern Standard Spoken Bengali is based. But since it has largely replaced *sādhu bhāṣā* as the language of literature, it is now just as much a literary language as the older *sādhu bhāṣā*. Moreover, *sādhu bhāṣā*, as handled by certain writers, can be racy and colloquial, and *calit bhāṣā* can be highly Sanskritic. Tagore's style here shows how hard it is to make a sharp distinction between *calit* and *sādhu*. It is breezy and spontaneous in tone, with loose punctuation and hardly any paragraphing. But the vocabulary is eclectic: literary words jostle with highly colloquial reduplicative forms such as খুৎখুৎ, থিটথিট, টানাটানি, কাটাকাটি, etc.

[1] কতক *(a few)*: a more literary form than কয়েক .

[2] -লুম instead of -লাম , -তুম instead of -তাম , etc. are West Bengali dialectal forms, common in Tagore's writing.

[3] মূর্তি can mean an image or statue: here it means *figure*.

[4] ওয়ালা entered British Indian English in *punkah-wallah, cha-wallah*: i.e. *the man who operates the punkah, the man who sells tea,* etc. Here it gives ছোট্-জানালা an adjectival reference: একটিছোট্-জানালা-ওয়ালা দরজা-বদ্ধ অন্ধকার ঘরে means literally *in a small-windowed door-fastened dark room.*

[5] In **Parts One** and **Two** of this book না has nearly always been attached to the verb: but you will often see it written as a separate word.

[6] একে . . . তাতে *(in the first place . . . on top of that)*. Cf. Note 6, Unit 28, p. 217.

[7] The verbal noun is here used an adjective, with the zero verb: *a curtain (is) drawn (thrown) over the window.* ঢাকা at the end of the next clause is also adjectival.

[8] *with Greek and Latin books.* বই in the instrumental case can be বইয়ে, বই-য়ে or বইতে ।.

[9] Lit. *If (you) enter the room (you) have to pant in a sort of enclosed air.* The participle from the extended verb হাঁপানো forms a colloquial compound with ওঠা in an impersonal obligation construction.

[10] Lit. *It is becoming a delay (for him) to put on tight boots*: another impersonal construction. Notice the gay abandon with which tenses are mixed up in this passage.

[11]A contraction of কুঁকড়িয়ে, the participle of the extended verb কুঁকড়ানো, *to shrink*. A more usual expression would be ভুরু কুঁচকানো.

[12] ভ্রুকুটি করা also means *to frown, screw up ones eyebrows*. উ–আ করা means, as you might guess, *to groan*.

[13]Normally যত *(so much)* has a correlative তত, but here it just seems to intensify আক্রোশ *all his fury*.

[14]থাকা combined with an infinitive or participle gives the meaning *keeps on, continually*.

[15] পাদ্রি *(padre)* is still used in Bengali for a Christian priest. Portuguese traders and missionaries gave quite a few words to Bengali in the pre-British period: জানালা *(window)* and চাবি *(key)* are others.

[16] অবধি here means *since*. Grammatically it would be possible to leave it out – *on some days having risen from his bed . . .* – but it emphasises that he works all day long. অবধি can also mean *until*: it had this meaning in the last sentence of the extract in Unit 29 (p. 222). জন্ম অবধি means *since birth*, but মরণ অবধি means *until death*.

[17]Lit. *However much age (she has) than that she looks older.* তার is the correlative of যত. In Bengali *looks, appears* is expressed by the causative form of দেখা used impersonally, with the person in the object case: তোমাকে সুন্দর দেখাচ্ছে *(You're looking beautiful).*

[18]Lit. *But that (one) says that between the two there is a lot of quarrelling that is not (so).* তা নয় is often associated with শুধু : তিনি যে শুধু সমালোচক তা নয়, তিনি নিজে একজন কবি : *That he is only a critic that is not (so), he's a poet himself.*

[19] দেখাশোনা করা can mean *to look after, take care of*: here the sense is simply that Mr and Mrs B didn't hear or see each other except at meal-times.

[20]An emphatic variant of এখানে. Tagore sometimes uses West Bengali dialectal forms. Cf. Note 2 above.

[21]থেকে with the possessive case *from the middle, from between them*. This is an obsolete usage: it would be মাঝ থেকে in present-day Bengali.

There are plenty of conjuncts in the passage, but the only novel ones are:

দ + ভ = দ্ভ
ত + ন = ত্ন

Notice also the হ + উ combination in হুঁচট (see Note 31, p. 255). It also occurred on p. 226, to spell 'wheel'.

Exercise

Bengali is very rich in reduplicative, onomatopeic expressions. Tagore called them ধ্বন্যাত্মক শব্দ *(sound-denoting words)* and included a long list of them in his collection of essays on the Bengali language *(Bāṃlā śabdatattva*, 1909). In the following sentences, see if you can guess which is the right word from the list given at the bottom. A bit of a lottery, perhaps, but an interesting experiment. Are sound values in words universal? Check your answers against the **Key to the exercises** on p. 289, and decide for yourself.

১ _____ করে বৃষ্টি পড়ছে ।

There's a light patter of rain.

২ ব্যাঙটি ভয় পেয়ে _____ করে চলে গেল ।

The frog hopped away in terror.

৩ সে পুরো গেলাস সরবত _____ করে খেয়ে ফেলল ।

He gulped the whole glass of sherbert down.

৪ কি _____ ছেলে ! ও কখনো চুপচাপ বসে থাকেনা ।

What a restless boy! He never sits quietly.

৫ _____ উঠে পড়, নইলে তোমার দেরি হবে ।

Get up quickly, otherwise you'll be late.

৬ ভদ্রলোকটির পোষাক দেখে মেয়েরা _____ করে হেসে উঠল ।

The girls giggled when they saw the clothes the gentleman was wearing.

৭ অন্ধকার ঘরে এক কোণে একটি বাতি _____ করছিল ।

A dim lamp was flickering in a corner of the dark room.

৮ বিরাট _____ চর – কোথাও কোনো লোক নেই ।

A huge desolate sandbank – not a soul anywhere.

৯ _____ করলেই সোনা হয় না ।

All that glitters is not gold.

১০ বাইরে একজন রিকশাওয়ালার ঘণ্টির _____ শব্দ শুনলাম ।

Outside I heard the tinkle of a rickshawallah's tiny bell.

১১ বাসে এত ভিড় - দারুণ _____ !

Such crowds on the bus – impossible pushing and shoving!

১২ চুড়ির _____ শুনে বুঝলাম সে আসছে ।

I could tell from the jingling of her bangles that she was approaching.

ছটফটে, টিপটিপ, রিনিঝিনি, মিটমিট, ঢকঢক, চকচক, চটপট, ধাক্কাধাক্কি, ধূ-ধূ, খিলখিল, থপথপ, টিং-টিং

(You will often see words of this sort written with the **হসন্ত** sign, indicating that the inherent vowel is not pronounced (see Unit 18, p. 95). Cf. খিট্‌খিট্‌ in the Tagore extract. But it is not really necessary, and contemporary writers frequently omit it.)

31

__ THE BANGLADESH __ WAR

From gentle humour, and the manners of a bygone age, we move to the brutal realities of Bangladesh's struggle for independence. The following passage is from একাত্তরের দিনগুলি *(The days of '71)*, Jahanara Imam's vivid diary of that year, when the Pakistani authorities used genocidal military force to try to suppress Bengali nationalist aspirations. The military clamp-down led to an exodus of ten million refugees, war between Pakistan and India, and the creation of the independent Republic of Bangladesh. The story is told from the point of view of a middle-class Dhaka family, many of whose members were caught up in the liberation struggle. The book has been translated into English by Mustafizur Rahman, under the title *Of Blood and Fire: The Untold Story of Bangladesh's War of Independence* (Academic Publishers, Dhaka, 1990).

২ জুলাই
শুক্রবার ১৯৭১

গতকাল সন্ধ্যার পর ডাক্তাররা[1] এসে পৌঁছেছেন ।[2] নিজেই গাড়ী ড্রাইভ করে[3] এসেছেন । পরশুদিন ট্রাংককলে বলেছিলেন সকালেই রওনা দেবেন । সে হিসাবে[4] তাঁদের বিকেল তিনটে-চারটের মধ্যে এসে

পৌঁছানোর কথা।[5] দেরী দেখে আমরা সবাই বেশ উদ্বিগ্ন হয়ে পড়েছিলাম। বিশেষ করে খুকুর যা অবস্থা।[6] দেরীর কারণ সম্বন্ধে বললেন, পথে বহু জায়গায় পাক আর্মী গাড়ি থামিয়ে চেক করেছে। উনি রওয়াল-পিণ্ডিতে মিটিং করতে যাচ্ছেন শুনে এবং করাচী থেকে আসা মিটিংয়ের চিঠি দেখে ওঁকে সব জায়গায় ছেড়ে দিয়েছে। গতকালই ওঁর কাছ থেকে রাজশাহীর কথা শুনতে খুব ইচ্ছে করছিল কিন্তু সারাদিন ধ'রে পথের ধকলে ওঁদের সবার যা বিধ্বস্ত চেহারা হয়েছে - তাতে[7] সে ইচ্ছে চেপে বললাম, 'আজ বিশ্রাম নিন। কাল সব শুনব।'

আজ সারাদিন ডাক্তার ব্যস্ত ছিলেন পি জি হাসপাতালের ডিরেক্টার ডাঃ নুরুল ইসলামের সঙ্গে দেখা করা, প্লেনের টিকিট ও যাত্রার অন্যান্য ব্যবস্থা করার জন্য। সন্ধ্যার পর এসে বসলেন আমাদের বসার ঘরে। সঙ্গে সানু - ডাক্তারের স্ত্রী।

ডাক্তার বললেন, 'আমরা তো প্রথমে ভেবেছিলাম ঢাকায় কিছু নেই। সব ভেঙে-চুরে জ্বালিয়ে পুড়িয়ে মিস্মার করে দিয়েছে।[8] কোনদিক থেকে কোন খবর পাবার উপায় নেই। শুধু ইণ্ডিয়ান রেডিয়ো, বিবিসি, রেডিয়ো অস্ট্রেলিয়া আর ভয়েস অব এমেরিকার খবর। তা সে সব খবর শুনে তো মাথা খারাপ।[9] ঢাকার সঠিক খবর পেতে অনেকদিন লেগেছে।'

'রাজশাহী ফল করে কবে?'[10]

'খুব সম্ভব ১৩ কি ১৪ এপ্রিল। ভোর বেলা নদীর ধার দিয়ে পাক আর্মী শহরে ঢুকে পড়ল। সেদিনের স্মৃতি ভয়াবহ। টাউনের চৌদ্দ আনা লোক বোধহয় পালিয়েছে, বাকী দুআনা[11] ঘরে দরজা-জানালা সেঁটে বসে ছিল। রাজশাহী টাউন সেদিন শ্মশানের মত দেখাচ্ছিল। পরে জেনেছি, পাক আর্মী পথের দু'পাশে সব জ্বালাতে জ্বালাতে শহরে ঢুকেছিল। বহু লোক মরেছে তাদের গুলিতে। ক'দিনের মধ্যেই[12] পাক বাহিনী রাজশাহী শহরের পুরো কন্ট্রোল নিয়ে নিল। আমাদের সবাইকে বলা হল, কাজে জয়েন করতে,[13] হাসপাতাল চালু করতে। আমরা প্রাণ হাতে করে হাসপাতালে যাতায়াত করতে লাগলাম।'

'হাসপাতালে রুগী ছিল?'

'মাঝে কিছুদিন ছিলনা। কিন্তু হাসপাতাল আবার চালু করার পর রুগী আসতে লাগল। খালি জখমের রুগী।'

'জখমের রুগী ?'

'হ্যাঁ। সাধারণ কোন রুগী বহুদিন হাসপাতালে কেউ আনেনি, এনেছে গুলি খাওয়া, বেয়নেট খোঁচানো, হাত-পা উড়ে যাওয়া রুগী।[14] আরো একরকম রুগী হাসপাতালে লোক আনত, তারা আমাদের জীবনে ব্যথা হয়ে আছে।'[15]

ডাক্তারের গলা ভারী হয়ে উঠল, আমরা সবাই নীরবে চেয়ে অপেক্ষা করতে লাগলাম।[16] ডাক্তার প্রায় আর্তনাদের মত স্বরে বললেন, 'ধর্ষিতা মহিলা। অল্প বয়সী মেয়ে থেকে শুরু করে প্রৌঢ়া মহিলা, মা, নানী, দাদী - কেউ রেহাই পাননি। অনেক বুড়ী মহিলা বাড়ী থেকে পালাননি, ভেবেছেন তাঁদের কিছু হবে না। অল্প বয়সী মেয়েদের সরিয়ে দিয়ে নিজেরা থেকেছেন, তাঁদেরও ছেড়ে দেয়নি পাকিস্তানী পাষণ্ডরা। এক মহিলা রুগীর কাছে শুনেছিলাম তিনি নামাজ পড়ছিলেন। সেই অবস্থায় তাঁকে টেনে রেপ করা হয়। আরেক মহিলা কোরান শরীফ পড়ছিলেন, শয়তানরা কোরান শরীফ টান দিয়ে ফেলে তাঁকে রেপ করে।'

ডাক্তার থমথমে মুখে চুপ করে মাটির দিকে চেয়ে রইলেন। আমরা খানিকক্ষণ স্তম্ভিত, বাকহারা[17] হয়ে বসে থাকলাম।

খানিকক্ষণ পর ডাক্তার আপন মনেই বললেন, 'যদি আল্লার অস্তিত্ব থাকে, তবে এই শয়তানের চেলা পাকিস্তানীদের ধ্বংস অবধারিত। আর যদি এরা ধ্বংস না হয়, তাহলে আল্লার অস্তিত্ব সম্বন্ধে আমাকে নতুন করে চিন্তা-ভাবনা করতে হবে।'[18]

Friday,
2nd July, 1971

Last evening the doctor and his wife arrived from Rajshahi. He had driven the car himself. He had told me the day before yesterday in a trunk-call that they would leave Rajshahi in the morning. So we were expecting them by about three or four in the afternoon. We had all been very worried by his lateness. Khuku was particularly anxious. The doctor said the reason for the delay was that at many places on the way the Pak army had stopped and checked the car. Hearing that he was going to Rawalpindi to attend a meeting and seeing the letters about the meeting from Karachi, they let him through at each place. I was very keen to hear about Rajshahi yesterday from him, but they all looked so shattered from the stress of travelling for the whole day that I suppressed that desire and said, 'Rest tonight. We'll hear everything tomorrow.'

The doctor was busy all today with seeing the P.G. Hospital Director Dr Nurul Islam, with his plane ticket and with various other arrangements for the journey. In the evening he came and sat in our sitting room. Shanu – his wife – was with him.

The doctor said, 'We thought at first that there was nothing left in Dhaka: that everything had been smashed and burnt and annihilated. There was no way of getting news from anywhere. Just the news from Indian radio, the BBC, Radio Australia and Voice of America. So hearing all that news we were very depressed. It took a long time to get correct news of Dhaka.'

'When did Rajshahi fall?'

'Probably on the 13th or 14th of April. Early in the morning, the Pakistani troops entered the city along the edge of the river. The memory of that day is terrible. Maybe eighty per cent of the people fled, and the rest sat in their houses with the doors and windows fastened. Rajshahi town that day looked like a cremation-ground. Later I learnt that the Pak army had entered the town setting fire to everything on either side of the road. Many people died from their bullets. Within a few days, the Pak military had taken full control of Rajshahi town. We were all told to go back to work and keep their hospital running. Taking our lives in our hands, we began to go to and from the hospital.'

'Were there patients in the hospital?'

'For some time there were none. But after the hospital started running again the patients started to come. Mostly gunshot victims.'

'Gunshot victims?'

'Yes. For a long time no one brought any ordinary patients to the hospital: they brought patients who had been shot, or stabbed with bayonets, or whose arms and legs had been blown off. People also brought another kind of patient to the hospital, whom I shall never ever forget.'

The doctor was choked for words: we all watched and waited silently. In a voice that was almost like a groan he said: 'Women who had been raped. From young girls to middle-aged women, mothers, grandmothers – none were spared. Many older ladies did not flee from their houses, they thought that nothing would happen to them. They stayed by themselves, having moved the young girls away, but the Pakistani brutes did not spare them *either. I heard from one lady patient that she was at her prayers. Even in that position, she was pulled away and raped. Another woman was reading the Holy Koran: they snatched it from her and raped her.'*

The doctor remained silent, looking at the ground, his face grief-stricken. For a while we were stunned: we sat speechless.

A little later, the doctor murmured to himself: 'If Allah exists, then these Pakistani followers of the devil must surely be destroyed. And if they are not destroyed, then I shall have to think again about the existence of Allah.'

Notes

[1]The doctor, a family friend, is named elsewhere in the book as Dr A. K. Khan. The plural ending -রা is added to ডাক্তার to indicate that he and his wife both arrived (see Unit 17, p. 84).

[2]Contracted form of the perfect tense of the extended verb পৌঁছানো. The full form would be পৌঁছিয়েছেন.

[3]As Jahanara Immam's diary is written in contemporary, conversational middle-class Bengali, she uses lots of English words. So in this extract we have ড্রাইভ করা, ট্রাংককল, চেক করা, etc. (*to drive, trunk-call, to check*, etc.).

[4] হিসাব (or হিসেব) means *calculation, reckoning, counting*, etc. The phrase here means *reckoning on that* (i.e. *so*).

[5]This is an important idiomatic use of কথা, used for events or things that are assumed, arranged or expected. It follows the verbal noun in the possessive case, and the person or thing that is expected goes into the possessive case, though in colloquial speech the possessive ending is sometimes dropped. There is zero verb if the sentence refers to the future:

ওর বিকেলে আসার কথা ।	*He's expected this afternoon.*
সামনের বছরে বইটার বেরনোর কথা ।	*The book should come out next year.*

If an expectation in the past is involved, ছিল is added:

গত বছরে বাংলাদেশে যাবার কথা ছিল, কিন্তু টাকা পাইনি ।	*(I) was supposed to be going to Bangladesh last year, but (I) didn't get the money.*

This use of কথা may be related to the verbal expression কথা দেওয়া, *to promise/give one's word*.

[6]An idiomatic and emphatic use of যা. Cf. যা গরম ! at the end of the Conversation in Unit 19 (p. 106). 'Khuku' is an affectionate form of

'Khuki', which means *young girl* and is often used as a name for the youngest daughter in a family.

[7] যা . . . তাতে – a relative/correlative construction: . . . *the shattered appearance which they all had, because of that* . . . The instrumental ending on তা gives it a causal meaning.

[8] মিসমার , a word of Persian origin meaning *utter destruction*.

[9] তা is just short for তাই, *so, therefore*; and সে সব খবর , *all that news*, would also perhaps more normally be written with the emphatic ই: সেই সব খবর.

[10] ফল is the English word *fall*. Nothing to do with fruit!

[11] Percentages can be expressed colloquially in Bengali by using the old 'anna' system. 16 annas = 1 rupee, so 12 annas = 75 per cent, 8 annas = 50 per cent, etc. (শতকরা পঁচাত্তর, শতকরা পঞ্চাশ). See the **Review of Part Two**, p. 194).

[12] ক'দিনের মধ্যেই (within a few days). The apostrophe has been used because ক'দিন is short for কয়দিন or কয়েকদিন – but Bengali writers never use apostrophes systematically, and there is really no need for them. In the previous sentence দু'পাশে is short for দুইপাশে , and earlier in the text you may have noticed ধ'রে . Participles are sometimes distinguished in this way from present tense forms. Thus you will see ক'রে (kôre – *having done*) to distinguish it from করে (kɔre – *he/she does*) – probably because of a residual feeling that the colloquial participle is a shortened form of the literary form করিয়া (see Unit 33). But this practice too has never been systematic and is falling into disuse.

[13] জয়েন করা (English *to join*) is commonly used in the sense of taking up a job, new post, etc.

[14] Notice the adjectival use of verbal nouns: Lit. *bullet-struck, bayonet-spiked, arms-and-legs-blown-off patients.*

[15] An idiomatic construction with ব্যথা (pain), suggesting permanency of pain, something that one can never forget.

[16] লাগা with the infinitive can mean *begin*, or it can mean *continued to*, *went on* . . . . The second meaning applies here.

[17] বাক means *speech*, and the verb হারা *(to lose)* is here used as an ending equivalent to English *-less*.

[18] Notice the conditional constructions using যদি . . . তবে/তাহলে (see Unit, 25 p. 185), with the negative coming before the verb in the যদি clause: আর যদি এরা ধ্বংস না হয় . . . The main clause in the sentence contains an obligation construction (see Unit 19, p. 109).

Note that in শ্মশান *(cremation ground)* the ম is silent ('ʃɔʃan'). The only other new conjunct is the predictable 'triple' ন + ট + র = ন্ট্র.

———— Exercise ————

See if you can find examples in the passage earlier in this unit of the following points of Bengali grammar, spelling and punctuation.

Paragraph 1
1   The emphatic particle ই added to the time of day.
2   An adjective turned into an adverb by the addition of করে.
3   A postposition that does not require the noun that it follows to be in the possessive case.
4   An extended verb participle meaning *having caused to stop.*
5   An impersonal construction expressing desire.

Paragraph 2
6   A word in which স is pronounced like an English 's', not 'sh'.
7   A postposition used elliptically: i.e. the noun or pronoun to which it refers has been left out.

Paragraph 3
8   The verbal noun in its alternative possessive form using -ব- (see Unit 24, p. 172).
9   The use of ভ to represent the English letter 'v'.
10 কোন – but does it mean *which* or *any*, and how is it pronounced? (see Unit 23, p. 158).

Paragraph 5
11 A compound verb meaning *to enter (suddenly).*
12 An example of an extended verb used in the past continuous tense.
13 An infinitive used to express *while doing something.*
14 A compound verb where both members of the compound come from the same verb – i.e. the verb is compounded with itself.
15 A passive construction.

Paragraph 9
16 An English word that has become 'naturalised' in Bengali: i.e. its sounds have changed to fit the phonology of the language.
17 The negative of the perfect tense.

Paragraph 10
18 A word with a silent ব-ফলা.
19 The particle ও used to mean *too, as well.*
20 The 'historic present': the present tense used to narrate past events.

32

— SHAMSUR RAHMAN —

By common consent, Shamsur Rahman is the leading poet of present-day Bangladesh, and arguably the finest poet writing in Bengali today. He has published more than twenty books of poems, which while being distinctively personal are also a public record of the tribulations and aspirations of Bangladesh. Like most Bangladeshi poets, he takes his public role seriously. Poetry is Bangladesh's most important art form, and poets are at the forefront of social and political debate. Shamsur Rahman has always stood for rationalism and secularism; his poetry makes full use of Bengal's varied poetic traditions, but is also responsive to European and Indian literature. He has, for example, written superb poems on classic Western subjects: Telemarchus, Samson, the Renaissance, etc. His verse forms are fluid and varied, and he comes up with striking and unexpected combinations of images.

Most of his poems are demanding for those still in the early stages of learning Bengali. The two poems given below are relatively simple. The reduplicating structure of the first poem (not typical of Shamsur's work, though other examples occur) makes it highly suitable for public recitation; and all Bengali audiences would be stirred by its theme: freedom.

 স্বাধীনতা তুমি

স্বাধীনতা তুমি
রবিঠাকুরের অজর কবিতা, অবিনাশী গান ।[1]

স্বাধীনতা তুমি
কাজী নজরুল, ঝাঁকড়া চুলের বাবরি দোলানো
মহান পুরুষ, সৃষ্টিসুখের উল্লাসে কাঁপা।[2]
স্বাধীনতা তুমি
শহীদ মিনারে অমর একুশে ফেব্রুয়ারির উজ্জ্বল সভা।[3]
স্বাধীনতা তুমি
পতাকা-শোভিত স্লোগান-মুখর ঝাঁঝালো মিছিল।
স্বাধীনতা তুমি
ফসলের মাঠে কৃষকের হাসি।
স্বাধীনতা তুমি
রোদেলা দুপুরে মধ্যপুকুরে গ্রাম্য মেয়ের অবাধ সাঁতার।
স্বাধীনতা তুমি
মজুর যুবার রোদে ঝলসিত দক্ষ বাহুর গ্রন্থিল পেশী।
স্বাধীনতা তুমি
অন্ধকারের খাঁ খাঁ সীমান্তে মুক্তিসেনার চোখের ঝিলিক।[4]
স্বাধীনতা তুমি
বটের ছায়ায় তরুণ মেধাবী শিক্ষার্থীর
শাণিত-কথার ঝলসানি-লাগা সতেজ ভাষণ।
স্বাধীনতা তুমি
চা-খানায় আর মাঠে-ময়দানে ঝোড়ো সংলাপ।[5]
স্বাধীনতা তুমি
কালবোশেখীর[6] দিগন্ত জোড়া মত্ত ঝাপটা।
স্বাধীনতা তুমি
শ্রাবণে অকূল মেঘনার বুক।[7]
স্বাধীনতা তুমি
পিতার কোমল জায়নামাজের উদার জমিন।[8]
স্বাধীনতা তুমি
উঠানে ছড়ানো মায়ের শুভ্র শাড়ির কাঁপন।[9]
স্বাধীনতা তুমি
বোনের হাতের নম্র পাতায় মেহেদীর রঙ।
স্বাধীনতা তুমি
বন্ধুর হাতে তারার মতন জ্বলজ্বলে এক রাঙা পোস্টার।

স্বাধীনতা তুমি
গৃহিণীর ঘন খোলা কালো চুল,
হাওয়ায় হাওয়ায় বুনো উদ্দাম ।[10]
স্বাধীনতা তুমি
খোকার গায়ের রঙিন কোর্তা,
খুকির অমন তুলতুলে গালে[11] রৌদ্রের খেলা ।[12]
স্বাধীনতা তুমি
বাগানে ঘর, কোকিলের গান,[13]
বয়েসী বটের ঝিলিমিলি পাতা,
যেমন ইচ্ছে লেখার আমার কবিতার খাতা ।

Freedom

Freedom
You are Rabi Thakur's ageless poems, indestructible songs.
Freedom
You are Kazi Nazrul, that great man with long shaggy hair swinging,
Trembling with pleasure at the joy of creation.
Freedom
You are the radiant meeting on immortal February 21st at the Shahid
    Minar.
Freedom
You are fiery meetings noisy with slogans and brilliant with banners.
Freedom
You are a farmer's smile in the harvest-fields.
Freedom
You are a village girl's unconstrained swimming out into a pond in the
    sunny noon.
Freedom
You are the knotty muscles of a young labourer's skilled arms shining in the
    sunshine.
Freedom
You are the glitter of a freedom fighter's eyes on the edge of the empty
    darkness.
Freedom
You are a bright young pupil in the shade of a banyan tree,
The lively speaking of sharp dazzling words.
Freedom

You are stormy conversation in tea-shops or on parks or Maidans.
Freedom
You are the mad slap of a kāl-baiśākhī *storm from horizon to horizon.*
Freedom
You are the breast of the shoreless Meghna in the month of Śrābaṇ
Freedom
You are my father's soft prayer-mat's welcoming realm.
Freedom
You are the fluttering of my mother's white saris spread out in the yard.
Freedom
You are the colour of henna on my sister's soft palms.
Freedom
You are a coloured poster shining like a star in the hand of a friend.
Freedom
You are a housewife's thick unbound black hair,
Blown about wildly in the wind.
Freedom
You are Khoka's coloured shirt,
You are the play of sunlight
On Khuki's such soft cheeks.
Freedom
You are a garden room, the koel-*bird's song,*
The old banyan tree's gleaming leaves,
My book of poems written as I please.

The second poem is touchingly personal and domestic: *Some Lines for a Cat.*

বেড়ালের জন্য কিছু পঙ্‌ক্তি

একটি বেড়াল ছিল ক'বছর আমার বাসায়
কুড়িয়ে আদর,[14] বিশেষত আমার কনিষ্ঠ কন্যা
ওর প্রতি ছিল বেশি মনোযোগী, নিয়মিত ওকে
দেখাশোনা করা, ওর প্রতীক্ষায় থাকা প্রতিদিন,
নাওয়ানো, ওর জন্যে নিজের ভাগের মাছ
তুলে রাখা ছিল তার নিত্যকার কাজ । একদিন
বলা-কওয়া[15] নেই, সে বেড়াল কোথায় উধাও হলো,
কিছুতে গেল না জানা,[16] খোঁজাখুঁজি হলো সার,[17] আর

আমার কনিষ্ঠ কন্যা ভীষণ খারাপ করে মন,
খেল না দুদিন কিছু, চুপচাপ নিলো সে বিছানা,
উপরন্তু বলেনি আমার সঙ্গে কথা অভিমানে,[18]
যেন বেড়ালের এই অন্তর্ধান আমারই কসুর !

কী করে বোঝাই তাকে ? 'আচ্ছা এবার তাহলে আসি[19]
আবার কখনো হবে দেখা' বলে দিব্যি[20] কোনো কোনো
মানুষও তো এভাবেই চলে যায় বিপুল শূন্যতা
দিয়ে উপহার,[21] তার সঙ্গে দেখা হয় না কখনো ।

Some Lines for a Cat

We had a cat for a few years in our house,
Always seeking attention, my youngest daughter especially
Was devoted to it, regularly
Looking after it, looking out for it every day,
Washing it, keeping her own share
Of fish for it was her daily task. One day
Without so much as a word, that cat vanished somewhere,
Not a trace of her, we searched everywhere,
And my little daughter was very downcast,
She didn't eat for two days, lay on her bed without talking,
She wouldn't even talk to me,
As if the disappearance of the cat were my fault!

How to explain to her? It was just like someone saying,
'OK, I'm off now, see you again sometime'
And then going off, never to be seen again,
Leaving as a present a great emptiness.

Notes

We are dealing now with the language of poetry: words can be combined more daringly than in prose, and literal meanings become harder to pin down. The translations above are therefore freer than the translations that have been given in previous chapters. You may need to use the **Glossary** extensively to arrive at a literal understanding of the lines.

[1]'Tagore' is an anglicised version of ঠাকুর. 'Rabi' is an affectionate abbreviation of 'Rabindranath'.

[2]The great 'rebel poet' Kazi Nazrul Islam (1899–1976) was famous for the flamboyance of his hair, clothes and personality. সৃষ্টিসুখের উল্লাসে is the title of a poem by Nazrul. Compound words such as সৃষ্টিসুখ *(creation-joy)* can be formed very easily in Bengali poetry.

[3]February 21st, শহীদ দিবস or 'Martyrs Day', is a very important date in the Bangladeshi calendar. There are ceremonies at the Shahid Minar ('Martyrs' Memorial') in Dhaka, and elsewhere in the country, to commemorate those who were shot dead for protesting against the Pakistan government's anti-Bengali language policy.

[4] খাঁ খাঁ – an expression of the kind that was discussed in Unit 30. It conveys desolation, loneliness, emptiness and also heat: the heat of the desert.

[5] খানা can be a definite article (see Unit 17, p. 82), but it can also mean *place*. চা-খানা is a place where you can buy and drink tea. A ময়দান is a park-like area of open grass in a town, where people can walk, play games or hold public meetings, as on the famous Calcutta Maidan.

[6] কালবোশেখী (কালবৈশাখী): see Unit 25, p. 190.

[7]*Śrābaṇ* is a monsoon month (July–August – see p. 195). The Meghna is one of the great rivers of Bangladesh.

[8] উদার– a complex adjective here conveying warm-heartedness, generosity, welcome, intimacy. জমিন is a variant of জমি *(land, space)*. The two words together convey the whole world of prayer extending beyond the prayer-mat, all the way to the K'aba Mosque in Mecca.

[9]Older Bengali women, both Hindu and Muslim, tend to wear white saris, with a coloured border if they are not widows. Widows traditionally dress completely in white – in what is technically a white dhoti not a sari.

[10]A woman's hair allowed to hang loose after bathing, blowing in the wind, is frequently a symbol of freedom and erotic allure in Bengali poetry.

[11]'Khoka' means *little boy*, just as 'Khuki' means *little girl* (see Note 6, p. 239), and is often used at a pet name for the youngest son in a family.

[12]Modern poets like Shamsur will freely mix literary with colloquial words, Persian words with Sanskrit words. You already know the word রোদ *(sunshine)*; রৌদ্র is the Sanskrit form of it. A distinction can be made between *tatsama* words: words that have been lifted direct into Bengali from Sanskrit; and *tatbhava* words: words that are derived from Sanskrit but have been modified or simplified over time. Bengali writers often have a choice between the two: Shamsur uses রোদ earlier in the poem (1.15) with a slight difference of nuance. The Sanskrit form here is grander and more intense than the colloquial.

[13] কোকিল is often translated as *cuckoo*. But the *koel*-bird, with its passionate call rising up the scale, is quite different from the European cuckoo, though it belongs to the same family.

[14] The language of the second poem is spontaneous, natural and colloquial, and the grammar is often quite loose. কুড়িয়ে আদর (Lit. *having picked up love*) suggests that the cat was always seeking affection.

[15] The linking of these two verbs meaning *to speak* (the second being dialectal, archaic or poetic in flavour) adds an informal, casual tone, and humorously personifies the cat.

[16] The word order has been switched round, and the tense is past, but this is none other than the verbal noun + যাওয়া construction: *Not at all could (anything) be known.* See Unit 22, p. 147.

[17] The reduplicated form of the verb খোঁজা *to search*, *look for* suggests searching high and low. সার means *essence* – searching became the essence, the be-all and end-all of everything.

[18] A classic use here of the word অভিমান for a feeling of being hurt or let down by someone you love: *Moreover she did not speak to me because of her hurt feelings.* Notice the free word order: a more normal 'prose' word order would be: অভিমানে আমার সঙ্গে কথা বলেনি.

[19] আসি is the first person imperative (*Let me . . ., May I . . .*); and remember, it is normal to speak of *coming* (again) when one takes one's leave of a person in Bengal (see Unit 21, p. 133).

[20] দিব্য (emphatic form দিবি্য) literally means *heavenly*, but is used here as a kind of particle, conveying an easy, pleasing, relaxed, casual manner of departure.

[21] Inverted word-order again: উপহার দিয়ে is the normal sequence.

Exercise

You have now been introduced to most of the common Bengali conjunct characters. Any unfamiliar ones (such as জ্ব and শ্ল in the first poem in this unit) should be readily recognisable. By way of revision and consolidation, however, see if you can complete the 'equations' for the following conjuncts, all of which occur in the poems in Unit 32. When pronouncing conjuncts, remember:

(a) Double consonants – ল্ল , ন্ন , etc. – should be properly double in sound.

(b) ব-ফলা – attached to a letter is generally silent, but lengthens the consonant to which it is attached (except where it occurs at the

beginning of a word). The exception to this rule is স্ব which can be pronounced 'mb', in English words such as nombôr, and in words derived from Sanskrit -mb- rather than -mv-. However, সম্বন্ধে (*about, concerning*) is often pronounced 'sommondhe'.

(c) য-ফলা – J – also lengthens the sound to which it is attached (except at the beginning of a word), and often changes a following **a** to **æ**. Occasionally it is followed by **e** (pronounced **æ**) or **o** (un-affected). An exception to the normal effect of য-ফলা is the conjunct হ + য = হ্য in the middle of a word, as in অসহ্য *(unbear-able)*, which is pronounced 'osôjjô'.

(d) শ and স in some conjuncts are pronounced 's' not 'sh' (see pp. 269–270).

১	স্ব =	১৪	স্ম =
২	ষ্ট =	১৫	জ্ব =
৩	ব্র =	১৬	ষ্ট =
৪	জ্জ্ব =	১৭	দ্দ =
৫	শ্ল =	১৮	র্ত =
৬	হ্ণ =	১৯	দ্র =
৭	গ্র =	২০	চ্ছ =
৮	ষ্ক =	২১	ষ্ঠ =
৯	ত্ত =	২২	ত্য =
১০	দ্ধ =	২৩	ন্তু * =
১১	ক্রু =	২৪	ঙ্ক =
১২	র্থ =	২৫	র্ধ =
১৩	ত্ত =		

*Be careful: there is a vowel here, as well as two consonants.

33

___ THE COMING OF ___
THE MONSOON

All the Bengali you have encountered so far has been in the so-called *calit bhāṣā* (চলিত ভাষা) or colloquial language. This is the normal form of Bengali both in speech and writing today. But in the nineteenth century and early part of the twentieth century, a more formal, literary form of Bengali, the *sādhu bhāṣā* (সাধু ভাষা) was used when writing Bengali. This was characterised not only by a more elaborate, Sanskritic vocabulary, but by longer verb endings and pronouns. Some of these forms – more archaic than the colloquial forms – survive in Bengali rural dialects. Thus the *sādhu bhāṣā* form for আমি খাচ্ছি is - আমি খাইতেছি, which you will frequently hear in Bangladesh (pronounced 'khaitesi'). The full range of the *sādhu bhāṣā* lies beyond the scope of this book; but to give you a taste of it, here is the end of one of Rabindranath Tagore's short stories of the 1890s. Tagore was a pioneer in writing in *calit bhāṣā*, and switched to using it in his later prose fiction; but his stories of the 1890s are all written in *sādhu bhāṣā*.

The passage below is taken from his story অতিথি *(Guest –* pronounced 'ôtithi' not 'ɔtithi': see p. 275). It's about a handsome young Brahmin boy, Tarapada, who has left his family to lead a roving life working for troupes of gymnasts, players, singers and the like. Matilal Babu and his family befriend him, and he lives with them for some time. Matilal arranges for him to have English lessons, and he and his wife begin to see him as a prospective bridegroom for their only daughter. But just before the wedding, Tarapada disappears, to return to the unfettered life that suits him best. The last three paragraphs of the story are written in Tagore's grandest manner, and are wonderfully evocative of East Bengal's riverine landscape. The translation is taken from my book *Selected Short Stories* of Tagore (Penguin, rev. 1994).

শ্রাবণ মাসে বিবাহের[1] শুভদিন স্থির করিয়া[2] মতিবাবু তারাপদর মা ও ভাইদের আনিতে পাঠাইলেন,[3] তারাপদকে তাহা জানিতে দিলেন না । কলিকাতার মুক্তারকে গড়ের বাদ্য বায়না দিতে[4] আদেশ করিলেন এবং জিনিসপত্রের ফর্দ পাঠাইয়া[5] দিলেন ।

আকাশে নববর্ষার মেঘ উঠিল । গ্রামের নদী এতদিন শুষ্কপ্রায়[6] হইয়াছিল, মাঝে মাঝে কেবল এক-একটা ডোবায় জল বাধিয়া থাকিত ; ছোটো ছোটো নৌকা সেই পঙ্কিল জলে ডোবানো ছিল এবং শুষ্ক নদীপথে গোরুর গাড়ি-চলাচলের সুগভীর[7] চক্রচিহ্ন ক্ষোদিত হইতেছিল[8] - এমন সময় একদিন পিতৃগৃহ-প্রত্যাগত পার্বতীর মতো,[9] কোথা হইতে[10] দ্রুতগামিনী[11] জলধারা কলহাস্য-সহকারে[12] গ্রামের শূন্যবক্ষে আসিয়া সমাগত হইল - উলঙ্গ বালকবালিকারা তীরে আসিয়া উচ্চৈঃস্বরে নৃত্য করিতে[13] লাগিল, অতৃপ্ত আনন্দে বারম্বার জলে ঝাঁপ দিয়া দিয়া[14] নদীকে যেন আলিঙ্গন করিয়া ধরিতে লাগিল, কুটিরবাসিনীরা তাহাদের পরিচিত প্রিয়সঙ্গিনীকে দেখিবার জন্য বাহির হইয়া আসিল[15] - শুষ্ক নির্জীব গ্রামের মধ্যে কোথা হইতে এক প্রবল বিপুল প্রাণহিল্লোল[16] আসিয়া প্রবেশ করিল । দেশবিদেশ হইতে বোঝাই হইয়া[17] ছোটো বড়ো আয়তনের নৌকা আসিতে লাগিল - বাজারের ঘাট সন্ধ্যাবেলায় বিদেশী মাঝির সঙ্গীতে ধ্বনিত হইয়া উঠিল । দুই তীরের গ্রামগুলি সম্বৎসর[18] আপনার[19] নিভৃত কোণে আপনার ক্ষুদ্র ঘরকন্না লইয়া একাকিনী দিনযাপন করিতে থাকে, বর্ষার সময় বাহিরের বৃহৎ পৃথিবী বিচিত্র পণ্যোপহার লইয়া[20] গৈরিকবর্ণ জলরথে চড়িয়া এই গ্রামকন্যাকাগুলির তত্ত্ব লইতে আসে ; তখন জগতের সঙ্গে আত্মীয়তাগর্বে কিছুদিনের জন্য তাহাদের ক্ষুদ্রতা ঘুচিয়া যায়, সমস্তই সচল সজাগ সজীব হইয়া উঠে এবং মৌন নিস্তব্ধ দেশের মধ্যে সুদূর রাজ্যের কলালাপধ্বনি আসিয়া চারি দিকের আকাশকে আন্দোলিত করিয়া তুলে ।[21]

এই সময়ে কুড়লকাটায় নাগবাবুদের এলাকায় বিখ্যাত রথযাত্রার মেলা হইবে।[21] জ্যোৎস্না-সন্ধ্যায় তারাপদ ঘাটে গিয়া দেখিল, কোনো নৌকা নাগরদোলা, কোনো নৌকা যাত্রার দল, কোনো নৌকা পণ্যদ্রব্য লইয়া প্রবল নবীন স্রোতের মুখে দ্রুতবেগে মেলা-অভিমুখে[22] চলিয়াছে ; কলিকাতার কনসর্টের দল বিপুলশব্দে দ্রুততালের বাজনা জুড়িয়া দিয়াছে, যাত্রার দল বেহালার সঙ্গে গান গাহিতেছে এবং সমের কাছে হাহাহাঃ শব্দে চিৎকার উঠিতেছে, পশ্চিমদেশী নৌকার দাঁড়ীমাল্লাগুলো কেবলমাত্র মাদল এবং করতাল লইয়া উন্মত্ত উৎসাহে বিনা সংগীতে খচমচ শব্দে আকাশ বিদীর্ণ করিতেছে - উদ্দীপনার সীমা নাই। দেখিতে দেখিতে[23] পূর্বদিগন্ত হইতে ঘন মেঘরাশি প্রকাণ্ড কালো পাল তুলিয়া দিয়া আকাশের মাঝখানে উঠিয়া পড়িল, চাঁদ আচ্ছন্ন হইল - পুবে-বাতাস[24] বেগে বহিতে[25] লাগিল, মেঘের পশ্চাতে মেঘ ছুটিয়া চলিল, নদীর জল খল খল হাস্যে স্ফীত হইয়া উঠিতে লাগিল - নদীতীরবর্তী আন্দোলিত বনশ্রেণীর মধ্যে অন্ধকার পুঞ্জীভূত হইয়া উঠিল, ভেক ডাকিতে আরম্ভ করিল, ঝিল্লিধ্বনি যেন[26] করাত দিয়া অন্ধকারকে চিরিতে লাগিল। তারাপদের সম্মুখে আজ যেন সমস্ত জগতের রথযাত্রা - চাকা ঘুরিয়াছে, ধ্বজা উড়িতেছে, পৃথিবী কাঁপিতেছে, মেঘ উড়িয়াছে, বাতাস ছুটিয়াছে, নদী বহিয়াছে, নৌকা চলিয়াছে, গান উঠিয়াছে ; দেখিতে দেখিতে গুরু গুরু শব্দে মেঘ ডাকিয়া উঠিল, বিদ্যুৎ আকাশকে কাটিয়া কাটিয়া ঝলসিয়া উঠিল, সুদূর অন্ধকার হইতে একটা মুষলধারাবর্ষী বৃষ্টির গন্ধ আসিতে লাগিল। কেবল নদীর এক তীরে এক পার্শ্বে কাঁঠালিয়া গ্রাম আপন[27] কুটিরদ্বার বন্ধ করিয়া দীপ নিবাইয়া দিয়া নিঃশব্দে[28] ঘুমাইতে লাগিল।

পরদিন তারাপদর মাতা ও ভ্রাতাগণ কাঁঠালিয়ায় আসিয়া অবতরণ করিলেন, পরদিন কলিকাতা হইতে বিবিধসামগ্রীপূর্ণ তিনখানা বড়ো নৌকা আসিয়া কাঁঠালিয়ার জমিদারি কাছারির ঘাটে লাগিল এবং পরদিন অতি প্রাতে সোনামণি কাগজে কিঞ্চিৎ আমসত্ত্ব এবং পাতার ঠোঙ্গায় কিঞ্চিৎ আচার লইয়া ভয়ে ভয়ে তারাপদর পাঠগৃহদ্বারে আসিয়া নিঃশব্দে দাঁড়াইল - কিন্তু পরদিন তারাপদকে দেখা গেল না। স্নেহ-প্রেম-বন্ধুত্বের ষড়যন্ত্রবন্ধন তাহাকে চারি দিক হইতে সম্পূর্ণরূপে[29] ঘিরিবার পূর্বেই[30] সমস্ত গ্রামের হৃদয়খানি[31] চুরি করিয়া একদা বর্ষার মেঘান্ধকার রাত্রে এই ব্রাহ্মণবালক আসক্তিবিহীন উদাসীন জননী বিশ্বপৃথিবীর নিকট চলিয়া গিয়াছে।[32]

Matilal Babu fixed the wedding for the month of Śrābaṇ *and sent word to Tarapada's mother and brothers; but he did not inform Tarapada himself. He told his* moktār *in Calcutta to hire a trumpet-and-drum band, and he ordered everything else that would be needed for the wedding.*

*Early monsoon clouds formed in the sky. The village-river had been dried up for weeks; there was water onl*ỵ *in holes here and there; small boats lay stuck in these pools of muddy water, and the dry river-bed was rutted with bullock-cart tracks. But now, like Parvati returning to her parents' home, gurgling waters returned to the empty arms of the village: naked children danced and shouted on the river-bank, jumped into the water with voracious joy as if trying to embrace the river; the villagers gazed at the river like a dear friend; a huge wave of life and delight rolled through the parched village. There were boats big and small with cargoes from far and wide; in the evenings the* ghāṭ *resounded with the songs of foreign boatmen. The villages along the river had spent the summer confined to their own small worlds: now, with the rains, the vast outside world had come in its earth-coloured watery chariot, carrying wondrous gifts to the villages, as if on a visit to its daughters. Rustic smallness was temporarily subsumed by pride of contact with the world; everything became more active; the bustle of distant cities came to this sleepy region, and the whole sky rang.*

Meanwhile at Kurulkata, on the Nag family estate, a famous chariot-festival was due to be held. One moonlit evening Tarapada went to the ghāṭ *and saw, on the swift flood-tide, boats with merry-go-rounds and* yātrā-*troupes; and cargo-boats rapidly making for the fair. An orchestra from Calcutta was practising loudly as it passed; the* yātrā- *troupe was singing to violin accompaniment, shouting out the beats; boatmen from lands to the west split the sky with cymbals and thudding drums. Such excitement! Then clouds from the east covered the moon with their huge black sails; an east wind blew sharply; cloud after cloud rolled by; the river gushed and swelled; darkness thickened in the swaying riverside trees; frogs croaked; crickets rasped like wood-saws. To Tarapada the whole world seemed like a chariot-festival: wheels turning, flags flying, earth trembling, clouds swirling, wind rushing, river flowing, boats sailing, songs rising! There were rumbles of thunder, and slashes of lightning in the sky: the smell of torrential rain approached from the dark distance. But Kathaliya village next to the river ignored all this: she shut her doors, turned out her lamps and went to sleep.*

The following morning Tarapada's mother and brothers arrived at Kathaliya; and that same morning three large boats from Calcutta, laden with things for the wedding, moored at the zamindar's ghāṭ; *and very early, that same morning, Sonamani brought some mango-juice preserve in paper and some pickle wrapped in a leaf, and timidly stood outside Tarapada's room – but Tarapada was not to be seen. In a cloudy monsoon night, before love and emotional ties could encircle him completely, this Brahmin boy, thief of all hearts in the village, had returned to the unconstraining, unemotional arms of his mother Earth.*

Notes

Most of the notes below simply refer you to *calit bhāṣā* equivalents to various words, verb forms, pronouns etc.

[1] বিবাহ is more formal than বিয়ে (*marriage*) so it tends to be used in *sādhu bhāṣā* writing.

[2] Equivalent to ঠিক করে (*having fixed*) in *calit bhāṣā*.

[3] Equivalent to আনতে পাঠালেন.

[4] Notice that not all verb forms are different in *sādhu bhāṣā*. The infinitive of দেওয়া is the same in both forms of Bengali.

[5] Equivalent to পাঠিয়ে – past participle of the extended verb পাঠানো, here combined with দেওয়া, as often happens (see Unit 23, p. 159).

[6] প্রায় used as an ending attached to an adjective means *nearly*.

[7] The prefix সু attached to an adjective intensifies the meaning: so সুগভীর means *very deep*.

[8] Equivalent to হচ্ছিল – past continuous tense.

[9] The kind of adjectival phrase, influenced by Sanskrit, that one would only find in *śādhu bhāṣā*: Lit. *like paternal-home-returned-Parvati*. No wonder nineteenth century German scholars took so readily to Sanskrit!

[10] Equivalent to the postposition থেকে in *calit bhāṣā*.

[11] *swiftly moving*: another Sanskrit compound. Notice that দ + র + উ = দ্রু.

[12] সহকারে (*with*) another *sādhu bhāṣā* word. Notice that it does not take the possessive case, unlike the *calit bhāṣā* সঙ্গে/সাথে.

[13] Equivalent to নাচতে.

[14] Equivalent to ঝাঁপ দিয়ে দিয়ে : the repetition of the past participle gives it a more 'continuous' meaning: *jumping into the water*.

[15] Equivalent to দেখবার জন্য বাইর হয়ে এল. Notice that where the *calit bhāṣā* has two vowels together – বাইর – the *sādhu bhāṣā* often has হ between them – বাহির.

[16] This kind of compound is as characteristic of a poetic style of writing as of *sādhu bhāṣā* as such: *a huge life-wave*.

[17] Equivalent to দেশবিদেশ থেকে বোঝাই হয়ে.

[18] *all year* – সারা বছর in *calit bhāṣā*. Notice the (now archaic) way of spelling the sound ch.

[19] আপনার can mean *one's own*, as here. The basic meaning of the root word আপন is *own*, not *your*.

²⁰ লওয়া is used instead of নেওয়া in *sādhu bhāṣā*, so লইয়া is equivalent to নিয়ে. পণ্যোপহার is a compound made up of পণ্য *(merchandise)* and উপহার *(gift)*. In Sanskrit, words change when they are joined together in compounds according to *sandhi* rules: ô + u = o, so pôṇyô + upôhar = pôṇyopôhar. When Sanskrit compounds occur in Bengali, *sandhi* rules generally apply, though speakers are not necessarily consciously aware of them.

²¹Note that Tagore writes তুলে and উঠে instead of তোলে and ওঠে for the third person familiar of the present tense.

²²A lengthy postposition typical of *sādhu bhāṣā*: the phrase is equivalent to *calit bhāṣā* মেলার দিকে চলেছে.

²³Equivalent to দেখতে দেখতে – an idiom meaning *immediately*.

²⁴*East wind*: notice that in this extract the *calit bhāṣā* form পুব is used as well as the *sādhu bhāṣā* form পূর্ব. A writer like Tagore can get away with mixing *sādhu bhāṣā* with *calit bhāṣā* sometimes.

²⁵Equivalent to বইতে. Even in *calit bhāṣā*, the verb বওয়া *(to blow, flow)* like চাওয়া *(to want, ask)* inserts an ই into many of its forms (see Unit 25, p. 186, and the **Verb tables** on p. 202).

²⁶Remember the use of যেন as a particle giving a sense of *seeming* (see Note 14, p. 218).

²⁷*own* – see Note 19 above.

²⁸Here we have (as often in Sanskritised Bengali) a word containing বিসর্গ (ঃ – see **Review of Part One**, p. 44). All it does here is lengthen the sound of the consonant that follows it: there is no aspiration. So নিঃশব্দ is pronounced 'niʃʃɔbdô'. In colloquial Bengali, the only common words containing বিসর্গ are দুঃখ *(sorrow)*, pronounced 'dukkhô' and বাঃ (see p. 81), pronounced with vigorous final aspiration.

²⁹ রূপে (rūpe) is often equivalent to রকমে or ভাবে in *calit bhāṣā*. Notice that র + ঊ = রূ.

³⁰Equivalent to আগে in *calit bhāṣā*.

³¹হৃদয় *(heart)* is commonly pronounced 'ridɔy' rather than the more correct 'hrɔdɔy'; hidɔy is also heard. Remember that in good typefaces হৃ appears as হৃ and হু appears as হু. Special consonant + vowel combinations as well as all the consonant conjuncts are given in the **Review of Part Three**, pp. 265–270.

³²Equivalent to বিশ্বপৃথিবীর কাছে চলে গেছে.

The more literary the Bengali, the more conjuncts occur!

ষ + ক = ষ্ক

হ + ন = হ্ন (pron. 'nn' – so চিহ্ন – *sign* – is pronounced 'cinnô')

ব + ধ = ব্ধ

ধ + ব = ধ্ব

——————— **Exercise** ———————

The extract in this unit introduced you to a number of *sādhu bhāṣā* verb-forms and pronouns. See if you can predict correct *sādhu bhāṣā* forms from the hints given below. They are not really very difficult, if your grasp of the *calit bhāṣā* forms are secure. A list of *sādhu bhāṣā* forms is given in the **Review of Part Three** (p. 270).

calit bhāṣā	*sādhu bhāṣā*
তার	তাহার
তাকে	১ _____
এ	ইহা
একে	২ _____
ও	উহা
ওর	৩ _____
ওদের	উহাদের
এদের	৪ _____
আমি বাঙালী নই	আমি বাঙালী নহি
সে বাঙালী নয়	৫ সে বাঙালী _____
আমি খেলাম	আমি খাইলাম
তিনি খেলেন	৬ তিনি _____
তুমি যাবে ?	তুমি যাইবে?
উনি যাবেন ?	৭ উনি _____ ?
আমি বুঝতে পারছিনা	আমি বুঝিতে পারিতেছিনা
তুমি বুঝতে পারছ ?	৮ তুমি _____ ?
হাত দিয়ে	হাত দিয়া
তারা হাত দিয়েছে	৯ _____ হাত _____

আমি ওকে দেখিয়েছি
আপনি একে দেখিয়েছেন ?

তাঁরা শুনেছিলেন
এঁরা বলেছিলেন

আমি তা করিনি
তিনিও করেননি

কাজ করলে শিখবে
চিঠি লিখলে সে আসবে

আমার চেয়ে বড়
ওর চেয়ে ছোট

শোনা যায়না
বোঝা যায়না

লেখার পরে
শেখার আগে

আমি উহাকে দেখাইয়াছি
১০ আপনি _____ ?

তাঁহারা শুনিয়াছিলেন
১১ _____

আমি তাহা করি নাই
১২ তিনিও _____

কাজ করিলে শিখিবে
১৩ চিঠি _____ সে _____

আমার চাইতে বড়
১৪ _____ ছোট

শুনা* যায় না
১৫ _____ যায় না

লিখার* পরে
১৬ _____ আগে

---

*These forms of the verbal noun for **o/u** and **e/i** verbs are used in dictionaries. See pp. 270–271 and the Notes at the beginning of the **Glossary** on p. 290. Verbal nouns for the other verb types are the same as for *calit bhāṣā*.

34

— JIBANANANDA DAS —

Finally, two poems by the finest of the modern Bengali poets who set out, in the 1920s and 1930s, to find a poetic style free of the all-pervasive influence of Rabindranath Tagore. Jibanananda Das (his name becomes easier to pronounce and spell if one understands that it means 'life-joy' – জীবন-আনন্দ) was born in 1899 in Barisal, the Ganges delta area of present-day Bangladesh, the son of a school-master who was also a preacher in the local branch of the Brahmo Samaj, the Hindu reform movement with which the Tagore family was connected. He went to Calcutta for his university education, and stayed there as a university teacher of English. He died in 1954, struck down by a Calcutta tram. His poems are characterised by expressive and surprising combinations of images, a deep feeling for the rural landscape of Bengal, and a modern awareness of the complexities and confusions of urban life. There is a melancholy, even morbid streak in his writing, but also a sensuous appreciation of beauty.

The first poem opposite, translated by Clinton B. Seely in his book *A Poet Apart: A Literary Biography of the Bengali Poet Jibanananda Das (1899–1954)* (University of Delaware Press, 1990), belongs to a group of poems that evoke the world of the Sundarbans, the mangrove swamps of South Bengal, home of the famous Bengal tiger, now a nature-reserve rather than the hunting-ground of Jibanananda's poem.

শিকার

ভোর ;
আকাশের রঙ ঘাসফড়িঙের দেহের মতো কোমল নীল :
চারিদিকে পেয়ারা ও নোনার গাছ টিয়ার পালকের মতো সবুজ ।
একটি তারা এখনো আকাশে রয়েছে -
পাড়াগাঁর বাসরঘরে সব চেয়ে গোধূলি-মদির মেয়েটির মতো ;
কিংবা মিশরের মানুষী তার বুকের থেকে যে মুক্তা আমার নীল মদের
        গেলাসে রেখেছিল
হাজার হাজার বছর আগে এক রাতে তেমনি -[1]
তেমনি একটি তারা আকাশে জ্বলছে এখনো ।[2]

হিমের রাতে শরীর 'উম'[3] রাখবার জন্য দেশোয়ালীরা সারারাতে মাঠে
        আগুন জ্বেলেছে -
মোরগফুলের মতো লাল আগুন ;
শুকনো অশ্বথপাতা দুমড়ে এখনো আগুন জ্বলছে তাদের ;[4]
সূর্যের আলোয় তার রঙ কুঙ্কুমের মতো নেই আর ;[5]
হ'য়ে গেছে রোগা শালিকের হৃদয়ের বিবর্ণ ইচ্ছার মতো ।
সকালের আলোয় টলমল শিশিরে চারিদিকের বন ও আকাশ ময়ূরের
        সবুজ নীল ডানার মতো ঝিলমিল করছে ।

ভোর ;
সারারাত চিতাবাঘিনীর হাত থেকে নিজেকে বাঁচিয়ে বাঁচিয়ে[6]
নক্ষত্রহীন,[7] মেহগনীর মতো অন্ধকারে সুন্দরীর বন থেকে অর্জুনের
        বনে ঘুরে ঘুরে
সুন্দর বাদামী হরিণ এই ভোরের জন্য অপেক্ষা করছিল ।
এসেছে সে ভোরের আলোয় নেমে ;
কচি বাতাবি-লেবুর মতো সবুজ সুগন্ধী ঘাস ছিঁড়ে ছিঁড়ে খাচ্ছে ;[8]
নদীর তীক্ষ্ণ শীতল ঢেউয়ে[9] সে নামল -
ঘুমহীন ক্লান্ত বিহ্বল[10] শরীরটাকে স্রোতের মতো
        একটা আবেগ দেওয়ার জন্য ;
অন্ধকারের হিম কুঞ্চিত জরায়ু ছিঁড়ে ভোরের রৌদ্রের মতো
        একটা বিস্তীর্ণ উল্লাস পাবার জন্য ;

এই নীল আকাশের নিচে সূর্যের সোনার বর্শার মতো জেগে উঠে সাহসে
সাধে সৌন্দর্যে হরিণীর পর হরিণীকে চমক লাগিয়ে দেবার জন্য ।[11]

একটা অদ্ভুত শব্দ ।
নদীর জল মচকাফুলের পাপড়ির মতো লাল ।
আগুন জ্বলল আবার – উষ্ণ লাল হরিণের মাংস তৈরী হয়ে এল ।
নক্ষত্রের নিচে ঘাসের বিছানায় ব'সে[12] অনেক পুরানো শিশিরভেজা গল্প ;
সিগারেটের ধোঁয়া ; ·
টেরিকাটা কয়েকটা মানুষের মাথা ;
এলোমেলো কয়েকটা বন্দুক – হিম – নিঃস্পন্দ নিরপরাধ ঘুম ।[13]

The Hunt

Dawn:
Sky, the soft blue of a grasshopper's belly.
Guava and custard apple trees all around, green as parrot feathers.
A single star lingers in the sky
Like the most twilight-intoxicated girl in some village bridal chamber,
Or that pearl from her bosom the Egyptian dipped into my Nile-blue
    wine-glass
One night some thousands of years ago –
Just so, in the sky shines a single star.

To warm their bodies through the cold night, up-country menials kept a
    fire going
In the field – red fire like a cockscomb blossom,
Still burning, contorting dry aśvattha *leaves.*

Its color in the light of sun is no longer that of saffron
But has become like wan desires of a sickly śālik *bird's heart.*
In the morning's light both sky and surrounding dewy forest sparkle like
    irridescent peacock wings.

Dawn:
All night long a sleak brown buck, bounding from sundarī *through* arjun
    forests
In starless, mahogany darkness, avoids the cheetah's grasp.
He has been waiting for this dawn.
Down he came in its glow,
Ripping, munching fragrant grass, green as green pomelo.

Down he came to the river's stinging, tingling ripples,
To instill his sleepless, weary, bewildered body with the current's drive,
To feel a thrill like that of dawn bursting through the cold and wizened
    womb of darkness,
To wake like gold sun-spears beneath this sky of blue and
Dazzle doe after doe with beauty, boldness, desire.

A strange sound.
The river's water red as macaka flower petals.
Again the fire crackled – red venison served warm.
Many an old dew-dampened yarn, while seated on a bed of grass beneath
    the stars.
Cigarette smoke.
Several human heads, hair neatly parted.
Guns here and there. Icy, calm, guiltless sleep.

Now a hauntingly pessimistic and ironic short poem, bitter words to utter whenever the world seems especially benighted.

অদ্ভুত আঁধার এক

অদ্ভুত আঁধার এক এসেছে এ-পৃথিবীতে আজ,
যারা অন্ধ সবচেয়ে বেশি আজ চোখে দ্যাখে[14] তারা ;
যাদের হৃদয়ে কোনো প্রেম নেই – প্রীতি নেই – করুণার আলোড়ন নেই
পৃথিবী অচল আজ তাদের[15] সুপরামর্শ[16] ছাড়া ।
যাদের গভীর আস্থা আছে আজো[17] মানুষের প্রতি
এখনো যাদের কাছে স্বাভাবিক ব'লে মনে হয়
মহৎ সত্য বা রীতি, কিংবা শিল্প অথবা[18] সাধনা
শকুন ও শেয়ালের খাদ্য আজ তাদের হৃদয় ।

A Strange Darkness

A strange darkness came upon the world today.
Those who are most blind now see.
Those who hearts lack love, lack warmth, lack pity's stirrings,
Without their fine advice, the world today dare not make a move.
Those who yet today possess an abiding faith in man,
To whom still now high truths or age-old customs
Or industry or austere practice all seem natural,
Their hearts are victuals for the vulture and the jackal.

Notes

[1]যে and তেমনি from a relative correlative pair here: *that pearl which . . . like that . . .*

[2]Clinton Seely writes about these lines: 'The twilight intoxicated girl warrants explanation. In many Hindu Bengali weddings, the ceremony takes place at the bride's home. Friends and relatives of the bride traditionally keep the newly married couple awake most of that first night, teasing the bride-groom and chatting with the bride . . . One maiden, undoubtedly excited by the whole affair, managed to stay awake the entire night. Juxtaposed to this thoroughly Bengali miss are the exotic Egyptian lady and her pearl pendant, drawn from Jibanananda's stock of Middle Eastern imagery.' (*A Poet Apart*, p. 130.)

[3]A Persian word meaning *warmth*.

[4]Notice the inverted word order: তাদের goes with আগুন *(their fire)*. To put a Bengali possessive pronoun at the end of a sentence is not uncommon in colloquial speech: this not necessarily a poeticism.

[5]Another inversion: normally আর meaning *any more* would go before the verb: আর নেই.

[6]*saving itself from the claws of the cheetah*: বাঁচা means *to live, survive*, and the extended verb বাঁচানো means *to cause to live, save, preserve*, etc.

[7]*starless*: the suffix -হীন means *without, -less*. Cf. The word for *friendless* in Unit 18, p. 93.

[8]The repetition of the past participle of the verb ছেঁড়া *(to tear)* in this compound makes it more like a present participle: *ripping, munching* as Clinton Seely has it.

[9]Note this way of spelling the locative case ending on ঢেউ *(wave)*.

[10]This word is pronounced either 'biuvɔl' or 'bibhɔl'. Cf. আহ্বান (*call, summons*), pronounced 'auvan'. Note the conjunct.

[11] চমক লাগা would mean *to feel alarm* and would be used impersonally. চমক লাগানো means *to startle, to alarm* in a transitive sense.

[12]Jibanananda often uses apostrophes in past participles (see Note 12, p. 240).

[13]There is no real grammar in this line: the fragmented phrases echo the sound of gunshots.

[14]This spelling of দেখে occurs sometimes: to indicate that এ is here pronounced æ.

[15]A straightforward relative/correlative construction, in a possessive form: যাদের . . . তাদের *(those who (have) . . ., those (have) . . .)*. The construction is repeated in the next sentence.

[16]The prefix সু- means *good*, so সুপরামর্শ means *good advice*.

¹⁷ আজ + the particle ও can be spelt in this way: *even today*.
¹⁸ কিংবা and অথবা both mean *or*: the variation is rhythmically satisfying here. Both words can be abbreviated to বা .

Line 11 of *The Hunt* has the conjunct: ত + থ = ত্থ . But if your appetite for conjuncts is sated, you can use a more colloquial form of the word for Indian fig (peepul) tree: অশথ, which occurs in the next poem.

Exercise

If you have worked your way through the two poems by Jibanananda Das above, you should be in a position now to enjoy a third poem by him as a poem rather than as a 'struggle with words and meanings'. So, for your final exercise, revel in the following exquisite, subtle example of poetic দেশ-প্রেম (love of one's country) by listening to the recording of it on the tape, trying to achieve the best possible pronunciation, and even – something that Westerners do not do easily these days but which still comes naturally to Bengalis – learning it by heart. There are references in it to one of the most famous of medieval Bengali poems, the *Manasā Mangal*, written in a genre known as *mangal kābya* – narrative poems describing the exploits of deities on earth.

Chand, a merchant, is punished in various ways by the snake goddess Manasa for his refusal to worship her. Six of his sons are killed by her. When the seventh, Lakindar, is killed by snakebite on his wedding night, his bride Behula refuses to give him up for dead, places him on a raft, and floats downstream with the body. She meets Manasa's assistant, Neto, who takes her to Amara, the abode of the gods. Behula's beautiful dancing so impresses Indra and the other gods, that they bring her husband back to life. The whole of Bengal, too, comes to life in the beauty of Jibanananda's poem. It is written in sonnet form, one of many untitled sonnets that were published posthumously in a book that the poet's brother called রূপসী বাংলা (*Bengal the Beautiful*).

Notice that it mixes *sādhu bhāṣā* and *calit bhāṣā* forms: e.g. দেখিয়াছি *(s.b.)* in line 1, but জেগে উঠে *(c.b.)* in l. 2. In Bengali *prose* the convention is that *s.b.* and *c.b.* forms should not be mixed. In poetry, however, there is no such restriction. Clinton Seely's translation is given in the **Key to the Exercises** on p. 287. Note the conjunct ষ + ণ = ষ্ণ, used to write 'Krishna', which in the poem here means *dark*.

বাংলার মুখ আমি দেখিয়াছি, তাই আমি পৃথিবীর রূপ
খুঁজিতে যাই না আর ; অন্ধকারে জেগে উঠে ডুমুরের গাছে
চেয়ে দেখি ছাতার মতন বড়ো পাতাটির নিচে ব'সে আছে
ভোরের দোয়েলপাখি - চারিদিকে চেয়ে দেখি পল্লবের স্তূপ
জাম-বট-কাঁঠালের-হিজলের অশথের ক'রে আছে চুপ ;
ফণিমনসার[a] ঝোপে শটিবনে তাহাদের ছায়া পড়িয়াছে ;
মধুকর ডিঙা থেকে না জানি সে কবে চাঁদ চম্পার কাছে
এমনই হিজল-বট-তমালের নীল ছায়া বাংলার অপরূপ রূপ
দেখেছিলো ; বেহুলাও একদিন গাঙুড়ের জলে ভেলা নিয়ে
- কৃষ্ণা দ্বাদশীর[b] জ্যোৎস্না যখন মরিয়া গেছে নদীর চড়ায় -
সোনালি ধানের পাশে অসংখ্য অশ্বথ বট দেখেছিলো, হায়,
শ্যামার নরম গান শুনেছিল, একদিন অমরায় গিয়ে
ছিন্ন খঞ্জনার মতো যখন সে নেচেছিল ইন্দ্রের সভায়
বাংলার নদী মাঠ ভাঁটফুল ঘুঙুরের মতো তার কেঁদেছিল পায় ।

[a]A cactus-like plant associated with Manasa rituals.
[b]The twelfth day of the 'dark' (কৃষ্ণপক্ষ) half of the lunar month.

35

_____ REVIEW OF _____
PART THREE

1 Conjunct consonants

The following lists of Bengali conjunct consonants are based on the table given in *Bāṃlā bānāner niyam* ('Rules of Bengali spelling') by Mahabubul Haq (Jatiya Sahitya Prakashini, Dhaka, 1991), p. 107. Conjuncts that can only be written by using the হসন্ত (্ – see Unit 18, p. 95) have been omitted. Pronunciations are given for conjuncts whose pronunciation is not easily predictable from their constituents or from the effect of ্য or ্ব (see Unit 7, p. 26). Remember that double sounds in Bengali must be fully doubled.

First letter	2 letters	3 letters
ক	ক + ক = ক্ক	ক + ল + য = ক্ল্য
	ক + ট = ক্ট	ক + ষ + ন = ক্ষ্ণ 'kkhn'
	ক + ত = ক্ত	ক + ষ + ম = ক্ষ্ম 'kkh'
	ক + ম = ক্ম	ক + ষ + য = ক্ষ্য 'kkh'
	ক + য = ক্য	
	ক + র = ক্র	
	ক + ল = ক্ল	
	ক + ব = ক্ব	
	ক + ষ = ক্ষ 'kkh' (p. 32)	
	ক + স = ক্স	

খ	খ + য = খ্য	
	খ + র = খ্র	
গ	গ + গ = গ্গ	গ + ন + য = গ্ন্য
	গ + ধ = গ্ধ	গ + র + য = গ্র্য
	গ + ন = গ্ন	
	গ + ম = গ্ম	
	গ + য = গ্য	
	গ + র = গ্র	
	গ + ল = গ্ল	
	গ + ব = গ্ব	
ঘ	ঘ + ন = ঘ্ন	
	ঘ + র = ঘ্র	
	ঘ + য = ঘ্য	
ঙ	ঙ + ক = ঙ্ক	ঙ + ক + ষ = ঙ্ক্ষ 'ŋkh'
	ঙ + খ = ঙ্খ	ঙ + খ + য = ঙ্খ্য
	ঙ + গ = ঙ্গ	ঙ + গ + য = ঙ্গ্য
	ঙ + ঘ = ঙ্ঘ	ঙ + ঘ + য = ঙ্ঘ্য
	ঙ + ম = ঙ্ম	
চ	চ + চ = চ্চ	চ + ছ + র = চ্ছ্র
	চ + ছ = চ্ছ	চ + ছ + ব = চ্ছ্ব 'cch'
	চ + এ঺ = চ্঺ঽ	
	চ + য = চ্য	
ছ	ছ + য = ছ্য	
জ	জ + জ = জ্জ	জ + জ + ব = জ্জ্ব 'jj'
	জ + ঝ = জ্ঝ	
	জ + এ঺ = জ্঺ঽ 'gg' (p. 82)	
	জ + য = জ্য	
	জ + র = জ্র	
	জ + ব = জ্ব	
এ঺(p. 44)	এ঺ + চ = ঞ্চ	
	এ঺ + ছ = ঞ্ছ	
	এ঺ + জ = ঞ্জ	
	এ঺ + ঝ = ঞ্ঝ	
ট	ট + ট = ট্ট	
	ট + য = ট্য	
	ট + র = ট্র	

ঠ ঠ + য = ঠ্য

ড ড + ড = ড্ড
ড + র = ড্র
ড + য = ড্য

ড় ড় + গ = ড়্গ

ঢ ঢ + য = ঢ্য

ণ ণ + ট = ণ্ট ণ + ঠ + য = ণ্ঠ্য
ণ + ঠ = ণ্ঠ ণ + ড + য = ণ্ড্য
ণ + ড = ণ্ড ণ + ড + র = ণ্ড্র
ণ + ঢ = ণ্ঢ
ণ + ণ = ণ্ণ
ণ + ম = ণ্ম
ণ + য = ণ্য
ণ + ব = ণ্ব

ত ত + ত = ত্ত ত + ত + য = ত্ত্য
ত + থ = ত্থ ত + ত + ব = ত্ত্ব
ত + ন = ত্ন ত + ম + য = ত্ম্য 'tt'
ত + ম = ত্ম 'tt' ত + র + য = ত্র্য
ত + য = ত্য
ত + র = ত্র
ত + ব = ত্ব 'tt'

থ থ + য = থ্য র + থ + য = র্থ্য
থ + র = থ্র
থ + ব = থ্ব 'tth'

দ দ + গ = দ্গ দ + ব + য = দ্ব্য 'dd'
দ + ঘ = দ্ঘ
দ + দ = দ্দ
দ + ধ = দ্ধ
দ + ভ = দ্ভ
দ + ম = দ্ম 'dd'
দ + য = দ্য
দ + র = দ্র
দ + ব = দ্ব 'dd'

ধ ধ + ন = ধ্ন
ধ + য = ধ্য
ধ + র = ধ্র

— 267 —

	ধ + ব = ধ্ব 'ddh'	
ন	ন + ত = ন্ত	ন + ত + য = ন্ত্য
	ন + থ = ন্থ	ন + ত + ব = ন্ত্ব
	ন + দ = ন্দ	ন + ত + র = ন্ত্র
	ন + ধ = ন্ধ	ন + দ + য = ন্দ্য
	ন + ন = ন্ন	ন + দ + র = ন্দ্র
	ন + য = ন্য	ন + দ + ব = ন্দ্ব
	ন + ব = ন্ব	ন + ধ + য = ন্ধ্য
	ন + ম = ন্ম	ন + ধ + র = ন্ধ্র
	ন + স = ন্স	ন + ন + য = ন্ন্য
প	প + ট = প্ট	প + ল + য = প্ল্য
	প + প = প্প	
	প + ন = প্ন	
	প + ত = প্ত	
	প + য = প্য	
	প + র = প্র	
	প + ল = প্ল	
	প + স = প্স	
ফ	ফ + য = ফ্য	ফ + ল + য = ফ্ল্য
	ফ + র = ফ্র	
	ফ + ল = ফ্ল	
ব	ব + জ = ব্জ	ব + ল + য = ব্ল্য
	ব + দ = ব্দ	
	ব + ধ = ব্ধ	
	ব + ব = ব্ব	
	ব + য = ব্য	
	ব + র = ব্র	
	ব + ল = ব্ল	
ভ	ভ + য = ভ্য	
	ভ + র = ভ্র	
ম	ম + ন = ম্ন	ম + প + র = ম্প্র
	ম + প = ম্প	ম + ভ + র = ম্ভ্র
	ম + ফ = ম্ফ	
	ম + ব = ম্ব 'mb/mm' (p. 249)	
	ম + ভ = ম্ভ	
	ম + ম = ম্ম	
	ম + য = ম্য	
	ম + র = ম্র	
	ম + ল = ম্ল	

য   য + য = য্য

র   র + ক = র্ক   র + ঘ + য = র্ঘ্য
     র + খ = র্খ, etc.   র + ণ + য = র্ণ্য
                              র + ত + য = র্ত্য
                              র + থ + য = র্থ্য
                              র + দ + র = র্দ্র
                              র + দ + য = র্দ্য
                              র + ব + য = র্ব্য
                              র + য + য = র্য্য
                              র + ধ + ব = র্ধ্ব
                              র + শ + ব = র্শ্ব
                              র + ষ + ণ = র্ষ্ণ

ল   ল + ক = ল্ক
     ল + গ = ল্গ
     ল + ট = ল্ট
     ল + ড = ল্ড
     ল + প = ল্প
     ল + ফ = ল্ফ
     ল + ব = ল্ব
     ল + ম = ল্ম 'll'
     ল + ল = ল্ল
     ল + য = ল্য

শ (pron. 'sh'   শ + চ = শ্চ
except when
indicated)

     শ + ছ = শ্ছ
     শ + ন = শ্ন
     শ + ম = শ্ম 'ʃʃ'
     শ + য = শ্য
     শ + র = শ্র 'sr'
     শ + ল = শ্ল
     শ + ব = শ্ব 'ʃʃ'

ষ (pron. 'sh')   ষ + ক = ষ্ক   ষ + ক + র = ষ্ক্র
                 ষ + ট = ষ্ট   ষ + ট + য = ষ্ট্য
                 ষ + ঠ = ষ্ঠ   ষ + ট + র = ষ্ট্র
                 ষ + ণ = ষ্ণ   ষ + ঠ + য = ষ্ঠ্য
                 ষ + প = ষ্প   ষ + ণ + য = ষ্ণ্য
                 ষ + ফ = ষ্ফ   ষ + ফ + য = ষ্ফ্য
                 ষ + ম = ষ্ম 'ss'   ষ + ম + য = ষ্ম্য
                 ষ + য = ষ্য

স (pron. 'sh' except when indicated)

স + ক = স্ক
স + খ = স্খ
স + ট = স্ট
স + ত = স্ত 'st'
স + থ = স্থ 'sth'
স + ন = স্ন 'sn'
স + প = স্প
স + ফ = স্ফ
স + ম = স্ম (p. 217.)
স + য = স্য
স + র = স্র
স + ল = স্ল
স + ব = স্ব

স + ট + র = স্ট্র
স + ট + য = স্ট্য
স + ত + য = স্ত্য 'stt'
স + ত + র = স্ত্র 'str'
স + থ + য = স্থ্য 'stth'
স + প + র = স্প্র

হ

হ + ণ = হ্ণ 'nh/nn'
হ + ন = হ্ন 'nh/nn'
হ + ম = হ্ম 'mh/mm'
হ + য = হ্য 'jj'
হ + র = হ্র
হ + ল = হ্ল
হ + ব = হ্ব (p. 262.)

Special consonant + vowel combinations

গ + উ = গু
ত + র + উ = ত্রু
ন + ত + উ = ন্তু
র + উ = রু
র + ঊ = রূ
শ + উ = শু
হ + ঋ = হৃ
হ + উ = হু

2 śādhu bhāṣā forms

Unit 33 introduced you to the *śādhu bhāṣā*, the literary form of Bengali which has now fallen into disuse but which you need to know to read classic Bengali literature. For the literary pronouns, see p. 256. As regards verbs, the present tense and present imperative are the same as in colloquial Bengali (but see Note 21, p. 255). In the other tenses, the

endings are the same as the colloquial forms, but the stems and participles are longer. It is only necessary to give three paradigms: a consonant stem verb (করা), a vowel stem (খাওয়া) and an extended verb (করানো), and for each tense the first person only. Note that for an **e/i** verb like লেখা the literary verbal noun is লিখা, and for an **o/u** verb like শোনা the literary verbal noun is শুনা (and these are the forms that are listed in dictionaries). The negative suffix নি, used for the negative of the perfect and past perfect tenses (see Unit 19, p. 113), is নাই in literary Bengali, written as a separate word, and নাই or নাহি is used for the negative of **ach-**.

Verbal noun	করা	খাওয়া	করানো
Infinitive	করিতে	খাইতে	করাইতে
Present continuous	করিতেছি	খাইতেছি	করাইতেছি
Future	করিব/করিবো	খাইব/খাইবো	করাইব/করাইবো
Simple past	করিলাম	খাইলাম	করাইলাম
Habitual past	করিতাম	খাইতাম	করাইতাম
Conditional participle	করিলে	খাইলে	করাইলে
Past participle	করিয়া	খাইয়া	করাইয়া
Perfect	করিয়াছি	খাইয়াছি	করাইয়াছি
Past perfect	করিয়াছিলাম	খাইয়াছিলাম	করাইয়াছিলাম
Past continuous	করিতেছিলাম	খাইতেছিলাম	করাইতেছিলাম
Future imperative	(তুই) করিস	খাইবি*	করাস
	(তুমি) করিও	খাইবে*	করাইবে*
	(আপনি) করিবেন	খাইবেন	করাইবেন

*Note that the future tense is used, rather than a special imperative form. করিবে would also be an alternative for করিও .

3 Muslim/Hindu distinctions

The following list consists mainly of the different kinship terms that are used by Hindus and Muslims in Bengal. A few additional words are added. In the case of সাথে the difference is more geographical than religious. There are plenty of Muslims in West Bengal, and a sizeable Hindu minority in Bangladesh. Where no Muslim kinship term is given, you can assume the same term is used by both Muslims and Hindus.

	Muslim/ Bangladesh	Hindu/ West Bengal
paternal grandfather	দাদা dada	ঠাকুরদা ṭhakurda
paternal grandmother	দাদী dadī	ঠাকুরমা ṭhakurma
maternal grandfather	নানা nana	দাদামশায় dadamôʃay
maternal grandmother	নানী nanī	দিদিমা didima
father	আব্বা abba	বাবা baba
mother	আম্মা amma	মা ma
elder brother	বড় ভাই bɔrô bhai	দাদা dada
elder sister		দিদি didi
younger brother		ভাই bhai
younger sister		বোন/ভগ্নী bon/bhɔgnī

Where there are a number of elder or younger brothers or sisters, বড় *(big)* মেজ *(middle)* or ছোট *(small)* + দা/দি/ভাই/বোন can be used: e.g. মেজদা , *middle elder brother*; ছোটদি , *youngest elder sister*; ছোটভাই , *youngest younger brother*, etc.

son		ছেলে chele

daughter		মেয়ে meye
son's wife		বউমা bouma
daughter's husband		জামাই jamai
grandson		নাতি nati
granddaughter		নাতনী natnī
father's elder brother		জ্যেঠা jyætha
his wife		জ্যেঠিমা jyethima
father's younger brother	চাচা caca	কাকা/খুড়ো kaka/khuɽo
his wife	চাচী cacī	কাকী/কাকীমা kakī/kakīma
his son	চাচাতো ভাই cacato bhai	খুড়তুতো ভাই khuɽtuto bhai
his daughter	চাচাতো বোন cacato bon	খুড়তুতো বোন khuɽtuto bon
father's sister	ফুফু phuphu	পিসী/পিসীমা pisī/pisīma
her husband	ফুফা phupha	পিসে/পিসেমশায় pise/pisemôʃay
her son	ফুফাতো ভাই phuphato bhai	পিসতুতো ভাই pistuto bhai
her daughter	ফুফাতো বোন phuphato bon	পিসতুতো বোন pistuto bon
mother's brother		মামা mama
his wife		মামী mamī
his son		মামাতো ভাই mamato bhai
his daughter		মামাতো বোন mamato bon
mother's sister	খালা khala	মাসী/মাসীমা masī/masīma

her husband	খালু khalu	মেসো/মেসোমশায় meso/mesomôʃay
her son	খালাতো ভাই khalato bhai	মাসতুতো ভাই mastuto bhai
her daughter	খালাতো বোন khalato bon	মাসতুতো বোন mastuto bon
elder brother's wife		বউদি boudi
younger brother's wife		বউমা bouma
elder sister's husband		দাদাবাবু dadababu
younger sister's husband		বোনাই/ভগ্নীপতি bonai/bhɔgnīpôti
brother's son		ভাইপো bhaipo
brother's daughter		ভাইঝি bhaijhi
sister's son		ভাগনে bhagne
sister's daughter		ভাগ্নী bhagnī
father-in-law		শ্বশুর ʃvɔʃur
mother-in-law		শাশুড়ী ʃaʃurī
wife's brother		শালা ʃala
wife's sister		শালী ʃalī
husband's elder brother		ভাশুর bhaʃur
husband's younger brother		দেওর/দেবর deor/debôr
husband's sister	ননদ nɔnôd	ঠাকুরঝি ʈhakurjhi

to bathe	গোসল করা gosɔl kɔra	স্নান করা snan kɔra
with	সাথে sathe	সঙ্গে sɔn̪ge
water	পানি pani	জল jɔl
salt	লবণ lɔbôn̪	নুন nun
God	আল্লা/খোদা alla/khoda	ঈশ্বর/ভগবান iʃvôr/bhɔgôban

4 Vowel Harmony

Many aspects of Bengali pronunciation that seem mysterious as first become less so once one is aware of its subtle system of 'vowel harmony'. As in German (*ich muß* but *wir müssen*), Bengali vowels are often modified through the influence of another vowel in the following syllable. A highly technical analysis of vowel harmony can be found in Chapter IV of S. K. Chatterji's book (see p. 276). A simpler formulation is given on p. 23 of *The Bengali Language* by E. M. Bîkova (tr. by M. E. Feldman, V. M. Breskrovny and V. D. Mazo, Nauka Publishing House, Moscow, 1981):

If the following syllable has i or u:	If the following syllable has ɔ, o, e or a:
o > u ɔ > o e > i æ > e	u > o o > ɔ i > e e > æ

You can easily see how this works with the verbs (ʃona becomes ʃuni, dækha becomes dekhi, kɔra becomes kôri etc.) and you will find it often accounts for the pronunciation of the inherent vowel (e.g. bôi or bôu not bɔi or bɔu) or the change from e to æ (ækhôn/ekhuni, æmôn/emni, etc.) The pronunciation of words like অতিথি or অনুবাদ (see Glossary), or a colloquial tendency to pronounce ইংরেজী 'imriji', can be similarly explained. There are many exceptions, but some users of this book may like to notice further examples.

5 Further reading

Dictionaries

The best modern Bengali–English dictionary is the *SAMSAD* dictionary, published in a full-size and student-size format by Shishu Sahitya Samsad Private Ltd., 32A Acharya Prafulla Chandra Rd., Calcutta 700009, India. English–Bengali dictionaries are not very useful to the foreign learner, as they tend to give descriptive definitions of English words rather than direct equivalents. For a basic English–Bengali vocabulary, Ghulam Murshid's pocket-sized *Bengali–English–Bengali Dictionary*, published by Ruposhi Bangla Ltd., 220 Tooting High St., London SW17 0SG, is recommended. Ruposhi Bangla has a large stock of Bengali books from Bangladesh and West Bengal, including children's primers, handwriting books, etc.

For pronunciation, consult the *Bāṅlā uccāraṇ abhidhān* ('Bengali pronunciation dictionary'), edited by Naren Biswas and published by the Bangla Academy in Dhaka.

Courses and grammars

Users of this book might wish to compare it with:
Edward C. Dimock, Somdev Bhattacharji, Suhas Chatterjee, *Introduction to Bengali, Part 1* (Chicago, 1964; New Delhi, Manohar, 1976)
Dušan Zbavitel, *Lehrbuch des Bengalischen* (Heidelberg, Julius Groos Verlag, 1970)
M. R. Hilali, *Learning Bengali* (London, Ruposhi Bangla, 1990)
France Bhattacharya, *Manuel de Bengali* (Paris, L'Asiathèque, 1992)

Bengali linguistics

For a summary article, see William Radice, 'Bengali' in *Encyclopedia of Language and Linguistics* (Oxford, Pergamon Press, 1994).

For those with a philological bent, Suniti Kumar Chatterji's monumental *The Origin and Development of the Bengali Language* (Calcutta, 1926; London, George Allen & Unwin, 1970) is indispensable.
For further bibliography, see Maniruzzaman, 'Linguistic Studies on Bangla' (*Chittagong University Studies* No. 2, pp. 55–94, 1986).

Literature and culture

For an overview, see article on Bengali literature by William Radice in *The Cambridge Encyclopedia of India* etc. (Cambridge, 1989)

Dušan Zbavitel, *Bengali Literature* (Wiesbaden, 1976)

Rabindranath Tagore, *Selected Poems*, tr. William Radice (Penguin, 1985, rev. 1987)

Rabindranath Tagore, *Selected Short Stories*, tr. William Radice (Penguin, 1991, rev. 1994)

Rabindranath Tagore, *I won't let you go: Selected Poems*, tr. Ketaki Kushari Dyson (Newcastle, Bloodaxe, 1991)

Rabindranath Tagore, *Quartet*, tr. Kaiser Haq (Oxford, Heinemann, 1993)

Geoffrey Moorhouse, *Calcutta: The City Revealed* (Penguin, 1974)

ed. Sukanta Chaudhuri, *Calcutta, the Living City* (2 Vols, Delhi, OUP 1990)

Nirad C. Chaudhuri, *The Autobiography of an Unknown Indian* (London, 1951)

Nirad C. Chaudhuri, *Thy Hand, Great Anarch! India 1921–1952* (London, 1987)

Sukumar Ray, *Collected Nonsense*, tr. Sukanta Chaudhuri (Delhi, OUP, 1988)

Bibhutibhusan Banerji, *Pather Panchali*, tr. T. W. Clark and Tarapada Mukherji (London, 1968)

Nemai Sadhan Bose, *The Indian Awakening and Bengal* (Calcutta, 1960, rev. 1969, 1976)

Tapan Raychaudhuri, *Europe Reconsidered: Perceptions of the West in Nineteenth Century Bengal* (Delhi, OUP, 1988)

Andrew Robinson, *Satyajit Ray: The Inner Eye* (London, 1989)

Betsy Hartman and James K. Boyce, *A Quiet Violence: View from a Bangladesh Village* (London, 1983)

Katy Gardner, *Songs at the River's Edge* (London, Virago, 1991)

Shamsur Rahman, *Selected Poems* tr. by Kaiser Haq (bilingual edition, Dhaka, Brac Prokashona, 1987)

Caroline Adams, *Across Seven Seas and Thirteen Rivers* (London, THAP Books, 1987)

Kalpana Bardhan, *Of Women, Outcastes, Peasants and Rebels: A Collection of Bengali Short Stories* (California, 1990)

KEY TO THE EXERCISES

Unit 1, Ex. 2

আম, মা, না, নাম, গা, গান, আমার, আবার, বাগান, আমি, নুন, ইনি, উনি, রুমাল, নীল, লাল, মূল, আমি আনিনি, আমি আনলাম, আমরা নিইনি, আমরা নিইনা, আম আনুন, নুন নিই ? নিন না, ইনি আমার মা, উনি আমার মামা, আমার নাম রাউল, আমার রুমাল নিন, উনি উমার বাবা ? না, উনি রিমির বাবা ।

Unit 2, Ex. 2

ও, ওরা, ওর, দশ, সব, দাদা, দিদি, দিন, আঙুল, মাসী, শুনুন ! বিষ, মানুষ, ও শুলনা, আমরা আসিনি, রবিবার আসুন, ও দিল, ওরা নিলনা, সোমবার আসবো ? আমরা শুনবো, ওই বইগুলো ওর ? ওরা দুই বোন, আমরা বাঙালী নই, আরো দই দাও, আমি শনিবার আসবোনা, ওর নাম বল, আমি আর বসবোনা, ওই সব আমার ? ওর দিদির নাম সরলা, উনি আমার বোন নন ।

Unit 3, Ex. 2

সে, এসে, এনে, এর, মেয়ে, বিয়ে, খায়, রাখে, খাবে, খাওয়া-দাওয়া, শেখে, খুব, অসুখ, নখ, মাংস, সঙ্গে, মঙ্গলবার, আমি খাব, আমি লিখবোনা, আমার সঙ্গে আসুন, আমাদের দেবেনা, ও এলে খাবে ? বইখানা নিয়ে এস, এখানে এসে বসুন, উনি আসেননি ? না, এ সব লিখে নেব ? ও এখুনি এল, সেখানে খুব গরম, আমি খেয়ে এলাম, সে মঙ্গলবার আসবেনা ।

Unit 4, Ex. 2

কি ? কে ? একে, ওকে, আমাকে, কার ? কেমন ? কেন, কেউ, কখন ? দিক, লোক, কাল, সকাল, সকল, কলম, এগার, নৌকো, গেল, আমি করি, উনি করেন, আমরা কিনি, কে কেনে ? ওর নাম কি ? এখানে গোলমাল করোনা, এ বইখানা কার ? এখন দেব ? কেউ আমাকে বলেনি, সে নৌকা করে অনেক দূর গেল, ওরা সবাই শুক্রবার গেল ।

Unit 5, Ex. 2

এঁকে, এঁরা, এঁদের, এঁর, ওঁকে, ওঁরা, ওঁদের, ওঁর, ছেলে, ছবি, ছয়, ছুরি, আমি আছি, আমরা ছিলাম, সে ছিলনা, আমরা খেয়েছিলাম, সে আসছে, আমি বসেছিলাম, আমি করছি, ওখানে রেখেছি, এঁকে আরো মাছ দাও, এঁর কাছে এসে বস, গোলমাল করছ কেন ? এঁকে বলবো না ওঁকে বলবো ? উনি খুব রাগ করেছেন, ওর খুব অসুখ করেছিল, মা এখনি আসছেন, বিছানা রোদে দাও, ওঁকে বল আমরা এসেছি, এঁরা মাছ মাংস কিছুই খাননা ।

Unit 6, Ex. 2

তুমি, তোমার, তোমাকে, তোমরা, তারা, তাঁরা, তাঁকে, টাকা, টুকরো, ছোট, টেবিল, একটা, দুটো, তিনটে, এটা, ওটা, কটা ? এটুকু, একটু, তোমরা আর দেরি করোনা, তুমি তবু বসে আছ ? এটুকু খেয়ে নিন, টেবিলটা তোমার কাছে টেনে নাও, তোমরা কাল কটার সময় এলে ? সাতটার সময়, মাছটা বেশ টাটকা, তোমরা মাটিতে শুয়েছ কেন ? তিনি এলে তাঁকে বসতে বলো, আমি কত টাকা দেব ? আমটা সুন্দর, কিন্তু টক ।

Unit 7, Ex. 2

যা, যে, জমিদার, জুতো, জল, জিনিস, স্বামী, আজকের কাজ, জায়গা, জ্বর, হাসি, আমার জন্য, তুমি যাও, আমার মনে হয়, একজন লোক, ব্যামো, শ্যাম, বিশ্বাস, ব্যবহার, বিশ্ববিদ্যালয়, ওতে হাত দিওনা, এত জোরে হাঁটবেনা, আলোটা কি জ্বেলে দেব ? জামা গায় দিয়ে এস, বল তো এখন কটা বাজে ? ওরা এক দিনের জন্য এসেছেন, তোমার কি জ্বর হয়েছে ? জানালা দিয়ে বেশ রোদ আসছে, ওঁরা এই মাত্র এলেন, তাঁরা এই মাত্র গেলেন ।

Unit 8, Ex. 2

মাথা, কথা, আমি থাকি, তুমি থাম, ফুল, ফল, তিনি ডাকেন, একটা বড় বাড়ি, ডাল আর তরকারি, মোটর গাড়ি, গরুর গাড়ি, ট্রেন কখন ছাড়বে ? এখানে থাম, তেল ফুরিয়ে গেছে, তুমি কোথায় থাক ? একটু দাঁড়ান, ছটায় ফিরে এস, কে ডাকছে ? ওগুলো দেশী ডিম ? সে বিড়ি খায়, আজ বাড়ি থেকে বেরিওনা, ওটা ফেলে দিওনা, দিদিকে ডাক, থাম,থাম – গাড়ি আসছে ! রোদে দাঁড়াবেননা, তোমার বাড়ি কোথায় ? ফলগুলি সব খেয়ে ফেলেছ ? ডান দিক দিয়ে গেলে তাড়াতাড়ি হবে, গাড়িটা থামলেই আমরা নামবো, আমার বড় বাক্সটা কোথায় ?

Unit 9, Ex. 2

পা, পথ, পরে, সে পড়ে, কৌসুলী, আপনি বাংলা বলতে পারেন ? আপনি কেমন আছেন ? টাকা-পয়সা, আপনাকে অপেক্ষা করতে হবে, পুরনো কাপড়, জামাটা ছিঁড়ে গেছে, এটা আমাদের পোষা বেড়াল, কি সুন্দর পাখি ! ওর ফুফু মারা গেছেন, পৌষ মাস, পয়লা তারিখ, আজ পর্যন্ত, একজন তরুণ কবি, আপনারা প্রত্যেকে অংশ নিন, তোমার মাথার উপর, আমি পা পিছলে পড়ে গেলাম, আপনি কখন পৌঁছলেন ? তোমাদের পড়াশোনা কেমন হয়েছে ? পাশের বাড়িতে কারা এসেছেন ? এখনো আলাপ হয়নি, এঁকে প্রণাম কর, জায়গাটার বিবরণ দিতে পার ? সেটা করুণ ব্যাপার, এটুকু পথ হেঁটে যেতে পারবো, পড়াশোনা না করলে, পরীক্ষায় পাশ করতে পারবেনা ।

Unit 10, Ex. 2

চা, চাল, চাবি, চোখ, চার, সে চায়, ভালো, ভুল, আমি ভুলে গেছি, ভাত, কি হচ্ছে ? চুপ কর ! ভদ্রলোক, চশমা, চৈত্র মাস, সে আমার চেয়ে বড়, ওর ভাইকে চিনিনা, চল, বেড়াতে যাই, উনি টাকা দিচ্ছেন, ভদ্রলোককে চা দাও, ভাত না খেয়ে লুচি খান, কয় চামচ চিনি দেব ? দুই চামচ দিন, আপনার ভাই কেমন আছে ? ভালো আছে, ভদ্রমহিলাটিকে চেন ? চাবিটা কোথায় রাখলে ?   আমার ভয়ানক ভূতের ভয় করে, বাড়িটা ভালো কিন্তু ভাড়া

বেশী, বাবার জন্য আমার খুব ভাবনা হয়, চোখে ভালো দেখতে পাইনা ।

Unit 11, Ex. 2

ঝোল, ঝড়, ঝি, ঝগড়া, মাঝি, ঠিক, ঠিকানা, ঠাট্টা, মাঠ, ঢেউ, সে বোঝে, তিনি ওঠেন, গাঢ় লাল, রাঢ় বঙ্গ, প্রৌঢ় বয়স, কথাটা ঠিক, ঝি মেঝে ঝাঁট দিচ্ছে, আমি বাংলা বুঝিনা, ঢিল মেরোনা, ভাত ঢাক, ঠিক আছে, আপনার ঠিকানাটা বলুন, আষাঢ় মাসের মাঝামাঝি, চিঠিটা পাঠিয়ে দাও, মেঝেতে শুয়ে ওর ঠান্ডা লেগেছে, এত ভোরে উঠোনা, ঝগড়া করছ কেন ? মাছের ঝোলে কি ঝাল হয়েছে ? এত বড় গাড়ি কি করে ঢুকবে ? হঠাৎ ঝড় উঠলো, মাঝি রওনা হতে রাজী হলনা ।

Unit 12, Ex. 2

ঘি, ঘাম, ঘাস, ঘর, ঘোড়া, ঘড়ি, ঘণ্টা, ধোপা, ধুলো, সে হাত ধোয়, এখানে বাস ধরা যায়, বাংলাদেশে ছটি ঋতু, আমার অনেক ঋণ, বৃষ্টি হচ্ছে, দোকানটা বন্ধ, আমরা শুধু বন্ধু, আমি আড়াই ঘণ্টা বসে আছি, আধ সের দুধ নেব, সে সমস্ত পৃথিবী ঘুরেছে, রোদে ঘুরবেননা – মাথা ধরবে, ওই বাড়ি থেকে ধোঁয়া আসছে ! এতক্ষণ ঘুমচ্ছিলে ! বুধবার কি স্কুল বন্ধ না খোলা ? বোধ হয় বন্ধ, এই রাস্তা ধরে বাজারে যাওয়া যায় ? ঘাটের পথে খুব ধুলো, এত সুখ আমার হৃদয়ে ! আজ দিনটা একেবারে বৃথা গেল, সে শুধু ধুতি পরে, ঘোড়াটা খুব ধীরে-ধীরে টানছে ।

Unit 14, 1   *(a)*

১ হ্যাঁ, উনি আমার মা । ২ হ্যাঁ, এ আমার ছোট ভাই । ৩ হ্যাঁ, ওর নাম জন । ৪ হ্যাঁ, এটা আমাদের বাড়ি । ৫ হ্যাঁ, এটা আমার সাইকেল । ৬ হ্যাঁ, ইনি আমার বোন । ৭ হ্যাঁ, উনি ওর স্বামী । ৮ হ্যাঁ, ইনি আমাদের প্রতিবেশী । ৯ হ্যাঁ, ওটা ওর । ১০ হ্যাঁ, এটা আমার ।

1   *(b)*

১ ওটা চেয়ার । ২ ওটা বল । ৩ ওটা টেলিফোন । ৪ ওটা ট্রেন । ৫ ওটা পেনসিল । ৬ ওটা প্যান্ট ।

2

১ তোমার নাম কি ? আমার নাম হাসান ।
২ আমি বাঙালী । আপনি কি ইংরেজ ?
৩ উনি কি টিচার ? না, উনি ডাক্তার । ৪ ওটা
কার ? ওটা আমার, ৫ আপনি কে ? আমি
রঞ্জিত । ৬ এটা কার ? ওর । ৭ ওটা ওর
কোট ? না, ওটা এর কোট । ৮ তারা কি
হিন্দু ? না, তারা খ্রিষ্টান । ৯ ওটা কি ওদের
বাড়ি ? হ্যাঁ, ওদের বাড়ি । ১০ তোমাদের
টিচার কে ? আমাদের টিচার মিস্টার হক ।

Unit 15, 1   *(a)*

১ ওর বাবার গাড়ি ছিলনা । ২ ওরা বাঙালী
নন । ৩ ওটা আপনার নয় । ৪ আমাদের
টেলিফোন নেই । ৫ ওদিকে ক্যামেরার দোকান
নেই । ৬ তুমি ওখানে ছিলেনা । ৭ ও আমার
ছেলে নয় । ৮ আপনারা বাঙালী নন । ৯ তুমি
চাষী নও । ১০ তিনি তখন এখানে ছিলেননা ।

1   *(b)*

১ ওই নিবটা সরু । ২ ওই বেড়ালটা রোগা ।
৩ ওই সুটকেসটা হালকা । ৪ ওই চেয়ারগুলো
ভাঙা । ৫ ওই সাটটা পুরনো । ৬ ওই ছবিটা
বিশ্রী ।

2

১ আপনাদের কি টেলিভিশন আছে ?
২ তোমার বাবা কোথায় ? ৩ তুমি কি ওখানে
ছিলে ? ৪ কলমটা আমার নয় ।
৫ ওর নতুন সাইকেল আছে । ৬ উনি বাঙালী
নন । ৭ ওই আমগাছটার আম খুব ভালো ।
৮ বইটার নাম কি ? ৯ ওদের অনেক
ছেলেমেয়ে আছে । ১০ আমাদের টিচার
এখানে আছেন / এখানে আমাদের টিচার
আছেন । ১১ এই সাটটা দাদার । ১২ আপনার
বাবার কি জমিজমা ছিল ?

Unit 16, 1   *(a)*

১ তিনটি মেয়ে ২ দশ টাকা । ৩ এক কিলো
চাল । ৪ দু চামচ চিনি । ৫ ছটা ডিম ।
৬ আড়াই-শ গ্রাম মাখন ।

1   *(b)*

১ টেবিলের উপর । ২ টেবিলের ডান
দিকে । ৩ দরজার কাছে । ৪ টেবিলের বাঁ
দিকে । ৫ দরজার ডান দিকে । ৬ টেবিলের
নিচে ।

2

১ আমার নাম জন । ২ আমার মায়ের নাম সু
আর আমার বাবার নাম পিটার । ৩ হ্যাঁ, আমার
ভাই-বোন আছে । ৪ দুটি ভাই আর একটি
বোন । ৫ পনের, তের আর দশ
বছর । ৬ হ্যাঁ, আমার একটি বাঙালী বন্ধু
আছে । ৭ হ্যাঁ, খুব কাছে । ৮ না, আমার
গাড়ি নেই । ৯ না, নতুন গাড়ি চাইনা ।
১০ নতুন গাড়ি চাইনা ! ১১ হ্যাঁ, খুব বেশী
দাম হবে । ১২ রাস্তা । ১৩ হ্যাঁ, একটা ছোট
বাগান । ১৪ আপেলগাছ আছে । ১৫ তিনটে ।
১৬ পার্ক আছে, কিন্তু একটু দূরে । ১৭ তিন
মাইল দূরে । ১৮ হ্যাঁ, খেলার মাঠ আছে ।
১৯ বেশ বড় । ২০ না, দুটো আছে ।

Unit 17, 1   *(a)*

১ না, ওরা একই উপজেলা থেকে আসেনা ।
২ হ্যাঁ, ওরা বাসে করে আসে । ৩ না, স্কুল
শেষ করার পর ওদের সবার বিয়ে হয়ে
যায়না । ৪ না, ক্লাস টুতে ওরা আলাদা আলাদা
বই থেকে শেখেনা । ৫ না, ওরা শক্ত বল
দিয়ে খেলেনা । ৬ না, ওরা খেলাধুলা
করেননা । ৭ না, ওরা ড্রিল করেননা । ৮ হ্যাঁ,
ওরা ইংরেজী শেখে । ৯ না, ওরা শুধু
সরকারের নির্দিষ্ট বই ব্যবহার করেনা । ১০ না,
ওরা সবসময় ইংরেজী কথা বলেননা ।

1   *(b)*

১ চট্টগ্রামে । ২ রাজশাহীতে ।
৩ রাজশাহীতে । ৪ ঢাকায় ।
৫ চট্টগ্রামে । ৬ চট্টগ্রামে । ৭ ঢাকায় । ৮
রাজশাহীতে । ৯ চট্টগ্রামে । ১০ খুলনায় ।

2

১ ওদের তিনটে গাড়ি আছে । ২ এই
হাসপাতালে শুধু পাঁচজন ডাক্তার । ৩ আপনার

বাড়িতে কি টেলিফোন নেই ? ৪ এই গ্রামে মেয়েদের জন্য স্কুল নেই। ৫ বাঙালীরা কবিতা ভালোবাসে। ৬ আপনার বাগানে কি কি ফুলের গাছ আছে ? ৭ বই ভালো। ৮ আপনি মদ খান ? ৯ তিনি কি ব্রাহ্মণ নন ? ১০ আমার ছোট ভাই খুব গান করে। ১১ এদেশে খাওয়া-দাওয়ার পরে আমরা মুখ ধুই। ১২ তুমি ক্রিকেট খেল ? ১৩ ওদের শুধু একটি মেয়ে। ১৪ আমি অনেক চিঠি লিখি। ১৫ আমার বাবা সবসময় ধুতি পরেন।

Unit 18, 1 *(a)*

১ আপনিও কি বাসে করে যাবেন ? ২ তুমিও কি বাংলায় কথা বলবে ? ৩ তোমার ছেলেমেয়েও কি আসবে ? ৪ তোমরাও কি পাঁচটায় খাবে ? ৫ তোমার বাবাও কি চিঠি লিখবেন ? ৬ তোমারও কি একা-একা লাগবে ? ৭ তুমিও কি চান-টান করবে ? ৮ আপনার স্বামীও কি যেতে চেষ্টা করবেন ? ৯ তোমারও কি খুব অসুবিধা হবে ? ১০ আপনিও কি কিছু বুঝবেননা ?

1 *(b)*

১ বুধবারে সরলা আসবেন। ২ বারটার সময়। ৩ শনিবারে। ৪ চারটেয়। ৫ মা-বাবার ওখানে। ৬ মাসিমাও যাবেন। ৭ বৃহস্পতিবারে। ৮ সকালে। ৯ উনি প্লেনে করে যাবেন। ১০ উনি রবিবারে ফিরবেন।

2

১ শনিবার সকালে আমি বাড়ি পরিষ্কার করবো। ২ শনিবার বিকেলে আমি দোকান করবো। ৩ শনিবার সন্ধ্যে বেলায় আমি টেলিভিশন দেখবো। ৪ রবিবার নটার সময় আমি স্নান করবো। ৫ দশটায় আমি ব্রেকফাস্ট খাব। ৬ বারটার সময় আমি চিঠি লিখবো। ৭ দুটোর সময় আমি খবরের কাগজ পড়বো। ৮ সাড়ে তিনটের সময় আমি পার্কে যাব। ৯ রবিবার সন্ধ্যে বেলায় আমি সিনেমা দেখতে যাব। ১০ সোমবার পাঁচটায় আমি জামা-কাপড় কাচবো। ১১ সন্ধ্যে বেলায় আমি পড়াশোনা করবো। ১২ মঙ্গলবার দুপুরে আমি আপিস থেকে ফিরবো। ১৩ বিকেলে আমি ডাক্তারকে দেখাতে যাব। ১৪ সন্ধ্যে বেলায় আমি বিশ্রাম করবো। ১৫ সাড়ে আটটার সময় আমি শুতে

যাব। ১৬ বৃহস্পতিবারে আমি কয়েকজন বন্ধুদের ফোন করবো। ১৭ শুক্রবারে আমি খুব ভোরে উঠবো। ১৮ আমি সারাদিন খাবার তৈরি করবো। ১৯ রাত্রে নটার সময় আমরা সকলে একসঙ্গে খাব। ২০ আমরা অনেক রাত পর্যন্ত গান শুনবো।

Unit 19, 1 *(a)*

১ সওয়া দুটো বাজে। ২ পাঁচটা বেজে কুড়ি। ৩ দেড়টা বাজে। ৪ পৌনে আটটা বাজে। ৫ এগারটা বাজে। ৬ সাড়ে ছটা বাজে।

or

১ দুটো বেজে পনের। ২ পাঁচটা বেজে কুড়ি। ৩ একটা বেজে ত্রিশ। ৪ সাতটা বেজে পঁয়তাল্লিশ। ৫ এগারটা বাজে। ৬ ছটা বেজে ত্রিশ।

1 *(b)*

১ আপনার শুতে যাওয়া উচিত। ২ আপনার সোয়েটার পরা উচিত। ৩ আপনার গরম চা খাওয়া উচিত। ৪ আপনার ঠাণ্ডা জল খাওয়া উচিত নয়। ৫ আপনার সুপ খাওয়া উচিত ৬ আপনার ওষুধ খাওয়া উচিত। ৭ আপনার কাজ করা উচিত নয়। ৮ আপনার সিগারেট খাওয়া উচিত নয়। ৯ আপনার মাফলার পরা উচিত। ১০ আপনার ডাক্তারকে দেখানো উচিত।

2

১ তুমি কে ? ২ উনি আমার বন্ধু। ৩ ওখানে ওটা কি ? ৪ আমাদের দুটি ছেলে আছে। ৫ আমার বোনের বাড়ি বড় নয়। ৬ গাছগুলো সুন্দর। ৭ তোমার বাবার বয়স কত ? ৮ পোস্টাপিস স্টেশনের কাছে। ৯ তোমাদের ক্লাসে কতজন ছেলেমেয়ে আছে ? ১০ ও কি বাঙালী নয় ? ১১ উনি ভাত খাননা। ১২ বইগুলো টেবিলে রাখ। ১৩ তোমার মা কটার সময় আসবেন ? ১৪ আপনারা নটার সময় খাবেন ? ১৫ তুমি কি গান করতে পার ? ১৬ সে কাজ করতে চায়না। ১৭ আপনার অসুবিধা হবেনা ? ১৮ তোমাকে বৃহস্পতিবারে ওখানে যেতে হবে। ১৯ আমার দাদার কাছে বসুন না। ২০ তোমার ঠাণ্ডা লাগেনি ?

Unit 20, 1 *(a)*

(i) ami **dekhe** esechi. (ii) se roj phuṭbɔl **khæle**. (iii) amra noũko **kôre** y̆abô. (iv) meyeṭi sundôr **kôre** ciṭhi lekhe. (v) uni ɔnekkṣôṇ **dhôre** bôse achen. (vi) ami suṭ **pôre** y̆abô. (vii) dɔṣṭar **pɔre** asun. (viii) se saradin ṭelibhiṣôn **dækhe**. (ix) cheleṭi khub pɔṛaṣona **kɔre**. (x) ora ei baṛi theke **côle** gæche.

1 *(b)*

১ উনি মেয়েটিকে উপহার দিয়েছেন । ২ ভদ্রলোকটি চিঠি পোস্ট করেছেন । ৩ ছেলেটি এক গেলাস জল খেয়েছে । ৪ গাছটা মরে গেছে । ৫ লোকটি ধুতি পরেছে ৬ ট্রেন স্টেশন ছেড়ে দিয়েছে ।

2

১ আমি ভাত খেয়ে আপিসে যাব । ২ আপনি কোট না পরে কেন এসেছেন ? ৩ তুমি পরীক্ষায় পাস করে কলেজে যেতে পারবে । ৪ আমি বাজার করে বাড়ি ফিরে আসবো । ৫ তিনি বাংলা শিখে এদেশে এসেছেন । ৬ সোজা গিয়ে বাঁ দিকে যান । ৭ বৃষ্টি হয়ে গিয়ে আকাশ বেশ পরিষ্কার হয়েছে । ৮ লোকটিকে শুধু তিন টাকা দিয়ে চলে আসুন । ৯ তুমি হাত না ধুয়ে খেতে আসতে পারনা । ১০ সে গাড়ি কিনে বড়লোক হয়ে গেছে । ১১ তুমি চলে গিয়ে আমাদের অসুবিধা হয়েছে । ১২ সে পাগল হয়ে স্ত্রী বাচ্চাদের খুন করেছে । ১৩ আমি বিশ্রাম নিয়ে অনেক ভালো আছি । ১৪ খুব বেশী মিষ্টি খেয়ে ছেলেটির বমি হয়েছে । ১৫ প্রধানমন্ত্রীর সঙ্গে কথা বলে আমি সব ব্যবস্থা করবো ।

সে খুব ভোরে উঠে চা খেয়ে দাঁত মেজে স্নান করে পাট-ভাঙা ধুতি পরে জুতো পালিশ করে বেশী ভাত না খেয়ে ছাতা নিয়ে তাড়াতাড়ি হেঁটে গিয়ে অপিসে এসে নটার মধ্যে কাজ করতে শুরু করে ।

Unit 21, 1 *(a)*

১ এই লোকটি ওই লোকটির চেয়ে বেঁটে । ২ এই মেয়েটি ওই মেয়েটির চেয়ে লম্বা । ৩ এই ছেলেটি ওই ছেলেটির চেয়ে মোটা । ৪ এই লোকটি ওই লোকটির চেয়ে কম বয়সের । ৫ এই লোকটি ওই লোকটির চেয়ে বয়সে ছোট । ৬ এই গরুটা ওই গরুটার চেয়ে রোগা ।

1 *(b)*

১ এই খাবার আমার ভালো লাগছেনা । ২ ফিল্মটা আমার ভালো লাগেনি । ৩ ওই মেয়েটিকে আমার খুবই ভালো লাগে । ৪ ওখানে যেতে আমার একটুও ভালো লাগবেনা । ৫ গানগুলি আমার খুব ভালো লেগেছে । ৬ বাগান করা আমার বেশী ভালো লাগনা । ৭ এখন আম খেতে আমার বেশী ভালো লাগবেনা । ৮ বাংলা শেখা আমার খুব ভালো লাগছে । ৯ ওর কবিতা আমার ভালো লেগেছে । ১০ বৃষ্টিতে হেঁটে যাওয়া আমার একটুও ভালো লাগেনা ।

2

১ আকাশে মেঘ করছে । ঝড় আসছে । ২ আমি বাজারে যাচ্ছি । তুমি বাড়িতে থাকবে, না আমার সঙ্গে আসবে ? ৩ এত বড় গাড়ি এই রাস্তায় ঢুকতে পারবেনা । ৪ আমি খুব ক্লান্ত । এখন আর পড়াশোনা করবোনা । ৫ দেখ কি হয়েছে ! কুকুরটা বেড়ালটিকে মেরে ফেলেছে । ৬ আমি রোজ দশ কাপ চা খাই । ৭ আপনি সমস্ত রবীন্দ্ররচনাবলী পড়েছেন ? ৮ আমরা তিন ঘণ্টা ধরে বসে আছি । ৯ না, এই জামাটা আমি কিনবোনা । এর রংটা আমার ভালো লাগেনা । ১০ আমাদের পড়াশোনা ভালো চলছে । আমরা অনেক শিখেছি । ১১ উনি বাংলা বলতে পারেননা । উনি বাঙালী নন । ১২ এখন আমাদের বাড়িতে বাথরুম হয়েছে । আগে আমাদের বাথরুম ছিলনা ১৩ সে সারাদিন নদীর ধারে বসে আছে, তবু কোনো মাছ পায়নি । ১৪ আপনার এত সুন্দর উপহার আমি প্রত্যাশা করিনি । ১৫ বাসটা কটার সময় ছাড়বে ? আমি অপেক্ষা করতে পারিনা ।

Unit 22, 1 *(a)*

১ আমি গত সপ্তাহেও ওকে চিঠি লিখেছিলাম । ২ ইনি গত রবিবারেও চিটাগাং গিয়েছিলেন । ৩ কয়েকদিন আগেও ওর সঙ্গে আমার দেখা হয়েছিল । ৪ গত পরশুদিনও উনি লণ্ডন থেকে ফোন করেছিলেন । ৫ গত বছরেও বাবার জন্মদিনে বৃষ্টি হয়েছিল । ৬ আমার ছেলেমেয়েরা গত বুধবারেও জাদুঘরে গিয়েছিল । ৭ কালকেও আমি পেট ভরে খেয়েছিলাম । ৮ উনি ১৯৪০ সালে ওকে দেখেছিলেন । ৯ আমার দাদাও গত বছরে আমেরিকায় চলে গিয়েছিল । ১০ সরলা বইটি গত মাসে পড়েছিল ।

1 *(b)*

ট্যাক্সি দেখা যায় । রিকশা দেখা যায় । গরু দেখা যায় । তিনটি বাচ্চাদের দেখা যায় । কয়েকটা গাছ দেখা যায় । গাছের উপরে পাখি দেখা যায় । ট্রেন দেখা যায় । একটা কুকুর আর একটা বেড়াল দেখা যায় । কুকুরটার ডাক শোনা যায় । কাগজওয়ালাকে দেখা যায় । কাগজওয়ালার ডাক শোনা যায় । পোস্ট-বাক্স দেখা যায় ।

2

১ বনের ভিতরের পথটা খুব অন্ধকার । ২ পুকুরের ওপারের মন্দিরটা পুরনো নয় । ৩ বাড়ির চারদিকের জঙ্গলে অনেক পাখি থাকে । ৪ ঈদের পরের ছুটিতে বাড়ি যাব । ৫ আমাদের উপরের একটা ঘরে তিনি থাকেন । ৬ বৃষ্টির পরের রোদে আমাদের চারাগুলো সতেজ হবে । ৭ ব্যাগের ভিতরের টাকাগুলো বিদেশী । ৮ আমার ডেস্কের নিচের বাক্সটা নিয়ে আসবো ? ৯ তাকের উপরের উপহারটি আমাকে দাও । ১০ দুপুরের আগের লেকচারটা খুব খারাপ ছিল ।

স্কুলটার পিছনের পুকুরের ধারের বনের মধ্যের পুরনো বাড়ির পাশের বটগাছের তলার পাথরের নিচের গর্তের ভিতরের বাক্সতে প্রচুর সোনার মোহর ছিল ।

Unit 23, 1 *(a)*

১ কোন বাস নেব ? ২ তোমার কাছে কিছু টাকা আছে ? ৩ হ্যাঁ আমার কাছে কিছু টাকা আছে । ৪ আপনি কোন দেশ থেকে এসেছেন ? ৫ ওখানে কিছু নেই । ৬ কোনো কোনো লোক রাস্তায় মারা যান । ৭ আপনি কোনটা কিনবেন ? ৮ বাচ্চাটি কিছু খেয়েছে ? ৯ না, ও কিছু খায়নি । ১০ বাংলাদেশে আমাদের কোনো গাড়ি ছিলনা ।

1 *(b)*

১ দামু, রামু আর শামু । ২ রামু । ৩ দামু । ৪ শামুর মাথায় । ৫ বটগাছটা । ৬ দামু । ৭ রামু । ৮ ও দেখল তার মাথায় একটুও চুল নেই । ৯ ও তাড়াতাড়ি উঠে আগুন জ্বালাল । ১০ ওরা খুব হাসতে লাগল ।

2

আমি আজ দেরি করে উঠলাম । ব্রেকফাস্ট খেতে খেতে খবরের কাগজ পড়লাম । তারপর আমি দুই-একটা চিঠি লিখলাম । দোকানে যেতে যেতে রাস্তায় দুর্ঘটনা দেখলাম । একজন বুড়ো ভদ্রলোক আঘাত পেলেন । পুলিশ আর অ্যাম্বুলান্স এল । পার্কের ভিতর দিয়ে ফিরে এসে আমার মনে পড়লো, কাল ভাইপোর জন্মদিন হবে । লান্চ-এর পরে আবার বেরিয়ে গিয়ে বই-এর দোকানে গেলাম । নাম করা ক্রিকেটার সম্বন্ধে একটা বই কিনলাম । বাড়ি ফিরে এসে দেখলাম, বাথরুমের সমস্ত মেঝেতে জল । মিস্ত্রীকে টেলিফোন করে বললাম । সে বলল, 'কালকে আবার আসবো ।' সব জল বন্ধ করার জন্য অসুবিধা হল । আমার খুব রাগ হল । অনিলকে টেলিফোন করলাম । ও ব্যস্ত ছিল – আমরা সামনের শনিবার দেখা করার ব্যবস্থা করলাম । টেলিভিশনে বিচ্ছিরি ছবি দেখলাম ।

Unit 24, 1 *(a)*

১ কালীঘাটে নামলে, কালীমন্দির দর্শন করে আসতে পারেন । ২ ভবানীপুরে নামলে, জগুবাবুর বাজারে যেতে পারবেন । ৩ রবীন্দ্রসদনে নামলে, তারামণ্ডল দেখে আসবেন । ৪ পার্ক স্ট্রীটে নামলে, জাদুঘরে যেতে পারেন । ৫ টালিগঞ্জে নামলে, গলফ ক্লাবে যেতে পারেন । ৬ বরীন্দ্রসরোবরে নামলে, রবীন্দ্রসরোবরের কাছে বেড়িয়ে আসতে পারেন । ৭ যতীন দাস পার্কে নামলে, আশুতোষ কলেজ দেখতে যেতে পারেন । ৮ ময়দানে নামলে, ময়দান সামনে পাবেন ।

TEACH YOURSELF BENGALI

1 *(b)*

১ কলম লাগবে। ২ পোস্টাপিসে যেতে হবে। ৩ দশটা এক টাকার টিকিট আনতে হবে। ৪ দিদির জন্য উপহার কিনতে হবে। ৫ শামসুর রাহমানের নতুন কবিতার বই কিনতে হবে। ৬ ভালো চা আনতে হবে। ৭ খাম লাগবে। ৮ আঠা লাগবেনা। ৯ ভালো আম পেলে কিনবো। ১০ ছাতা কিনতেই হবে।

2 (i) Will he/she have something to eat when he/she comes? (ii) If (you) give (me) that (I) shall go. (iii) Don't come if it rains. (iv) He/she fell ill and died. (v) If (you) go there (you) will get (it). (vi) Don't pay too much (for it). (vii) It will be better if (you) do (it) later. (viii) (You) ought to say that. (ix) It would have been better if (we) had eaten earlier. (x) (I) got delayed, so (I) didn't go. (xi) If there had been a taxi (I) would have taken (it). (xii) If the mango is sweet (I)'ll eat (it). (xiii) (One) shouldn't get angry. (xiv) (I)'ll sit in an easy chair and eat (it). (xv) (I) wasn't happy when (I) bought that. (xvi) Go up on to the roof when the moon rises. (xvii) If necessary (I) shall come. (xviii) What is the point of going there? (xix) (You) won't need (any) money. (xx) When (I) went there (I) couldn't find (it).

Unit 25, 1 *(a)*

১ বৃষ্টি হলে, আমাদের ভিতরে খেতে হবে। ২ ও চিঠি লিখলে আমি রাগ করতাম না। ৩ তুমি পড়াশোনা করলে পরীক্ষায় পাস করবে। ৪ বেশী আম খেলে ছেলেটার অসুখ হবে। ৫ ভদ্রভাবে না বললে তোমার অসুবিধা হবে। ৬ টাকা থাকলে আমি আমেরিকায় চলে যেতাম। ৭ ওইভাবে ব্যবহার করলে তার স্ত্রীর তাকে ছেড়ে দেওয়া উচিত। ৮ আপনি সাহায্য না করলে আমি কাজটা করতে পারতামনা। ৯ তুমি টাকা দিলে আমি করবো। ১০ এই বইটা শেষ করলে আপনি অনেক বাংলা জেনে যাবেন।

1 *(b)*

১ মাস্টারমশাই মেয়েটিকে সেতার শেখাতে চেষ্টা করছেন, কিন্তু ও শিখতে চাইছেনা। ২ মা রেলগাড়িতে বাচ্চাকে বসাতে চেষ্টা করছেন, কিন্তু ও বসছেনা। ৩ মা তাঁর মেয়েকে জাগাতে চেষ্টা করছেন, কিন্তু ও জাগছেনা। ৪ মা তাঁর ছেলেকে স্কুলে হাঁটিয়ে নিয়ে যেতে চেষ্টা করছেন, কিন্তু ও হেঁটে যেতে চাইছেনা। ৫ ব্রাহ্মণ ছেলেটিকে বেদ পড়াতে চেষ্টা করছেন, কিন্তু ও পড়তে চায়না। ৬ মা মেয়েকে শাড়ী পরাতে চেষ্টা করছেন, কিন্তু ও শাড়ী পড়তে চায়না।

2

আমি শীতের দেশের লোক, তবে বাংলাদেশের গরম আমার খারাপ লাগেনা। রাস্তায় আমি ইউরোপীয় পোশাক পরি কিন্তু বাড়িতে আমি বাঙালী পোশাক পরতে ভালোবাসি। আমি রোজ খুব ভোরে উঠি। চা খেতে খেতে আমি পাখির ডাক শুনি আর সূর্যোদয় দেখি। তখন আমার মনে গভীর ভাব জাগে। তার পরে আমি বই পড়ি বা চিঠি লিখি।

গতকাল আমার বন্ধু নরেন এসেছিল ব্রেকফাস্টের আগে। তার আশি বছরের মায়ের জন্য তার খুব ভাবনা হচ্ছে। উনি বাতের ব্যথায় খুব ভোগেন আর হাঁটতে পারেননা। তাছাড়া নরেন একটা নতুন মাটির ঘর করাচ্ছে। কাজটা নিজে তদারক করবার জন্য সে যথেষ্ট সময় পাচ্ছেনা। কয়েক দিন আগে একটা কাল-বৈশাখীর ঝড় উঠেছিল – নতুন ঘরটার অর্ধেক শেষ করা ছাদ বাতাসের ঝাপটায় উড়ে গিয়েছিল। এখন তাকে আবার শুরু করতে হবে – খালিখালি অনেকগুলি টাকা নষ্ট হয়েছে।

মনে হয় আমার এখন তাকে কিছু টাকা ধার দেওয়া উচিত। তাতে তার একটু সাহায্য হবে। নরেন আমার জন্য আগে অনেক করেছে।

Unit 27

বেঁধেছে	perfect	3F	বাঁধা		has built
হাঁ করে	present	3F	হাঁ করা		gape
ভাবে	present	3F	ভাবা		thinks
খাব	future	1	খাওয়া		will eat
হেঁট হয়ে	participle	—	হেঁট হওয়া		having bowed
চলে গেল	simple past	3F	চলে যাওয়া		went away
চলে যায়	present	3F	চলে যাওয়া		goes away
উড়তে	infinitive	—	ওড়া		to fly
পারব	future	1	পারা		will be able
বসতে	infinitive	—	বসা		to sit/perch
এসে	participle	—	আসা		having come
পালাল	simple past	3F	পালানো		fled
লাফিয়ে	participle	—	লাফানো		having jumped
ধরতে	infinitive	—	ধরা		to catch
ফিরল	simple past	3F	ফেরা		returned

Unit 28

১ যে লোকটি পাশের বাড়িতে থাকতো সে হঠাৎ মারা গেল। ২ যে চেয়ারের কথা আপনাকে বলেছিলাম সেটা এই। ৩ তোমাদের মধ্যে যারা বাঙালী, তারা আমার সাথে এস। ৪ যে চাবি দিয়ে এই আলমারি খোলা যায় সেটা কোথায়? ৫ যে জায়গা থেকে পাহাড় দেখা যায় সেখানে থাকতে চাই। ৬ রবীন্দ্রনাথের যে গল্পগুলি তুমি পড়েছ, সেগুলির মধ্যে কোনটি তোমার সবচেয়ে প্রিয়? ৭ যে জামা-কাপড় ধোয় তাকে ধোপা বলে। ৮ যার দোষ নেই সে মানুষ নয়। ৯ যা অসম্ভব তা কেউ করতে পারেনা। ১০ যেখানে জল নেই সেখানে কি করে থাকবো? ১১ তুমি আমাকে যা-ই দেবে তা-ই আমি সারাজীবন কাছে রাখবো। ১২ যা পরিষ্কার নয় তা ব্যবহার না করাই ভালো।

Unit 29

The circus still comes every year, but in those days in the Harmstone Circus Europeans used to perform, and nowadays they're mainly Madrasi circuses. The thing that can't be seen nowadays is the Carnival. In our childhood there were large open spaces either side of Central Avenue. Calcutta's first 'high-rise' ten-storey tower blocks had not yet been built; the Electric Supply's Victoria House had not yet been built. In one of these open spaces, right next to the circus, the Carnival was held.

It is hard to convey to today's children just how much fun the Carnival was. Everyone has seen Big Wheels at fairs, but the Carnival's wheel – its 'Giant Wheel' – was as high as a five-storey building. The revolving wheel's lights could be seen from far away. Besides the wheel, there were merry-go-rounds, whirling aeroplanes, dodgem-cars, a switchback Alpine railway, and much else. Various kinds of gambling stall were scattered round all of this. Such enticing things were arranged on these stalls that it was difficult to suppress the desire to gamble. Eventually, because the Government made public gambling illegal, the Carnival disappeared from Calcutta. Its actual earnings were probably from this gambling.

Unit 30

১ টিপটিপ করে বৃষ্টি পড়ছে। ২ ব্যাঙটি ভয় পেয়ে থপথপ করে চলে গেল। ৩ সে পুরো গেলাস সরবত ঢকঢক করে খেয়ে ফেলল। ৪ কি ছটফটে ছেলে ! ও কখনও চুপচাপ বসে থাকেনা। ৫ চটপট উঠে পড়, নইলে তোমার দেরি হবে। ৬ ভদ্রলোকটির পোসাক দেখে মেয়েরা খিলখিল করে হেসে উঠল। ৭ অন্ধকার ঘরে এক কোণে একটি বাতি মিটমিট করছিল। ৮ বিরাট ধু-ধু চর - কোথাও কোনো লোক নেই। ৯ চকচক করলেই সোনা হয় না। ১০ বাইরে একজন রিকশাওয়ালার ঘন্টির টিং-টিং শব্দ শুনলাম। ১১ বাসে এত ভিড় - দারুণ ধাকাধাকি। ১২ চুড়ির রিনিঝিনি শুনে বুঝলাম সে আসছে।

Unit 31

১ সকালেই ২ বিশেষ করে ৩ সম্বন্ধে ৪ থামিয়ে ৫ শুনতে (আমার) খুব ইচ্ছে করছিল ৬ ব্যস্ত ৭ সঙ্গে ৮ পাবার ৯ ভয়েস (Voice) ১০ কোনদিক থেকে কোন খবর (konô . . . konô = any . . . any) ১১ ঢুকে পড়ল ১২ দেখাচ্ছিল ১৩ জ্বালাতে জ্বালাতে ১৪ নিয়ে নিল ১৫ আমাদের সবাইকে বলা হল ১৬ হাসপাতাল ১৭ আনেনি ১৮ স্বর ১৯ তাঁদেরও ২০ রেপ করে

Unit 32

১ স্ব = স + ব, ২ ষ্ট = ষ + ট, ৩ ব্র = ব + র, ৪ জ্জ = জ + জ + ব, ৫ শ্ল = শ + ল, ৬ স্থ = ন + থ, ৭ গ্র = গ + র, ৮ ক্ষ = ক + ষ, ৯ স্ত = ন + ত, ১০ স্ধ = ন + ধ, ১১ ক্র = ক + ত, ১২ র্থ = র + থ, ১৩ ত্ত = ত + ত, ১৪ ম্র = ম + র, ১৫ জ্ব = জ + ব, ১৬ স্ট = স + ট, ১৭ দ্দ = দ + দ, ১৮ র্ত = র + ত, ১৯ দ্র = দ + র, ২০ চ্ছ = চ + ছ, ২১ ষ্ঠ = ষ + ঠ, ২২ ত্য = ত + য(য়), ২৩ ন্ত = ন + ত + উ, ২৪ ঙ্গ = ঙ + গ, ২৫ র্ধ = র + ধ।

Unit 33

১ তাহাকে ২ ইহাকে ৩ উহার ৪ ইহাদের ৫ সে বাঙালী নহে ৬ তিনি খাইলেন ৭ উনি যাইবেন ? ৮ তুমি বুঝিতে পারিতেছ ? ৯ তাহারা হাত দিয়াছে ১০ আপনি ইহাকে দেখাইয়াছিলেন ? ১১ ইঁহারা শুনিয়াছিলেন ১২ তিনিও করেন নাই ১৩ চিঠি লিখিলে সে আসিবে ১৪ উহার চাইতে ছোট ১৫ বুঝা যায় না ১৬ শিখার আগে

Unit 34

I have looked upon the face of Bengal – the world's beauty
I need no longer seek: in the darkness I awake and glimpse
In a fig tree, sitting beneath umbrella-like foliage,
The early morning magpie – I see all around piles of leaves
Of jām, *banyan, jackfruit, cashew,* aśvattha, *lying still;*
Shade falls upon the cactus clump, upon the śaṭi *grove.*
I know not when Chand from Champa, from his boat the Honeybee,
Had seen Bengal's exquisite beauty, the same blue shadows
Of cashew, banyan, tamāl. *Behula once on a raft upon the river –*
When the moon's sliver died away behind some sandy shoal –
Had seen many an aśvattha *and banyan beside the golden paddy,*
Had heard the śyāmā *bird's soft song, once had gone to Amara and*
when
She danced like a clip-winged wagtail bird at Indra's court, Bengal's
Rivers, fields, bhāṭ *blossoms wept like ankle bells upon her feet.*

The tape accompanying this book ends with a recording of Tagore's song
আমার সোনার বাংলা . Here are the words of the complete song (the first
two verses are sung as the National Anthem of Bangladesh), with an
English translation:

আমার সোনার বাংলা, আমি তোমায় ভালোবাসি ।
চিরদিন তোমার আকাশ, তোমার বাতাস, আমার প্রাণে বাজায় বাঁশি ॥
ও মা, ফাগুনে তোর আমের বনে ঘ্রাণে পাগল করে,
মরি হায়, হায়, রে –
ও মা, অঘ্রানে তোর ভরা ক্ষেতে আমি কী দেখেছি মধুর হাসি ॥

কী শোভা, কী ছায়া গো, কী স্নেহ, কী মায়া গো –
কী আঁচল বিছায়েছ বটের মূলে, নদীর কূলে কূলে ।
মা, তোর মুখের বাণী আমার কানে লাগে সুধার মতো,
মরি হায়, হায় রে –
মা, তোর বদনখানি মলিন হলে, ও মা, আমি নয়নজলে ভাসি ॥

তোমার এই খেলাঘরে শিশুকাল কাটিল রে,
তোমারি ধুলামাটি অঙ্গে মাখি ধন্য জীবন মানি ।
তুই দিন ফুরালে সন্ধ্যাকালে কী দীপ জ্বালিস ঘরে,

মরি হায়, হায় রে –
তখন খেলাধুলা সকল ফেলে, ও মা, তোমার কোলে ছুটে আসি ॥

ধেনু-চরা তোমার মাঠে, পারে যাবার খেয়াঘাটে,
সারা দিন পাখি-ডাকা ছায়ায়-ঢাকা তোমার পল্লীবাটে,
তোমার ধানে-ভরা আঙিনাতে জীবনের দিন কাটে,
মরি হায়, হায় রে –
ও মা, আমার যে ভাই তারা সবাই, ও মা, তোমার রাখাল
তোমার চাষি ॥
ও মা, তোর চরণেতে দিলেম এই মাথা পেতে –
দে গো তোর পায়ের ধূলা, সে যে আমার মাথার মানিক হবে ।
ও মা, গরিবের ধন যা আছে তাই দিব চরণতলে,
মরি হায়, হায় রে –
আমি পরের ঘরে কিনব না আর, মা, তোর ভূষণ ব'লে গলার ফাঁসি ॥

My golden Bengal, I love you.
Your skies, your breezes, play an everlasting flutesong in my being.
O mother, the scents in your mango-groves in Phālgun *send me mad,*
Ah! Ecstasy!
O mother, what enchanting smiles I see in your full fields in Agrahāyaṇ.

What beauty, what shade, what love and tenderness –
How you spread your sari at the banyan's foot, on the river-bank.
Mother, your message in my ears is like nectar,
Ah! Ecstasy!
Mother, if your face turns angry, I swim in tears.

I spent my childhood in this nursery of yours –
To smear my limbs with your earth glorifies my life.
When day ends, what a lamp you light in the evening,
Ah! Ecstasy!
We throw aside our toys then, O mother, and rush to your lap.

In your fields where cattle graze, at your ghats where ferries cross,
In your shaded villages where birds sing all day,
In your yards piled with harvested paddy, we pass our days,
Ah! Ecstasy!
Your herd-boys and farmers, O mother, are all my brothers.

O mother, I place my head at your feet –
Give me the dust of your feet as jewels for my head.
O mother, I shall place whatever humble treasures I have at your feet,
Ah! Ecstasy!
Never again shall I buy in a stranger's house a rope for your neck as
*your ornament.**

*An allusion to colonial domination, rejected from now on.

GLOSSARY

It takes time to learn to use a Bengali dictionary, so do not be disheartened if it initially takes you a long time to locate a word – even in a glossary like this. The order of letters follows the table on p. 45, read across (i.e. অ comes before আ, ক comes before খ etc.). ং ঃ ঁ come between the vowels and consonants: so all words beginning with বাঁ, say, are grouped after বাউল but before বা + ক, বা + কি, বা + খ etc. ব-ফলা comes after ল.

Be prepared to find inconsistency in the spelling of o/ô (see p. 8). In **Part Two** of the book, spelling of the future first person ending for verbs (consonant stems), for example, was consistently given as **-bo**, and the word for *good* was always spelt bhalo. The texts in **Part Three** are taken from different authors, so spellings vary. The **Glossary** gives both spellings if they occur commonly in current Bengali usage.

Some Bengali words are idiosyncratic in their pronunciation, and the transcription system used in this book will not indicate fully how they are pronounced. These pronunciations are explained in the notes to the **Conversations** and texts in **Part Two** and **Three**, and the **Glossary** will refer you to these explanations.

The **Glossary** aims to include all the Bengali words used in this book, except for pronouns, demonstratives, numbers, the words in the onomatopeic exercise in Unit 30, some names of plants and birds, and verb forms other than the verbal noun. The verbal noun forms are the colloquial forms you have learnt, but in dictionaries you will find the more literary forms লিখা for লেখা and শুনা for শোনা (though cross-references are usually given). Some English words, so naturalised into Bengali that they are hard to recognise, have been included.

E = East Bengal (Muslim); W = West Bengal (Hindu)

অ

অংশ	ɔmʃô	*part*
অংশ নেওয়া	ɔmʃô neoya	*to take part*
অকারণে	ɔkarône	*for no reason*
অকূল	ɔkūl	*shoreless, limitless*
অগাধ	ɔgadh	*bottomless*
অঙ্ক	ɔŋkô	*mathematics*

অঙ্গ	ɔŋgô	*limb*
অঙ্গুল/আঙ্গুল	ôŋgul/aŋgul	*finger*
অচল	ɔcɔl	*unmoving*
অজর	ɔjôr	*ageless*
অত	ɔtô	*so, so much*
অতি–	ôti-	*over-, hyper-*
অতিথি	ôtithi	*guest*
অতৃপ্ত	ɔtr̥ptô	*unsatisfied*
অত্যন্ত	ɔtyôntô	*extremely*
অথচ	ɔthôcô	*yet, still*
অথবা	ɔthôba	*or*
অদ্ভুত	ɔdbhut	*strange*
অধ্যাপক	ôdhyapôk	*professor*
অনাদর	ɔnadôr	*neglect, slight*
অনিয়মিত	ɔniyômitô	*irregular*
অনুবাদ	ônubad	*translation*
অনুষদ	ônuʃɔd	*university faculty*
অনুষ্ঠান	ônuʃṭhan	*function, concert*
অনেক	ɔnek	*much, a lot*
অনেকক্ষণ	ɔnekkʃôṇ	*a long time*
অন্তর্ধান	ɔntôrdhan	*disappearance*
অন্ধ	ɔndhô	*blind*
অন্ধকার	ɔndhôkar	*dark*
অন্বেষণ	ɔnveʂɔṇ	*search*
অন্য	ônyô	*other*
অন্যান্য	ônyænyô	*various other*
অপমান	ɔpôman	*insult*
অপমান করা	ɔpôman kɔra	*to insult*
অপরাধ	ɔpôradh	*fault, crime*
অপরিষ্কার	ɔpôriʂkar	*unclean*
অপরূপ	ɔpôrūp	*amazing*
অপেক্ষা	ɔpekʂa	*wait*
অপেক্ষা করা	ɔpekʂa kɔra	*to wait for*
অপ্রস্তুত	ɔprôstut	*unready*
অবকাশ	ɔbôkaʃ	*leisure*
অবতরণ করা	ɔbôtɔrôṇ kɔra	*to disembark*
অবধারিত	ɔbôdharitô	*determined, fixed*
অবধি	ɔbôdhi	*since, until* (p. 232)
অবশ্য/অবশ্যই	ɔbôʃyô/ɔbôʃyôi	*needless to say*
অবস্থা	ɔbɔstha	*state, condition*
অবাধ	ɔbadh	*unobstructed*
অবিনাশী	ɔbinaʃī	*indestructible*

অভাব	ɔbhab	lack
অভিজ্ঞতা	ôbhiɲɲôta	experience (p. 82)
অভিধান	ôbhidhan	dictionary
অভিমান	ôbhiman	hurt pride (p. 217)
অভিমানী	ôbhimanī	proud, haughty
অভিমুখে	ôbhimukhe	in the direction of (+ poss.)
অভিশাপ	ôbhiʃap	curse
অভিসম্পাত করা	ôbhisɔmpat kɔra	to curse
অভ্যাস	ôbhyæs	practice, habit
অমন	ɔmôn	such
অমনি	ômni	just like that, at once
অমর	ɔmôr	immortal
অমিল	ɔmil	discord
অর্জুন	ôrjun	foxglove
অর্থনীতি	ɔrthônīti	economics
অর্থনৈতিক	ɔrthônɔïtik	economic
অর্থাৎ	ɔrthat	that is, i.e.
অর্ধেক	ɔrdhek	a half
অল্প	ɔlpô	a little
অল্প-কিছু	ɔlpô-kichu	a small amount
অল্প-বয়সী	ɔlpô-bɔyôsī	young
অশান্তি	ɔʃanti	lack of peace
অশথ/অশ্বথ	ɔʃɔth/ɔʃvɔtthô	peepul-tree
অসংখ্য	ɔsɔmkhyô	countless
অসম্ভব	ɔsɔmbhôb	impossible
অসহ্য	ɔsôhyô	unbearable (p. 249)
অসুখ	ɔsukh	illness
অসুবিধা/অসুবিধে	ɔsubidha/ɔsubidhe	inconvenience
অস্তিত্ব	ôstitvô	existence

আ		
আংটি/আঙটি	amṭi/aŋṭi	ring
আঁকা	āka	to draw, paint
আঁচল	ācôl	loose end of a sari
আঁট	āṭ	tight
আঁধার	ādhar	dark
আকার	akar	shape, form
আকাশ	akaʃ	sky
আক্রোশ	akroʃ	wrath
আগে	age	before (+ poss.)
আগুন	agun	fire
আঘাত	aghat	blow, hit

আচার	acar	*pickle*
আচ্ছন্ন	acchɔnnô	*covered, overcast*
আচ্ছা	accha	*fine, well, OK*
আছ-	ach-	*to be present* (p. 60)
আজ/আজকে	aj/ajke	*today*
আজকাল	ajkal	*nowadays*
আটকান/আটকানো	aṭkanô/aṭkano	*to obstruct, jam*
আড্ডা	aḍḍa	*coterie* (p. 120)
আড়ম্বর	arômbôr	*pomp*
আড়াই	arai	*two-and-a-half*
আত্মীয়-স্বজন	atmīyô-svɔjôn	*family circle* (p. 145)
আত্মীয়তা	atmīyôta	*relationship*
আদর	adôr	*affection*
আদেশ করা	adeʃ kɔra	*to command*
আধ	adh	*half*
আধবুড়ো	adhburo	*middle-aged*
আনন্দ	anôndô	*joy*
আনমনে	anômɔne	*absent-mindedly*
আনা	ana	*to bring, buy* (p. 174)
আনা	ana	*anna* (p. 71)
আন্দোলিত	andolitô	*swung, stirred*
আপন	apôn	*one's own*
আপিস	apis	*office*
আবার	abar	*again, but*
আবেগ	abeg	*passion, force*
আব্বা	abba	*father* (E)
আম	am	*mango*
আমসত্ত্ব	amsɔttvô	*mango-juice preserve*
আম্মা	amma	*mother* (E)
আয়	ay	*earnings*
আয়তন	ayôtôn	*breadth, volume*
আয়না	ayna	*mirror*
আয়োজন করা	ayojɔn kɔra	*to prepare*
আর	ar	*and, yet more*
আরও/আরো	ar-o/āro	*more*
আরম্ভ করা	arômbhô kɔra	*to begin*
আর্তনাদ	artônad	*groaning*
আলমারি	almari	*cupboard*
আলাদা	alada	*separate, different*
আলাপ	alap	*introduction*
আলাপ করা	alap kɔra	*to introduce*
আলিঙ্গন করা	aliŋgɔn kɔra	*to embrace*

আলু	alu	*potato*
আলো	alo	*light*
আলোচনা করা	alocôna kɔra	*to discuss*
আলোড়ন	alorɔn	*agitation*
আশা করা	aʃa kɔra	*to hope*
আশ্চর্য	aʃcôrỹô	*surprise*
আষাঢ়	aʂaɽh	*Bengali month* (p. 195)
আসক্তি	asôkti	*attachment*
আসন	asôn	*seat*
আসল	asôl	*real*
আসলে	asôle	*really*
আসা	asa	*to come*
আস্তে-আস্তে	aste-aste	*slowly, gently*
আস্থা	astha	*trust*

ই

ইউরোপীয়	iuropīyô	*European*
ইংরেজ	im̩rej	*English*
ইংরিজী/ইংরেজী	im̩rijī/im̩rejī	*English language*
ইচ্ছা/ইচ্ছে	iccha/icche	*desire*
ইচ্ছা/ইচ্ছে করা	iccha/icche kɔra	*to desire*
ইতিহাস	itihas	*history*
ইস্কাপন	iskapɔn	*spades* (in cards)

ঈ

| ঈদ | īd | *Eid* |

উ

উঁচু	ūcu	*height*
উচ্চারণ	uccarɔn̩	*pronunciation*
উচ্চৈঃস্বর	uccoĩhsvɔr	*loud voice*
উজ্জ্বল	ujjvɔl	*radiant*
উঠন/উঠান	uʈhôn/uʈhan	*yard*
উড়ে যাওয়া	uɽe ỹaoya	*to fly off*
উৎসাহ	utsahô	*encouragement, zest*
উদার	udar	*generous, liberal*
উদাসীন	udasīn	*detached*
উদ্দাম	uddam	*violent, wild*
উদ্দীপনা	uddīpôna	*incitement, impetus*
উদ্দেশ করা	uddeʃ kɔra	*to aim*
উদ্ধত	uddhôtô	*high and mighty*
উদ্বিগ্ন	udbignô	*anxious*

উধাও	udhao	*vanished*
উন্নতি	unnôti	*improvement*
উন্মত্ত	unmɔttô	*insane, furious*
উপজেলা	upôjela	*sub-district* (p. 81)
উপবন	upôbɔn	*garden, grove*
উপর/উ·রে	upôr/upôre	*on, on top of*
উপরন্তু	upôrôntu	*in addition, besides*
উপস্থিত	upôsthit	*present, arrived*
উপহার	upôhar	*gift*
উপায়	upay	*way, means*
উলঙ্গ	ulɔŋgô	*nude*
উলটো	ulṭo	*opposite, reverse*
উল্লাস	ullas	*delight*
উষ্ণ	uṣṇô	*hot*

ঋ

ঋণ	ṛṇ	*debt*
ঋতু	ṛtu	*season*
ঋষি	ṛiṣi	*sage, saint*

এ

এই মাত্র	ei matrô	*only just now*
একা-একা	æka-æka	*lonely*
একাকার করা	ækakar kɔra	*to turn into a mass*
একটু	ekṭu	*a little*
একটুও	ekṭuo	*at all* (p. 138)
একদম	ækdɔm	*absolutely*
একদা	ækda	*once upon a time*
একদিন	ækdin	*one day*
একবার	ækbar	*once*
একরকম	ækrɔkôm	*so-so*
একসঙ্গে	æksɔŋge	*together* (W)
একসময়	æksɔmɔy	*at the same time*
একসাথে	æksathe	*together* (E)
একাকিনী	ækakinī	*alone* (female)
এক্ষণি	ekṣôṇi	*immediately*
এখন	ækhôn	*now*
এখনই/এখনি	ækhôn-i/ækhôni	*immediately*
এখনও/এখনো	ækhôn-o/ækhôno	*still*
এখানে	ekhane	*here*
এখুনি	ekhuni	*immediately*
এটুকু	eṭuku	*this little bit*

এত	ætô	so, so much
এতক্ষণ	ætôkṣôṇ	so long (within a day)
এতদিন	ætôdin	so long
এদিকে	edike	in this direction
এপারে	epare	on this side/shore
এবং	ebɔŋ	and
এমন	æmôn	such
এমন সময়	æmôn sɔmɔy	at such a time (p. 217)
এলাকা	elaka	area
এলো করা	elo kɔra	to ruffle up
এলোমেলো	elomelo	dishevelled

ও

ওখানে	okhane	there
ওঠা	oṭha	to rise
ওঠান/ওঠানো	oṭhanô/oṭhano	to raise
ওড়া	oṛa	to fly
ওদিকে	odike	in that direction
ওপর/ওপরে	opôr/opôre	(see উপর)
ওপারে	opare	on that side/shore
-ওয়ালা	-oyala	wallah (p. 231)
ওষুধ	oṣudh	medicine

ঔ

| ওষুধ | oṣudh | medicine |
| ঔষধ | oŭṣɔdh | medicine |

ক

কওয়া	kɔoya	to speak (archaic)
কখন	kɔkhôn	when (within a day)
কখনও/কখনো	kɔkhôn-o/kɔkhôno	never
কচি	kôci	fresh, green
কটা	kɔta	how many (p. 73)
কটাক্ষপাত করা	kɔṭakṣôpat kɔra	to cast a glance
কঠিন	kôṭhin	difficult
কত	kɔtô	how much/many (p. 72)
কতক	kɔtôk	some, somewhat
কথা	kɔtha	word, story, statement about (+poss.)
কথা বলা	kɔtha bɔla	to speak
কথাবার্তা	kɔthabarta	conversation
কনিষ্ঠা	kôniṣṭha	youngest (daughter)

কন্যা	kônya	daughter, bride
কন্যাকাল	kɔnyakal	maidenhood
কবি	kôbi	poet
কবিতা	kôbita	poem
কম	kɔm	a few, a little
কয়েক	kɔyek	a few
কয়েকদিন	kɔyekdin	a few days
কর	kɔr	hand
করতাল	kɔrtal	cymbal
করাত	kɔrat	saw
করুণ	kôruṇ	sad
করুণা	kôruṇa	compassion
কলম	kɔlôm	pen
কলহাস্য	kɔlhasyô	sweet cackling
কলালাপ	kɔlalap	amorous tête-à-tête
কলেজ	kɔlej	college
কসুর	kôsur	fault, shortcoming
কাঁচা	kāca	unripe
কাঁটা	kāṭa	thorn, fishbone
কাঁঠাল	kāṭhal	jackfruit
কাঁদা	kāda	to weep
কাঁধ	kādh	shoulder
কাঁপন	kāpôn	trembling
কাঁপা	kāpa	to tremble
কাকুতি-মিনতি	kakuti-minôti	repeated pleading
কাগজ	kagôj	paper
কাচা	kaca	to wash (clothes)
কাছ থেকে	kach theke	from (a person, + poss.)
কাছারি	kachari	zamindar's office
কাছে	kache	near (+ poss.)
কাজ	kaj	work
কাজকর্ম	kajkɔrmô	work
কাটা	kaṭa	to cut
কাটাকাটি	kaṭakaṭi	cutting, slaughtering
কাঠি	kaṭhi	small stick, chip
কান	kan	ear
কাপ	kap	cup
কাপড়	kapôṛ	cloth, garment
কাপড়-চোপড়	kapôṛ-copôṛ	clothing
কামান/কামানো	kamanô/kamano	to shave
কারণ	karôṇ	because
কারসাজি	karsaji	trickery

কাল/কালকে	kal/kalke	*tomorrow/yesterday* (p. 150)
কালবৈশাখী/কালবোশেখী	kalboïʃakhī/kalboʃekhī	*summer storm* (p. 190)
কালো/কাল	kalo/kalô	*black*
কাশি	kaʃi	*cough*
কি	ki	*what* (p. 51)
কিংবা	kiṃba	*or*
কিছু	kichu	*some, something*
কিছুতে	kichute	*in any way*
কিঞ্চিৎ	kiñcit	*a little*
কিন্তু	kintu	*but*
কিম্বা	kimba	*(see কিংবা)*
কিরণ	kirôṇ	*ray, beam*
কিলো	kilo	*kilo*
কুঁকড়ান/কুঁকড়ানো	kūkṛanô/kūkṛano	*to shrivel*
কুঁচকান/কুঁচকানো	kūckanô/kūckano	*to shrivel* (p. 232)
কুকুর	kukur	*dog*
কুঙ্কুম	kuṇkum	*saffron flower*
কুঞ্চিত	kuñcitô	*curled*
কুটির	kuṭir	*hut, cottage*
কুমির	kumir	*crocodile*
কৃতজ্ঞ	kṛtôjñô	*grateful* (p. 82)
কৃষক	kṛʂɔk	*farmer*
কে	ke	*who*
কেউ	keu	*anyone*
কেন	kænô	*why*
কেনা	kena	*to buy*
কেবল	kebôl	*only, just*
কেবলমাত্র	kebôlmatrô	*only, just*
কেমন	kæmôn	*how*
কোকিল	kokil	*koil-bird, cuckoo*
কোট	koṭ	*coat*
কোণ	koṇ	*corner*
কোথায়	kothay	*where* (interrogative)
কোন	kon	*which* (interrogative)
কোন/কোনো	konô/kono	*any* (p. 158)
কোমল	komɔl	*soft*
কোরান শরীফ	koran ʃôrīph	*Holy Koran*
কোর্তা/কুর্তা	korta/kurta	*Indian shirt*
কৌসুলী	kōūsulī	*legal counsel*
ক্যামেরা	kyæmera	*camera*
ক্যাম্পাস	kyæmpas	*campus*

ক্রিয়াপদ	kriyapɔd	*verb*
ক্লান্ত	klantô	*tired*
ক্লাস	klas	*class*

ক্ষ

ক্ষণ	kṣôṇ	*moment*
ক্ষমতা	kṣɔmôta	*power, skill*
ক্ষান্ত	kṣantô	*ceased*
ক্ষুদ্র	kṣudrô	*small, trifling*
ক্ষুদ্রতা	kṣudrôta	*smallness, meanness*
ক্ষোদিত	kṣoditô	*engraved, carved*

খ

খচমচ	khɔcmoc	= *irritation*
খঞ্জনা	khɔñjôna	*wag-tail (female)*
খবর	khɔbôr	*news*
খবরের কাগজ	khɔbôrer kagôj	*newspaper*
খল খল	khɔl khɔl	= *bubbling*
খসড়া	khɔsôɽa	*draft, sketch*
খাঁ খাঁ	khā khā	= *heat, loneliness*
খাওয়া	khaoya	*to eat, drink, receive*
খাওয়া-দাওয়া	khaoya-daoya	*meal*
খাওয়ান/খাওয়ানো	khaoyanô/khaoyano	*to feed*
খাট	khaṭ	*bed*
খাটা	khaṭa	*to toil*
খাতা	khata	*exercise-book*
খাদ্য	khadyô	*food*
খানিক	khanik	*a little, a while*
খানিকক্ষণ	khanikkṣôṇ	*a little while*
খাবার	khabar	*food*
খারাপ	kharap	*bad*
খালি	khali	*empty, bare, merely*
খালিখালি	khalikhali	*for nothing*
খিটখিট	khiṭkhiṭ	= *displeasure*
খিদে	khide	*hunger*
খুঁৎখুঁৎ	khūtkhūt	= *peevishness*
খুকী/খুকু	khukī/khuku	*little girl (p. 239)*
খুন করা	khun kɔra	*to murder*
খুব/খুবই	khub/khub-i	*very*
খুশি	khuʃi	*happy*
খেঁচান/খেঁচানো	khæ̃canô/khæ̃cano	*to grit, clench*
খেয়ে ফেলা	kheye phæla	*to eat up*
খেলনা	khælna	*toy*

খেলা	khæla	sport, game; to play
খেলাধুলা	khæladhula	sports
খেলান/খেলানো	khælanô/khælano	to cause to play
খেলার মাঠ	khælar maṭh	playing field
খোঁচা	khõca	prick, jab
খোঁচান/খোঁচানো	khõcanô/khõcano	to prick, jab
খোঁজা	khõja	to seek, search for
খোঁজাখুঁজি	khõjakhũji	looking and searching
খোকা	khoka	little boy (p. 247)
খোদা হাফিজ	khoda haphiz	'May God protect you' (p. 145)
খোলা	khola	open; to open
খ্রিষ্টান	khriṣṭan	Christian

গ

গত	gotô	last, previous
গতকাল	gotôkal	yesterday
গন্ধ	gondhô	scent, smell
গভীর	gôbhīr	deep, profound
গড়	goɽ	fort
গড়া	goɽa	to mould, shape
গড়ান/গড়ানো	goɽanô/goɽano	to roll
গড়িয়ে যাওয়া	goɽiye ẙaoya	to roll along
গরম	gorôm	warm, hot
গরিব	gôrib	poor
গরু	gôru	cow, cattle
গর্জন	gorjôn	roar
গর্ত	gortô	hole
গর্ব	gorbô	pride
গলা	gola	throat, voice
গল্প	golpô	story
গল্প করা	golpô kora	to chat
গা	ga	body
গাওয়া	gaoya	to sing (p. 202)
গাছ	gach	tree, plant
গাড়ি/গাড়ী	gaɽi/gaɽī	car, vehicle
গাঢ়	gaɽhô	solid, deep
গান	gan	song
গান করা	gan kora	to sing
গাল	gal	cheek
গুরুগুরু	guruguru	= rumbling
গুলি	guli	bullet, pill

গুলি খাওয়া	guli khaoya	to be shot
গৃহ	grhô	room, house
গৃহস্থ	grhôsthô	householder
গৃহিণী	grhiṇī	housewife
গেলাস	gelas	glass
গৈরিক	goïrik	red ochre
গোঁ গোঁ	gõ gõ	= groaning
গোধূলি	ghodhūli	dusk
গোলমাল	golmal	noise, trouble
গোলাপ	golap	rose
গোসল করা	gosɔl kɔra	to have a bath (E)
গ্রন্থিল	grônthil	knot
গ্রাম	gram	gramme
গ্রাম	gram	village
গ্রাম্য	gramyô	rustic

ঘ

ঘণ্টা	ghɔṇṭa	hour
ঘড়ি	ghôṛi	watch, clock
ঘন	ghɔnô	dense, thick
ঘর	ghɔr	room, house
ঘরকন্না	ghɔrkɔnna	housekeeping
ঘাট	ghaṭ	steps, mooring-place
ঘাবড়ান/ঘাবড়ানো	ghabṛanô/ghabṛano	to be taken aback
ঘাম	gham	sweat
ঘামা	ghama	to sweat
ঘাস	ghas	grass
ঘাসফরিং	ghasphôṛiṃ	grasshopper
ঘি	ghi	ghee, clarified butter
ঘুঙুর	ghuṇur	ankle-bells
ঘুম	ghum	sleep
ঘুরন্ত	ghurôntô	turning, spinning
ঘুরে আসা	ghure asa	to go out for a stroll
ঘূর্ণি	ghūrṇi	whirlpool, whirling
ঘোচা	ghoca	to be destroyed
ঘোড়া	ghoṛa	horse
ঘোমনো	ghomôno	to sleep (p. 183)
ঘোমান/ঘোমানো	ghomanô/ghomano	to sleep
ঘোর	ghor	severe, dark
ঘোরা	ghora	to wander

চ

চক্র	cɔkrô	wheel

চটা	cɔṭa	to get angry
চড়া	cɔṛa	to ride, climb
চমক	cɔmôk	alarm, amazement
চমৎকার	cɔmôtkar	fine, excellent
চলা	cɔla	to move, go
চলাচল	cɔlacɔl	movement, travel
চলে আসা	côle asa	to come, turn up
চলে যাওয়া	côle ÿaoya	to go away
চশমা	cɔʃma	spectacles
চা	ca	tea
চা-খানা	ca-khana	tea-stall
চাওয়া	caoya	to want, ask for (p. 202)
চাঁদ	cād	moon
চাকা	caka	wheel
চাকরি/চাকরী	cakri/cakrī	job, employment
চান করা	can kɔra	to have a bath (W)
চাপা	capa	to press
চাবি	cabi	key
চামচ	camôc	spoon
চারদিকে/চারিদিকে	cardike/caridike	all around
চারা	cara	shoot, seedling
চাল	cal	rice (uncooked)
চালাক	calak	clever
চালু করা	calu kɔra	to introduce, start up
চাষ করা	caṣ kɔra	to farm
চাষী	caṣī	farmer
টি টি করা	cī cī kɔra	to cheep
চিকণ	cikɔṇ	glossy
চিঠি	ciṭhi	letter
চিঠিপত্র	ciṭhipɔtrô	letters
চিৎকার/চীৎকার	citkar/cītkar	shouting
চিতাবাঘিনী	citabaghinī	(female) cheetah
চিন্তাধারা	cintadhara	flow of thought
চিন্তা-ভাবনা করা	cinta-bhabna kɔra	to think, worry
চিহ্ন	cinhô	sign (p. 255)
চুপ	cup	silence
চুপ করা	cup kɔra	to be silent
চুপ-চাপ	cup-cap	silent, peaceful
চুরি করা	curi kɔra	to steal
চুল	cul	hair
চেঁচামেচি	cæ̃cameci	hullabaloo
চেনা	cena	to know (a person)

চেয়ার	ceyar	*chair*
চেয়ে নেওয়া	ceye neoya	*to ask for something*
চেরা	cera	*to cleave, split*
চেলা	cæla	*disciple*
চেষ্টা করা	cesṭa kɔra	*to try*
চেহারা	cehara	*appearance*
চৈত্র মাস	coitrô	*Bengali month* (p. 195)
চোখ	cokh	*eye*
চৌকাঠ	coûkaṭh	*doorframe, threshold*

ছ

ছড়ান/ছড়ানো	chɔɽanô/chɔɽano	*to scatter*
ছবি	chôbi	*picture*
ছাড়া	chaɽa	*to leave; besides*
ছাতা	chata	*umbrella*
ছাত্র	chatrô	*pupil*
ছানা	chana	*chick, puppy*, etc.
ছাপ	chap	*impression*
ছাপ ফেলা	chap phæla	*to make an impression*
ছায়া	chaya	*shadow*
ছিটান/ছিটানো	chiṭanô/chiṭano	*to sprinkle, scatter*
ছিন্ন	chinnô	*torn*
ছুটি	chuṭi	*holiday*
ছুটোছুটি করা	chuṭochuṭi kɔra	*to rush about*
ছুরি	churi	*knife*
ছেঁড়া	chēɽa	*to tear*
ছেড়ে দেওয়া	chere deoya	*to leave, give up*
ছেলে	chele	*boy*
ছেলেপিলে	chelepile	*children, kids*
ছেলেবেলা	chelebæla	*childhood*
ছেলেমেয়ে	chelemeye	*children*
ছোট/ছোটো	choṭô/choṭo	*small*
ছোটা	choṭa	*to rush*
ছোট্ট	choṭṭô	*tiny* (p. 210)

জ

জখম	jɔkhôm	*wound*
জগৎ	jɔgôt	*world*
জঙ্গল	jɔngôl	*jungle*
জটিল	jôṭil	*complex*
জননী	jɔnônī	*mother*
জনপ্রিয়	jɔnôpriyô	*popular*

জনসংখ্যা	jɔnôsɔŋkhya	*population*
জন্ম	jɔnmô	*birth*
জন্মদিন	jɔnmôdin	*birthday*
জন্য/জন্যে	jônyô/jônye	*for, because of* (+ poss.
জমিজমা	jômijɔma	*land*
জমিদার	jômidar	*zamindar, landowner*
জমিদারি	jômidari	*zamindari, estate*
জমিন	jômin	*land, space* (p. 247)
জরায়ু	jɔrayu	*womb*
জল	jɔl	*water* (W)
জলধারা	jɔlôdhara	*stream, fountain*
জাগা	jaga	*to wake*
জাগান/জাগানো	jaganô/jagano	*to wake someone up*
জাদুকর	jadukɔr	*magician*
জাদুঘর	jadughɔr	*museum*
জানা	jana	*to know* (a thing)
জানালা	janala	*window*
জাম	jam	*rose-apple*
জামা	jama	*shirt, dress* (p. 33)
জামা-কাপড়	jama-kapôɽ	*clothes*
জায়গা	jayga	*place*
জার্মান	jarman	*German*
জি	ji	*yes* (E)
জিনিস	jinis	*thing*
জিনিসপত্র	jinispɔtrô	*things*
জিরা	jira	*cummin*
জুতো	juto	*shoe(s)*
জুয়া	juya	*gambling*
জেগে ওঠা	jege oṭha	*to wake up*
জোটা	joṭa	*to gather, assemble*
জোড়া	joɽa	*pair*
জোর	jor	*force, strength*
জ্ঞান	jñæn	*knowledge* (p. 82)
জ্যোৎস্না	jyotsna	*moonlight* (p. 249)
জ্বর	jvɔr	*fever*
জ্বলজ্বলে	jvɔljvôle	*blazing, sparkling*
জ্বলা	jvɔla	*to burn, blaze*
জ্বালান/জ্বালানো	jvalanô/jvalano	*to light, set on fire*

ঝ

| ঝগড়া | jhɔgɽa | *quarrel* |
| ঝগড়াঝাঁটি | jhɔgɽajhãṭi | *bickering* |

ঝড়	jhoɽ	*storm*
ঝলসান/ঝলসানো	jholsanô/jholsano	*to daze, dazzle*
ঝলসানি	jholsani	*daze, dazzle*
ঝলসিত	jholôsitô	*dazzled*
ঝাঁকড়া	jhākɽa	*shaggy, clustering*
ঝাঁঝালো	jhājhalo	*very hot, pungent*
ঝাঁপ দেওয়া	jhāp deoya	*to jump*
ঝাঁট দেওয়া	jhāṭ deoya	*to sweep*
ঝাপটা	jhapṭa	*gust, flap*
ঝাল	jhal	*hot, spicy*
ঝি	jhi	*maid-servant*
ঝিঝি	jhījhī	*cricket*
ঝিলমিল	jhilmil	*= sparkling*
ঝিলিক	jhilik	*mild flash*
ঝিলিমিলি	jhilimili	*sparkling, glittering*
ঝিল্লি	jhilli	*cricket*
ঝুড়ি/ঝোড়া	jhuɽi/jhoɽa	*basket*
ঝোড়ো	jhoɽo	*stormy*
ঝোপ	jhop	*bush*
ঝোল	jhol	*sauce* (of curry)

ট

টক	ṭok	*sour*
টকা	ṭoka	*to turn sour*
টমেটো	ṭomeṭo	*tomato*
টলমল	ṭolmol	*= agitation*
টাক	ṭak	*bald patch*
টাকা	ṭaka	*money, rupee*
টাকা-পয়সা	ṭaka-poysa	*money*
টাটকা	ṭaṭka	*fresh*
টান দেওয়া	ṭan deoya	*to pull*
টানা	ṭana	*to pull*
টানাটানি	ṭanaṭani	*= pulling, tugging*
টিচার	ṭicar	*teacher*
টিয়া	ṭiya	*parrot*
টুকরো	ṭukro	*piece, bit*
টুনটুনি	ṭunṭuni	*tailor-bird*
টেকো	ṭeko	*bald*
টেক্কা	ṭekka	*ace* (in cards)
টেবিল	ṭebil	*table*
টেরিকাটা	ṭerikaṭa	*hair-parting*
টেলিফোন	ṭeliphon	*telephone*

| টেলিভিশন | ţelibhiʃon | *television* |
| ট্যাক্সি | <u>ţyæ</u><u>k</u>si | *taxi* |

ঠ

ঠাট্টা	ţhaţţa	*teasing*
ঠাণ্ডা	ţhan̠ḍa	*cold*
ঠিক	ţhik	*right, correct*
ঠিক আছে	ţhik ache	*OK, all right*
ঠিকানা	ţhikana	*address*
ঠেকান/ঠেকানো	ţhekanô/ţhekano	*to obstruct* (p. 181)
ঠোঁট	ţhõţ	*lip, beak*
ঠোকাঠুকি	ţhokaţhuki	*hitting, hammering*
ঠোঙ্গা	ţhon̠ga	*container*

ড

ডগা	ḍɔga	*tip, point*
ডাক দেওয়া	ḍak deoya	*to call, shout*
ডাক-নাম	ḍak-nam	*pet name* (p. 50)
ডাকা	ḍaka	*to call, name*
ডাক্তার	ḍa<u>k</u>tar	*doctor*
ডান	ḍa<u>n</u>	*right* (opp. of left)
ডানা	ḍana	*wing*
ডায়েরি	ḍayeri	*diary*
ডাল	ḍal	*dal, lentils; branch*
ডিঙা/ডিঙ্গা	ḍin̠a/ḍin̠ga	*boat, dinghy*
ডিম	ḍim	*egg*
ডুমুর	ḍumur	*fig*
ডোবা	ḍoba	*to sink, drown*
ডোবান/ডোবানো	ḍobanô/ḍobano	*to cause to drown*

ঢ

ঢাকা	ḍhaka	*to cover, lid*
ঢিল	ḍhil	*clod, lump*
ঢেউ	ḍheu	*wave, billow*
ঢোকা	ḍhoka	*to enter*
ঢাঁড়স	<u>ḍhyæ</u>ŗôs	*lady's finger*

ত

তখন	tɔkhôn	*then*
তখনও/তখনো	tɔkhôn-o/tɔkhôno	*still*
তখনকার	tɔkhônkar	*of then*
তত	tɔtô	*so much, so many*
ততদিন	tɔtôdin	*so many days*

তত্ত্ব	tɔttvô	essence, truth, knowledge, news
তদারক করা	tɔdarôk kɔra	to manage, look after
তফাৎ	tɔphat	difference
তবে	tɔbe	but, then
তবু	tôbu	yet, nevertheless
তরকারি	tɔrkari	vegetables
তরুণ	tôruŋ	young, fresh
তলা	tɔla	floor, storey
তলায়	tɔlay	at the foot of (+ poss.)
তাই/তা	tai/ta	so, therefore
তাই নাকি !	tai naki!	is that so!
তাঁবু	tābu	tent
তাক	tak	shelf
তাছাড়া	tachaɽa	apart from that
তাজ্জব	tajjôb	amazing, odd
তাড়া	taɽa	hurry, urgency
তাড়াতাড়ি	taɽataɽi	quickly
তারপর/তার পরে	tarpɔr/tar pɔre	then, after that
তারা	tara	star
তারামণ্ডল	taramɔnɖôl	planetarium
তারিখ	tarikh	date (p. 195)
তাল/তালগাছ	tal/talgach	palm tree
তাস	tas	playing cards
তাহলে	tahôle	in that case (p. 185)
তীক্ষ্ণ	tīkṣṇô	sharp, keen
তীর	tīr	shore, coast
তীর্থ	tīrthô	place of pilgrimage
তুলতুলে	tultule	= delightful softness
তুলনা করা	tulôna kɔra	to compare
তুলে ধরা	tule dhɔra	to lift up
তেমন	tæmôn	such, so
তেমনি	temni	in such a way
তৈরি/তৈরী করা	tôiri/tôirī kɔra	to make, prepare
তৈরি/তৈরী হওয়া	tôiri/tôirī hɔoya	to be made, prepared
তো	to	('adversative' particle, p. 95)
তোলা	tola	to lift, take (a photo)

থ

| থমথমে | thɔmthôme | = glumness, gloom |
| থরথর করা | thɔrthɔr kɔra | to tremble violently |

থাকা	thaka	*to stay*
থামা	thama	*to stop*
থেকে	theke	*from* (**not** + poss.)

দ

দই	dôi	*curds, yoghurt*
দক্ষ	dôkṣô	*skilful*
দরজা	dorôja/dorja	*door*
দরকার	dorkar	*need* (p. 172)
দর্শন	dorʃôn	*seeing, homage, philosophy*
দল	dɔl	*group, faction*
দাঁড়ান/দাঁড়ানো	dãɽanô/dãɽano	*to stand, wait*
দাঁড়ী	dãɽī	*oarsman*
দাঁত	dãt	*tooth, teeth*
দাদা	dada	*elder brother, grandfather* (p. 272)
দাদী	dadī	*grandmother* (p. 272)
দাম	dam	*price, cost*
দারুণ	daruṇ	*severe, very great*
দাসী	dasī	*maid-servant*
দিক	dik	*direction*
দিগন্ত	digɔntô	*horizon*
দিদি	didi	*elder sister* (p. 272)
দিদিমা	didima	*grandmother* (p. 272)
দিন	din	*day*
দিনযাপন করা	dinŷapôn kɔra	*to spend time*
দিব্যি	dibyi	*divine, pleasant* (p. 248)
দিয়ে	diye	*by, with* (**not** + poss.)
দীপ	dīp	*lamp*
দুধারে	dudhare	*on both sides*
দুপুর	dupur	*noon* (p. 103)
দুমড়ান/দুমড়ানো	dumɽanô/dumɽano	*to fold, twist*
দুয়ার	duyar	*door*
দুর্ঘটনা	durghɔţôna	*accident*
দুর্বল	durbôl	*weak*
দুষ্টু	duṣţu	*mischievous, naughty*
দূর	dūr	*distance; distant*
দৃঢ়	dṛɽhô	*firm, sound*

দেওয়া	deoya	to give
দেওয়াল	deoyal	wall
দেখা	dækha	to see; meeting
দেখান/দেখানো	dækhanô/dækhano	to show
দেখাশোনা	dækhaʃona	meeting
দেখাশোনা করা	dækhaʃona kɔra	to look after
দেড়	deɾ	one-and-a-half
দেরাজ	deraj	drawer
দেরি/দেরী	deri/derī	delay, lateness
দেরি করা	deri kɔra	to delay
দেশ	deʃ	land
দেশলাই	deʃlai	matches
দেশী	deʃī	of the country
দেশোয়ালী	deʃoyalī	countryman, rustic
দেহ	dehô	body
দোকান	dokan	shop
দোকান করা	dokan kɔra	to shop
দোয়েল	doyel	magpie-robin
দোলান/দোলানো	dolanô/dolano	to cause to swing
দ্রুত	drutô	quick, swift
দ্রুতগামিনী	drutôgaminī	swiftly moving
দ্বার	dvar	door, gate
দ্বারা	dvara	by (p. 158)
দ্বিগুণ	dvigun	twice
দ্বিতীয়	dvitiyô	second

ধ

ধকল	dhɔkôl	stress, impact
ধন্যবাদ	dhônyôbad	thank you
ধমকান/ধমকানো	dhɔmkanô/dhɔmkano	to scold, rebuke
ধরন	dhɔrôn	way, sort
ধরা	dhɔra	to hold
ধরান/ধরানো	dhɔranô/dhɔrano	to cause to hold
ধরে	dhôre	for (a span of time, p. 125)
ধর্ম	dhɔrmô	religion
ধর্ষিতা	dhôrṣita	raped, ravished
ধাঁধান/ধাঁধনো	dhādhanô/dhādhano	to daze
ধান	dhan	paddy
ধার	dhar	edge, side
ধার দেওয়া	dhar deoya	to lend
ধার নেওয়া	dhar neoya	to borrow

ধীরে-ধীরে	dhīre-dhīre	slowly
ধুতি	dhuti	dhoti, loincloth
ধূমপান করা	dhūmpan kɔra	to smoke
ধূলো	dhūlo	dust
ধোঁয়া	dhõya	smoke
ধোপা	dhopa	washerman
ধোয়া	dhoya	to wash
ধ্বংস	dhvɔmsô	destruction
ধ্বনি	dhvôni	sound
ধ্বনিত	dhvônitô	sounded, played
ধ্বজা	dhvɔja	flag, banner

ন

ন-	nɔ-	(verb 'not to be', p. 63)
নখ	nɔkh	finger/toe nail
নক্ষত্র	nɔkṣotrô	star
নববর্ষা	nɔbôbɔrṣa	new rain
নবীন	nôbīn	new
নড়াচড়া	nɔɽacɔɽa	movement, strolling
নতুন	nôtun	new
নদী	nôdī	river
নমস্কার	nɔmôskar	(Hindu greeting, p. 95)
নম্র	nɔmrô	soft, gentle
নম্বর	nɔmbôr	number
নরক	nɔrôk	hell
নরম	nɔrôm	soft
নষ্ট করা	nɔṣṭô kɔra	to spoil, waste
নষ্ট হওয়া	nɔṣṭô hɔoya	to be spoilt, wasted
না	na	no; not; please (p. 112); or (p. 77)
নাওয়ান/নাওয়ানো	naoyanô/naoyano	to cause to bathe
নাকাল	nakal	embarrassed
নাগরদোলা	nagôrdola	big wheel
নাচ	nac	dance
নাচা	naca	to dance
নাচানাচি করা	nacanaci kɔra	to dance about
নাচান/নাচানো	nacanô/nacano	to cause to dance
নাগাদ	nagad	by, up to (**not** + poss.)
নাড়া	naɽa	to move, shake

নানা/নানান	nana/nanan	*various*
নানী	nanī	*grandmother* (p. 272)
নাপিত	napit	*barber*
নাম	nam	*name*
নাম করা	nam kɔra	*to name; famous*
নামা	nama	*to get down*
নামাজ পরা	namaj pɽa	*to say* (Muslim) *prayers*
নিঃশব্দ	nihʃɔbdô	*without sound*
নিঃস্পন্দ	nihspɔndô	*without pulse, lifeless*
নিকট	nikɔṭ	*near* (+ poss.)
নিচে/নীচে	nice/nīce	*below* (+ poss.)
নিজে/নিজের	nije/nijer	*oneself/one's own* (p. 85)
নিত্যকাল	nityôkal	*eternity*
নিদেন	niden	*at least*
নিভৃত	nibhṛtô	*secret, private*
নিমন্ত্রিত	nimôntritô	*invited*
নিয়মিত	niyômitô	*regular*
নিয়ে	niye	*with, by* (**not** + poss.)
নিয়ে আসা	niye asa	*to bring, fetch*
নিয়ে যাওয়া	niye y̆aoya	*to take, transport*
নিরপরাধ	nirɔpôradh	*guiltless*
নিরুপায়	nirupay	*helpless*
নিজীব	nirjīb	*lifeless*
নির্দিষ্ট	nirdiṣṭô	*fixed, defined*
নিষেধ করা	niṣedh kɔra	*to forbid*
নিশ্চয়/নিশ্চয়ই	niʃcɔy/niʃcôy-i	*certainly*
নিস্তব্ধ	nistɔbdhô	*completely still*
নীরবে	nīrɔbe	*noiselessly*
নীল	nīl	*blue*
নুন	nun	*salt* (W)
নূতন	nūtôn	*new*
নৃত্য করা	nṛtyô kɔra	*to dance*
নেওয়া	neoya	*to take*
নেশা	neʃa	*intoxication*
নোট	noṭ	*note*
নোনা	nona	*salty*
নৌকা/নৌকো	noŭka/noûko	*boat*

প

পক্ষ	pôkṣô	*wing, flank, side*
পক্ষে	pôkṣe	*for, on behalf of*
পঙ্কিল	pôṇkil	*muddy*
পঙ্ক্তি	pôṇkti	*line*
পছন্দ করা	pɔchôndô kɔra	*to like, prefer*
পড়া	pɔɽa	*to fall*
পড়া	pɔɽa	*to read, study*
পড়াশোনা করা	pɔɽaʃona kɔra	*to study*
পড়ান/পড়ানো	pɔɽanô/pɔɽano	*to teach*
পণ্যদ্রব্য	pôṇyôdrɔbyô	*merchandise, wares*
পণ্যোপহার	pôṇyopôhar	*gift of merchandise (p. 255)*
পতাকা	pɔtaka	*flag, banner*
পত্রিকা	pôtrika	*journal*
পথ	pɔth	*path, road*
পদ	pɔd	*foot, pace, position*
পদক্রম	pɔdôkrɔm	*series*
পয়লা	pɔyla	*first of the month*
পর	pɔr	*after (+ poss.)*
পরদা/পর্দা	pɔrda/pɔrda	*curtain, purdah*
পরদিন	pɔrdin	*next day*
পরন	pɔrôn	*wearing, putting on*
পরশুদিন	pôrʃudin	*day before yesterday/ after tomorrow (p. 150)*
পরস্পর	pɔrôspôr	*reciprocal, mutual*
পরা	pɔra	*to wear, put on*
পরিচিত	pôricitô	*acquainted*
পরিবার	pôribar	*family*
পরিসংখ্যান	pôrisɔmkhyan	*statistics*
পরিষ্কার	pôriṣkar	*clean*
পরিষ্কার করা	pôriṣkar kɔra	*to clean*
পরীক্ষা	pôrīkṣa	*examination*
পরীক্ষা করা	pôrīkṣa kɔra	*to examine, test*
পরে	pɔre	*(see পর); later*
পর্যন্ত	pôryôntô	*until (not + poss.)*
পল্লব	pɔllôb	*leaf*
পশু	pôʃu	*animal*
পশ্চাৎ	pôʃcat	*behind (+ poss.)*
পশ্চিম	pôʃcim	*west, western*

পা	pa	*foot, leg*
পাওয়া	paoya	*to get, receive*
পাখা	pakha	*fan*
পাখি/পাখী	pakhi/pakhī	*bird*
পাগড়ি	pagɾi	*pugree, turban*
পাগল	pagôl	*mad*
পাট-ভাঙা	paṭ-bhaŋa	*crisply folded, pressed*
পাঠ	paṭh	*text*
পাঠক	paṭhôk	*reader*
পাঠান/পাঠানো	paṭhanô/paṭhano	*to send*
পাঠিয়ে দেওয়া	paṭhiye deoya	*to send*
পাড়াগাঁ	paɾagā	*rural area, village*
পাতা	pata	*leaf, page*
পাতা	pata	*to spread*
পাথর	pathôr	*stone*
পাপিয়সী	papīyôsī	*sinful* (female)
পায়জামা	payjama	*pyjamas*
পারা	para	*to be able*
পার্ক	paɾk	*park*
পার্শ্ব	paɾʃvô	*side, flank, edge*
পাল	pal	*sail*
পালক	palôk	*guardian*
পালান/পালানো	palanô/palano	*to flee*
পালিশ করা	paliʃ kɔra	*to polish*
পাশ	paʃ	*side, flank, edge*
পাশে	paʃe	*next to* (+ poss.)
পাশ্চাত্য	paʃcatyô	*western*
পাষণ্ড	paṣôṇḍô	*inveterate sinner*
পাস করা	pas kɔra	*to pass (an exam)*
পিছন	pichôn	*back, rear*
পিছনে	pichône	*behind* (+ poss.)
পিছলান/পিছলানো	pichlanô/pichlano	*to slip*
পিতা	pita	*father*
পিতৃগৃহ	pitɾgɾhô	*paternal home*
পুকুর	pukur	*pond, tank*
পুঞ্জীভূত	puñjībhūtô	*piled up*
পুবে-বাতাস	pube-batas	*east wind*
পুরস্কার	purôskar	*prize*
পুরানো/পুরনো	purano/purôno	*old*
পুরুষ	puruṣ	*man, male*
পুরো	puro	*all, whole*

পুলিশ	puliʃ	police
পূর্ণ	pūrṇô	full, whole, complete
পূর্ব	pūrbô	east, past, former
পূর্বে	pūrbe	before (+ poss.)
পৃথিবী	pr̥thibī	world
পেট	peṭ	stomach
পেনসিল	pensil	pencil
পেয়ারা	peyara	guava
পেরেক	perek	nail, spike
পেশী	peʃī	muscle
পোড়ান/পোড়ানো	poṛanô/poṛano	to burn
পোষা	poṣa	tame, pet
পোশাক/পোষাক	poʃak/poṣak	clothes
পোস্টাপিস	posṭapis	post-office
পৌছান/পৌছানো	pôŭchanô/pôŭchano	to arrive
পৌষ	poŭṣ	Bengali month (p. 195)
প্যাণ্ডেল	pyæṇḍel	pandal (p. 224)
প্রকাণ্ড	prôkaṇḍô	huge
প্রকার	prôkar	way, kind
প্রকাশ করা	prôkaʃ kɔra	to publish, express
প্রকাশিত	prôkaʃitô	published
প্রকাশ্যে	prôkaʃye	publicly, openly
প্রকৃতি	prôkr̥ti	nature
প্রচুর	prôcur	profuse, huge in amount
প্রণাম	prôṇam	(obeisance, p. 33)
প্রতি-	prôti-	each, every (prefix)
প্রতিদিন	prôtidin	every day
প্রতিবেশী	prôtibeʃī	neighbour
প্রতিহিংসা	prôtihimsa	revenge, retaliation
প্রতীক্ষা	prôtīkṣa	waiting, expectation
প্রত্যাগত	prôtyægɔtô	returned
প্রত্যাশা	prôtyaʃa	expectation
প্রত্যেক	prôtyek	each
প্রত্যেকে	prôtyeke	each one, everyone
প্রথম	prôthôm	first
প্রথমে	prôthôme	at first
প্রধান	prôdhan	chief
প্রধানত	prôdhanôtô	chiefly
প্রধানমন্ত্রী	prôdhanmôntrī	prime minister
প্রবন্ধ	prôbɔndhô	essay, article
প্রবল	prôbɔl	very strong, mighty

প্রবেশ করা	prôbeʃ kɔra	to enter
প্রশংসা	prôʃɔmsa	praise
প্রাত	prat	morning
প্রাণ	praṇ	life-breath, vitality
প্রায়	pray	nearly, about
প্রায়ই	pray-i	often, usually
প্রিয়	priyô	dear
প্রিয়সঙ্গিনী	priyôsɔŋginī	dear companion (female)
প্রীতি	prīti	affection, pleasure
প্রেম	prem	love
প্রৌঢ়	proûṛhô	middle-aged
প্রৌঢ়া	proûṛha	middle-aged (female)
প্লেট	pleṭ	plate

ফ

ফটো	phôṭo	photo
ফরাস	phɔras	floor-covering, durrie
ফর্দ	phɔrdô	list, inventory
ফল	phol	fruit
ফলে	phole	as a result
ফসল	phɔsôl	harvest
ফাঁক	phãk	gap, space
ফিরে আসা	phire asa	to come back
ফিরে যাওয়া	phire y̆aoya	to go back
ফিল্ম	philm	film
ফুড়ুক	phuṛuk	= sudden flying away
ফুফু	phuphu	aunt (p. 273)
ফুরিয়ে যাওয়া	phuriye y̆aoya	to run out
ফুল	phul	flower
ফুলকপি/ফুলকফি	phulkôpi/phulkôphi	cauliflower
ফেরৎ দেওয়া	pherôt deoya	to return, give back
ফেরা	phera	to come/go back
ফেলা	phæla	to throw
ফেলে দেওয়া	phele deoya	to throw away
ফ্যান	phyæn	fan

ব

বই	bôi	book
বকা	bɔka	to scold
বক্তৃতা	bôktrta	speech, lecture
বক্ষ	bôkṣô	breast, chest

বছর	bɔchôr	year
বট/বটগাছ	bɔṭ/bɔṭgach	banyan tree
বটে	bɔṭe	indeed, of course
বড়/বড়ো	bɔrô/bɔro	big
বড়লোক	bɔrôlok	rich person
বদ্ধ	bɔddhô	fastened, caught
বন	bɔn/bôn	forest, wood
বনপথ	bɔnôpɔth	forest path
বনা	bɔna	to be reduced to
বন্দুক	bônduk	gun
বদ্ধ	bɔndhô	closed
বদ্ধ করা	bɔndhô kɔra	to close
বন্ধন	bɔndhôn	binding, tie
বন্ধু	bôndhu	friend
বন্ধুবিহীন	bôndhubihīn	friendless
বন্ধুত্ব	bôndhutvô	friendship
বন্যা	bônya	flood
বমি	bômi	vomiting
বয়স	bɔyôs	age
বয়সী	bɔyôsī	aged
বরং	bɔrôŋ	rather, in preference
বর্ণ	bɔrṇô	colour, letter of the alphabet
বর্ষাকাল	bɔrṣakal	monsoon
বল	bɔl	ball
বলা	bɔla	to speak, say, tell
বলে	bôle	because
বসা	bɔsa	to sit
বহা	bɔha	to blow, flow (p. 255)
বহু	bôhu	many, much
বহুদিন	bôhudin	a long time
বাংলা	baŋla	Bengali (language)
বাংলাদেশ	baŋladeʃ	Bangladesh; Bengal (p. 190)
বাইরে	baire	outside (+ poss.)
বাঃ	bah	Bravo! (p. 81)
বাঁ	bā	left
বাঁচা	bāca	to live, survive (p. 156)
বাঁচান/বাঁচানো	bācanô/bācano	to save, revive
বাঁধা	bādha	to bind, tie
বাঁধাকপি/বাঁধাকফি	bādhakôpi/bādhakôphi	cabbage
বাকহারা	bak-hara	speechless

বাকী	bakī	remaining, the rest
বাক্য	bakyô	speech, sentence
বাক্স	baksô	box, suitcase
বাগান	bagan	garden
বাঘ	bagh	tiger
বাঙালী	baŋalī	Bengali (race, nation)
বাচ্চা/বাচ্ছা/বাছা	bacca/baccha/bacha	child, kid
বাজনা	bajna	playing, musical instrument
বাজা	baja	to ring, strike (p. 108)
বাজার	bajar	bazaar
বাজার করা	bajar kɔra	to do the shopping
বাতাবি/বাতাবি-লেবু	batabi/batabi-lebu	pomelo
বার করা	bar kɔra	to bring out
বারম্বার	barômbar	again and again
বাড়া	baɽa	to grow
বাড়ান/বাড়ানো	baɽanô/baɽano	to cause to grow
বাড়ি/বাড়ী	baɽi/baɽī	house, home
বাত	bat	rheumatism
বাতাস	batas	wind
বাথরুম	bathrum	bathroom
বাদ দেওয়া	bad deoya	to omit
বাদে	bade	afterwards, later
বাদামী	badamī	brown, nut-coloured
বাদ্য	badyô	music, band
বাধা	badha	to stick, be obstructed
বাধ্য	badhyô	obedient, compelled
বাবরি	babri	long hair, mane
বাবা	baba	father (W)
বায়না	bayna	earnest money
বারান্দা	baranda	verandah
বালক	balôk	boy
বালিকা	balika	girl
বাস	bas	dwelling; garment
বাস করা	bas kɔra	to dwell, live
বাসরঘর	basôrghɔr	bridal chamber
বাসা	basa	residence
-বাসিনী	-basinī	residing (female)
বাহিনী	bahinī	army, battalion
বাহির	bahir	outside
বাহু	bahu	arm
বিকাল/বিকেল	bikal/bikel	afternoon (p. 103)

বিক্রি করা	bikri kɔra	to sell
বিক্রি হওয়া	bikri hɔoya	to be sold
বিখ্যাত	bikhyætô	famous
বিচিত্র	bicitrô	varied, wonderful
বিছান/বিছানো	bichanô/bichano	to spread, strew
বিছানা	bichana	bedding
বিচ্ছিরি	bicchiri	ugly, nasty (p. 67)
বিজ্ঞান	bijñæn	science (p. 82)
বিড়াল	biɽal	cat
বিড়ালনী	biɽalnī	female cat
বিদীর্ণ করা	bidīrɳô kɔra	to split
বিদেশ	bideʃ	foreign land, abroad
বিদেশী	bideʃī	foreign
বিদ্যুৎ	bidyut	lightning, electricity
বিধ্বস্ত	bidhvɔstô	utterly ruined
বিনা	bina	without
বিপুল	bipul	huge
বিবরণ দেওয়া	bibɔrôɳ deoya	to describe
বিবর্ণ	bibɔrɳô	discoloured, pale
বিবাহ	bibahô	marriage, wedding
বিবিধ	bibidh	various
বিব্রত	bibrôtô	embarrassed
বিভাগ	bibhag	division, department
বিভিন্ন	bibhinnô	various
বিভীষিকা	bibhīṣika	horror, panic
বিয়ে	biye	marriage, wedding
বিয়ে করা	biye kɔra	to marry
বিয়ে হওয়া	biye hɔoya	to get married (p. 100)
বিরক্ত	birɔktô	annoyed
বিলম্ব	bilɔmbô	delay, lateness
বিলেত	bilet	England
বিশাল	biʃal	huge, vast
বিশেষ	biʃeṣ	special, particular
বিশেষ করে	biʃeṣ kôre	specially
বিশেষত	biʃeṣɔtô	specially
বিশ্রী	biʃrī	ugly (p. 67)
বিশ্ব	biʃvô	world, universe
বিশ্ববিদ্যালয়	biʃvôbidyælɔy	university
বিশ্বাস	biʃvas	belief, trust
বিশ্রাম	biʃram	rest
বিশ্রাম করা/নেওয়া	biʃram kɔra/neoya	to rest
বিষ	biṣ	poison

বিষয়	biṣɔy	*subject*
বিষয়ক	biṣɔyôk	*denoting, relating to*
বিস্ফোরণ	bisphorôṇ	*explosion*
বিস্তীর্ণ	bistīrṇô	*spread out, extensive*
বিহ্বল	bihvɔl	*bewildered* (p. 262)
বীর	bīr	*hero, warrior*
বুক	buk	*breast, chest*
বুড়ী	buṛī	*old woman*
বুড়ো	buṛo	*old man*
বুদ্ধিমতী	buddhimôtī	*intelligent* (female)
বুদ্ধিমান	buddhiman	*intelligent* (male)
বুধবার	budhbar	*Wednesday* (p. 103)
বুনো	buno	*wild, savage*
বৃথা	bṛtha	*futile, in vain*
বৃষ্টি	bṛṣṭi	*rain*
বৃহৎ	bṛhɔt	*huge, large*
বৃহস্পতিবার	bṛhɔspôtibar	*Thursday* (p. 103)
বেআইনী	beainī	*illegal*
বেঁটে	bēṭe	*short*
বেকার	bekar	*unemployed; unemployment*
বেগ	beg	*speed, impetus*
বেগুন	begun	*brinjal, aubergine*
বেড়াল	beṛal	*see* বিড়াল
বেদ	bed	*Veda(s)*
বেরান/বেরানো	beranô/berano	*to go out*
বেরন/বেরনো	berônô/berôno	*to go out* (p. 183)
বেরিয়ে যাওয়া	beriye y̆aoya	*to go out* (p. 163)
বেলা	bæla	*time of day* (p. 103)
বেশ	beʃ	*fine, nice, very*
বেশি/বেশী	beʃi/beʃī	*many, much* (p. 138)
বেশিরভাগ	beʃirbhag	*the mostpart, majority*
বেহালা	behala	*violin*
বোকা	boka	*stupid*
বোজা	boja	*to shut* (eyes, p. 211)
বোঝা	bojha	*to understand*
বোঝাই	bojhai	*load, burden*
বোঝান/বোঝানো	bojhanô/bojhano	*to explain*
বোধ করা	bodh kɔra	*to feel*
বোধ হয়	bodh hɔy	*perhaps, probably*
বোন	bon	*sister* (p. 272)
ব্যক্তি	bykti	*person* (p. 26)

ব্যঞ্জনবর্ণ	byñjônbɔrṇô	*consonant*
ব্যথা	bytha	*pain*
ব্যবস্থা	bybɔstha	*arrangement*
ব্যবস্থা করা	bybôstha kɔra	*to arrange, fix up*
ব্যবহার	bybôhar	*behaviour, usage*
ব্যবহার করা	bybôhar kɔra	*to behave, use*
ব্যস্ত	bystô	*busy, fussed*
ব্যস্ততা	bystôta	*bustle, excitement*
ব্যাকরণ	byækɔrôṇ	*grammar*
ব্যাগ	byæg	*bag*
ব্যাঙ্ক	byæŋk	*bank*
ব্যাপার	byæpar	*matter, affair*
ব্যামো	byæmo	*illness*
ব্রাহ্মণ	brahmôṇ	*Brahmin* (p. 90)

ভ

ভঙ্গি	bhôŋgi	*style, posture*
ভদ্রমহিলা	bhɔdrômôhila	*lady*
ভদ্রলোক	bhɔdrôlok	*gentleman*
ভয়	bhɔy	*fear*
ভয়ানক	bhɔyanôk	*dreadful, frightful*
ভয়াবহ	bhɔyabɔhô	*dreadful, frightful*
ভরা	bhɔra	*to fill; full*
ভরান/ভরানো	bhɔranô/bhɔrano	*to cause to fill*
ভস্ম করা	bhɔsmô kɔra	*to burn to ashes*
ভাই	bhai	*brother* (p. 272)
ভাইপো	bhaipo	*nephew* (p. 274)
ভাগ	bhag	*part, share*
ভাগ্য	bhagyô	*fortune, luck*
ভাঙা/ভাঙ্গা	baŋa/baŋga	*to break; broken*
ভাঙান/ভাঙানো	bhaŋanô/bhaŋano	*to break something, change* (a banknote)
ভাড়া	bhaṛa	*rent, fare*
ভাত	bhat	*cooked rice, meal*
ভাব	bhab	*way, mood*
-ভাবে	-bhabe	*in a way* (p. 122)
ভাবনা	bhabna	*worry*
ভাবা	bhaba	*to think, devise*
ভারী	bharī	*heavy*
ভাল/ভালো	bhalô/bhalo	*good*
ভালোবাসা	bhalobasa	*love; to love*

ভাষণ	bhaṣôṇ	speech, utterance
ভাষা	bhaṣa	language
ভাসান/ভাসানো	bhasanô/bhasano	to set afloat
ভিজে	bhije	wet
ভিড়	bhiṛ	crowd
ভিতর/ভিতরে	bhitôr/bhitôre	in, inside (+ poss.)
ভিতর দিয়ে	bhitôr diye	through
ভিসা	bhisa	visa
ভীষণ	bhīṣôṇ	terrible, awful
ভুরু	bhuru	eyebrow
ভুল	bhul	mistake
ভুল করা	bhul kɔra	to make a mistake
ভুলে যাওয়া	bhule ẏaoya	to forget
ভূগোল	bhūgol	geography
ভূত	bhūt	ghost
ভেক	bhek	frog
ভেঙে যাওয়া	bheṇe ẏaoya	to break up, collapse
ভেঙে-চুরে	bheṇge-cure	broken, crumbled
ভেজা	bheja	wet; to get wet
ভেতর/ভেতরে	bhetôr/bhetôre	see
ভেলা	bhæla	raft
ভোগা	bhoga	to suffer
ভোর	bhor	dawn
ভোলা	bhola	to forget, be charmed
ভ্রাতা	bhrata	brother
ভ্রুকুটি	bhrūkuṭi	frown

ম

মঙ্গলবার	mɔṇgôlbar	Tuesday (p. 103)
মজা	mɔja	joke, fun
মজার	mɔjar	funny
মজুর	môjur	labourer
মত	mɔt	opinion
মত/মতন/মতো	mɔtô/mɔtôn/mɔto	like, similar to (+ poss.)
মত্ত	mɔttô	drunk, mad
মদ	mɔd	alcoholic drink
মদির	môdir	intoxicating
মধুকর	môdhukɔr	bee
মধ্যবিত্ত	môdhyôbittô	middle-class
মধ্য	môdhyô	middle

মধ্যে	môdhye	*in, inside* (+ poss.)
মন	mɔn/môn	*mind*
মনযোগ দেওয়া	mɔnôy̆og deoya	*to concentrate*
মনযোগী	mɔnôy̆ogī	*attentive*
মন্ত্রী	môntrī	*minister*
মন্দির	môndir	*temple*
ময়দান	mɔydan	*open area, maidan* (p. 247)
ময়ূর	môyūr	*peacock*
মরা	mɔra	*to die, whither*
মর্মভেদী	mɔrmôbhedī	*heart-rending*
মস্ত	mɔstô	*big, great*
মহৎ	mɔhôt	*large, noble*
মহর্ষি	mɔhôrṣi	*great sage*
মহা/মহান	mɔha/mɔhan	*great*
মহামানী	mɔhamani	*very proud*
মহারানী	mɔharanī	*queen*
মহিলা	môhila	*woman*
মা	ma	*mother* (W)
মা-বাবা	ma-baba	*parents* (W)
মাইল	mail	*mile*
মাংস	maṃsô	*meat*
মাখা	makha	*daub, smear, knead*
মাছ	mach	*fish*
মাছের ঝোল	macher jhol	*fish curry*
মাজা	maja	*to scrub, brush*
মাঝ	majh	*middle*
মাঝখানে	majhkhane	*in the middle* (+ poss.)
মাঝামাঝি	majhamajhi	*about the middle*
মাঝি	majhi	*boatman*
মাঝে	majhe	*in, inside* (+ poss.)
মাঝে-মাঝে	majhe-majhe	*sometimes*
মাঝে-সাঝে	majhe-sajhe	*sometimes*
মাতা	mata	*mother*
মাটি	maṭi	*earth, soil, ground*
মাঠ	maṭh	*open cultivated land*
মাত্র	matrô	*only*
মাথা	matha	*head*
মাথা ধরা	matha dhɔra	*to have a headache*
মাদল	madôl	*drum*

মাধ্যম	madhyôm	medium, means
মানুষ	manuṣ	human race/being
মানুষী	manuṣī	woman
মানে	mane	meaning
মামা	mama	uncle (p. 273)
মামুলি	mamuli	trite, hackneyed
মারা	mara	beat, kill
মাল্লা	malla	oarsman
মাস	mas	month
মাসিক	masik	monthly
মাসী	masī	aunt (p. 273)
মিছিল	michil	rally, demonstration
মিথ্যে	mithye	lie, falsehood
মিনার	minar	tower
মিশর/মিসর	miʃɔr/misɔr	Egypt
মিশে যাওয়া	miʃe ẙaoya	to get mixed up
মিষ্টি	miṣṭi	sweet(s)
মিসমার করা	mismar kɔra	to destroy utterly (p. 240)
মিস্ত্রী	mistrī	artisan, tradesman
মুক্তা	mukta	pearl
মুক্তি	mukti	freedom, deliverance
মুখ	mukh	face, mouth
মুখর	mukhôr	garrulous
মুষলধারাবর্ষী	muṣôldharabôrṣī	torrentially raining
মুশকিল	muʃkil	trouble, difficulty
মুসলমান	musôlman	Muslim
মূর্তি	mūrti	image, statue
মূল	mūl	root
-মূলক	-mūlôk	originating from
মৃদু	mr̥du	soft, delicate
মেঘ	megh	cloud
মেঝে	mejhe	floor
মেধাবী	medhabī	intelligent, gifted
মেয়ে	meye	girl, daughter, woman
মেরে ফেলা	mere phæla	to kill
মেলা	mæla	fair, fête
মেলা	mela	to fit, combine
মেলামেশা	melameʃa	mixing, social contact
মেলামেশা করা	melameʃa kɔra	to mix socially
মেহগনী	mehôgônī	mahogany
মেহেদী	mehedī	henna

মোক্তার	moktar	*attorney, agent*
মোটর	moṭôr	*motor*
মোটামুটি	moṭamuṭi	*more-or-less, so-so*
মোড়	moṛ	*street corner, crossing*
মোরগ	morɔg	*cock*
মোরগফুল	morɔgphul	*cockscomb*
মোহর	mohɔr	*mohur, gold coin*
মৌন	moŭnô	*silent, reticent*

য

যখন	y̆ɔkhôn	*when (p. 181)*
যত	y̆ɔtô	*as much, as many*
যতদিন	y̆ɔtôdin	*as many days*
যত্ন করা	y̆ɔtnô kɔra	*to take care of*
যথেষ্ট	y̆ôtheṣṭô	*sufficient, abundant*
যদি	y̆ôdi	*if (p. 184)*
যন্ত্রপাতি	y̆ɔntrôpati	*tools and implements*
যা হোক	y̆a hok	*Oh well*
যাওয়া	y̆aoya	*to go*
যাতায়াত করা	y̆atayat kɔra	*to come and go*
যাত্রা	y̆atra	*journey; stage-show*
যুদ্ধ	y̆uddhô	*war*
যুবা	y̆uba	*young man*
যেন	y̆æno	*as if, seemingly (p. 218)*
যেমন	y̆æmôn	*as like, just as*
যোগাযোগ করা	y̆ogay̆og kɔra	*to make contact*

র

রওনা হওয়া/দেওয়া	rɔona hɔoya/deoya	*to start out*
রওয়া	rɔoya	*to remain (p. 219)*
রং/রঙ	rɔŋ/rɔŋ	*colour*
রং করা	rɔŋ kɔra	*to colour, paint*
রকম	rɔkôm	*sort, kind, way*
রঙিন/রঙীন	rôŋin/rôŋīn	*coloured*
রঙ্গভরে	rɔŋgôbhôre	*playfully*
রথ	rɔth	*chariot*
রথযাত্রা	rɔthy̆atra	*chariot journey*
রবিবার	rôbibar	*Sunday (p. 103)*
রাঁধা	rādha	*to cook*
রাঁধা-বাড়া	rādha-baṛa	*cooking and serving food*

রাখা	rakha	*to put, keep*
রাগ	rag	*musical raga*
রাগ	rag	*anger*
রাগী	ragī	*hot-tempered*
রাঙা	raṇa	*red, flushed*
রাজনীতি	rajnīti	*politics*
রাজনৈতিক	rajnoĭtik	*political*
রাজপুর	rajpur	*royal city, capital*
রাজা	raja	*king, rajah*
রাজী হওয়া	rajī hɔoya	*to be willing*
রাজ্য	rajyô	*realm*
রাত	rat	*night*
রাত্রি/রাত্রি বেলা	ratri/ratri bæla	*night, night time*
রাত্রে	ratre	*at night*
রান্না করা	ranna kɔra	*to cook*
রান্নাঘর	rannaghɔr	*kitchen*
রাস্তা	rasta	*street*
রিকশা	rikʃa	*rickshaw*
রীতি	rīti	*method, custom*
রুগী	rugī	*ill, sick*
রুমাল	rumal	*handkerchief*
রূপ	rūp	*form, figure, beauty*
রূপে	-rūpe	*in a way* (p. 255)
রূপো	rūpo	*silver*
রেস্টুরেন্ট	resturent	*restaurant*
রেহাই	rehai	*exemption, acquittal*
রোগা	roga	*thin*
রোজ	roj	*every day*
রোজগার	rojgar	*earnings*
রোজগার করা	rojgar kɔra	*to earn*
রোদ	rod	*sunshine*
রোদেলা	rodela	*sunny*
রোপা	ropa	*to plant, sow*
রৌদ্র	roŭdrô	*sunshine* (p. 247)

ল

লওয়া	lɔoya	*to take* (p. 255)
লক্ষ্মীছাড়ী	lôksmīchaɽī	*good-for-nothing* (female)
লণ্ডনী	lɔṇḍônī	*Sylheti resident in London* (p. 80)
লম্বা	lɔmba	*long, tall*

লাইন	lain	line, queue
লাগা	laga	to strike (p. 134, 172)
লাঠি	laṭhi	stick
লাফান/লাফানো	laphanô/laphano	to jump
লাথি	lathi	kick
লান্চ	lanc	lunch
লাল	lal	red
লুটান/লুটানো	luṭanô/luṭano	to roll on the ground
লুটিয়ে পড়া	luṭiye pɔṛa	to roll down
লেকচার	lekcar	lecture
লেখা	lekha	to write
লেবু	lebu	lemon, lime
লোক	lok	person
লোভ	lobh	greed
লোভনীয়	lobhônīyô	alluring

শ

শকুন	ʃôkun	vulture
শক্ত	ʃɔktô	hard, difficult
শখ	ʃɔkh	craze, hobby
শনিবার	ʃônibar	Saturday (p. 103)
শব্দ	ʃɔbdô	word, sound
শব্দকোষ	ʃɔbdôkoʃ	vocabulary, glossary
শয়তান	ʃɔytan	Satan, devil
শরীফ	ʃôrīph	holy (to Muslims)
শরীর	ʃôrīr	body, health
শহর	ʃɔhôr	city, town
শহিদ	ʃôhid	martyr
শাড়ি/শাড়ী	ʃaṛi/ʃaṛī	sari
শাণিত	ʃaṇitô	sharpened
শান্ত	ʃantô	peaceful
শাপ	ʃap	curse
শাপান্ত	ʃapantô	lifting of a curse (p. 218)
শিক্ষক	ʃikṣɔk	teacher
শিক্ষার্থী	ʃikṣarthī	student; seeking instruction
শিক্ষিত	ʃikṣitô	educated
শিক্ষিতা	ʃikṣita	educated (female)
শিগগির	ʃiggir	soon
শিল্প	ʃilpô	art, industry
শিল্পী	ʃilpī	artist

শিশির	ʃiʃir	dew, frost
শিষ্য	ʃi_s_yô	pupil
শীত	ʃīt	cold
শীতল	ʃītɔl	cold, cool
শুকনো	ʃukno	dry
শুক্রবার	ʃu_k_rôbar	Friday (p. 103)
শুতে যাওয়া	ʃute y̌aoya	to go to bed
শুধু	ʃudhu	only
শুভ	ʃubhô	well-being; beneficial
শুভরাত্রি	ʃubhôratri	Good night (p. 169)
শুভ্র	ʃubhrô	white
শুরু	ʃuru	beginning
শুরু করা	ʃuru kɔra	to begin
শুষ্ক	ʃu_s_kô	dry, withered
শূন্য	ʃūnyô	empty; zero
শূন্যতা	ʃūnyôta	emptiness
শেখা	ʃekha	to learn
শেয়াল	ʃeyal	jackal
শেষ	ʃeʂ	end
শেষ করা	ʃeʂ kɔra	to end
শেষ পর্যন্ত	ʃeʂ pôry̌ôn_tô	ultimately
শেষে	ʃeʂe	finally
শোনা	ʃona	to hear
শোনান/শোনানো	ʃonanô/ʃonano	to cause to hear, play
শোভিত	ʃobhitô	adorned
শ্মাশান	ʃmɔʃan	cremation-ground (p. 240)
শ্যাম	ʃyæm	blue-green
শ্রাবণ	ʃrabôn̩	Bengali month (p. 195)
শ্রেণী	ʃren̩ī	class, series, row
শ্রেষ্ঠ	ʃre_s_thô	excellent, best
শ্রোতা	ʃrota	listener
ষ		
ষড়যন্ত্র	ʂɔɽôyɔn_trô	conspiracy
স		
সংখ্যা/সঙ্খ্যা	sɔm̩khya/sɔn̩khya	number
সংগীত/সঙ্গীত	ʃôm̩gīt/ʃôn̩gīt	music
সংলাপ	sɔm̩lap	conversation
সংসার	sɔm̩sar	world, family
সকল	sɔkôl	all (people)

সকলে	sokôle	*everyone*
সকাল	sɔkal	*morning* (p. 103)
সকাল-সকাল	sɔkal-sɔkal	*early*
সখী	sôkhī	*confidante*
সঙ্গীহীন	sôŋgīhīn	*companionless*
সঙ্গে	sɔŋge	*with* (+ poss. W)
সঙ্গে-সঙ্গে	sɔŋge-sɔŋge	*straightaway*
সচল	sɔcôl	*moving, active*
সজাগ	sɔjag	*wakeful, alert*
সজীব	sɔjīb	*alive, vivacious*
সঠিক	sɔṭhik	*correct*
সড়াৎ	sɔɾat̪	*= sudden darting*
সতেজ	sɔtej	*vigorous*
সত্য	sôt̪yô	*truth*
সন্তান	sɔntan	*child, offspring*
সন্ধ্যা/সন্ধ্যে	sôndhya/sôndhye	*evening* (p. 103)
সব	sɔb	*all*
সবচেয়ে/সবথেকে	sɔbceye/sɔbtheke	*than all* (p. 134)
সবচাইতে	sɔbcaite	*than all* (p. 257)
সবসময়	sɔbsɔmɔy	*all the time, always*
সবাই	sɔbai	*everyone*
সবুজ	sôbuj	*green*
সভা	sɔbha	*meeting, court*
সম	sɔm	*first beat in a rhythmic cycle*
সময়	sɔmɔy	*time; at the time of* (+ poss., p. 95)
সমস্ত	sɔmɔst̪ô	*all, whole*
সমস্যা	sɔmôsya	*problem*
সমাগত	sɔmagɔt̪ô	*arrived, assembled*
সমাজ	sɔmaj	*society*
সমান	sɔman	*equal, level*
সমুদ্র	sômud̪rô	*sea*
সম্পূর্ণ	sɔmpūrṇô	*complete, whole*
সম্বন্ধে	sɔmbondhe	*concerning* (**not** + poss., p. 148)
সম্বৎসর	sɔmbɔtsôr	*all year*
সম্বোধন করা	sɔmbodhɔn kɔra	*to address*
সম্ভব	sɔmbhôb	*possible*
সম্মুখে	sɔmmukhe	*in front of* (+ poss.)
সরান/সরানো	sɔranô/sɔrano	*to cause something to move*

সরকার	sɔrkar	*government*
সরু	sôru	*narrow, thin*
সর্দি	sôrdi	*cold*
সর্দি-কাশি	sordi-kaʃi	*cold and cough*
সর্বদাই	sɔrbôdai	*always*
সর্বাঙ্গ	sɔrbaŋgô	*all limbs, body*
সস্তা	sɔsta	*cheap*
সহকারে	sɔhôkare	*with* (+ poss.)
সহজ	sɔhôj	*easy*
সহজে	sɔhôje	*easily*
সাইকেল	saikel	*bicycle*
সাঁটা	sãʈa	*to grip*
সাঁতার	sãtar	*swimming*
সাজগোজ	sajgoj	*dressing*
সাজান/সাজানো	sajanô/sajano	*to dress, decorate, play a rôle*
সাড়ি/সাড়ী	saɽi/saɽī	*see* শাড়ি
সাথে	sathe	*with* (+ poss., E)
সাধ	sadh	*desire*
সাধনা	sadhôna	*spiritual endeavour*
সাধারণ	sadharɔn	*ordinary, general*
সাধারণত	sadharɔnɔtô	*generally, usually*
সাধ্য-সাধনা	sadhyô-sadhôna	*repeated demands*
সাফাই	saphai	*cleansing, vindication*
সামগ্রী	samôgrī	*things, articles*
সামনে	samne	*in front of* (+ poss.)
সামলান/সামলানো	samlanô/samlano	*to restrain*
সামান্য	samanyô	*ordinary, trifling*
সার	sar	*essence*
সারাদিন	saradin	*all day*
সারারাত	sararat	*all night*
সাহস	sahôs	*courage*
সাহায্য	sahay̆yô	*help*
সাহিত্য	sahityô	*literature*
সিনেমা	sinema	*cinema, film*
সীমন্ত	sīmɔntô	*woman's hair-parting*
সীমা	sīma	*limit*
সুখ	sukh	*pleasure*
সুগন্ধি	sugôndhi	*scent, sweet smell*
সুটকেস	suʈkes	*suitcase*
সুতরাং	sutôraŋ	*therefore*
সুদূর	sudūr	*remote*

সুন্দর	sundôr	*beautiful*
সুন্দরী	sundôrī	*beautiful* (female)
সুপ	sup	*soup*
সুপরামর্শ	supɔramɔrʃô	*fine advice*
সুবিধা/সুবিধে	subidha/subhidhe	*convénience*
সুযোগ	suў̃og	*opportunity*
সূর্য	sūrў̃ô	*sun*
সূর্যোদয়	sūrў̃odɔy	*sunrise*
সৃষ্টি	sr̥ṣṭi	*creation*
সেই	sei	*that's right* (p. 181)
সেকেলে	sekele	*old-fashioned*
সেখানে	sekhane	*there*
সেনা	sena	*army*
সেবা	seba	*service, waiting upon*
সেলাই করা	selai kɔra	*to sew*
সোজা	soja	*straight*
সোনার	sonar	*golden*
সোনালী	sonalī	*golden*
সোমবার	sombar	*Monday* (p. 103)
সৌন্দর্য	soũndôrў̃ô	*beauty*
স্কুল	skul	*school*
স্কুল-মাস্টারী	skul-masṭarī	*schoolmastering*
স্তম্ভিত	stômbhitô	*stunned*
স্তুপ	stūp	*mound*, stūpa
স্ত্রী	strī	*wife*
স্থির করা	sthir kɔra	*to decide*
স্নান করা	snan kɔra	*to have a bath* (W)
স্নেহ করা	snehô kɔra	*to be affectionate to-wards*
স্পষ্ট	spɔṣṭô	*clear*
স্ফীত	sphītô	*swollen*
স্মৃতি	smr̥ti	*memory* (p. 217)
স্রোত	srot	*stream*
স্বর	svɔr	*sound, vowel*
স্বরবর্ণ	svɔrbɔrn̥ô	*vowel*
স্বাধীনতা	svadhīnôta	*freedom*
স্বাভাবিক	svabhabik	*natural*
স্বামী	svamī	*husband* (p. 26)

হ

| হয়তো | hɔyto | *perhaps* |
| হরিণ | hôrin̥ | *deer* |

হরিণী	hôriṇī	*doe*
হঠাৎ	hɔṭhat	*suddenly*
হল	hɔl	*(student) hall*
হলদে	hôlde	*yellow, turmeric* (W)
হলুদ	hôlud	*yellow, turmeric* (E)
হাঁটা	hāṭa	*to walk*
হাঁপান/হাঁপানো	hāpanô/hāpano	*to pant*
হাওয়া	haoya	*breeze*
হাজির হওয়া	hajir hɔoya	*to appear, turn up*
হাত	hat	*hand, arm*
হাত দেওয়া	hat deoya	*to touch*
হাতের লেখা	hater lekha	*handwriting*
হাসা	hasa	*to laugh, smile*
হাসি	hasi	*laugh, smile*
হাসিমুখ	hasimukh	*smiling face*
হাসপাতাল	haspatal	*hospital*
হাস্য	hasyô	*laugh, smile*
হায়	hay	*alas*
হারান/হারানো	haranô/harano	*to lose, defeat*
হিন্দী	hindī	*Hindi*
হিন্দু	hindu	*Hindu*
হিম	him	*snow, frost*
হিল্লোল	hillol	*wave, billow*
হিসাব/হিসেব	hisab/hiseb	*calculation*
হিসাবে/হিসেবে	hisabe/hisebe	*as* (**not** + poss., p. 239)
-হীন	-hīn	*without, -less*
হুঁচট খাওয়া	hūcɔṭ khaoya	*to trip*
হৃদয়	hrdɔy	*heart* (p. 255)
হেঁট হওয়া	hēṭ hɔoya	*to bend, bow*
হেঁটে যাওয়া	hēṭe y̆aoya	*to walk*
হ্যাঁ	hyæ̃	*yes*

GRAMMATICAL INDEX

In this index below the bold numbers refer to the unit number and the number after the slash is the Grammar point from that unit. Other numbers are named as such: note, exercise and so on.

ACKNOWLEDGEMENTS

The author and publishers would like to thank the following for permission to reproduce material in this title: Associated University Presses for the three translations, 'The Hunt', 'A Strange Darkness' and 'I have looked upon the face of Bengal' from *A Poet Apart: A Literary Biography of the Bengali Poet Jibanananda Das (1899–1954)* by Clinton B. Seely; Oxford University Press, Delhi, for an extract from *Ānanda Pāṭh*; Shamsur Rahman for his two poems 'Freedom' and 'Some Lines for a Cat'; and Mrs Bijoya Ray for an extract from *Yakhan choṭa chilām* by Satyajit Ray.

In the absence of any response to their enquiries, the author and publisher would also like to acknowledge Gazi Shahabuddin Ahmad for an extract from Jahanara Imam's *Ekāttarer Dinguli*, and Bharabi Publishers for three poems by Jibanananda Das.